JUDGES

JUDGES

Donald Dale Jackson

Atheneum New York

1974

FERNALD LIBRARY
COLBY-SAWYER COLLEGE
NEW LONDON, N. H. 03257

KF
8775
.J3

Grateful acknowledgments is made for use of excerpts from the following books:

THE FACES OF JUSTICE, *copyright © 1961 by Sybille Bedford; reprinted by permission of Simon & Schuster, Inc.*
THE LAWYERS, *copyright © 1967 by Martin Mayer; reprinted by permission of Harper & Row, Publishers, Inc.*
IN HIS OWN IMAGE, *copyright © 1973 by James Simon; reprinted by permission of David McKay Company, Inc.*
THE CORRUPT JUDGE, *copyright © 1962 by Joseph Borkin; reprinted by permission of Joseph Borkin.*

Portions of Chapter III, "The Goodoleboys," are adapted from the Life article, "Good Old Boy Justice," July 7, 1972. Portions of Chapter XVI, "Agony and Essence," appeared in New Times magazine, January 11, 1974.

67765

Copyright © 1974 by Donald Dale Jackson
All rights reserved
Library of Congress catalog card number 73–91633
ISBN *0–689–10595–9*
Published simultaneously in Canada by McClelland and Stewart Ltd.
Manufactured in the United States of America by H. Wolff, New York
Designed by Harry Ford
First Edition

For M. J. and Z. B.

———

Preface

THIS BOOK is an attempt to illuminate the character and quality of American judges. My premise is that we ought to know more than we do about any group of people with such power over our lives.

Judges are not, as many believe, impartial umpires who hand down decisions in accordance with clear and unwavering rules. This view of the judge as an invisible interpreter of the law, as a part of the courtroom with no more individual personality than a witness chair or a jury box, is a fiction that judges themselves have done much to perpetuate.

The reality is that judges are enormously potent public servants who usually have a broad range of options in any given instance: they may allow or disallow a contested piece of evidence; they set bail and revoke it; they pronounce final judgment in non-jury trials; they establish a trial's ground rules in their decisions on motions; they circumscribe and guide the verdicts of juries with their charges; and—most demanding and fateful of all—they select the appropriate punishment for convicted criminals. And these are only the most obvious illustrations of judicial authority. A judge may influence the course of justice in a dozen subtler ways—with an eyebrow raised in skepticism, a tone harsh or gentle, a pointed question, or a disparaging comment.

A judge's character and personality are vital variables in every decision he makes. His own experience is the frame of reference he brings to the judgment of his peers. Judges are no more and no less than human, struggling with their own imperfections and those of others, and their human reactions have as profound an influence on their decisions as the law they are sworn to serve. "Men's judg-

vii

ments are a parcel of their fortunes," Shakespeare wrote, "and things outward do draw the inward quality after them, to suffer all alike." The quality of our justice is a direct reflection of the quality—and qualities—of our judges.

So this is a book about people, the people who happen to be judges, and only secondarily about our "system" and the "justice" it does or does not dispense. I am interested in who they are, how they think, how they got there, how they approach their job, how they see themselves and their country and their fellow men. There is no attempt here to pin labels on them or to fit them into a particular vision of the society, but rather an effort to present them as themselves, as a gallery of individuals whose power makes them worth our attention.

I don't know if the judges in these pages are "typical" or not; I don't know that any judges are. I tried to corral as broad a sample as possible—geographically, politically, and in terms of the hierarchy of courts and the varying methods of selection. There are Republicans and Democrats here, Northerners, Southerners, and Westerners, elected and appointed judges, and a panorama of jurisdictions stretching from a West Virginia justice of the peace to the United States Supreme Court.

My only other criterion for inclusion in this collective portrait was access—their willingness to open their minds and methods to me. In some instances I approached them cold; I explained my purpose and asked their cooperation. In other cases my way was pointed by friends who felt that a particular judge would be amenable to talking with me. I chose two judges for special reasons—one because she was the first woman to campaign for the highest court in her state, and another, also a woman, because she was a black judge in the South.

The risk in this technique is that a judge will perform differently under journalistic scrutiny than he does normally. I tried to minimize that danger in several ways: by sitting in a judge's courtroom before I introduced myself; by interviewing lawyers and others who knew them; and by simple saturation—just *being there* persistently enough to penetrate their façades. Nevertheless the danger is inherent in the method, and must be acknowledged.

A few more technicalities should be mentioned: where courtroom dialogue occurs, I report it faithfully but not comprehensively, eliminating some exchanges for purposes of economy and easier digestion; I change the names of all criminal defendants to protect their privacy; lawyers' opinions on individual judges are frequently unattributed, for the good and sufficient reason that lawyers are loath to criticize them openly—hence the frequency of the veiled ascription "a lawyer said"; one judge asked for anonymity in exchange for candor, and I gave it to him; and I permitted two judges to read what I wrote about them, with no censorship privilege asked and none granted. As a hedge against inaccuracy, I asked people I considered experts in particular areas (sentencing, appellate courts, and federal judicial selection are examples) to read my chapters on those subjects. I offer them (they are listed in my acknowledgments) the customary bow of gratitude, and I volunteer my equally customary acceptance of responsibility for any errors.

A book like this is at best a photograph of a transitory phenomenon. I am describing people and circumstances as they exist *now*. I make no real attempt to explain causation or to chart the currents of history that brought us to this point, nor do I try to predict the direction of the future. The state of the American judiciary is a shifting vista, a response to the drift and dynamics of a society in constant flux.

Like any photograph, it is of course subjective, a reflection of my own biases and perceptions, strengths and weaknesses. I am no more able to elevate myself to a plateau of "objectivity" than a judge is. We can each invoke the mythology of our craft—theirs is legal truth, mine journalistic truth. But in the end we all see only what our own eyes show us.

D.D.J.

October 8, 1973

Contents

xii   CONTENTS

JUDGES

I

Introduction to an American Elite

IN BOSTON MUNICIPAL COURT, the flour-faced old judge sits between two large, high windows that frame him evenly and fill his bench with morning light, as if he enjoyed heavenly blessing. Everyone else—defendants, witnesses, lawyers, families —is in shadow. The defendant stands behind a railing, hands clasped in back of him, and hears the policeman say the narcotics test was negative, the material they found on him was nothing identifiably illegal. The judge scans the paper on his desk. "Well, I guess there's not much we can do about it, is there?" he says. It sounds like a complaint. Then he finds something. "Wait. What about this carrying-a-weapon charge?" "It's an old case, Judge," the policeman says, "it's been disposed of." The judge shakes his head in exasperation and turns at last to the defendant. "How long you been locked up?" he asks. "A week." The judge chuckles, a mirth-less cackle. "All right," he says, "you'll get compensated," and he waves the man away. . . .

In Washington Family Court, a black mother tries to explain to the white judge that her delinquent thirteen-year-old son is not a bad child. "He just resents somethin', y'know? He wants to be

3

recognized." The judge looks up from the forms he is filling out, asks two or three questions, and orders the boy to a detention center. The mother collapses in sobs, hugging her son. "I love you, I'm so sorry," she cries. "You're breaking my heart. I don't want nothin' to happen to you, I don't want you to go nowhere. Oh, I'm so sorry." Her son begins to cry too, and the sound of their heavy sobs fills the small courtroom. The lawyers and social workers stare at the wall, while the judge continues to fill out forms. "What's the date of that report?" he asks a social worker. Finally he can no longer ignore the weeping mother and son. "I want to tell you a story, James," he says. "I had a young security guard come up to me the other day when I was parking my car. He said I had put him in the detention center once for delinquency. He said he learned a lot, got a good education, and now he was a guard. You've got a lot of good in you, James. You'll do okay if you cooperate. . . ."

The trial is over, and the easy-going, red-faced Texas judge is relaxing in chambers, his cowboy-booted feet on his desk. "Did you see those two niggers sittin' in the back of the courtroom when the jury came in?" he asks. The two were the only spectators at the trial of a black man who was convicted of carrying a pistol and placed on probation. "Well, I never saw 'em before, y'know, but I kind of quietly sent the assistant DA back there to stand close to them when the verdict was read. He was a Golden Gloves boxer, see? I figured it was a good idea." I ask why. "You know, I don't know," he says in what appears to be genuine perplexity. "I guess I'm just scared-a niggers. . . ."

The Connecticut judge picks at his low-calorie lunch and broods about the injustice in his own life. He has a large head and large, strong features. He looks rather like Golda Meir, except for the eyes, which look hurt and vulnerable. "When you get bypassed," he is saying, "it does something to your ego. It makes you a defeated man. There's nothing worse psychologically." The judge has been repeatedly passed over for promotion to a higher court, and he has identified the reason: politics. He didn't toil for the party. "Sure, you do your work," he continues, "you strive, but you don't have that same wonderful, alert"—there is a long pause—"sense of well-being. You can content yourself with being a good man in a bad system, sure. But you have to look at yourself in the mirror in the morning and ask, 'What's wrong with me?' I'm in a vicious system where merit has no meaning whatever, none. I've never seen judges promoted on merit, and I'm sixty-four. It's politics. It's who you know and who you're going to help. . . ."

The judiciary, more than any other American institution, has traditionally enjoyed a warm and uncritical public trust. We have given judges our deference. In past years judges regularly topped the public-opinion polls comparing the prestige of various professions. The mystique—the robes and gavels and the "All rise"—has promoted and preserved the deference. And it endures: when an event occurs which baffles and frightens the public, a presidential assassination or an Attica massacre, politicians still turn to the judiciary for serene investigation and guidance; what emerges is a judge-led commission.

But the dreamy insulation of the judiciary has been punctured. Judges are more visible, partly because they have taken a few tentative steps out of the shadows, and partly because new floodlights of public attention have been turned on them. The Warren Court was the turning point. Its liberal, expansive decisions made the Supreme Court a constant focus of criticism and provoked a personal animosity that justices had never known before. No billboard ever demanded the impeachment of Justice Holmes.

The awe barrier was down, and critics of all hues galloped through the breach. The law's delay, its cumbersome mechanics, became a high-decibel public complaint: a system that deferred decisions for months and even years no longer bore any resemblance to justice, and was no longer tolerable. The pervasive practice of "plea bargaining" in the crowded, shabby criminal courts became recognized as a somewhat unsavory compromise with the raw facts of the system's inadequacy—a shortage of judges and courtrooms. Out of their own bleak experiences, Americans began to withhold the automatic respect for courts and judges that they had so long conferred. The resignation under pressure of Justice Abe Fortas inspired a reexamination of standards of judicial ethics, and the legal profession drew up a new code of conduct for its priests. The Supreme Court nominations of Clement Haynsworth and G. Harrold Carswell buckled under the gaze of an awakened public. The highly publicized political trials of an era of confrontation exposed the vanities and weaknesses of judges to a polarized audience. When California Judge Harold Haley was abducted from his courtroom and shot to death, judges throughout the country were shocked and courtroom security was tightened.

Our judges emerged gingerly into the glare, rubbing their eyes and blinking. They generally agree that respect for the judiciary has diminished. "You see it in everything," a Connecticut judge sighed, "in attitudes, mannerisms, courtroom dress, promptness. It's the prevailing mood of the society—it's loose, restless, and disrespectful."

The change in public attitude is confirmed by public-opinion polls. A National Opinion Research Center poll in 1947 asked Americans to rank ninety occupations in order of their prestige. U.S. Supreme Court justices were rated first (physicians were second, governors third, county judges twelfth). A similar poll taken by the Louis Harris organization in 1971 found U.S. Supreme Court justices eleventh, right behind psychiatrists. By 1972 the justices had climbed to ninth, tied with retail businessmen.

A cross-section of Connecticut citizens, asked in 1970 whether they had "confidence in the basic integrity of our court system," voted "no" 117 to 48. On whether majority and minority groups are treated equally by the courts, the vote was a lop-sided 159 to 15 against. Asked if the men presently appointed judges are the best qualified for the job, 113 said "no" and 17 "yes."

A 1971 Harris poll in Utah found that 60 percent of the public had a negative opinion of the courts, and that 28 percent thought the courts had changed for the worse in the preceding five years. Forty-two percent of the Utah citizens rated incompetent judges a serious problem; 57 percent believed that judges were vulnerable to political pressure.

The view of the unpolled public is probably close to that described by Howard James, author of Crisis in the Courts. "When forced to generalize about the public attitude toward the judiciary," he said, "I can only reply that it is a mixture of reverence and outrage, respect and anger—tempered with the cooling waters of indifference."

The most vocal segments of the public, clustered in angry bands at opposite ends of the political battleground, are equally harsh on judges. Right-wing critics believe that judges are too "permissive" with criminals. Policemen, particularly, and large elements of the letter-writing public (judges invariably get more mail from the right than from the left) accuse judges of excessive leniency. Many charge them with contributing to a general decline in respect for law, authority, and public morality.

On the left, the argument is that judges are agents of an oppressive state, dedicated to perpetuating its own power and blind to the principle of equal justice. "Justice means just us white folks," H. Rap Brown has said. "The court system," says Chicago Seven defendant Tom Hayden, "is just another part of this rigged apparatus that is passed off as 'open and impartial.' "

"It's not so nice to be a judge now," New York Judge George Tilzer recently lamented, and another reason is that so many people are watching. Organized groups of "court-watchers" have appeared in Massachusetts, Michigan, Pennsylvania, and other states. Especially alert to judicial violations of civil liberties, court-watchers keep track of judicial performance: Is a defendant told of his right to an attorney and a jury trial? Is he given a chance to cross-examine witnesses? Are interpreters present for those who need them?

A more significant long-run change is the recent introduction of judicial disciplinary commissions. Their effectiveness has been uneven, but their mere presence offers the unfairly treated citizen a recourse he has never had before.

"Scratch the average person's idea of what a judge should be and it's basically Solomon," says Yale law professor Geoffrey C. Hazard, Jr. "If you had a benign father, that's probably whom you envision. We demand more from them, we look for miracles from them and spit on them when they don't produce them. It's romantic, emotional, unexamined, unadmitted, and almost undiscussable."

We expect them to be honest, wise, patient, tolerant, compassionate, strong, decisive, articulate, courageous—the list of virtues stretches on with the dogged unreality of a Boy Scout handbook. Every few years a new attempt is made to define the essential qualities of a good judge, and each time the fantasy is spun anew.

"No man can be the sort of judge we expect an American judge to be," wrote Justice John Parker two generations ago, "unless he is absolutely honest, absolutely courageous, and blessed by God with an understanding heart. . . . And a judge should be a kindly man. The power he exercises is so great—he can so easily make or break an ordinary man—that no one but a kindly man should be entrusted with it."

A current attempt by the American Bar Association to set forth general standards for courts and judges informs us that judges should be "of good moral character, emotionally stable and mature, patient, courteous, and decisive." Then it has the good grace to subside.

Our expectations, desperately romantic as they are, are grounded in historical and social reality. America is a law-ridden nation. And in such a society the judges, the interpreters of the law, acquire the status of a priesthood; they are the bearers of The Word.

"Each generation in America recasts the social institutions," Professor Hazard says. "This makes for an unstable environment, and in such circumstances the law is a tremendously vital element. And the judge is the personification of the law." The judge is the rock in the stormy sea of American social change.

Yet the impulse to lift judges above the ordinary run of mankind persists, even after its fantasy content is conceded. Try as I may, I confess, I cannot put down the notion that a good judge, a *truly* good judge, is something beautiful, something beyond the normal attainment of men, something one feels an almost pathetic urge to venerate. And so the corollary: a bad judge is worse than a bad anything else. A bad judge enters another dimension of evil, another circle of hell. The bad judge has betrayed our innocent trust, and such betrayal permits no forgiveness.

The melancholy fact is that there is no checklist for the attributes of a good judge, no convenient formula, not even any generally agreed-upon objective criteria. The same words keep recurring, words such as "temperament" and "integrity" and "compassion," but their meaning is lost in individual perception.

Allan Ashman, research director of the American Judicature Society, is a man whose gorge rises as he contemplates such murkiness. He yearns for the establishment of objective standards.

"We ought to be able to develop a mathematical formula of some kind to determine whether a judge is qualified or not," he declares.

"For example, demeanor. How important is it? There should be a way to measure it. Is a man learned in the law? Is that subjective? How often are his decisions reversed? We should have hard-core criteria for selecting and evaluating. I don't like the idea of quantifying, but if we're going to say a judge is incompetent and should not be retained in office, we have to have something more than a poll saying thirty-five percent of those interviewed think he's a jerk.

"I admit that it may be impossible," he continues, "but I think we ought to try it. How does he handle witnesses? What are his administrative abilities? How does he handle the calendar? Some parts can be measured and others can't. How does he instruct the jury, what's his policy on the advisory of rights . . . ?" Ashman's eyes are lit with a zealot's flame, but somehow he reminds me of a man in the Department of Interior I met once who had devised a numerical scale by which he proposed to measure the beauty of a given piece of wilderness, with so many points for the view of a mountain, the presence of animals, or the depth of a canyon.

Columbia law professor Harry Jones, in a brilliant essay on the subject, delineated what he considers the essential qualities of a trial judge:

"The demands and strains of his courtroom task require unusual emotional stability, exceptional firmness and serenity of temperament, and . . . great intellectual and psychic endurance." He must have "unusual talents of communication." He needs to be "empathetic and endlessly patient" with jurors and witnesses, "compassionate without being mushy-headed" in sentencing, "at once sensitive and austere.

"By these criteria," he asks, "has any lawyer ever been 'qualified' for selection as a trial court judge? *Fully* qualified? Of course not. . . . But every lawyer knows at least a few trial judges who have come wonderfully close to the ideal." And almost every lawyer, Jones might have added, has his own ideal.

"He must be able to take a lot of pressure," says F. Lee Bailey. "He should be strong and compassionate, he should have a quick mind and be right a fair amount of the time. If he's right all the time, he's slowing the trial so much that he's killing it, because he's looking everything up. Common sense helps, and so does knowledge of the community."

"Fairness, judicial temperament—by which I mean courtroom

demeanor, courtesy, patience, and the ability to cut through the shrubbery and get to the heart of a case," says a Connecticut public defender. "And he has to move the business."

"I define a good judge," says William Kunstler, "as a person who understands the realities of American life and who is consciously doing something to change them." Kunstler adds that he knows of no judges who meet this standard.

"The most important prerequisite," says New York Civil Court Judge Irving Younger, "is a vivid sense of fairness. Everything else is acquired."

Buffalo law professor Herman Schwartz yields to total subjectivity. "A good judge," he says, "is a guy who thinks the way I do."

Judicial failings are more easily identified. A flaw in a judge's character is painfully visible, magnified by his power. The weaknesses of judges span the human landscape, from greed and bigotry to laziness and stupidity, from the indisputable venality of a corrupt judge to the subtle misdirection of an intolerant judge.

Every lawyer seems to know at least one alcoholic judge, and perhaps three who are senile. Still other judges are clearly psychotic, a claim U.S. District Judge Marvin Frankel of New York says is supported by both "statistical probability and direct personal knowledge."

There are bigots on the bench and arrogant martinets. There are the dull-witted, the narrow-minded, the harsh, and the lazy. There are those who are merely weak, mediocre, the "gray mice" of the judiciary. And there are the callous and insensitive, judges whose exposure to human pride and folly has encrusted their own humanity.

"The horrible thing about all legal officials, even the best," British author G. K. Chesterton wrote, "about all judges, magistrates, barristers, detectives, and policemen, is not that they are wicked (some of them are good), not that they are stupid (several of them are quite intelligent), it is simply that they have got used to it. Strictly they do not see the prisoner in the dock; all they see is the usual man in the usual place. They do not see the awful court of judgment; they see only their own workshop."

The American court system is a bewildering maze of parallel, perpendicular, crisscrossing, and overlapping lines. Our history of dividing legal authority among the federal government, states, counties, and municipalities has created a residue of courts and jurisdictions which is incomprehensible to all but the best-traveled lawyers. No two states have precisely the same hierarchical court structure; courts with the same name (circuit court, say, or district court) may have totally different responsibilities in neighboring states; courts may be burdened with archaic names (chancery, surrogate's, common pleas) that have no relation to their function. And coursing alongside (or above, or around) the grand quagmire of state and local courts is the federal system, sometimes sharing jurisdiction with state courts, other times holding its own exclusive mandate, and in still other instances empowered to snatch a case from the grasp of state courts. A chart maker would collapse in despair.

At the bottom are justices of the peace and magistrates. Halfway to obsolescence, the surviving JP courts usually deal with nothing more serious than traffic violations and the collection of debts. Some have the authority to commit an offender to jail and others don't. The presiding justices are usually small-town merchants or politicians, locally knowledgeable but untrained in the law. Magistrates, who operate in forums known variously as police court, magistrate's court, county court, and others, are a slightly elevated urban version of the JP. Magistrates commonly have the power to arraign criminal defendants and set bail, to issue warrants, and to pass judgment on the simplest categories of crime—petty larceny, say, or traffic offenses. Jury trials are rare at this level. Magistrates may or may not be lawyers.

The next tier of courts appears in a dozen different guises, but its common ingredient is jurisdiction over misdemeanor crimes and civil cases where the amount of money in question does not exceed a specified figure, perhaps $5000. These are the courts which are generally lumped together under the vaguely demeaning label of "lower courts" (judges prefer to call them "special courts"). Almost all judges at this level work full-time, and the great majority attended law school. Most municipal courts are in this category, as are "county courts" in many states. They are also known, in one precinct or another, as circuit, district, common pleas, and criminal courts.

Misdemeanors, the main business of the lower-special courts, are again differently defined by different state statutes. Drunk-driving cases are a staple of these courts, as are shoplifting and possession of lesser drugs such as marijuana. Divorces are often dispensed at this level. This is also the arena of plea bargaining, where lawyers and prosecutors barter for a reduced charge in exchange for a guilty plea; the broad range of categories and degrees of crime (robbery, burglary, and assault, for example, may fall anywhere between first- and fourth-degree, from a serious felony with a penalty of ten years and more to a minor misdemeanor carrying a sentence of ninety days or less) gives the bargainers plenty of flexibility.

Judges of the lower courts are the judicial foot soldiers, the arbiters of the daily confrontations of the law—a neighborhood quarrel that escalates into an assault charge, an attempt by the state to remove a child from negligent parents, a condemnation of property to make room for a new highway, an auto accident that cannot be settled by the insurance companies. Judges at this level are the tribunes and guardians of everyday American justice, which is only as good as they are. This is also the plateau of the specialists: juvenile courts, probate courts, small-claims courts, family courts; an urban lower court may be broken into a half-dozen "special" parts; the small-town lower-court judge must deal singly with every kind of issue a contentious populace can offer.

The smoke clears somewhat at the next level, the state trial court of general jurisdiction. This is the "higher court," where lawyers walk more softly and choose their words more carefully, and judges speak airily of "the law," "principles," and even "the Constitution." The stakes are greater: felonies are tried at this level, and a man can be sentenced to death or life imprisonment. Heroin dealers, kidnappers, armed robbers, and sex criminals turn up in these courts. There are fewer guilty pleas here, and more trials—both jury and non-jury. A judge's ruling on a given piece of evidence, his decision whether to admit it or not, is crucially important at this level, as is his charge to the jury. His character, wisdom, and compassion are tested in the gnarly legal questions he must resolve and the sentences he imposes.

The weightiest civil conflicts—where property and not liberty is usually at stake—are argued here as well: bankruptcy proceedings, corporate disputes, injunctions. The authority of the general-jurisdiction trial judge frequently overlaps the lower courts, giving the pleader a choice of battlefields. Judges of these courts must frequently put their decisions in writing and produce "opinions" that are scrutinized by lawyers and appellate judges. These courts too bear a dizzy variety of labels—"superior" in California, Arizona, and fourteen other states; "district" in Minnesota, Texas, and another fourteen; "circuit" in still others. To muddy the picture further, New York calls its highest trial court the "supreme court," and its judges "justices."

Appellate courts, known in most states as the "supreme court" and in others as the "court of appeals," are near the top of the judicial pyramid. Appellate courts belong to a different and softer world. Opinions issue forth from them like tablets of granite, freighted with the highest authority in law. But there are no trials, no witnesses, no defendants—just well-modulated argument.

Each state has such a court of last resort, which has the final word on all civil and criminal cases heard in its trial courts except the few that, for varying reasons, are transferred to federal courts. Many states have an intermediate appellate court as well, a way-station between the trial court and the supreme court which deflects many appeals away from the highest tribunal.

Federal courts form a separate, self-contained system that operates alongside state courts. Judges of the trial court, the federal district bench, are appointed for life, paid $40,000 a year, and accorded the earnest deference of everyone who comes in sight of them.

Federal district judges are distributed throughout the country in proportion to the population. They are constitutionally empowered to hear (1) cases in which the federal government is a party—a federal anti-trust suit, for example, or a citizen's suit against the National Park Service; (2) certain cases involving a conflict between the citizens of different states; (3) cases concerning foreign governments or nationals of foreign countries; and (4) trials for violation of federal laws, such as selective-service cases, crimes at federal banks, counterfeiting, and the interstate transportation of stolen goods. Federal judges also referee a wide variety of cases involving constitutional principles—petitions for *habeas corpus* (challenging the state's right to hold a prisoner), arguments claiming violation of the "due process of law" clause of the Fourteenth Amendment, and many others. State-court cases with a constitutional issue may be moved to federal court.

Above the district courts are the eleven circuit courts of appeal, each responsible for a geographic region. These courts hear appeals from cases argued in district courts and occasionally take an appeal from a state court. In addition, there are several special-purpose federal courts—the court of customs and patent appeals, the court of military appeals, the court of claims. Finally, in the highest aerie of all, passing judgment on the most critical and far-reaching constitutional issues, there are the nine robed philosophers of the U.S. Supreme Court.

"A judge," in Curtis Bok's epigram, "is a member of the Bar who once knew a Governor." The change of a single word—read "Senator" for Governor—extends the application of Bok's law to the federal district courts. For Supreme Court justices, crank it up another notch—"A Supreme Court justice is a member of the Bar who once knew a President."

Far more than their brothers under the robe in other civilized nations, American judges are products of the political arena. In France and most other countries in Europe, judges are civil servants who undergo an apprenticeship and spend their career on the bench. In England they are selected from among the barristers, an elite corps of trial specialists. In Japan, would-be judges must survive a two-year, post-law-school regimen of courses, field training, and special examinations.

By contrast, an American judge received, until recent years, no specialized training whatever for the particular demands of his job. Even now, judicial training is limited to an occasional three-day institute and longer voluntary sessions. An American lawyer can ascend the bench knowing no more about the law than what he recalls from law school, what he has picked up in his years of active or inactive practice, and what he has read.

The backgrounds of judges, and often their qualifications as well, are political. The immersion of American judges in the foamy sea of politics at every level, in every sense, is close to total.

The political judiciary is no accident. It derives in part from the same pervasive power of law that leads us to esteem judges so highly. This is a society dependent on law for the resolution of every important social, economic, or cultural issue, from abortion to suburban zoning, taxes to racial equality, obscenity to wiretapping.

"Historically, we've always needed lawyers," says Herman Schwartz, "and what that means is that the judiciary is not sacred or a priesthood, but that it partakes of the blood and guts and dirt and filth of the accumulation of conflicts in a conflict-ridden society. Judges can't stay aloof. Nixon packed the court, the Federalists packed the court, everybody packs the court; the court is a political instrument.

"The pervasiveness of politics is a fact of life. It's no more right or wrong than a thunderstorm is right or wrong. Courts have always been enmeshed in political, social, and economic disputes, and judges have always been in the middle of them. The judges come out of that conflict. Because of the power of law and thus the judiciary in America, it must be that way. And nobody's going to turn that kind of power over to a priesthood."

The politics of judicial selection is politics in both the broad and narrow senses. In the narrow sense it is Republican and Democratic partisanship, but in the broader sense it reflects, at least theoretically, a commitment to the principles of democracy.

That commitment, the belief that Americans should have a major role in selecting their judges, has had an uneven history. None of the thirteen original states provided for the choice of judges by popular election. Seven left judicial selection to the legislatures, and the other six entrusted it to a combination of the governor and either the legislature or an executive council.

With the eruption of Jacksonian Democracy in the 1820s and 1830s, however, one state after another switched to an elective system. Judges were elected in Georgia as early as 1812. Mississippi, in 1832, became the first state with an all-elective judiciary. From 1846, when New York decided to elect its judges, until Alaska joined the Union in 1958, every new state arrived with a provision for an elected judiciary.

The abuse of the elective system by self-serving politicians inspired sporadic outbursts of discontent and reform. Several states reinstated the appointive method, and others, in the early twentieth century, turned to the non-partisan ballot.

The current phase began in 1940, when Missouri voters adopted the concept of merit selection which became known as the "Missouri Plan," a system by which the governor selects a judge from a list of names drawn up by a commission, and the judge subsequently goes before the voters, without opposition, on a retention ballot.

The Missouri Plan has steadily gained adherents ever since, despite the almost reflexive opposition of most politicians. The American Bar Association endorsed it early on, and an occasional giddy reformer has even proposed that it be extended to the federal judiciary, where the President appoints judges with the consent of the Senate.

By 1973 the currents and cross-currents in judicial selection had left the United States with four distinct systems, each prevailing in a different part of the country and each dominant in at least nine states.

Appointment by the governor or legislature survives in ten states, primarily in the East. The governor's appointments commonly must be confirmed by either the legislature or an executive council. Connecticut, Delaware, Massachusetts, Maine, New Hampshire, New Jersey, Rhode Island, South Carolina, Virginia, and Hawaii choose their judges this way.

Fifteen states, chiefly in the Far West and northern Midwest, use non-partisan ballots, on which judicial candidates are not identified by party. Usually, however, the candidates are nominated by parties. These states are California, Arizona, Oregon, Washington, Idaho, Nevada, Montana, North Dakota, South Dakota, Minnesota, Michigan, Wisconsin, Ohio, Oklahoma, and Kentucky.

Another fifteen, principally in the South, choose judges on partisan ballots, though in most of them the real contest, if any, is in the primary. This is the dominant method in Alabama, Georgia, Arkansas, Louisiana, Mississippi, Maryland, North Carolina, Tennessee, Texas, West Virginia, New Mexico, Kansas, Indiana, Pennsylvania, and New York.

And, finally, nine—concentrated in the prairie and mountain states—have opted for the method of the moment, the Missouri or "merit selection" plan. The nine are Colorado, Iowa, Missouri, Nebraska, Utah, Alaska, Wyoming, Vermont, and Florida.

The variations and combinations are almost infinite. Some states use merit selection for their appellate judges and partisan or non-partisan elections for the rest; others appoint lower-court judges and elect their higher-court brothers. It's a changing vista: no fewer than nine states tampered with one aspect or another of their judiciaries in the 1972 elections. So richly pluralistic is the American republic, so jealously individualistic are its member states, that no two of the fifty have identical systems of courts and selection from top to bottom.

"We see the judges move like lions," John Selden wrote more than three centuries ago, "but we do not see what moves them." They prefer it that way. By tradition and often by temperament as well, judges usually choose to remain as close to invisible as possible. Many of them believe that their role precludes acknowledgment of their own humanity. To them, a judge is the personification of law, and thus an instrument. He decides by code or statute or precedent, by an accumulation of weight on one side of the scale or the other, and his own character, values, experiences, and prejudices are sublimely irrelevant.

Acknowledging his own humanity, for a judge, is no simple exercise. It requires unlearning hard-won lore. "Judges think the law is the law," says Chief Justice Franklin Flaschner of the Massachusetts District Court. "They don't like to concede the extent to which their own attitudes and ideas and personality pervade the exercise of their function. It's a scary thing for a judge to get into, to say that his personality and attitude are largely responsible for the decisions he makes. It's in effect saying that it's not a matter of what's in the books, and practically every judge believes that—that he is interpreting the books and not unloading his own ideas."

There are, of course, other, less honorable reasons for the judicial taste for invisibility. To wall off one's humanity is also to deny the existence of prejudice, cruelty, mental or physical laziness, greed, and the dozens of other entries in the unlimited edition of human frailties.

But, for all his professional inhibitions, a judge can no more avoid feeling than he can avoid being who and what he is. "All their lives, forces which they do not recognize and cannot name, have been tugging at them," Justice Benjamin Cardozo wrote of judges, "inherited instincts, traditional beliefs, acquired convictions; and the result is an outlook on life, a conception of social needs, a sense . . . of 'the total push and pressure of the cosmos' which, when reasons are nicely balanced, must determine where choice shall fall. . . . We may try to see things as objectively as we please. None the less, we can never see them with any eyes except our own."

And what our senses tell us is inevitably filtered by memory, through blurred scenes edited by time, down the dim corridors of our own experience. A judge's own past, Justice Jerome Frank wrote, "may have created plus or minus reactions to women, or blonde women, or men with beards, or Southerners, or Italians, or Englishmen, or plumbers, or ministers, or college graduates, or Democrats. A certain facial twitch or cough or gesture may start up memories, painful or pleasant."

Most judges would sooner admit to grand larceny than confess a political interest or motivation. It is so rare as to approach the charming to hear a judge concede that the power, prestige, or security of the bench holds some attraction for him. Find a judge who admits to political calculation or, worse, ambition, and you've found one who may shortly be blackballed for violating the lodge rules. The curtain is thick, and judges are apt to swat at anyone who tiptoes forward to rustle it and look behind it. This is what I try to do in the pages that follow.

II

Learnin' Judgin' Down in Reno

A unique college where judges get their consciousness raised

O N A H O T N I G H T in the second week of their course at the National College of the State Judiciary in Reno, Nevada, nine lower-court judges found themselves seated in a bare, cement-floored room in the basement of the Washoe County jail. Eleven inmates, clad in prison-blue workshirts, dungarees, and white slippers, were brought in to join them. Plain, straight-backed chairs were arranged in a circle, prisoners alternating with judges. "Watch what you say," one inmate said to another as they entered, "or you'll lose your 'good time.' " Two guards sat near the door.

The college had set up the meeting to promote some contact between judges and prisoners, who often see each other through layers of glass tinted by pride, ignorance, fear, prejudice, or self-justification. In 1970 twenty-three judges had volunteered to spend a night in Nevada State Prison. Five were manacled and lodged in the maximum-security unit, where they listened to the eerie howls of fellow inmates through the night.

The following year a bogus arrest was staged without the judges' knowledge, and five were picked up at a bar and hauled off to a drunk tank. But with that the college "blew its cover," Dean Laurance M. Hyde explained, and the practice was abandoned. This meeting was a milder attempt to achieve the same purpose.

19

The director of the course for lower-court judges, Thomas Russell, told the inmates that the judges were there to learn. The prisoners, all serving a year or less on misdemeanor convictions, introduced themselves by their crimes: possession of firearms, larceny, drug possession, manslaughter, burglary, forgery. Neither judges nor prisoners had names; the judges had shucked their name tags for the occasion.

One by one, the prisoners spoke, some angrily and others calmly. A thin young man with a frizzly goatee claimed that he had pleaded guilty after he was threatened with a longer sentence if he went to trial. A pasty-faced, wrinkled old alcoholic said his prosecutor had reneged on a bargained plea. "The judge didn't know nothin' about me," an angular young black cried. "He only saw me for ten minutes."

The judge from South Carolina folded his arms across his chest. The long-legged judge from Oregon slouched in his chair and squinted. The Idaho judge, youngest in the class at thirty, sat on the edge of his chair and looked skeptical.

"None of us would be here if we had any money," one inmate said. "You don't see any rich boys here."

"Right on," several others chorused.

"I'm doing time for nothin'," said a stocky black. "I did three years in Missouri for assault and got picked up here because they were after the guy I was with. They found a joint on me—one lousy joint—and I got a year for parole violation."

"That's not fair," one judge said.

"I'm paying for what I did when I was a kid," the prisoner continued.

"Is there a habitual-criminal statute here?" a judge asked.

"WAIT A MINUTE, MAN!" the goateed youth shouted. "The dude's *talkin'*." He glared at the offending judge.

"I mean, what's a fucking joint, man? Why do I have to keep paying because I got a record?"

"That's why," said Judge South Carolina.

The goateed man and another inmate stood up to leave. The judges ignored them as they walked out.

"Let's hear about the manslaughter," a judge said. "Was it alcohol or narcotics?"

"What difference does it make?" the prisoner shot back. He was narrow-faced and tense. "I almost motherfucking died. Hey! Dig it!

I ran off the road and my wife was killed." Judge Oregon, sitting next to him, slumped further in his chair. "Okay, I was on stuff." Several judges nodded. "Hey, you can shake your head, right? That's okay with you. That clears it all up, doesn't it? I copped to manslaughter."

"Why?"

" 'Cause I was scared, and my lawyer told me to."

"You could have had a trial."

"Who am I?"

"Did the judge advise you?"

"He said either cop or don't cop, kid."

"You had an attorney."

"He wasn't elected, was he?"

"What difference does that make?"

"You tell me." The inmate smiled.

The judges, all rational men, seemed offended by the logical imprecision. The prisoners' arguments, free from the intervention of lawyers, were untidy and emotional. The distance between judges and inmates seemed as vast as ever. The nervous inmate got up and left.

"Which one of you looks past the probation report and talks to the man himself?" the angular black demanded.

Judge South Carolina, sitting next to him, jabbed him on the knee. "All the judges I know will listen," he said emphatically.

"Look, man, my public defender didn't tell me nothin' about my constitutional rights."

"Did you ask?"

The prisoner was relaxed. He smiled. "He didn't give me *nothin'*, man."

"What law did he violate?" South Carolina asked.

"He lied."

"Did he let you make a statement?"

"No."

"Did they beat you with a rubber hose?"

"I wasn't advised of my rights," the inmate insisted.

"There was no harm done," said South Carolina.

"Jesus." The prisoner shook his head.

"It doesn't make you any less guilty, does it?" another judge said.

The prisoner was exasperated but still not angry. "You know, you dudes are just flipping me the bird," he said after a moment. "We hear each other, but we don't *see* each other." He smiled and stood up. "I'm gonna be leaving. Later, man." Seven of the original eleven prisoners now remained.

Only a few of the judges had spoken. Most merely listened, their attitudes hidden behind their judicial masks. If they were shocked, discouraged, amused, hopeful, or cynical, they didn't let on. One or two betrayed an occasional smug smile, but that was all.

"You guys ever take someone into chambers and talk to him man to man?" a red-haired prisoner asked. Judge Oregon nodded. "I just want to talk eye to eye," the prisoner continued, "not looking up at this guy all in black like the Grim Reaper or somethin'. Across the desk I'm a man and you're a man."

"I believe that," said Oregon. "I think we can level with each other across a desk."

Judge South Carolina, several minutes earlier, had looked at Director Russell and tapped his watch. He was ready to leave, but walking out was not his style.

Now Russell searched for a closing line. "I know it's frustrating," he said. "And there's nothing we can do to help you. But at least you know that judges are learning a bit about their job from you, and maybe you're helping some guys you've never met."

A deputy unlocked a gate to let the judges out. "You know those two hotheads who left, the one with the goatee and the other one?" he said.

"That one guy was fourteen feet off the ground," a judge said.

"Well, they went upstairs and got into a fight. They're both in solitary."

The guards led the prisoners into an elevator for the ride back to their cells.

Judge Idaho, who had been silent, shook his head. "Maybe it's just a quirk that they're there and we're not," he said.

The National College of the State Judiciary, financed by private foundations and supervised by the American Bar Association, has operated since 1964. Each summer it accepts several hundred judges for two- and four-week courses on their craft at its University of Nevada headquarters. The judge-students live in dormitories, eat institutional food, make timid forays into the casinos of Reno, tell each other stories of the legal wars, and listen to lectures on everything from prisons to public relations.

By 1972 the college had graduated two thousand judges. In that year it inaugurated its two-week course for lower-court judges of limited jurisdiction. Seventy-four of them, divided into six seminar-sized discussion groups, showed up for the opening session in the first week of August.

Like so many short-haired sophomores, the thirteen judges of Discussion Group K chatted easily as they entered the classroom and settled into their assigned seats. Their names were printed on cards attached to their chairs, and as further insurance against awkward lapses of memory, each judge wore a name tag pinned to his shirt. They dressed in conservative short-sleeved shirts and slacks, though two of the more adventurous wore Bermuda shorts, their extended white legs looking extraordinarily naked and vulnerable to the Nevada sun. One or two wore lapelled coats and buttoned the top button of their shirts.

Three were from the East, seven from the West, one from the Midwest, and two from the South. The Easterners—judges from Massachusetts, Rhode Island, and Connecticut—were all short, dark, and pudgy. The judge from Oregon was rangy, rawboned, open-faced, and younger, as were the judge from Washington, the appointed leader of the group, and another from Utah. Judge Colorado was broad-shouldered and powerfully built. Judge South Carolina was soft and puffy like a powdered pastry. Judge Idaho was a thin, dark, intense young man. Michigan was handsome and dignified, but was rendered faintly ridiculous by an enormous beach ball of a stomach. The others were Judge Alaska, bespectacled and thin-lipped; sandy-haired, pink-faced Judge Tennessee; and slight, wiry Judge Hawaii. Their ages ranged from thirty to fifty-five: Massachusetts, Rhode Island, South Carolina, and Michigan were in their fifties, Idaho and Alaska in their thirties, and the rest between forty and fifty, but closer to forty.

The personalities ranged from the gregarious conventioneer heartiness of Tennessee and Colorado to the almost monastic shyness of Idaho and Hawaii. Most judges in concert tend to adjust to the level of the quietest; the inhibitions of office persist even away from home, though some carry their dignity naturally while others never quite get the hang of it. Most of the thirteen were serious, anxious to look good and do well, and uncomfortable with frivolity or temptation, both of which waited just down the street.

The subject under discussion, as they dropped their identical thick green binders on their desks and commenced, was the mechanics of criminal cases—advising defendants of their rights, guilty pleas, and plea bargaining.

"You-all know we'll do anything that we damn well please," said Judge Tennessee, "as long as we don't get appealed. We're all protecting ourselves." He was the least inhibited of the group. The others smiled at his candor. "I look at each situation in the light of whether I think there might be an appeal. If I think so, I'll go through all the advising of rights, all that rigamarole."

"I let them convict themselves out of their own mouths," said portly Judge Michigan. "I put their rights in, but make sure they admit their guilt. How can they appeal from that? How can they tell an appeals court they didn't know what they were doing?"

Their opinions reflected the fact that the large majority of lower-court cases end in guilty verdicts, most often as the result of bargained guilty pleas. No one mentioned the presumption of innocence.

"I won't take a guilty plea until the police prove a *prima facie* case," Judge Connecticut said. "If they bring a lawyer along, then we have some plea bargaining and everybody winds up happy."

Judge Utah frowned under his wheat-blond hair and furrowed brow. "I think plea bargaining is destructive of the judicial process. . . ."

"I love it," chirped Judge Rhode Island.

"It's allowing others to do our job," Utah went on. "It's supposed to cut down the backlogs, but it's backfired. The more plea bargaining we do, the more there is."

"Hell," drawled Judge Tennessee, "our courts would stop dead if we didn't have it."

"They should plead guilty to the original charge, not a reduced charge," Utah insisted. "I don't like the prosecutors and attorneys determining the penalities. If they can do that, then they don't need a judge. We can go play golf."

Washington pointed out that a reduced charge—reduced sentence, really—is often the only inducement available to persuade a guilty defendant to plead guilty. Otherwise they will plead not guilty, trials will back up, and some percentage of them will be acquitted.

"If the prosecutor has a weak case," Utah continued, "then that's a legitimate occasion for plea bargaining."

"You mean it's okay if it looks like he might be acquitted?"

"Right."

"It seems to me we look for the easiest way to take care of the backlog," Washington said. "If we get devoted to expediency, we can eliminate the judge's function altogether."

"A lot of them go home at one o'clock now," said Rhode Island.

"It's the lawyers," Judge Massachusetts growled. "We all know that lawyers are the laziest bunch of bastards that ever lived."

"We ought to," said Rhode Island, "we're among them."

"What time do *you* go home?" Washington asked Massachusetts.

"After two I just sign warrants," he replied. "I'm usually out by three thirty."

Following the discussion, according to their printed schedule, the judges were to engage in "corridor conferences." The faculty envisioned excited huddles of judges extending and deepening their classroom dialogues at impromptu meetings. The sportier members of Discussion Group K, however, eschewed the corridors. Instead Judges Tennessee, Colorado, and Michigan went to a nearby beer-and-pizza emporium called The Library, where they drank several pitchers of beer and conferred through the afternoon.

They discussed juries. "I believe in 'em," said Tennessee. "I think you can go out and stop five people on the street, any five people, and they know what justice is. They can do justice as well as we can. We don't have to hold back anything with 'em, or send 'em out so they don't hear some technicality. They know what's right."

"But we have to protect the little guy," Michigan said. "It's like Cassius Clay fighting some hundred-twenty-pound guy. We have to make sure that it's a fair fight. And we know more than the jurors do."

Judge Tennessee, the defiant democrat, shook his head. "I don't," he drawled. "I'm no damn better than the people on that jury. Oh, maybe I know a little law that they don't, but they know some things I don't too."

The three had taken different routes to the bench. Tennessee won his job in a Democratic primary ("I had to kiss a few of those politicians' asses"), Michigan was selected on a non-partisan ballot ("The Republican organization supported me"), and Colorado, also a Republican, was chosen by his local city council.

Despite the range of their political and geographic backgrounds, they had more similarities than differences. All believed, for example, that judicial sternness was important in the face of increasing crime, that "respect for law and order" was declining, that all lawyers secretly yearned to be judges, and that a judge was a fine thing to be.

"The prestige, the robe, all that means a lot," said Judge Michigan, "and don't believe them if they tell you differently."

"I got tired of watching them other sonsabitches playin' God," Tennessee explained. "*I* wanted to play God awhile."

All three were worried about "niggers." "We got a nigger judge in Denver now," Judge Colorado reported. "There's been all kinds of complaints about him."

"We got a bundle of 'em in Michigan."

"You know, justice is different in the black part of town," Tennessee said. "These bleeding hearts talk about equal justice. Hell, the black part of town's different, that's all. It's a different world, different kind of people, different standards. So you have to deal with them differently." The other two nodded and sipped their beer.

The conversation moved to capital punishment. As misdemeanor judges, none of them had ever presided at a capital trial. But all three favored it.

"If they're cold-blooded killers, no better than animals," Michigan demanded, "what purpose does it serve to let them live?"

"What purpose does it serve to kill them?" I asked.

"It keeps them from doing it again," Colorado replied.

I asked if they aspired to be federal judges. "Hell, yes," said Michigan, "that's the best deal around. But it's a long shot for somebody like me. You have to know the big boys or be a big contributor. With the kind of system we have, it's lucky we get as good federal judges as we have."

"What's wrong with the system?" Tennessee wanted to know.

"It's politics. That's how it works. That's what it's all about. If I was going for it, I'd become friendly with everyone who could possibly help me, and so what? I ain't proud."

The talk drifted into descriptions of their somewhat tepid adventures the night before. Colorado and Michigan had visited a topless bar and discovered three brother judges there. "They were buying drinks for the girls," Colorado said. Michigan shook his head. "I can't even go into a place like that at home," he sighed. They had watched discreetly from the bar, played the slot machines briefly, and left before eleven.

"Only one of those girls was good-looking, if you noticed," Colorado said. "One of the others looked like her mother and the other looked like her grandmother."

Tennessee smiled broadly and raised his glass. "Why, you-all are just plain *devils*, you know that?"

Later that evening, on my way to accompany a group of judges to a teenage drug-rehabilitation center, I passed the motel where Judge Tennessee was staying. He was in front of the building, leaning against a wall. I stopped and asked if he wanted a ride.

"Where you headin'?" he asked.

I told him.

"Naw, reckon I'll pass on that," he said. "You're answering the call of duty. I'm feeling the call of desire." He waved cheerfully as I drove off.

The drug center, Omega House, occupied two large rooms on the second floor of a wooden building in downtown Reno. The rooms were filled with overstuffed furniture, musical instruments, and soft-drink machines. Messages of exhortation ("One Day at a Time") were posted on the walls.

The idea was to expose the judges to the experiences and thinking of teenage drug users. Cross-exposure, kids to judges, was secondary: the aim was to educate the judges. Most of the teenagers, who were between thirteen and eighteen, had used marijuana, LSD, or "speed"; one in five had sampled heroin.

The confrontation hobbled off to a self-conscious start. The twenty judges, leaderless, stood inside the door for an awkward minute until the program director, an intense, shiny-eyed Japanese-American, invited them into one of the rooms. Eight or nine teenagers lounged on the floor, smoking cigarettes. A few parents sat in couches and chairs around the periphery of the room; some judges had brought their wives.

The director described the program ("The kids look after each other. It's fifteen hours a day seven days a week"), its tentative successes and frustrations ("The first time they come in they only give us half their stash"), and the kids' attitudes ("They need to be accepted. They think the traditional institutions are uncool. Courts are uncool"). The judges listened solemnly.

"The old-fashioned remedy was to get a job and get a haircut," he continued. "That doesn't work. That doesn't change what's inside their heads. We're trying to change that, and to turn out kids who don't need grass or booze or anything else. Okay, let's begin." He turned toward a red-haired fourteen-year-old boy. "Tell them when you started, Billy."

"I was eleven."

"What did you take?"

"Reds."

"What's that?" a judge inquired.

"Reds. Barbiturates," the director said.

"How much of a habit?"

"Couple or three times a day," the boy said lazily. "Then I got into acid."

"How'd you pay for it?"

"I'd rip stuff off and sell it."

"You understand ripping off?" the director asked. Several judges nodded.

Gradually the discussion opened up. The judges, afraid of exposing their ignorance to the kids or each other, were more self-conscious than the kids. A pretty, long-haired girl told them that many of the student leaders used dope. They listened intently. Finally the judges began to snap questions at the kids.

"What about the 'jocks,' do they do it too?"

Several of the kids laughed. "The football players drop speed before their games," one said.

"Forty-eight percent of the kids in the county have tried some drug by the time they're high-school seniors," the director said.

"What if you get arrested? Does that change anything?"

"Getting busted just pisses you off."

"What about the films they show in school?"

"They don't help for shit," a girl said. "Ssssshh," said two of the kids, assuming four-letter words were forbidden. "It's all right," one judge said, "we've heard the word before."

"The films tell you how to do it."

"What's the matter with judges?" one asked.

Several answers came at once: "They like to send people up." "They represent the society." "They're like hardhats."

"Don't you think judges want to help you?"

"No. They just want to get rid of you."

One judge couldn't contain himself. "Don't you realize we often have no alternative . . . ?" he began. It was a whine, and vividly out of place. He was ignored.

"Some of these kids get threatened when they turn straight," the director said. "It's tough on them. They call it a rat pack, when the others are down on them."

"You know what they call my kid at school?" a judge asked. "Peter Narc. Just because he's the judge's son. Peter Narc."

The judges were learning a little, and trying not to appear shocked. The teenagers were warming to the show. ("All those judges listening to me," one said later. "It was far out.")

"Where do you get the dope?" a judge asked.

Billy, the laconic redhead, had been waiting. "You may not believe this," he said in his dreamy way, "but the best place in town to score dope is in front of the courthouse."

The judges in this course had been especially recruited. "We wanted the best," said Dean Hyde, a former Missouri judge who has directed the college since 1965. "We were interested in the potential future leadership. We wrote our graduates in each state and asked for recommendations." Two of the all-male class were black (one Northern, one Southern) and three were Orientals (all from Hawaii). "The idea was to create a cadre," Hyde said, to spread the message of judicial education through the states.

Judicial education in America caught on in the 1960s. Until then the idea that judges might actually sit in a room and be lectured at was regarded by the legal fraternity as heretical and somewhat laughable. Almost everyone assumed they would resent and reject it.

But under prodding by the American Bar Association and former Supreme Court Justice Tom Clark, the resistance began to give way. The Institute for Judicial Administration at New York University was inviting state appeals-court judges to seminars as early as 1956. The federal judiciary opened its own academy, the

Federal Judicial Center, in Washington in 1968. The American Academy of Judicial Education in Tuscaloosa, Alabama, began offering programs similar to those at the Reno college in 1970. More than a dozen states now have judicial-training institutes.

"The schools arose out of a hunger close to starvation," Hyde said, "which was apparent whenever judges got together. They were eager for more education." Hyde believes that today's judges are in some ways a new breed. "They're younger, and they look at the judiciary as a career now rather than the capstone to a lifetime practicing law. And they're more educable." The product of a Missouri Plan state, Hyde sees younger, more reachable judges as the first consequence of the advance of merit selection. The average age of judges at the lower-court session was forty-two.

The college gives a four-week course for felony-level trial judges and a shorter course for juvenile judges in addition to the lower-court session. The cost for the short course is about $200 for the judge who leaves his family home, as most do. It is borne either by the judge's court or by the college, which has scholarships available.

Between their discussions, "corridor conferences," and side excursions, the student judges sat through about thirty-two hours of lectures covering criminal law, evidence, traffic and juvenile procedure, sentencing, drugs, alcohol, and half a dozen other subjects. They had two thick binders of assigned reading plus other assorted homework. "The pace is tougher than I expected," one judge complained near the end. "It's like being back in the military—you do something different every hour."

Such diligence cries out for relief. "Your biggest problem in community relations," they were told by an instructor in that subject the first night, "is to convince the voters back home that you stayed two weeks in a place with legalized cathouses and gambling and spent all your time going to classes." Returning from a night at the tables, one band of judges explained that they were "examining contemporary community standards." Another judge rose to announce to the class that he had won $500. Several took advantage of locally legal prostitution.

But the majority did no more than drop a fleeting handful of coins into slot machines. Their level of gambling sophistication was probably illustrated by the Connecticut judge who asked me whether a face card in blackjack counts ten points or half a point.

"I think we get judges who are bright and trying to improve,"

Hyde contends. "The ones who already know the answers don't come." He concedes that some come to play golf or gamble, "some just like conferences," and others "are ticket-punching to get promoted." No grades are given, and only six out of two thousand dropped out before the conclusion of their course. "The most important thing we offer," says Hyde, "is the chance to exchange viewpoints and experiences, and to give them a sense of a national picture.

"We don't sell a point of view. We try to give a balanced presentation on judicial issues." He added that most of the faculty (primarily judges) tend to be "activists" who believe in "judicial involvement" in the community, as opposed to traditionalists who feel that judges should stick to judging, period.

Hyde believes that state judges are "more responsive to the Bill of Rights now" than they were ten years ago. "The federal courts expanded their scope at least partly because of distrust of state judges," he said. "That might have been justified in 1963, but it isn't now. The state courts have unquestionably improved in preserving people's rights."

Dr. Andrew Watson, a rotund University of Michigan psychiatrist with a Karl Marx beard, stood before the assembled class and studied them a moment. Across the gulf separating the disciplines of law and psychiatry, the judges returned the scrutiny. "I'm here to talk about the subjective processes of judging," Watson began, confirming their suspicions. Most of them were uncomfortable with the notion of "subjective processes of judging," and uneasy-to-hostile with psychiatrists. They stirred in their padded lecture-hall seats.

"There are stresses in your job," Watson told them. "You have to stick your neck out and rule, and sometimes you don't know the answer. Sometimes you don't give the reason for your ruling, and it's because you might be wrong. You're afraid you might be shot down.

"I suspect most of you are not that impressed with the usefulness of psychiatry," he went on, pacing behind the rostrum. The judges sat in tiered rows above him, neatly distributed in every other seat so they could take notes more easily. A blind judge, his seeing-eye dog beside him, sat at the end of one row. "I know you would unhesitatingly rule in my field," Watson said. "I had a judge overrule my interpretation of a Rorschach test once and make his own. The fact is I can speak your language but you haven't learned much of mine."

He had their attention. Except for Judge Mississippi, who muttered under his breath more or less continually, and Judge Missouri, who slept peacefully, they were silent and attentive. A few took notes.

"There's comfort on that bench," Watson declared. "It's nice to be thought of as godlike, but don't ever believe it."

The psychiatrist stopped in front of the rostrum and suddenly pointed at Judge South Carolina, who sat near the front. "How did you come to be a judge?" he asked gently.

"I was appointed on the recommendation of the local bar," the judge replied.

"I mean," Watson said, "how did you *come to be* a judge?"

South Carolina hesitated. "Since I was a little boy I always wanted to be a judge," he said.

The judges laughed.

Watson's eyes raced around the room. "Why did you laugh?" he demanded.

They fell silent. No one spoke for thirty seconds. "Because it's true," one judge said finally.

Watson then began questioning another judge, only this time his tone was sarcastic and aggressive. "What made *you* qualified to be a judge?" he asked.

"I applied," the man answered.

"Didn't anyone else apply?" the psychiatrist sneered.

The judge muttered something inaudible.

Watson stepped back and unloaded his point. "Demeanor evidence—the manner of the questioner, the inflection in the voice— that can have a lot to do with a trial, can't it? I'd think there would be a lot of legal arguments about it, but I've never heard a judge say, 'Let the record show the witness squirmed or his face got red at this point.' I say that more than fifty percent of the significant messages in a trial are non-verbal."

Judge Michigan raised his hand. "Aren't you playing God when you consider something like that as evidence? You can't assume guilt or innocence from it."

"I say it happens now," Watson replied, "and it's a game played without regulation. I can count on the fingers of one hand the judges I've seen who can handle it."

Watson then asked the judges to read a hypothetical case description which they had in their binders. The case concerned a twenty-two-year-old college student who had been found guilty of thirteen counts of petty larceny. The description said:

"You have read his pre-sentence report which makes it clear that he probably has been 'ripping off' the community for some time. He seems to feel justified in doing so since he thoroughly disparages the 'industrial-military complexion of our corrupt and polluted society.' He has been living in an urban campus area for the past seven years and has little direct contact with his parents, although they still provide him with tuition and a substantial allowance. His current address is a kind of commune where he shares a room with a 'wife' who is six months pregnant. . . . Although he has no prior criminal record, his long-haired, straggly-bearded mien hardly reflects contrition." At Watson's suggestion, Judge Oregon read the description to the blind judge.

When they had finished, Watson asked the class what their sentence would be.

"I'd throw his ass in jail," came a reply from high up in the room. The judges tittered.

"Why?" Watson asked.

"Because he's nothing but a parasite," the judge said. "I'd say he's polluting and contaminating the economy. Not only that, he's a male and he's committing a female crime in twenty-five counts of shoplifting. . . ."

Watson turned to another judge. "What would *you* do with him?"

"I'd send him to the mental-health department."

"Why dump him on us?"

"Because you know all the answers."

The judges roared. It was the squelch they'd been waiting for.

Watson let the laughter subside and then asked softly, "Did anyone notice what happened to the facts? Petty larceny became shoplifting, thirteen counts became twenty-five. The fact is that we don't know much about him, and you didn't ask much about him. You assumed that the report told you all you needed to know, and most of it was conclusions."

57765

FERNALD LIBRARY
COLBY-SAWYER COLLEGE
NEW LONDON, N. H. 03257

"Psychiatrists always try to protect themselves," a judge said. "All we want is facts."

Watson stroked his great beard. "Very few of you," he said, "know what you want from us."

"We want to know why he did what he did."

"All right, he did it because of an Oedipal conflict. Now what do you do?"

"Give him psychotherapy," one judge said.

"Give him shock therapy—jail," suggested another.

"Hell, it was just a few thefts and only one girl pregnant," a third said. "I think he's probably doing pretty good."

"I say he's a man," came a new voice from the rear, "and it's time to talk about punishment."

"Ah," said Watson, as if springing a trap. "Why?"

"He deserves it. That's why we have laws."

"*Why* do we have laws?"

"To punish people. Why not tell him to go back and do it thirteen more times if you're not going to punish him?"

Watson stood with hands on hips and eyes narrowed. "The law is to punish people?" he repeated.

"Yes, sir," the judge replied.

The psychiatrist stared at the judge, then retreated behind the rostrum.

"What I want to leave with you," Watson said, returning to his lecture, "is the idea that you should watch your own impulses when you sentence. Don't let your impulses get in the way of your reasoning. Know yourself. Learn something about psychology. Allow for your own hang-ups. You have to learn who you are because you can't make a rational sentence until you do."

A whistle sounded, ending the lecture. The judges talked animatedly as they filed out.

"Absolutely the best thing that's happened here," said Connecticut. "It was exciting."

Mississippi was still muttering. "Goddam judges ain't s'posed to be in sociology," he said. "S'posed to ad-JU-dicate."

"The thing about this job," Michigan was saying, "is that the only measuring stick is yourself. You can't go by what anyone else does. You can't tell if you're doing well or not. You're alone."

They had assembled at The Library for a departure-eve drink. That night was the final banquet, and they were leaving the next day. Judges Colorado, Tennessee, and Massachusetts were there along with Michigan.

"You have to play tricks on yourself," Colorado said. "Like when you have to sentence a man and you're inclined to be easy on him, but you know the community is howling for vengeance. I won't sacrifice a man to please the public, but on the other hand I can see their point. You just have to take the heat, bite the bullet. You know any other way?"

"We're not free, that's for sure," said Michigan.

"Educate the public," Tennessee said.

The others laughed. "There's no way."

"You know," said Massachusetts, "some days I feel lousy and I'll give a guy six months. Other days I feel good and I might fine somebody fifty dollars for the same thing. I figure it all evens out."

They agreed that the course had helped them. "Hell, it was the first conference I went to that was actually interesting," Tennessee said.

The final banquet was all sentiment and fellowship. The class skit detailed the trial of a luckless defendant accused of "assault with a friendly weapon" perpetrated on a prostitute at a locally well-known brothel. Someone in the college office blue-penciled the script, changing "ass" to "duff," "son of a bitch" to "son of a gun," and "stop, you're hurting me" to "stop." But the cast, displaying judicial independence, presented it unexpurgated.

Following the skit, a quartet of judges leaned together in new-found harmony as they grafted their own words onto the sturdy melody of "I've Been Working on the Railroad."

> "*Learnin' judgin' down in Reno*
> *At the Judges' School,*
> *We've been workin' down in Reno*
> *Just to learn to keep our cool. . . .*"

III

The Goodoleboys

The justice of the peace is alive and reasonably well in West Virginia

JOHN D. HERRON is bent slightly forward over the large desk that dominates his courtroom-office. A calendar picture of a highway accident, distributed by the Fraternal Order of Police, decorates the paneled wall behind him. To his right, an old-fashioned adding machine sits atop an antique wooden cabinet, and above that hangs a framed diploma from "The University of Hard Knocks," proclaiming Herron a graduate. A copy of *You and the Law* by the editors of *Reader's Digest* is on the desk.

The furniture is plain and spare: linoleum floor, a beige vinyl couch, vinyl chairs with stuffing peeping through the seams, straw curtains, American Legion magazines on the table. The only visible judicial furnishing is a glass gavel, which is filled with Avon No. 5 spicy aftershave lotion.

The sign on the glass door says "John D. Herron, Justice of the Peace and General Insurance." The JP's office—two small rooms plus a dank storeroom where witnesses often wait and lawyers sometimes settle—is in an old building a block from the Ohio River in New Cumberland, West Virginia, population 2500. The building was once wood-frame, but Herron has sided it with aluminum and brick. He rents out an apartment on the second floor.

Herron takes notes occasionally as he talks with a calm, dark-haired woman. The JP is a short man with a square pinkish face and wavy silver hair. Now fifty-five, he has the look of a once-handsome rustic dandy gone slightly florid and fleshy. His voice and manner, except when he's riled, are grandfatherly, patient, often sympathetic. He dresses in tailored double-knit suits and colored shirts. His eyes are small and full of secrets.

He talks amiably with the woman. She is attractive in a world-weary way, a sort of slump-shouldered Patricia Neal. They seem comfortable with one another, as if their memories include a selection of each other's follies. She wants to report a missing husband.

"I want to have him picked up, John D.," she says softly. "I've got the rent and the utilities due."

Herron nods and makes a note. "Any idea where he went?"

"Well, he might be at his mother's." She smiles wryly. "He says he stays at the mill sometimes."

"The mill" is the Weirton Steel Co., in nearby Weirton ("Home of the Mighty Tin Can," the welcoming sign says), which employs a majority of the residents of New Cumberland and the neighboring towns. Herron himself worked there for fourteen years before he became a full-time justice of the peace.

Herron smiles across his desk. "You've been by this way before a time or two."

"You know, John D., I divorced a drunk and married a gambler. I don't know which is worse. Next time I'll live with him a while first."

"Now you're talkin' sense."

"It wouldn't be so bad if I didn't get pregnant so fast."

"Well . . ."

"Well, the man said he loved me, and he said he wanted a child. God knows I try to please." She smiles. "So here I am."

Herron stands and hands his notes to one of his two secretaries, who types up a warrant for him to sign. The woman puts out her cigarette and gets up to leave.

"I imagine I'll be seeing you again," Herron says pleasantly.

"I imagine so," she replies.

Herron's business is his neighbors' troubles. Five days a week and half a day Saturday he listens to their problems, mediates their feuds, admonishes and fines and jails them, orders their paychecks "attached" to meet their bills, and lectures their children. In return they solemnly plunk their one- and five-dollar bills on his desk, tip their hats to him, and vote their confidence in him at four-year intervals.

John Herron, unlike most JPs, works reasonably hard at his job. The years have given him a certain familiarity with procedure and even with precedent. He gets calls from lawyers inquiring about points of law. He is frequently addressed as "Squire," and in sleepy, river-hugging New Cumberland, a town of general stores, fire-department picnics, and car-chasing dogs, the title is appropriate. The nineteenth-century flavor endures here, along with its institutions.

He is the busiest of six JPs in the county, a man of substance in the community. He can fine an offender $1000 or sentence him to a year in the county jail. He can decide civil disputes up to $300. He is respected by all.

Yet John Herron has no training in the law except what he has learned on the job. He graduated from high school, went to work at the mill, served in the Navy, and came home to become a judge. His qualification is his election; he took no test, earned no license, and works without supervision. "All we have to do is get elected," he says, "that and post a bond so we won't steal the state's money."

He is one of the folks, a "goodoleboy," an easy-mannerd politician with an avuncular charm. His values are plain, small-town, and Middle American; he is conservative, patriotic, don't-rock-the-boat, wary of outsiders and "big-city types," tolerant of what he understands and intolerant of what he doesn't, kindly in the face of contrition, stern with defiance.

The U.S. Constitution, with its protections refined through years of struggle, is a long way from John Herron's adding machine. "I know I'm supposed to have lawyers in here on some of these cases," he says, "but hell's fire, they'd be wasting their time with these family fights. Hell, all the attorneys in the county would be mad at me." His court-required reading of a defendant's rights ("Youhave-therighttohaveanattorneyyouhavetherighttocallanyrelativeorfriend.
. . .") is an incomprehensible fusillade of words. Due process of law, the right to a jury trial, the right of cross-examination, the presumption of innocence are chancy commodities in the JP court. Herron is living proof of the dictum of legal scholar Eugen Ehrlich: "There is no guarantee of justice except the personality of the

judge." The quality of John Herron's justice is the character of the man.

The woman is heavy and bespectacled. Her lower lip seems afflicted with a permanent downward curl. She sits on the edge of the couch, four furious feet from her husband, who is thin and sandy-haired. He fastens his eyes on the scuffed linoleum floor, pitted by the cigarette ashes of a thousand anxious supplicants.

The woman has asked for a "peace warrant" to place her husband under bond not to hurt her. West Virginia is one of the few states that authorize such bonds, issued when the judge believes there is reasonable danger of a crime but none has actually been committed.

Husband and wife are separated. She has brought her daughter, and the two sit tensely, oozing indignation. He has brought a lawyer.

"He makes threats, says he's gonna kill the children, he's gonna kill me. . . ."

"Did you threaten to commit suicide?" the lawyer asks.

"I acted like I was sick so he wouldn't bother my children. . . . He had a gun on me. I was scared to death." Her lips are quivering.

Herron is leaning back in his chair in the posture he assumes when hearing evidence: eyes nearly closed, a long, manicured fingernail barely touching his nose. He looks like he might be applying nose drops.

"I gotta hide like a *con-vick*. Can't work. Can't do nothin'."

"What about it, Tyrone?"

"I love this woman with everything that's in me," he declares. "No, I did not threaten her, never." His eyes doggedly hold the floor. "I run into her . . . she was with her ex-husband. I said let's work it out. We went to a motel."

A burst explodes from his wife. "Whyn't you tell him about the gun you had on me that night?" Husband, lawyer, and judge all ignore her. She looks disgusted. She is clearly trapped, surrounded by unfeeling males.

"It would make me the happiest man in the world if she came back to me," says Tyrone, eyes still downcast.

Herron rocks forward in his chair. The evidence is in and the decision ready. "The purpose of a peace warrant," he says in his soft mountain drawl, "is to prevent a crime from happening before it does." He knows the family, and he has made a judicious estimate of the potential for physical harm, the only issue that really concerns him. "Now I'm gonna order you, Tyrone, to stay away from Eula here and you, Eula, to stay away from him."

Eula bites her nails.

"I order you to split the costs of this case. That will be three fifty each." The seven dollars is Herron's fee for the paperwork and the hearing.

Tyrone rises to his feet. "I'll pay it all," he announces, "I'm her husband."

Mother and daughter, unimpressed, steam out of the room like twin diesels.

"Hell's fire," Herron observes after they leave, "this is the third one he's been through like that. It was the same thing with both other wives—threats, peace warrants. I know damn well he was lying to me when he denied threatening her, but he's just a big bag of wind. He never hurts 'em."

Herron shakes his head. "I just have to try to keep 'em away from each other. She had a pretty good husband before, you know, and she left him for this gook here. Well," he concludes, "I've got to take my daughter to the dentist."

Herron likes to call his court "the little man's court." In the sense that a poor man can get a hearing, unencumbered by the expense of a lawyer or the bureaucracy of the courthouse, the point is valid. "This is the first place they come," he says, "just to find out what to do. They can talk to me on a man-to-man basis. I'm not somebody sitting on a pedestal, I'm accessible. For eighty percent of these people, I'm the only judge they'll ever see. The older people mistrust the paperwork, the newer, faster methods, the bigness of the law. It scares them. To them I'm just a man sitting here on their level. I'm a link with the past, something that's been here before and they know how to deal with. I'm the local man. To them I'm knowledge."

Common-sense justice, he calls it, and the idea has a powerful attraction. "I know who's lying and who's telling the truth, who's living with who. I've heard all the stories. If the local grocer's not doing too well, I know it, if he can't afford to carry somebody and the man can't afford the bill." The attraction of the idea may lie in its presumption of moral certainty, its righteousness; it's the pull of the absolute, romantic and foredoomed. "I may not know the law," a Texas municipal judge told me, "but I know the difference between right and wrong." Blessed are the certain.

"The state of West Virginia versus Ronald Dante," Herron reads. "The charge is assault."

Dante is a service-station owner, well built and luxuriantly mustached. He chews gum aggressively and smokes, his arms folded sternly on his chest. He looks a little like a Turkish terrorist.

His accuser is John Minnick, a thin, whiny, fox-faced young man in a leatherette jacket. Minnick, also a mechanic, contends that Dante assaulted him. He seems pleased to learn that the entire state of West Virginia is on his side.

"I drove up to his station," Minnick says. "He came out and put his finger in my face, stuck up his fist. I thought it was a joke. He grabbed me by the shirt and pushed me on the hood of a car. He said get the, uh, get the eff out of here. He said if I ever came back he'd whip my ass."

Dante is a man of property. He has an attorney, a young man with the bulldog manner of a good criminal lawyer. Minnick, who is not wearing socks, does not. The county's assistant prosecutors represent the state at only the more important trials, which do not include this one. Now the state's case rests entirely on Minnick's narrow and inadequate shoulders.

"I went up to him," Dante testifies, "and I said, 'Look, John, I'm tired of you coming in here and telling my customers that after I finish screwing up their cars they should take them to you to fix.' He told my customers he would do it cheaper. I told him to hit the road, now, and I shoved him."

Dante has a witness, a black-eyed girl who says Minnick did indeed try to solicit business at Dante's station. She is about to leave when Minnick pipes up timidly, "Uh, Your Honor, don't I have the right to ask the witness some questions?"

This assertion of his right of cross-examination seems somehow out of place; things had been moving along so smoothly. The judge, taken aback by the impertinence, nevertheless permits Minnick to inquire. "But don't argue with the witness," he cautions.

"The other kid had the Volkswagen, he came out and—"

"Objection," says the lawyer. "He's making a statement." Sustained.

"Oh, uh, right," Minnick says. "And then I asked him what he was gonna have done—"

"OBJECTION." Sustained.

Minnick is unable to refine his argument into a question, the art of the attorney. At last he manages one: "Do you remember what I said?" She doesn't. "No further questions," says Minnick brightly. His case appears to be exhausted.

The lawyer delivers a learned summation. "The question is whether it was unprivileged touching, Your Honor. . . ." Minnick is slumped in his chair with a hooded-eye glower. What had seemed like a simple injustice has become snarled in a thicket of legal foliage. "A man can remove people from his property," the lawyer is saying. "He was not an invitee on the gas-station property. . . ."

The odds were stacked, and the outcome was foreordained. No lawyer had helped Minnick uncover and emphasize facts to his advantage; no one had advised him on the law. "This warrant calls for assault, beat, and wound," Herron intones. He looks down at his glass gavel and his metal letter-opener, which says "Wyoming, The Equality State." "There was an assault, but the threat made had an 'if' in it—'if you come back here, I'll whip your ass.' No one appears to have been hurt. I cannot see justifiable grounds for an assault conviction, so I find the defendant not guilty and order you, Mr. Minnick, to pay the costs. Seven dollars."

Minnick climbs slowly to his feet and reaches for his wallet. His encounter with the law has left him unfulfilled, poorer, and cynical. "Wow," he says to a friend as he pays Herron, "did you know you had to be *invited* to a gas station?"

"All he had to do was stay the hell away from there," Herron says afterward. But he seems aware that justice in this case was something less than perfect. "I hate these cases where only one side has a lawyer," he says. "The other side always feels taken advantage of." He prefers a case where neither side has a lawyer. Then he can work justice out in his own way, free from legal ambushes—and appeals.

John Herron belongs to a tradition that began in fourteenth-century England. The first JPs were landed gentry, appointed by the crown and responsible for administering local affairs and settling disputes. They were the original squires. "Men of property and prestige," a historian wrote, "they knew their neighbors and they understood the needs and nature of their communities."

The English squires' authority touched all facets of life. They administered the poor laws, licensed beggars, determined public wages, ran the prisons, and supervised public works in addition to sitting in judgment. They were unpaid, often enough independent-minded, and apparently successful: "Never in any commonwealth," Sir Thomas Smith wrote contentedly in the sixteenth century, "was there devised a more wise, a more dulce and gentle, nor a more certain way to rule the people, whereby they are kept always, as it were, in a bridle of good order."

The JP system was transported to the American colonies, where it survived the revolution and was established in every state of the new republic. Each state that subsequently entered the Union included a provision for justices of the peace. Their authority was limited to minor civil and criminal matters, though details varied from state to state. They were distinguished from village and municipal courts, which are generally set up to enforce local ordinances. From the beginning the JPs were rural laymen who sat part-time, won office by election, and were paid in fees rather than salaries. And almost from the beginning, lawyers complained about them.

New York University's Institute for Judicial Administration succinctly listed the main grievances in a 1965 book detailing the JP's steady decline in the twentieth century: "Lack of legal training, part-time service, compensation by fee, inadequate supervision, archaic procedures, makeshift facilities." The same rustic, down-home qualities that so endear the JP system to its defenders have always affronted its critics, primarily lawyers, who view it as hopelessly out of keeping with a consistent and orderly rule of law.

The opponents began to gather strength in the 1920s, focusing particularly on the fee-collection system that made payment contingent on conviction in criminal cases. The Supreme Court declared the practice unconstitutional in 1927, but JPs in many states continued it anyway.

By the 1930s several states were chipping away at the jurisdiction and authority of JP courts. The general trend was to replace them with salaried, full-time magistrates, sometimes but not always required to be lawyers. Missouri, ever the leader in judicial reform, abolished JP courts in 1945. New Jersey followed, and in the next twenty years the JP was rendered extinct in a dozen more states. Another 10 states eliminated JP courts between 1965 and 1972, leaving 26 states where JPs retained some judicial power—and only 21 where they had substantial criminal authority. The rural justice seemed inexorably headed the way of the ferryboat and the trolley car, a vestige of a simpler time, quaint but inefficient. Even in the states where JPs endured, the abolitionist pressure was relentless. "Every year I'm down in Charleston lobbying with the legislators," says John Herron, "because they have something new in against us."

Trying to calculate the exact number of JPs remaining in America is like trying to take a census of jackrabbits. They do not lend themselves to efficient record-keeping. "No one knows how many justices of the peace there are in the state of Washington," one writer despaired, "much less who they are, where they are located, and the extent to which they do or do not function." As many as 2000 are believed to be relatively operative in Texas, and that many more in New York. Herron, who is president of the Minor Judiciary Association of West Virginia, can only estimate that the number in his state is perhaps 300.

The states where JPs survive are primarily in the South and West, but there are some in all sections of the country. Delaware, Pennsylvania, and a few other states have retained JPs while requiring them to pass frequent examinations and paying them a salary.

In Alabama, Arkansas, Kentucky, New York, and West Virginia the maximum sentence a justice may impose is one year. In Delaware, where JPs are appointed, it is eighteen months; in the remainder it is between thirty days and six months. JPs are paid by a combination of fees and salary in some states, by salary alone in others, and by fees only in seven states: Alabama, Arkansas,

Georgia, Mississippi, Nebraska, Utah, and John Herron's West Virginia. "We don't cost the taxpayers a cent," he brags.

The strongest case against JP justice is that it is more business than justice. "It's just like any other business," says Herron, "it builds up over a period of years." And the way it grows, as with any other business, is by satisfying the customers. "The squire has to satisfy them to keep them coming back," says West Virginia legislator Ron Wilson. "The customers are the state police and the merchants who sue to collect bills. The merchants extend easy credit because they know the JP will get them their money back and collect his fee at the same time."

The President's Crime Commission, in its 1967 report, deplored the use of the fee system in criminal cases. The report quoted law professor Eldon Sunderland:

". . . Most criminal complaints are made by officers exercising police powers. These officers naturally seek convictions, and would be expected to patronize justices who aid them in their efforts rather than those who insist too rigidly upon protecting the rights of the defendants. A sympathetic attitude toward the views of the police is therefore quite likely to result in more business and an increase in the justice's income."

The report added that in states such as West Virginia, where justices are paid by the county for cases ending in acquittal, the justices "tend to convict to avoid having to wait for the county to pay." The commission urged total abolition of the JP system, condemning specifically the fee policy, the lack of legal training, and the absence of administrative accountability.

The "little man's court" too often exploits rather than protects the little man. The commonsense-justice argument has taken its lumps as well.

"That's okay if you want an adviser," says Chief Justice Edward Pringle of the Colorado Supreme Court, "but not a judge. It may be old-shoe, but it's not a court of justice."

Local knowledge may be a liability to equal justice. "A judge personally acquainted with the circumstances of the litigants," Professor Sunderland writes, "is likely to be influenced in his decisions by prejudice and personal opinion rather than by the merits of the cases. Discrimination against non-residents . . . is frequent. And local contacts too often lead to judicial action based upon personal and political expediency."

Tales of JPs overpowered by temptation are part of American

folklore. There are a dozen devious ways in which a JP can bend justice to his own profit, from "speed traps" in collusion with state police to the convenient misplacement of a summons ordering a debtor to appear for a hearing. Herron collects a large stack of creditor complaints every Monday. Only a few people bother to answer the summons he orders, which is served by a constable. The great majority of these cases result in "default judgments" and, frequently, the attachment of part of the debtor's paycheck until the debt, plus the JP's fee, is paid. Many JPs are accused of "sewer service"—failing to see that the summons is served.

The more bizarre antics of JPs are almost lovingly collected by legal connoisseurs. Dean Dorothy Nelson of the University of Southern California law school tells of one JP who polled his gallery of courtroom kibitzers after each case and based his verdict on their decision. She knows another whose habit was to sniff each witness before he testified, in the belief that he could tell an honest or dishonest witness by his scent.

In San Andreas, California, Justice Howard (Bluejay) Blewett cited a local newspaper publisher for contempt in February 1973 after an editorial critical of the justice appeared in the paper. When a photographer went to the café Blewett owned to take a picture of the judge scouring pots and pans, Blewett reportedly slapped him and grabbed his camera.

Justice John Klarich of Gilroy, California, took offense when two utility-company repairmen disturbed his peace while working on a pole behind his house in 1972. The justice warned them to quiet down, punctuating the warning by firing a shotgun blast in the air. He was found guilty of brandishing a weapon and sentenced to six months' probation and a $250 fine.

In Norristown, Pennsylvania, Justice Leonard Flack attracted the interest of the local American Civil Liberties Union branch last year following reports that he held hearings in a police squadroom. He rejected a request by ACLU court-watchers to see his records, which are supposed to be public. When the ACLU persisted, he filed a $10-million damage suit, charging slander.

"I don't know anything more about the law than a hog does about the Fourth of July," Justice Vernon Hilliard of Murrieta, California, confessed a few years ago. The elderly judge told a reporter that he frequently drove eighty-five and ninety miles an hour because he knew no policeman would give him a ticket. Confronted with the suggestion of race prejudice in his court, he denied any bias, adding, "I don't have anything against the black bastards—even though they lie and steal all the time."

Another California justice (there are not necessarily more JP degradations in California; they are just better documented), Hugh Keating of El Centro, was so enraged when a lawyer accused him of lying that he threw hot coffee in the attorney's face and scuffled with him in a hallway.

JP fiction barely outruns JP fact. Herron likes the story about the time a state trooper brought a young man before a JP and told him that the charge was arson. "There's been too much of that stuff going on around here," the JP said indignantly. "You're gonna have to marry the girl."

"This court has in hand a check from the plaintiff for $10,000," goes another JP story, "and a check from the defendant for $15,000. The court will return $5000 to the defendant and then we will try the case on its merits."

But most JPs probably see more of themselves in the story about the judge who listened to the plaintiff's case and promptly declared, "Plaintiff wins." Informed that the defense had not presented its case yet, he reluctantly agreed to hear it. After the defense testimony he looked around in purest perplexity. "Don't that just beat all!" he exclaimed. "Now defendant wins."

JPs, who may rank among the least-organized citizens in the society, lack the unity and sophistication to campaign in their own defense. Other judges—those of New York's Civil Court bench, for example—have hired public-relations consultants to gloss their image. A talented PR man could build a formidable case for the justice of the peace as an endangered American species, which he is.

But there have been no campaigns. The JPs are inclined to plug along as they always have and hope for the best. They don't deny the abuses; they even laugh at the JP jokes. The occasional statement in defense of the system has invariably come in response to a question or a direct threat, and the tenor is usually mild-mannered and unpretentious.

"You have a personal understanding," California Justice Robert Stewart told an inquiring law student, "so that a judge is in a better position to render a judgment. . . . There are few violators [in a small town], and I am familiar with their family status and background."

"I delve into something and find out it's a family affair," said

Justice Charles Spaugh of Reddington, Indiana. "I warn them that
if the charge goes through, it could reach a higher court. I tell
them it's smarter to bury the hatchet. Most times they do."

"Neighborhood justice"—nothing highfalutin about it, just us
plain folks working it out among ourselves. Accessibility, understanding, the avoidance of red tape and a fifty-dollar lawyer's fee,
the JP as an embodiment of the principle underlying the jury
system. "If the JPs go, it will be the people's loss and not the
lawyer's," says West Virginia attorney Martin Bogarad.

But in other ways it will be the people's gain. Perhaps, as Martin
Mayer has written in his book *The Lawyers*, "what went wrong in
the JP courts was less the system than the people who manned it."
Mayer maintains that common-sense justice "does greater service
than law on this level . . . and for this purpose an alert and
public-spirited druggist with easy access to legal advice from a
centralized clerk's office may be more effective than a third-rate
lawyer who couldn't make it in private practice and has been
running little errands for a political party."

The pale self-justifications of the JPs have a sort of winning
modesty. All the resentments engendered by a technological, super-
organized age work in their favor. When West Virginia Supreme
Court Justice Thornton Berry urges the end of the JP because "all
of modern life is rapidly moving in the direction of scientific,
technological, and managerial advancement," one feels an impulse
to gallop furiously to the rear, shooting fretful glances back at the
machine. The JP is suspended in time and hounded by change. In
isolated patches of America—in New Cumberland, West Virginia,
for one—it is still 1921 and the JP lives. But in most places it isn't
and he shouldn't—at least not in his present incarnation.

Professor Willard Lorensen, dean of the University of West
Virginia law school, believes that "there can and should be a
competent system of lay judges." He regards the JP's bias for
police and plaintiff as "built in," but feels that training and supervision could correct it. "Our legal system isn't set up to deliver the
kind of common-sense service they offer," he says. "It's easy to see a
nationwide reform program, but it's a little frightening too. We'd
probably get the standard *solution*, a flat-footed, uncompromising
plan that ignores the good the JP does, the local knowledge he has,
and his flexibility.

"What we have to do is balance the allegiance to a more professional administration of justice with the provincial allegiance to the public being served." He proposes placing the JPs under trained regional supervisors who would monitor their performance.

John Herron is regarded by most of the lawyers in Hancock County as competent, honest, and reasonably knowledgeable. The most frequent criticism is that he runs a "collection agency," which is an indictment of the system rather than the man. "Herron's one of the best," one lawyer says. "He knows the law and he's been at it a long time. You can't snow him."

"He's not knowledgeable in depth," another says, "but he's fair and honest, and he tries to do the best he can."

"He's an exception," a third insists. "They're elected in popularity contests, and it's unusual to get a good one."

Herron was born a few miles from his office, on a dairy farm tucked in a mountain hollow above New Cumberland, on January 9, 1918. ("My birthday and Nixon's are the same, but he's got a few years on me.") Like many judges, he finds moral lessons in his background. "When I was ten I milked the cows. I'd get twenty-five cents a week and go roller-skating. I think being raised on a farm is the best thing that can happen to a kid. The kids nowadays don't have work to do. You can build a community center and they tear the damn thing down."

As a high-school student he developed a taste for law and legislation. "My ambition was to be in the legislature," he says. "I just love legislation. When I was in high school we had a debate on the NRA. I argued that it was unconstitutional, and the teacher was arguing against me. I remember going down to the poolroom that noon and seeing a newspaper headline saying the Supreme Court declared the NRA unconstitutional. I spent three cents for the paper and put it on the teacher's desk. I got throwed out of English class."

With other boys he would climb to the roof of the next-door courthouse and sneak into a balcony to watch trials. "We'd play hookey for the afternoon and listen to murder and rape cases. I'd watch them attorneys. They used to say if you want to get away with murder, bring 'em to Hancock County and murder 'em here." He is one of the law's jilted lovers. "I guess I got about as close to it as I could," he says, "but, God, I'd-a loved to be a criminal lawyer, like that F. Lee Bailey. I used to watch Perry Mason and I'd always tell my daughter who was guilty, because I read all the books."

But at seventeen he did what most working-age males do in Hancock County: he went to work at the mill. "I was a scrap piler," he recalls, "carrying oil and loading boxcars. It was the lowest job there." He finished high school, but college was out of the question.

He and his fourteen-year-old girl friend eloped. "I only had ten dollars, and I gave that to a taxi driver to get us married. We told her father we was going to the county fair. Shee-it, I thought they'd annul it." They lived together a year.

He advanced steadily at the mill, working his way up to the job of "sticker." "I'd stick the coil in the finished stand and put it into a roll," which was later pressed into tin. "If I was still there today," he says proudly, "I'd be a roller." He was industrious and eager to learn, though not averse to having a good time. He had an easy charm with women and a formidable capacity for beer.

A generation earlier he probably could have "read law" in an attorney's office—a custom that was abandoned before he came of age—and, with luck, qualified for the bar. But in semi-feudal Hancock County his world was the mill, a world of grime and smoke and soot-blackened windows, all-night furnaces and work-ingmen's bars. The women in Hancock County look haggard at twenty-eight, their eyes dead. Children of ten wear the grave expressions of their fathers. Herron shared the narrow horizons of his neighbors. He didn't dream of escape, only of making the best of it. He is not a reflective man. "I say worrying is like a rocking chair," he likes to say. "It gives you something to do, but it doesn't get you anywhere." He doesn't brood about the causes of crime. Abstractions, inconsistencies, or the search for root causes don't concern him.

In 1942, when he was twenty-four, he made his first bid for the office of JP, but the political leaders told him he was too young. Two years later he filed for election on his own. But before the election his Navy draft notice came. "I was sent to Norfolk," he remembers, "and I'd come home and campaign on weekends. I called the morning after the election and found out I'd won, and the next day we shoved off for the South Pacific. I was the only Repub-lican to win in the whole damn state."

Herron's partisanship was more a matter of family heritage than deep conviction. "My dad and granddad wouldn't have voted for me if I was a Democrat," he says. "My granddad was a protective-tariff Republican. Nowadays I don't know the difference between the parties. I consider myself a rugged individualist. The Republican organization here thinks I'm a maverick." His district is overwhelmingly Democratic.

He served as quartermaster to a sixty-five-man crew on a Navy LCS, a picture of which still hangs in his office. His ship took part in the amphibious assault at Okinawa. He was known as "the judge" to his shipmates, the name he signed to an advice-to-the-lovelorn column he wrote for the ship's paper.

His only experience on the wrong side of the law came in the Navy. "The war was over," he recalls, "and we hadn't seen any civilization for months except Japan and the Philippines, and you can't call that civilized. I went off limits when we docked at Honolulu and spent a night in jail. I took a lot of razzing."

He returned to New Cumberland in 1946, went back to work at the mill, and handled his JP business in his off hours. "The first real case I had was when the state police raided a casino in Weirton. They came to me at the mill to sign the warrants. I was green as hell. They raided the place and afterwards the gamblers offered me money to throw the warrants out. I turned 'em down." He married a local girl and fathered two daughters. By 1949 he had built up his JP clientele to the point that he could quit to become a full-time squire.

In most ways Herron shares the values of his narrow Ohio Valley society. The only exception is religion. "I think religion's more habit than anything else," he says. He regards himself as "an existentialist, maybe, or even a nihilist. I believe that man lives in a purposeless universe, that we're here to die and that's all. They'd think I was an atheist if they heard me say it, but I think man lives for pleasure and that's all. People are bad, and they have to be taught to be good."

Shanahan sits tranquilly in the vinyl chair with the stuffing showing. He is blond and hook-nosed and somehow comical. He looks as if he is about to do something foolish, as if he might at any moment make an animal sound or stick his fingers in his ears and go "nyah nyah" at Herron. Maybe he just feels liberated. He spent the last three days in jail.

Mrs. Riley, dark and somber-eyed, sits on the couch and does not look at Shanahan. She says he removed $200 from her purse at the Paradise Club.

The prosecutor is dark and swarthy with a vaguely Latin flavor to his speech. He asks her how it happened.

"I left my purse on the lunch counter and went to dance. Came back and it was gone." She twiddles her thumbs. "I found it at the table where he had been sitting. The money was gone."

Shanahan studies the clouds over the valley. He is contented.

"Did you see the defendant take your purse?"

"No . . . Mrs. Adkins said she seen him take it through the doorway into the other room."

Mrs. Adkins is thin and birdlike, her cheeks pinched and her eyes wary. "I saw him pick it up."

"What were you doing at the time?"

"I was at the counter gettin' me a hot dog."

"Did you see the defendant take anything from the purse?" The defense lawyer has taken over.

"No, sir."

Shanahan seems to know some secret. Mrs. Riley seems preoccupied with an unrelated sorrow.

The testimony drifts away, trails off into dim murmurs, then into nothing. The judge is in his contemplative posture, head back, finger on nose, eyes nearly closed. He has asked no questions.

"Your Honor," the defense lawyer says, "I move for dismissal. There is hardly a *scintilla* of even *circumstantial* evidence showing this defendant could have stolen that money. The only evidence is that he carried the purse into the room *where the complainant was.*"

The prosecutor seizes his witness and takes her into a corner, though no corner in this room is really private. "Did you see him take anything?" he whispers urgently. No. "Don't you have *any* other witnesses?" No. She seems calmer about it than he.

The prosecutor returns to his seat. "Your Honor, all the state can show is that this gentleman had possession of the purse in that room. What happened thereafter we, uh, cannot offer."

"Motion granted." It is over.

Mrs. Riley walks over to Shanahan. Prosecutor, lawyer, and judge all watch in fascination. She is close to smiling for the first time since she came in. She shakes his hand. "No hard feelings," she says. He looks away and scratches his stomach.

The prosecutor looks at the judge. He spreads his arms out, palms up. "Why do we bother with cases like this?" he asks in exasperation.

Herron chuckles. "Why·did I get up at three in the morning to arraign him?"

No one asks why Shanahan spent three days in jail.

What became of the $200? "Ah," says the judge, "in insurance cases we call that a 'mysterious disappearance.' "

Herron has the touch and feel of a successful small-town politician: his warmth is carefully rationed, but his geniality is spent freely. He has a quick and handsome smile and a reassuring manner. He belongs to everything—Lions, VFW, Elks, American Legion. "The Lions Club is my religion," he says. There is a trace of some long-ago riverboat about him: the sunglasses he sometimes wears indoors, the hint of flash in his clothes. He is a man who Knows the Ropes. He is a country slicker.

"There was a man who ran against me one time," he confides, "and damned if the candidate's father didn't accuse me of having an affair with his wife, my opponent's mother. I was separated at the time, but that was lowdown campaigning." Was the charge true? The eyes narrow, the corners of the mouth turn up in a small, sly smile. "They couldn't prove it," he says.

His second marriage ended in divorce in 1967, and he remarried the following year. "It was brought up in the campaign," he says. "It was kind of messy, there were detectives involved and all. But I refused to discuss it, and I won." His relationship with his daughters is still close. One of them is married to the town's chief of police.

He politicks ceaselessly. "When the Lions Club has a fair," he says, "I'm at the mike announcing the acts. If there's a minstrel show, I'm out there again, thanking the crowd. If there's a Loyalty Day banquet, I'm the toastmaster. Memorial Day, Veterans Day, I'm the MC. My name and face are in front of the public all the time." He notarizes documents free of charge—"for political reasons," he says. Besides his JP job and his insurance business, he is the county coroner, the police judge for New Cumberland, part owner of a finance company, and an investor in a Florida drive-in theater. "We almost lost our movie business when the government made us integrate," he complains.

He admires political organization and believes in political loyalty. "Bobby Kennedy was in the office here once, just in and out," he recalls. "Hell's fire, they knew how to campaign. That makes an impression when somebody like that comes into your office. Down in Charleston they said they never saw nothing before that Kennedy outfit came in." When a local legislator proposed a bill requiring elected officials to disclose the source of their contributions, he opposed it. "You don't do that to your own buddies," he says.

He enjoys the job—"I wake up thinking about it"—but recognizes its limitations. "I have the title of judge, but it doesn't mean much," he says. "It's a prestige thing—but that's enough." In the evenings he naps for forty-five minutes after dinner, then feels ready for whatever meeting is on. He likes to tend his flower garden on weekends: "I'm still a farmer."

The office has its dangers. "A big colored man came over the desk at me one time," he remembers, and since that time he has kept a can of Mace in a desk drawer next to his cash box. He received a bomb threat after arraigning a group of "the local hippies" on drug charges. And when rumors spread that Weirton blacks planned to riot after Martin Luther King was killed, he bought a .32 pistol and a shotgun. "I figured my office would be one of the first places they'd smash, with all the wages I've attached. But nothing happened. I still don't know how to load the shotgun."

On one occasion he could have used it. "I was at the Wellsville Legion to a dance, and afterwards we were at a tavern having a couple of beers. A woman came by and said, 'You wanna watch Sonny, he's going to get you.' I paid the check and walked to the door and this fella blocked me. He said, 'You're on my side of the river now, and I got a knife.' He said I gave him a year in jail once. I didn't even remember him. He grabbed me and we went to wrestling, and he was a big sonofabitch and wearing construction boots. I grabbed him by the throat and rammed his head against a wall, but that didn't seem to faze him. Then a crowd started coming toward us, and I thought this was the end. But they just drug him back in. I brought charges. Hell's fire, I couldn't just let it go. He'd brag he got me and everyone I ever fined would figure they could take a crack at me. I looked him up in our files and I did give him a year for non-support, but he got out after a few days because his father made the support payments."

An elderly black couple comes into the office. The woman is angry, the man bewildered and apologetic. "How you think we gonna live?" she demands. "We're trying to budget what little we have, and you put a lien on his itty-bitty pension." The man offers an embarrassed smile.

The couple had failed to repay a finance-company loan, and Herron had ordered their bank account frozen until they began payment. They complained to the finance company, but were told they had to see Herron.

"You promised you'd pay thirty dollars a month after the first of March," Herron says crisply. His expression is cold and indifferent. "You went over my head to the finance company."

She is boiling. The telephone rings and Herron seizes it gratefully. "Let's go," the woman huffs, grabbing her husband by the elbow.

"They confessed judgment," he explains after they leave, "and then never came in with the money. He refused to pay the loan after he retired. They were trying to get out of paying court costs by going to the finance company." There is no compassion or humanity in his explanation; they owed, they tried to get out of it, they'll pay.

Now a deputy sheriff enters with an old red-nosed man in a threadbare overcoat. He is charged with drunk driving. The man gazes at the judge with an expression of humble gratitude for small official favors. Herron reads the charge.

"I had two beers, Mr. Herron," the man declares.

"You know every man in here on drunk charges says that," Herron replies easily. "I've never seen a man didn't say he had two beers. Never one or three." Herron, a constant smoker, lights another Camel.

"All I can do is just lay it out," the man continues. His eyes are begging. "My Social Security don't go too far. I don't think I was going more than thirty miles an hour."

Herron is smiling. He seems to feel comfortable—it has to do with this man's color and age and manner. He seems more at ease with older people, and with contrition.

"How do you wish to plead?"

"I'd like for you to do the best you can for me. I'm sixty-six."

"How do you plead?"

"Well, I have to plead guilty."

"Upon your plea, I fine you one hundred dollars and costs or ten days in the county jail, and revoke your driver's license for six months."

The man appears relieved. He leans back on the couch, a lounger now on the courthouse steps. "Wal, okay," he says. "I ain't been in the ketch for over a year now."

"You can still pay the fine if you want to get out," Herron says.

"No, I reckon I'll just serve it, John." The man leaves to join the deputy in the outer office.

"I had compassion for him," Herron says afterward. "I've heard so many stories I can pretty well tell who's lying. I believed that fella. He was on Social Security and he didn't have any money. Normally I give 'em thirty days on drunk driving, but I made it ten in his case." The court has compassion, but it is selectively administered. "Let's go for a ride," Herron suddenly suggests.

Fifteen minutes later he is driving his Buick Riviera along the road paralleling the tea-colored Ohio. A dusty haze fills the valley. Smoke and fire spurt out of Weirton's stacks. "There's graphite a foot deep under some of them houses," he says, "the ones where the foreign element lives. I guess they've breathed it all their lives." The Age of Ecology has not dawned in this place. "People in Weirton just ain't gonna say anything against the Weirton Steel Company."

He drives into a neighborhood of rundown frame houses with sagging porches and black windows. "We had a murder right on that porch," he says animatedly, pointing to a house. "Five shots. She'd taken him for a ride. She was twenty-seven and he was fifty. He got second-degree." He points at another house a block down the street. "Guy shot his wife through a window with a shotgun right there," he says. "She was washing the dishes."

He passes a cluster of dull, institutional-looking two-story buildings. Government housing. "This is the low-rise," he says. "Probably the best a lot of these people ever lived. I bet you can get anything you want in that place, including a knife in the back."

He heads into the rolling hills and smoothly sculpted hollows east of the river. "You know, I read Hugh Hefner," he says. "I'm not against anybody gambling or committing adultery if they don't get caught. I don't say I don't violate the laws, and some are silly. But if you're caught and you come before me, it's too bad for you. What I *feel* about a law doesn't matter.

"I had a woman once swore out an adultery warrant against her husband and his girlfriend. The damn fools pleaded guilty. Right about that time the mayor of Weirton cut out all the booze in town because of bootlegging. So around here they were saying the mayor cut out whiskey in Weirton and Herron cut out screwin' in New Cumberland. Hell, if we enforced adultery, we'd lose half the population in the county.

"I remember a rape trial we had here once. The evidence was pretty strong against this fella, but the only choice the jury had was twenty years or acquittal. Well, the girl didn't have much of a reputation, and the jury came in with acquittal. The man shook everybody's hand on that jury and said, 'I want to thank you and I'll never do it again.' "

He passes a ranch-style house with a big lawn. "That's the house I lost in the divorce," he says. Everything he sees in these hills seems to have meaning for him. "See that old church? They had witch trials there long ago. . . . There's the cemetery. My plot's there. . . . Used to play football on that field."

He waves to an overalled farmer. "My idea of a crime is where somebody hurts somebody else," he says. "But I go by the book and the code. If it's a bad law, then the legislature or the Supreme Court can change it, but I'll administer it whether it's good or bad.

"There are three kinds of laws," he says, enunciating a JP's-eye view of legal authority and its source. "There's God-given laws, like the Ten Commandments, and very few people today give a damn about them. There are man-made laws, and people aren't afraid of them either, because it's so easy to get off. People are afraid of only one law: the law of society. What your next-door neighbor's gonna say. Talk."

He slows the car as we come in sight of a house topping a rise and an unpainted old barn tucked between hillocks. Much of the land has been scraped clean of trees. "That's the homeplace." He is quiet for a moment. "See that springhouse? It was the best in the county. We had an apple orchard in back. You talk about strip mining." His voice rises. "When I think about what they've done to this place—they've stripped this old farm, by God!—it just makes me damn sick."

We ride awhile in silence, then pass a black man walking along the road. "I don't think a black revolutionary can get a fair trial here," he says, "but that's probably true anyplace. Hell, a longhair couldn't get a fair trial around here a year or two ago, but we've changed some since then. There's a black girl agitator here who filed a petition against me because I levied against her car. But the older colored, they're contented. Hell's fire, all these federal judges and the FBI jump three feet in the air when anybody mentions civil rights.

"If I was that Judge Hoffman in Chicago," he continues, "I'd have been tempted to bring a gun and shoot those guys [the Chicago Seven]. That judge put up with a lot in *plain radicalism*."

Back at his office, Herron arbitrates another husband-and-wife conflict. They had been drinking at a tavern when the man punched her, blackening her eye. "I don't get too excited about them any more," he says afterward. "Plenty of times they forget about it the next day and they're back in bed together." He orders them to stay apart, "but I know they won't."

Finding a way to divide one meager income into sustenance for a separated family is a drain on both his local knowledge and his judiciousness. "Some of these people have never done anything other than work, get drunk, and come home to the same old poverty," he says. "I have to come up with a figure—and it seems like the husband can never afford any more and the wife can't accept any less." Frequently he orders a husband to pay one third of his income to his wife.

"People come in here and ask how much the fine would be for an assault, like they're deciding whether it's worth it or not," he says. Once he changed a man's second drunk-driving conviction to nonsupport, allowing the man to work each day and return to jail at night and thus keep his family off welfare.

"But I don't feel I'm superior to them," he says. "Hell, I'm still the same old farm boy. I've maybe accumulated a little money, but it doesn't make me any better. I still feel more comfortable loafing down at the VFW than I do at the country club."

Jesse is twenty, hot-eyed and truculent. His facial hair is striving eagerly to attain muttonchops. He roars into the courtroom, trailing his adoring girlfriend. He has come to fight.

Along the windows are arrayed the Gump family: a wizened little man, black-haired and toothless, probably ten years younger than he looks; his dumpling-cheeked wife; and two of their many sons, one tall and mottled with red bumps, the other plump and earnest-eyed like his mother.

Jesse is charged with hazardous driving, the complaint brought by the family Gump. No lawyers. It is Herron's show.

"He come around the corner," Gump begins. "I asked him to slow down. He said some bad language. He spun his wheels and sent the gravel a-flying. I went and called the law."

"Who's your next witness?"

"Young Roger here."

Young Roger, the tall one, clamps his eyes on the far wall at about the level of Herron's diploma from the University of Hard Knocks. "We was all out on the porch. He came speeding around the corner. . . ."

Jesse is blowing angry smoke rings. "I was going real slow, I was in first gear," Jesse declares. "There's big chuckholes there. Young Roger, he yells, 'Slow down or I'll let the air out of your tires.' I said, 'You touch my car and I'll beat your head in.' The old man threatened to slap me in the mouth, so I said, 'Come on, old man, do your thing.' "

Herron interrupts. "How much do you weigh?"

"One hundred fifty pounds."

"How much do you think Mr. Gump weighs?"

"Don't know."

"You know he's a cripple?"

"Yessir."

"That makes you a brave boy, doesn't it?"

"No, sir."

"Your Honor," Gump says, "I told him he *needed* his mouth slapped."

"In view of the testimony presented here, I find you guilty as charged and fine you the sum of twenty-five dollars plus—"

Jesse doesn't let him finish. "I appeal your decision," he says, spitting each word.

Herron does not break stride. "You will be committed to jail until you furnish an appeal bond."

Jesse is startled. *Jail?* The truculence begins to drain from his voice. "Who do I have to get to sign a bond?" he asks.

It seems that it is too late in the afternoon to get a bond. The county clerk's office is closed. Jesse is hooked and squirming.

"Can I use your phone, Mr. Herron?"

"They'll let you use the one at the jail."

Jesse cracks his knuckles. The Gumps depart in ragged triumph. The girlfriend's father arrives and offers to help. "I'm afraid the clerk's office is closed," Herron says evenly.

Jesse makes a final try. "Ah, Mr. Herron, I have ten days to file an appeal, right?"

Herron is ready for this one. "You . . . have . . . already . . . filed . . . your . . . appeal."

Jesse leaves in the company of a deputy. The phone rings. "He's filed an appeal and has to post bond," Herron says. It rings again: "Tell his lawyer I'll explain the code to him or read it to him. The clerk's office is closed." Again: "No, it has to be an *appeal* bond. I don't think the bondsman's got any."

At the time Jesse appealed, Herron knew (as Jesse did not) that the clerk's office was closed and that obtaining a bond would probably be impossible. Jesse—more specifically, Jesse's mouth—was therefore buying a ticket to a night in jail. But the judge told Jesse none of this.

It was a sort of vindictiveness by default: you appeal my decision, perhaps embarrass me in front of a higher-court judge, you go to jail. But it was also a carefully reasoned judgment. "I think that boy's going to sit up there and think tonight," he says after Jesse leaves. "I think his attitude has been complete, utter defiance. He thinks he's above the law. His parents have been able to buy him out of everything. He doesn't care about anyone. I think jail might help—I've had it help 'em before. And, well, he wanted it legal and he got it legal.

"Besides, that's a dangerous little street they live on. Hell's fire, old Gump's got about ten kids. That boy could have hit one. Gump probably can't afford to lose any of 'em."

The judge is through for the day. "Got to get home," he says. "My wife is running the illegal bingo tonight."

IV

Snakepit Justice

"Moving the business" through a congested criminal court in Connecticut

ITS FORMAL NAME is Courtroom 1, Second Circuit of the Connecticut Circuit Court, but even the judges call it "the snakepit." The courthouse is a shabby ex-factory building indistinguishable from the warehouses that surround it on Bridgeport's south side. The five courtrooms—1 for criminal arraignments, pleas, and dispositions, 2 for criminal trials, 3 for civil cases, 4 for traffic, and 5 for small claims—are on the fourth floor.

It is 9:30 on a weekday morning, and the narrow hall outside the courtroom is full of smoke, anxiety, and anger. Young blacks lounging against a dingy wall exchange glowers with red-faced Irish bailiffs. Mothers with folded arms stand a few feet apart from their uncomfortable-looking sons, the generations gazing past each other in silence. Groups of young men smoke and talk animatedly, hooting and spinning in little circles when they laugh. Dull-eyed civil servants weave importantly through the crowd, clutching sheets of paper. The smell is of sweat, urine, fear, and bureaucracy. On the wall of the men's room down the hall someone has written, "Free the Bridgeport 160,000." Another has penciled, "Flush twice, it's a long way to Africa," and someone else has crossed out "Africa" and written in "Ireland."

The business of the moment is going on in the prosecutor's office, where defense lawyers and prosecutors sustain a steady hum of barter. No court is yet in session. Directly across the hall from the entrance to Courtroom 1 is a door with a little window in it, guarded by an officer. Several women press close to the window, trying to talk to prisoners behind the door. A line of people wait to fill out forms at a half-door marked "Public Defender."

In a few minutes the doors to Courtroom 1 are opened, and the majority of the people in the hall move into a narrow, low-ceilinged room, perhaps forty feet long and sixteen feet wide. The judge's bench, at one end of the room, is two steps up from the floor, and behind it are the flags of the United States and Connecticut. Straight-back, armless chairs are arranged in reasonably even rows behind the wooden railing separating the spectator section from the court. Dirty windows offering a view of an equally dirty courtyard fill one wall, but they are covered by lowered blinds. One chair-filled area about eight feet square is separated from the rest of the room by a low railing; the prisoners will sit here when they are brought in from their cage across the hall.

The seats fill up with perhaps a hundred people. Many of them are young, between sixteen and twenty-five. Half or more are black, the rest divided between Puerto Ricans and whites. A young, bespectacled public defender carrying a stack of file folders enters and walks up and down the aisle, calling out names. "Brown," he calls, "Samuel Brown?" He looks up without curiosity when a young man says, "Here." "Okay, see you in a minute," the attorney says. He calls another name: "Tesqueria?" In a few moments he stops and begins a series of whispered conferences in the spectator section, relaying a prosecutor's offer and then waiting for a reply. When a defendant hesitates, the attorney purses his lips and drums his fingers on his files. "It's up to you," he says.

The bartering has now moved from the prosecutor's office to the well of the court, where a prosecutor has set up an auction post at a table in front of the bench. Lawyers converge on him like coyotes honing in on a lost calf. Five voices are working at once: "Can I make him a youthful offender?" "Evans, what can you do for Evans?" "Where's the file? Who the hell took the file?" "Who's got Rodrigues?" "Okay, we can get you a larceny." "He wants to cop." "If he doesn't make it in the program, you can reopen it." Justice in the urban criminal court is being dealt out, the DA dealing. The lawyers stand on their tiptoes and reach over one another's shoulders to gain the prosecutor's eye, then scribble on their calendar sheets. It looks like a scene on the floor of the New York Stock Exchange. The difference is that here there are no winners, only losers.

The door opposite the prisoners' cage opens and a dozen men come in, some unshaven and in workclothes. It is 9:50 when another door opens, this one behind the bench, and a pink-faced, white-haired judge with long woolly sideburns ascends the bench.

"All rise!" cries bailiff Martin Reedy. "Oyez, oyez, oyez, Circuit Court of Circuit Number Two at Bridgeport in the state of Connecticut is now open and in session in this place. All persons having cause or action pending or having been summoned or bound to appear, give your attention according to law. The honorable Judge Rodney Eielson presiding. Be seated and pay attention to His Honor. Good morning, Your Honor." Reedy's cry is delivered in the accent of his native Tralee.

Judge Eielson is a short man with a thick torso and short legs. His complexion is permanently pink and his eyes are lively beneath his longish, wavy, white hair. He has the semi-genial, semi-pugnacious look of a traffic cop with twenty years in, or a ward politician. When he raises his eyebrows he looks like Archie Bunker. He lets his eyes cruise around the room as the lawyers find chairs in front of the railing, then nods at his clerk.

"All defendants are advised of their right to engage an attorney for the purpose of their defense," the clerk says in a rapid-fire monotone, "and of their right to remain silent. You are advised that any statements you may make may be used against you. If you are without funds, you may make application to the public defender's office for a lawyer to represent you. If you are incarcerated, you are entitled to a hearing on your bond and to a continuance to give you time to consult with your own attorney or with the public defender." An olive-skinned young man, facing the spectators with his hands folded behind him like a schoolboy giving a recitation, translates the clerk's words into Spanish.

The prosecutor stands at a table in front of the judge and to his right. A large pile of files is stacked on the table, listing precariously. At least twenty people sit on the business side of the railing: lawyers, clerks, a woman from the family-relations department, a police liaison officer, a court reporter, two representatives of the court's narcotics liaison staff, a bail commissioner, a matron, and three women prisoners, one of whom is falling asleep. Two uniformed guards stand by the male prisoners, warning them frequently to be quiet.

"Number twelve, Jordan," says the prosecutor, a tired-looking man in his forties. A lean young man rises in the rear of the courtroom and walks up the aisle. He is joined by a lawyer.

"The charge is non-support, Your Honor," says the prosecutor, reading from a file.

"Are we ready to plead today?" asks the judge.

"No, Your Honor, we'd like to ask for a three-week continuance."

The judge frowns. "I believe in men supporting their families, and I'm going to give him speedy justice," he says, making it sound like a threat. "One-week continuance."

Jordan and his lawyer turn to leave.

"Number seventeen, Charles Higgins, Your Honor," the prosecutor says. Higgins is a stocky young black, free on bond on a possession-of-narcotics charge. He asks for a public defender.

The judge reaches for a document handed up by the bail commissioner. "You own a 1971 Buick?" he asks. Higgins nods. "You have a job?" Another nod. "Your application for the public defender is denied. You may hire your own attorney." Higgins leaves.

The next case is another non-support. "The state would ask for a nollie, Your Honor," says the family-relations officer, using the local shorthand for a *nolle prosequi*, a decision not to prosecute. "His wife has left the state and we have no case." "Nollie's noted," says the judge.

Another half-dozen cases are called. In each instance the defendant stands in front of the judge for no more than a minute. A continuance is granted, a nollie, a plea entered, the public defender assigned—bang, bang, shuffle, shuffle.

"All right, we'll take the overnights," the prosecutor says.

The "overnights" are the prisoners held in jail since they were arrested, which was usually within the past twenty-four hours. The first is a sleepy, bare-armed young black man. He stands with feet apart and gazes at the floor.

"Charge is breach of the peace, Your Honor."

"Are you going to get a lawyer?" the judge asks.

"No."

"Do you wish to plead?"

"Guilty, I guess."

"No prior history, Your Honor," the prosecutor says.

"What happened?" the judge asks.

"He was causing a disturbance at a bar, Your Honor," the prosecutor reads from a police report. "He became violent, had to be subdued."

The defendant shifts his feet, but continues staring at the floor.

"Do you wish to speak?"

"I was drinkin', I dunno what happened," he mumbles.

"You working?"

"No."

"How long you been here?"

"Two or three days. Came up from South Carolina."

"Thirty days suspended," Eielson says. "You may leave."

"Rodrigues? Pepe Rodrigues?"

Rodrigues, a twenty-year-old with a sullen expression, stands next to the public defender. He is charged with first-degree assault, a felony beyond the jurisdiction of this court. The Circuit Court is Connecticut's equivalent of the police or municipal court. The forty-four judges, who move from one city to another every three months, have authority to hear misdemeanors punishable by sentences up to five years and civil cases involving up to $7500. In more serious cases, such as the assault charge against Rodrigues, the circuit judge arraigns the defendant and sets bail. The case is then usually "bound over" to the Superior Court.

"We would ask for a reduction of bail," the public defender says. "We believe that five thousand dollars bail in this case is excessive. Mr. Rodrigues has a job."

"Your Honor," the prosecutor says, "there were thirty stitches taken on the cut he gave his brother-in-law."

The public defender smiles and holds up his index finger. "*Alleged* cut, Your Honor."

"Alleged cut," the prosecutor mutters. "It took thirty stitches to sew him up."

"They were small stitches," the public defender says.

The judge smiles. Rodrigues looks bored.

"All right, bail is reduced to a thousand dollars." A $1000 bail bond means a bondsman's fee (at 7½ percent in Bridgeport) of seventy-five dollars, plus security (title to a house, for example, or a bankbook) posted by whomever guarantees his appearance.

"William Simpson." A young black in a ragged T-shirt comes forward from the prisoners' section. "To the charge of assault in the third degree, how do you plead?"

"Uh, not to no assault. The wife and me was having a ruckus." Simpson is without an attorney.

"This is legally known as assault in the third degree, how do you plead?" the prosecutor exhales.

"Oh. Guilty."

The prosecutor reads from his file. "The wife was cut on the neck and right eye—"

Simpson interrupts: "She hit me up the side of my head with a glass. I think she was cut when I pushed her down on the floor."

The judge is listening with apparent interest and smiling thinly. "How long have you been married?" he asks Simpson.

"Seven years."

"Did she forgive you?"

"Uh, we're still together, yes."

The judge glances around the room. "People do have an unusual way of showing affection these days. The fine will be fifteen dollars."

Gradually the seats in the spectator area are emptying as one defendant after another comes forth for his minute or two in court, receives "speedy justice" or a postponement, and moves on to make room for the next one. The judge flips the pages of his calendar and calls out dates. The prosecutor rarely looks at the defendants. The public defender does not always recognize the names of his clients when they are called. Clerks and other court officers gaze dully at windows or wall.

The momentum is so fast, the pressure so constant that any concept of "justice" is lost. No one asks *why* a crime was committed. No one questions the police reports, or how a defendant was apprehended. No one pursues whatever the truth of a given incident may be. There is no time for an exploration of human circumstances. This is mass-production justice, snakepit justice. Bargained pleas of guilty grease the wheels and keep it moving. "We move the business," Eielson likes to say. He is proud of his reputation for efficiency. The defendant sacrifices his right to a trial, the state gives up its interest in protecting society—nobody gains, everybody loses. The system operates on its own ethic, churning on in a mindless internal rhythm with no relation to principles of any kind. Step up, step down, how do you plead, were you promised anything, let's see the record, next case. After a while it becomes almost hypnotic, like a recurrent melody half heard in a stupor, like the endlessly repeated language of a recorded message.

"Ralph Bodega."

Bodega is a man in his thirties, wearing a sport shirt. He holds a piece of paper in his hand. The charge is disorderly conduct.

"Do you wish to plead or to get a lawyer?"

Bodega looks at the judge and squares his shoulders. "I wish to explain the circumstances."

"Do you wish to plead or to get a lawyer?"

"I, uh . . . to get a lawyer."

"Prior record?" the judge asks, reaching for the file.

Bodega waves the paper in his hand. "But—"

"All right, released on your own recognizance. Get a lawyer."

Bodega no longer interests the court. "Freeman," the prosecutor calls.

Freeman is up and down in thirty seconds, and Bodega is suddenly back, making an unscheduled appearance, waving his piece of paper. The prosecutor looks at him as if he were a mosquito.

"What I wanted to explain is I was going to the store—"

The judge cuts him off. "I don't want to hear any of the facts," he says. "We won't go into that today. You come back with a lawyer."

Bodega is talking to himself and shaking his head. "Yates," the prosecutor says. "Number forty-two, Yates." Bodega retreats in confusion.

Yates is a long-legged young black in raspberry slacks. He pleads guilty to possession of narcotics.

"Was any promise made to you as regards your plea of guilty?"

"Uh, yes."

"What?"

"That I'd be sent to a drug program."

"All right," the judge says. "Any others?"

"No."

"You understand," the judge says, "that I could send you to jail for five years if I chose to." Yates nods. "I know your prior record, which is atrocious. You deserve jail. But the Daytop program is willing to work with you, and as long as they are, I might as well give you a chance. You better face it, young man, this is *it* for you. Two and a half to five years suspended, three years probation on condition that you participate in in-patient treatment at Daytop until they phase you out. If you leave the program, you go to jail for two and a half years." Yates has occupied the system for almost five minutes.

The judge is growing irritated. He has decreed that there will be no morning recess today because "I'm getting a little distressed at this four-in-the-afternoon business." Judge Eielson likes to clean up his court calendar by one o'clock. "I don't want to be here if we have to work with him this afternoon," one of the court staff whispers.

"Evans, Duane Evans." There is no response. The prosecutor calls the name again.

"All right, the bond is forfeited," Eielson says. "How much is it?"

"Five thousand," the bail commissioner says.

Two minutes later an attorney hurries up the aisle. "I was right outside," he says. "The defendant was here at nine thirty."

The judge glares at him. "So was I," he says. "Your client was called twice. I know a lot of attorneys who like to come in at ten or eleven o'clock. If I have to be here, you can be here." Grudgingly he reinstates the bond.

On the next case the prosecutor is unable to find the file. "I'll give the state two weeks to come up with the original document or else we'll dismiss it," the judge snaps. The prosecutor, red-faced, says nothing. The judge kicks the wastebasket under his desk petulantly and drops a pencil on the floor. His eyes dart around belligerently.

"Lamar Clark." Clark is a sixteen-year-old who has pleaded guilty to a narcotics charge. He is appearing for sentence. "He's very weak, Your Honor," his guardian tells the judge.

"How are we going to strengthen him?" the judge asks. "I'll help," he continues. "One hundred and eighty days, execution suspended, two years probation. You get in trouble again while I'm sitting here and you better bring your toothpaste because you'll need it. You're either going to behave or go to jail."

Every case seems to trigger another judicial peeve. The public defender argues that he has been unable to meet with his client.

"Every time I appoint you public defender on a case, you should give them time certain to see you," the judge fumes. "Or else I'll begin to be your appointments secretary and make your appointments for you and I have enough to do." The young attorney looks stunned.

"Phillips, number sixty-eight," the prosecutor says. "The charge is possession of heroin and conspiracy to sell." The public defender asks for a reduction of the $5000 bond.

"You want a refresher course on his record?" the judge asks. "I'd have to have my head examined if I reduced that, and I'm not ready for that yet."

"Your Honor, on the companion case—"

"Keep talking and I'll increase the bond," the judge threatens.

"He's really very compassionate," the family-relations officer whispers to me. "He gets in these moods, but they may be an act. Sometimes he gets a kick out of riding people."

The atmosphere in court has become tense. Prosecutor and public defender are both nervous and eager to finish the calendar. They avert their eyes from the judge's as he looks down at them.

"Monti," the prosecutor says. "Intoxication. I think there's a mental problem, Your Honor."

"It would be nice if you read the report last night," Eielson says.

"It would be nice if I could do it, Your Honor, but I'm quite overburdened. I don't have time."

"Better find time," the judge says, smiling coolly. Monti's case is postponed.

"Let's get lunch, I'm hungry," the prosecutor says under his breath to a clerk.

The judge is watching him, and the room falls suddenly still. "Are you finished?" the judge says.

The prosecutor looks at his files.

"Now may we proceed?" Eielson asks sarcastically.

"Marilyn Holmes, number eighty-one." A heavy-set, bespectacled woman comes forward, her hands shaking. "How do you plead to the charge of issuing bad checks, seven counts?"

Her plea of guilty is almost inaudible.

"She has three children, Your Honor," the public defender says. "She says she will make restitution." The woman begins to cry. "The money was for family needs. She's divorced."

"One hundred eighty days suspended on each count," the judge says, "and two years probation on the condition that she pays off the checks."

"That's three and a half years," a policeman whispers.

"Will you pay off the checks?" the judge asks her. She is unable to speak, finally manages a nod. "The sentences are to run concurrently," Judge Eielson says, and the policeman looks up—it's not three and a half years after all.

"Platnik, Robert Platnik." Platnik is a middle-aged white man in an open-necked white shirt. He looks uncowed and faintly amused. "To the charge of breach of the peace how do you plead?"

Platnik begins a dialogue with himself. "Well, if I plead guilty, I go back to work, right? But it's hard to plead guilty to what you didn't do."

The prosecutor turns toward him. "How do you plead?"

The judge begins to smile.

"Well," says Platnik, "I'll plead guilty."

"Wait a minute," the judge says. "Don't plead guilty if you—"

"I can't afford to come back," Platnik says.

"Let's pass it and have the police report read to him," the judge says.

"No, I'll plead guilty. I want to plead guilty."

"Enter a plea of not guilty," the judge orders.

Another case is called, also a breach of the peace. The defendant is a defiant-looking young black. "I think he has troubles, Your Honor," the public defender says.

"I see the report says he's a chronic schizophrenic," Eielson says.

"I don't think I have no troubles," the defendant mutters. "I think I can go back home." He pleads guilty.

"He made an obscene gesture to customers in a store," the prosecutor reads. "The report says he seemed to be in a daze. I think he has mental problems, Your Honor."

"One hundred eighty days suspended, two years probation," the judge rules. "You either behave or go to jail." There is no mention of psychiatric treatment, although a probation officer's report has recommended it.

Now Platnik returns, still talking to himself. He reaffirms his plea of guilty. His manner seems to break the tension. The judge appears relaxed and the lawyers follow his lead.

"The complaint says his wife took his wallet and he pushed her," the prosecutor reads.

"Are you living with her?" the judge asks.

"Right at the moment I do," he replies. "I gave her a check last night. I have a room, let's put it that way."

The family-relations officer knows them. "She's as bad as he is, Judge," she says.

"Today's fine is twenty-five dollars," Eielson says.

Platnik looks crestfallen. "I haven't got it," he says. He thinks a minute. "How about my vacation pay when I get it?"

"It's always the man that gets arrested," the woman family-relations officer whispers. "Both of them are going at it all the time, but he takes the rap."

"Stay of execution for two weeks until you get your vacation pay," the judge decrees.

Platnik smiles merrily. He resumes his conversation with himself as he turns to leave: "I have no more straight pay coming, let's see . . ." He turns around when he reaches the railing. "Could you make that on a Friday?"

The judge smiles. "Okay."

It is almost one o'clock and the room is nearly empty. The day's business has been moved. Despite the judge's shifts of mood, he has generally treated defendants leniently. The narcotics offenders who promised to cooperate with various drug programs have been given suspended sentences and assigned to programs. Most of the drunks, disorderly conducts, and petty thefts have been dealt with by fines. Non-support cases are likely to draw a jail sentence from Eielson, but there have been none up for sentencing today. Some first offenders have been dismissed. The only defendants in jail are those who were there before the session began.

"White, Ted White," the prosecutor calls. A reed-thin, unsteady young white man approaches the bench. He leans slightly forward. He looks as if he might topple, then steadies himself by resting his fingers on a table. The charge is possession of "controlled drugs," in his case LSD.

White wants to enter a drug program. He pleads guilty. He looks at once arrogant and near tears. "He needs help, Your Honor," the public defender says. White gulps.

The judge looks at him, and something changes in his expression. His eyes show a warmth not visible before. "Didn't I dismiss a glue-sniffing case against you some years ago, Teddy?" White nods. "You went the whole way, huh?" the judge continues, looking at him. Eielson shakes his head sadly. "He needs help. I'm glad he realizes it. What a *waste* of a life. Good kid, too."

"I'm not going to sentence him today," the judge says, "I'm going to commit him to Fairfield Hills and ask for a pre-sentence investigation. It's obvious he's drug dependent."

The drug liaison officer stands up. "But if he's adjudged drug dependent, they don't treat him," he says. "They just put him down as dependent and don't do anything for him."

The judge thinks a minute. "I have to sentence him, then," he says. "I sentence you to three hundred sixty days, execution suspended, and two years probation, and order you committed to the Connecticut Department of Mental Health for a period of ninety days to twenty-four months." White is looking down at the table and weaving slightly. "Good luck to you, Ted." The judge stares after him as he leaves.

"Okay, that's it," he says. "Court's adjourned."

The Bridgeport snakepit is a phenomenon of contemporary American justice. Almost every city in America has its miasmic equivalent. In Boston it is the Municipal Court, in Detroit the Recorder's Court, in New York the Criminal Court, but always the atmosphere is the same—hustle them through, "move the business," get through the calendar any way you can. Trials are a luxury the system cannot afford, and out with the trial go the carefully written and preserved safeguards of the law—the rules, the search for truth, the right to confront your accuser, the promise of fairness, the presumption of innocence. The "rights" upheld by the Supreme Court—the right to an attorney, the right to appeal, and to a jury trial—are sometimes granted lip-service, sometimes not. A suspended sentence in Boston Municipal Court is coupled with a waiver of the right to appeal. In virtually every lower court in the land, to demand a trial is to risk a higher sentence. The judicial rationale is that a guilty plea is an "admission of wrong" and thus deserves consideration, but the real reasons are expediency, the press of numbers on an antiquated structure, and bureaucratic inertia.

Leonard Downie summed it up in his book *Justice Denied:*

"A lawyer who knows next to nothing about his client or the facts of the crime with which he is charged barters away a man's right to a trial, and, along with it, the presumption that a defendant is innocent until proved guilty—the presumption on which the

American system of criminal justice rests. A prosecutor who knows little more about the case than what a policeman tells him hurriedly trades off one of American society's most important responsibilities—the responsibility for providing a full hearing for those charged with criminal acts and the levying of appropriate sanctions upon those convicted of crimes against that society. The judge, who has abdicated his authority to bartering lawyers, acquiesces to all this and sanctifies it for 'the record.'

". . . An indifferent public has allowed the system to become overwhelmed with work: too many cases for too few judges, too few lawyers, too few clerks. An uncaring legal community has failed to modernize the system to cope with the inundation. How else can the system survive, except by trying to dispose of cases as fast as it can?"

"The system of criminal justice in the lower courts is well on its way to collapse," political scientist Richard Pious wrote in 1971. "It forces judges, prosecutors, and defense attorneys, no matter how interested they are in justice, to engage in practices which provide neither speedy trials nor justice. At best only a rough equity is provided, and that at the cost of the deterrent power of the criminal code."

Plea bargaining is defended as essential by judges at every level, including the highest. Chief Justice Warren E. Burger, who prefers the dressier phrase "plea discussions," upholds the practice as desirable as well as necessary. ". . . The disposition of criminal charges by agreement between the prosecutor and the accused, sometimes loosely called 'plea bargaining,' " he wrote in a 1971 decision, "is an essential component of the administration of justice. Properly administered, it is to be encouraged. If every criminal charge were subjected to a full-scale trial, the states and the federal government would need to multiply by many times the number of judges and court facilities."

But one must question a rationale built on court congestion. Courts *are* under heavy pressure, unarguably. And we *are* in a period of escalating litigation, at every level, indisputably. But judges and others have bemoaned the law's delay for centuries. Hammurabi complained about it 3700 years ago. Shakespeare included it in Hamlet's catalog of life's frustrations. It is not peculiar to twentieth-century America.

In addition, close observation of the snakepit courts raises other questions. If the press of business is so great, how are so many

judges able to complete their calendars by lunchtime? Judicial laziness and bureaucratic sluggishness certainly play a part. It is rare
to find a court operating after 4:00 p.m. or before 9:30 a.m. The
routine of the snakepit becomes comfortable for those who live in
it. It sets a rhythm to their days. And it has other advantages. A
criminal lawyer who handles ten cases in a morning, as many do in
Eielson's court, can make more money in three hours of pleading
than he can in two days of trial work. "They love the way he moves
it along," one court officer said of Eielson. "They get fat off him."

If congestion is the excuse for mass-production justice, then
judges themselves must bear part of the responsibility. Judges who
work four-hour days or postpone decisions for long periods increase
the congestion, as do archaic administrative practices. The simple
expedient of shifting several judges from civil to criminal work
helped reduce backlogs in San Francisco. Increasing the daily caseload of individual judges from four to nine did the same in
Portland.

Appellate courts have recognized the crippling injustice of long-
delayed trials and have tried to enforce rules to overcome it, sometimes without success. The chief judge of the New York state
Court of Appeals ordered New York criminal courts to dismiss any
case delayed longer than six months before trial, and gave the
courts a year to prepare. When the year was up, in May 1972, the
state legislature responded to massed prosecutorial opposition by,
in effect, negating the rule. The prosecutors argued that the possibility of a dismissal removed any incentive for a defendant to plead
guilty.

President Nixon has proposed that non-lawyer "parajudges" be
given responsibility for many of the routine judicial tasks, and that
drunkenness, minor traffic offenses, and other lesser crimes be
handled by other agencies—which would free judges to deal more
effectively with their oppressive caseloads. Senator Henry M. Jackson introduced a bill that would provide for more judges and other
staff and simultaneously assure all criminal defendants the right to
a trial within sixty days.

But greater efficiency, especially if it is at the expense of constitutional protections, is no panacea. "I think there is a grave danger
we have been oversold on the benefits of judicial efficiency," writes
Chief Judge David L. Bazelon of the U.S. Court of Appeals for the
District of Columbia Circuit. ". . . In our current stampede for
faster convictions and fewer appeals, we are in danger of throwing

out the baby and serving the bathwater for soup." Bazelon argues
that the courts are inefficient by their nature, and must be to perform their proper function.

So the snakepits persist, with few signs of genuine reform in
sight. Libertarians bellow, policemen grumble, and judges can
only shrug and doggedly seek a silver lining. "There's a discount in
justice for pleading guilty to a lesser offense because there's an
admission of wrong," says Rodney Eielson. "If we didn't have plea
bargaining, we'd need as many courtrooms in Connecticut as there
are gymnasiums. Anyone who condemns it doesn't know the problems. Besides," he adds disingenuously, "without it you assume the
police are always right. Plea bargaining knocks down the original
police charges."

Eielson has a zest absent in most judges, a taste for the dapper
and dashing, a willingness to hang around as long as the party
lasts. He favors bright print shirts and white shoes, prefers middlebrow music—"I don't like the heavies"—and drives a classic Mer-
cedes sport car. He sometimes fishes in Long Island Sound before
coming to court, and hurries back to his forty-foot fishing boat
after a morning of moving the business.

He is also a bridge-burner who has alienated every segment of
his judicial constituency—prosecutors, defense lawyers, police,
defendants, other judges—at one time or another, as well as the
politicians who put him on the bench in the first place. He is mer-
curial, quirky, melancholy, even fanciful. He is more romantic than
rational. He seems at times to operate on raw emotion, to react to
feelings much more than facts, though he is clever enough to hide
his feelings in legal language. His personality puts him forever at
odds with the profession he serves.

"He's . . . the word is fickle," says an attorney who knows him
well. "He's self-centered, sarcastic, volatile, and sometimes quite
fair. You can't predict him. You can have a case where a suspended
sentence and commitment to a drug program seems logical, and he
might do it, or he might do something else altogether. Sometimes
he'll give everyone in court a high bond, and sometimes he'll lean
over the other way."

"He has the courtroom demeanor of a drill instructor," says another. "I think he's unstable. He has the kind of clout that not only stings but breaks your jaw in two places. He can destroy a lawyer, and then be amiable as hell after court. Once I was in his court and it was close to one o'clock, and everyone knew he wanted to get out early. He was hearing a marijuana case, and the state wanted to put a fifteen-year-old kid on the stand as an expert witness. The lawyer objected and cited precedent. Eielson didn't even blink, he overruled it. Then the lawyer said, 'Your Honor, may I have the basis for your ruling?' Jesus, he wheeled in his chair, banged his hand on the desk, his eyes bugged out, and he said, 'Don't you EVER dare ask me again for the basis for one of my rulings or I'll hold you in contempt.' He looked like he wanted to kill that lawyer. Then later that afternoon he gave a very lucid explanation for the ruling."

"The easiest thing would be to send everybody to jail," Eielson says, "and everyone would congratulate you. It's so easy for a judge to lean in the direction of the state because you're dealing with the same prosecutors all the time. You know them, you're familiar with their method. But I try not to. You sit up there and you begin to appreciate the awesomeness of the power you have. There's an aura to a courtroom which I've never gotten over, the idea of it, the awesomeness of justice. You're acting as God for that moment. You can live with it, but you never get used to it.

"You know, they say that judges are pessimists, teachers are realists, and ministers are optimists. I'm not cynical to the point that I still won't take a chance and hope for the best. But I guess I really expect the worst. I know what's going to happen, but I still have to give a man one last chance before I put him in jail, because jail is the end of the road. I have no illusions that a prisoner is going to be rehabilitated. I'm not sending them to jail for rehabilitation, but for punishment and to protect society. I'd rather be accused of leniency and give them a chance than lock them up and throw the key away.

"I'm not consistent in sentencing because I take a person's background into consideration. You demand more of an educated person. A fine of fifteen dollars to a Negro in a housing project means as much as fifty dollars to someone in Fairfield."

Eielson grew up in a middle-class neighborhood in a New Haven suburb. His father, a minister of the Evangelical Free Church in

New Haven, had immigrated to America from Norway as a youth. His mother was a Swede from Minnesota.

At seventeen he left home to join the Navy, serving four years as an enlisted man aboard amphibious landing craft during the war. He returned to Connecticut and rushed through Bridgeport University and the University of Connecticut law school in five years. He was in a hurry to get into politics.

He set up a law practice in Bridgeport, dealing mainly in real estate, and immediately became a member of the local Republican organization. He was elected to the Republican town committee in suburban Trumbull and joined the Young Republicans. He married a high-school science teacher.

In 1955, at thirty-one, he was elected to the lower house of the state legislature. He became a protégé of Bill Brennan, the leader of Fairfield County Republicans and a power in state politics, and for the next few years he was a rising star in the Connecticut GOP.

"Bill Brennan was like a father to me," he says. "I was one of his boys. I can remember riding into New York one day with Bill, and he said to me, 'Rod, where would you say the seat of financial and political power in the United States is?' And I just automatically said, 'Why, Washington.' He said, 'Now, think about it, where do you think the power really is?' And I still said Washington. And he said, 'No, it's the Waldorf Towers.' Because at that time MacArthur was living there, and Hoover, and Jim Farley, and Luce, and I think Joe Kennedy. He was a very astute man and a good politician. He was like [Connecticut Democratic leader] John Bailey. It was hard to get a promise out of him, but once he made one he stuck to it."

Brennan guided Eielson's career. Reelected to the state House of Representatives in 1957, he was named assistant minority leader with Brennan's backing. He sat on the labor and judiciary committees. When Governor Abraham Ribicoff proposed in 1957 that the state's system of local courts be replaced with a single statewide circuit court, future Circuit Judge Eielson opposed it.

In 1958 Connecticut Republicans nominated the thirty-four-year-old Eielson to run for state controller. "I got trounced in the Ribicoff landslide," he recalls, "and retired from politics at the overwhelming wishes of the people of Connecticut." The meteor had crashed. His quick rise and early fall in state politics had spanned just four years.

He declined an opportunity to run for first selectman (mayor) of his hometown of Trumbull, and returned to his law practice. But Brennan was still looking out for him.

Ribicoff's court-reform bill, buttressed considerably when Brennan gave it his support, was enacted into law in 1959. Forty-four new judgeships were created, a patronage bonanza that drew a reported two hundred applications from the faithful of both parties. The bill required that the forty-four appointments be split evenly between Republicans and Democrats, apparently the price exacted by Brennan for his support.

"Bill thought it would be a good idea if I went on the bench," Eielson recalls. "When he first suggested it I turned it down. I thought I was too young, and I never aspired to be a judge anyway. But my first love was still politics, and the judgeship was a way to stay in politics. Brennan figured that the Republicans were out for eight years at least, and there was no better place to sit out a political famine than on the bench." Eielson was persuaded, and he was one of the charter members of the new court when it began in January 1961. At thirty-six, he was the youngest circuit judge.

"I liked the bench from the start," he says. "It's a good job. I have no problem making decisions." In time his political ardor ebbed. "It took me about four years to make up my mind. I wouldn't go back into politics now. It's a new machine from my days and I don't have the patience or the tenacity any more."

Like many judges with political backgrounds, Eielson views his as an asset. "You can't survive in politics unless you have the art of listening to the other side and unless you're willing to compromise," he says. "Without that and the ability to project yourself, you're no good in politics. And it's the same with judging. You can't sit up there unless you can listen to both sides and keep an open mind. Only we don't call it compromising on the bench, we call it understanding."

Eielson's natural ebullience was never inhibited by the robe. He popped into the newspapers often enough to inspire muttering in outlying chambers. Publicity doesn't come easy to lower-court judges, who patrol a world of shoplifters and derelicts, but he had a gift for it. On one occasion in the early 1960s he banished a woman from his court for wearing slacks, but not without quoting Ogden Nash: "Sure, deck your lower limbs in pants; yours are the limbs, my sweeting. You look divine when you advance—have you seen yourself retreating?"

He became known for his consistently harsh sentences to fathers guilty of non-support. "My feeling is that a man should support his family and especially his children, and a man who won't do that is less than an animal," he says. "If he's on welfare, he's a moocher. I have one sentence for them and it's well known—three hundred and sixty days in jail. That's for any man who works but doesn't support his kids, or who doesn't work if there's work available. It's funny how they'll get the money for support payments when jail is threatened."

When a stripper named Hope Diamond plunged topless into a lake near Hartford, Eielson ordered her bound over to the Superior Court for indecent exposure and "risk of injury to a minor" (because a young boy was present). This was headline stuff, and inspired an original Eielson literary effort: "Intrigue is greater when you conceal, 'tis far far better than to reveal. Allurement is all to a degree; this is true even above the knee."

He was in the papers again when a seventeen-year-old black girl got her conversational needle stuck in court. "I asked her a question and she said, 'Fuck you.' I said very well, that will be thirty days. Then her mother and father tried to restrain her, and she told them to go fuck themselves. So I gave her thirty more. The matron came up and she said the same thing to her. I gave her another thirty and said take her away. I found out afterward that the reason she was arrested was because she walked up to a cop in a car and told him to go fuck himself. The story in the paper said, 'Girl loses numbers game with judge.' "

But his biggest burst of publicity came in 1964, when he ordered the arrest of the parents of several teenagers in Darien for serving liquor to their children. The arrests followed the auto death of a seventeen-year-old girl who had been drinking at home. Three corporate executives and a psychiatrist were among the arrested parents, who were ultimately fined. Eielson became nationally known as "the Darien Case judge," received dozens of speaking invitations, wrote an article for *McCall's* magazine, and enjoyed a brief vogue as an expert on the decline of parental responsibility.

He sailed through the mandatory legislative reconfirmation of his first four-year term in 1965. But when he came up again in 1969, all the resentments and animosity he had engendered through the years boiled to the surface and he nearly lost his job. 1969 brought both personal and professional disaster for him. He and his wife separated in January, and nine months later she died of a heart attack. Their only son, a high-school student, was arrested that year on a narcotics charge; he was later given a suspended sentence in Superior Court.

By 1969 Eielson's free-wheeling, let-the-chips-fall judicial style, sporadic irascibility, and arrogance had littered Connecticut courthouses with his enemies. Lawyers openly complained about him, and a state-bar poll found that most of the anonymous lawyers who replied regarded him as unfit for his job. His brother judges grumbled among themselves that he didn't pull his weight. He feuded with police and prosecutors constantly. They said he released suspects out of personal pique. He accused policemen of "insolence"—one had given him a speeding ticket back in 1957— and prosecutors of failure to prepare.

"I saw a guy brought into his court once for speeding," a lawyer remembers. "The state police said he was doing seventy-six. The guy was contesting it, defending himself, and the state didn't have the tuning-fork expert who could testify that their radar was accurate. Eielson told the guy to 'make a motion.' He didn't understand, he thought he was being railroaded. Finally the judge said, 'I am ready to entertain a motion to dismiss.' Eielson dismissed it, and the state troopers were standing in back of the court with their mouths open."

But the most important enemies he made were the attorneys who serve in the legislature. Under the Connecticut system, the same legislative lawyers who must pass on a judge's appointment may frequently appear in his court. Eielson, whose bouts of ill temper were politically non-partisan, had offended enough of them to jeopardize his reconfirmation.

The judiciary committee of the lower house called him to Hartford to answer the complaints against him in a secret session. They asked about an occasion when he said in open court that he hadn't yet sentenced his "quota" to jail that day. They were concerned about a day in Waterbury when he heard 264 separate criminal cases. He was accused of refusing to refer children to Juvenile Court. After the hearing he conferred privately with committee chairman John A. Carrozzella of Wallingford, and Carrozzella reported that he had admitted making mistakes and promised to reform.

In the customary smooth-it-over, don't-rock-the-boat ambience of

Connecticut judicial politics, that would have been that. But when the resolution on Eielson's reconfirmation was introduced on the floor of the house, the debate on his fitness swirled into the open, a development unprecedented in state history. It was a "public display," wrote a Hartford political reporter, "that startled and amazed the most hard-bitten politicians."

The floor debate included all the earlier complaints and added a few more. Representative Bernard L. Avcollie of Naugatuck claimed that Eielson's "morals are strongly in question," citing an incident when he allegedly brought a girlfriend to court and "noontime drinking with attorneys." Representative Carl R. Ajello of Ansonia said Eielson had once threatened to put him in jail. Representative Howard M. Klebanoff of Hartford complained that Eielson announced in court that he had "to be at my boat by eleven thirty." Several legislators spoke in his favor, and others criticized the debate itself as a "star chamber" proceeding with the judge unable to defend himself. In all, 14 legislators spoke for his confirmation and 6 against it. The vote of the full house was 90 to 66 to confirm.

Eielson was staggered. "There were so many things thrown at me that I began to feel just shot," he says. "I felt physically and mentally destroyed. Everything came at once. I'd start crying sometimes for no reason. I couldn't eat." In September he took a two-month sick leave and sailed his boat down to Florida and back with his son.

He believes the attack on him was motivated by legislative lawyers who expected special treatment and didn't get it. "A judge is a sitting duck for any lawyer with a beef, particularly one with political muscle." He denies that he promised any change in his judicial behavior. "They wanted me to grovel," he says, "and I wouldn't. I told them that's the way I am."

He became melancholy. "I thought about retiring," he says, "and maybe going into some kind of business connected with fishing or boating. I wanted to get out of law and politics altogether." But after a few months his interest in the job revived. "There were so many hurts so fast that I got numb," he says, "but I got through it. I decided that this is my life's work. Whatever happens now is aftermath."

His son's experience with drugs made him "personally aware of the drug problem in a way I hadn't been before," he says. "Before, I had what you might call the casual judicial approach. I think I'm more knowledgeable now." He and his son participated in encounter therapy. "That shook me up," he says. Once a youth up for sentencing on drug charges accused him in court of being the father of a drug-user. "The guards grabbed the kid," a court officer recalls, "and the judge just stepped down from the bench and declared a recess. We all had some coffee. The guy was sentenced to two years, but Eielson later reduced it to three months."

By 1973 most of the forty-four judges originally appointed to the Circuit bench had been promoted. Of the twenty-two Republicans named in 1961, only Eielson and one other judge remained. He says he prefers the lower court. "The Circuit Court is more human," he says. "It's the working court, the court of first impression. I like that type of atmosphere. You're dealing with problems of people in everyday life. I have no great ambition," he declares. "Promotion is all muscle here anyway—it doesn't have anything to do with merit. I never asked to be promoted." The legislature reconfirmed his appointment for another four years in 1973, this time without any debate.

The lawyers who appear before him regard him with a strange mixture of fear, admiration, and disapproval. "He's independent and decisive," one says. "A lot of judges worry about appeals or the legislature, but he doesn't seem to care. He's the absolute boss in the courtroom, and he wants you to be grateful when he does anything short of send someone to jail. He has no racial prejudice, but he's quirky and sarcastic. He doesn't decide on the basis of neutral principles, but rather on what he infers from an attitude or an expression."

"A judge can show too much personality on the bench," another attorney says, "and the result is a loss of respect for the system. He's a notorious bug-out, but it's more complicated than that. It's just that he wants to do it his way, and he thinks it shouldn't take that long. He's too lazy to look up the law, but he knows enough of it to bullshit about it. No judge should be as sarcastic as he is, but he can also be very reasonable. Ultimately, I think he's a tyrant."

Eielson contends that sarcasm is preferable to moralizing. "I don't believe in lecturing," he says, "but I'll make a sarcastic remark because I think it's more penetrating. He'll remember it. You have to reach a person, and you do that by projecting yourself and your humanity, your personality.

"A judge shouldn't be detached. We're always fighting to keep from treating people as numbers, even though we have to expedite the business. It makes a difference to me if a defendant is penitent. I try to read character. I look for defiance in the eyes. If they look ashamed, that's a good sign."

"Eielson is qualified," a critical lawyer says, "precisely because there are no standards. In the real world we get judges through politics, they go up through the chain of command and get the party leader's blessing. We get good ones and bad ones, and we've had them better and worse than him. So in those terms he's fit. But in a better system, maybe in a better world, he wouldn't be a judge."

The system of judicial selection that produced Rodney Eielson lives on in Connecticut. The governor, often with the advice of the state party chairman, nominates judicial candidates, who are then confirmed by the legislature. The bar association, which screens potential judges in many states, is ineffectual in Connecticut. The choice is the governor's, and behind him are the party men. Promotions are based not on merit, but on service to the party and on seniority. One result is that the average age of Connecticut judges —fifty-eight on the Circuit and Common Pleas courts, sixty on the Superior Court—is one of the highest in the nation. Another result is that the quality of the judges is erratic but tending to mediocre.

"A judge without political clout is lost, he wouldn't stand a chance," says a prosecutor. "Occasionally the politicians step out of line and appoint a good judge, but it's a fluke."

"The Circuit Court appointments are mainly controlled by the state chairmen and any local party chairmen with power," a defense attorney says. "The guy says he wants to be a judge, he tells the party leader, and the party leader decides whether they owe him a favor.

"There are some good ones, but mainly the bench attracts lawyers who aren't making it in private practice, or those to whom the retirement benefits look good, or those with money who just want to be called Your Honor, or failed politicians. I don't know any who think it's their calling, even among those I admire most. There have been only two instances where judges were persuaded to retire; it's essentially a lifetime job as long as they don't commit rape."

"You're appointed for what it does for the party," says a circuit judge, "and for no other reason. Some men become judges by ringing doorbells, hustling for the party. If you want to spend time at a law library, you have no time to develop political influence, and you're lost." One Connecticut judge won his job through his brother's political contributions. Another tried for six years after losing a mayoralty election before he was finally rewarded. A third was the brother of a high state official; a fourth was making too many waves in an appointive job.

"The system almost guarantees incompetence," another attorney said. "It's like asking fish to walk when you take politicians or office lawyers [as opposed to trial lawyers] and put them on the bench. Many of them have failed in politics or law, and when they get on the bench it's a rebirth—people have to listen to them now. And then when they have to rule, it's like sitting behind the wheel of a racing car that goes two hundred and forty miles an hour and you have to drive it and you can't."

A Judicial Review Council was set up in 1969 to receive complaints about judges, but the council's only power is to recommend impeachment to the governor and legislature. Not surprisingly, no such recommendations have been made. To its somewhat tepid credit, Connecticut has remained free of the revelations of judicial venality that have afflicted many other states, including neighboring New York and Massachusetts.

In 1972 an *ad hoc* group called the Committee on Judicial Modernization, backed by the state bar association, recommended adoption of merit selection and the creation of an effective removal commission. "Merit selection isn't perfect," says one member of the reform group, "but it's the best system short of a visitation by an angel tapping a man and designating him God. If nothing else, it destroys the basis for belief that politics is the primary consideration, among judges along with everyone else. Eielson would never have made it through a selection commission." The Connecticut legislature commissioned a study of court reform, including merit selection, but no recommendations were expected until 1974.

It is four o'clock on a Wednesday afternoon, and Rodney Eielson is sitting with his feet up on the small metal desk in his chambers.

The office is devoid of charm. It is spare and uncarpeted, with a few wooden chairs and blank walls. There is none of the oak-and-leather atmosphere one associates with "chambers."

It has been a long and difficult day. The morning calendar spilled into the afternoon, and then there was a hearing on whether a sixteen-year-old boy was mentally competent to plead. The judge ruled that he was, but he still hasn't decided what to do with him.

The door opens and the public defender comes in. "You moved a lot of business today," the judge says admiringly.

The attorney is pleased. "Twenty-four," he says.

"That's really moving it," says Eielson.

"Yeah, but you're still getting paid the same," the prosecutor says sourly.

"You know, these doctors take the day off to come down here and testify," the judge says, referring to two Asian physicians who had testified in the competency hearing. "Then they charge the state for it. Everybody's found a way to get a buck." He shakes his head.

A black Youth Services worker comes in to report on the case. "I think the boy is mentally defective," he says.

"Yes," the judge replies, "but unfortunately there's no place to keep him. He can't go back to Fairfield Hills. They don't want him. He's not committable."

"He's a retardate," the public defender says. "But he can't go to Southbury. He's too old."

"He would have been perfect for it too," Eielson says.

"And I don't want him on the street," the youth worker says. "I know he's in trouble on the street."

"Do you think you can find a place for him?" Eielson asks.

"I don't know. I can try."

"I can continue it for a few days if you want to try."

The public defender and the youth worker leave.

"That's a good man," the judge says of the youth worker. "He's a very soft-spoken Negro."

The door opens again and another lawyer comes in, a good friend of the judge. "You allow Jews in here?" he says.

"Is there one *here?*" Eielson asks in mock anger.

Eielson and the lawyer are plainly comfortable in each other's company. They begin to exchange stories about each other.

"You remember that time you came to court hung-over and you

were representing a client on an intoxication charge?" Eielson says, laughing.

The lawyer picks up the story. "Yeah, and you said you didn't know which of us to send to honor camp."

"Another time," the judge continues, "this hero was representing a guy paying twenty dollars a week in non-support and I said to him in court, 'I bet you wish *you* could get that.'" Eielson smiles and looks at him. "But I like you anyway. You've always been pleasantly obnoxious."

Eielson goes on. "We used to have a guy here named Charley the Drunk. He had the longest drunk record of anybody in town, but the problem was he couldn't control his bladder." The lawyers chuckle at the memory. "So what we'd do is keep him out of the courtroom. He'd stand over in the hall by the door, and we'd yell out, 'Charley, how do you plead?' and he'd say guilty. And if I gave him a jail sentence, the police wouldn't like it because he'd stink up the place. It would take a day to delouse him and they'd have to fumigate after he was there awhile."

The public defender and the youth worker return. "He can go to Fairfield Hills," the lawyer reports, "because he's charged with intoxication."

"Yes, but they won't let him stay," the judge says. "They'll throw him out after thirty days and then what?"

"Well, we can get him there anyway."

"His IQ is sixty-nine," Eielson says. "Isn't there some way we can get him to Southbury?"

"I'll try it," the youth worker says, and he goes out again.

"No recesses tomorrow," Eielson says to the public defender and prosecutor. "I'm not getting off the bench. I have to be out by twelve thirty for a judges' meeting." They nod.

The youth worker returns. "He says he's afraid to go to North Avenue jail because he testified against some people there and they're looking for him. We can send him to the hospital as an alcoholic, but it's only good for thirty days. It's no solution." He leaves to continue checking.

"I want to give him whatever chance I can," the judge says. "The problem is finding a place to put him."

"It's enough to give you ulcers," the prosecutor says.

"Not me," says the judge. "I always say I give ulcers, I don't get 'em."

The judge's friend gets up to leave. "You stay out of trouble," Eielson says. "That legislator rapped me for drinking with lawyers," the judge goes on. "You know, there's not a judge around who doesn't do that."

"You do it better than most, though," his friend says. The judge laughs.

The youth worker returns as the judge's friend leaves. "The phone's busy, I can't get through to Southbury," he says.

"Okay, let's put him in Fairfield Hills," the judge says. "It's just a temporary solution, but it's all we have."

"I'll keep working on it," the youth worker says.

The judge puts on his robe. "I think I'm assigned to New London after this," he sighs. "I'm due for an easy one." He goes into court to take the boy's guilty plea and assign him to the hospital.

Twenty minutes later I was stalled in a line of traffic on a two-lane road heading north out of Bridgeport. Suddenly a light-blue sports car with the top down buzzed by me on the right, where there wasn't room for a full-sized car. I glanced over and saw Eielson, in his baby-blue blazer and big sunglasses, running a judicial hand through his long, wavy hair.

V

Just Plain Frank

A Texas judge lets his gut reaction be his guide

I'LL CALL HIM FRANK BRYANT, which is not his real
name, because I promised that I would disguise his identity and
that of the good-sized Texas city where he works. Bryant presides
over a criminal court where the business is misdemeanor crimes:
drunk driving, carrying a pistol without a permit, simple assault,
shoplifting—offenses with a penalty of no more than two years in
jail.

The judge is a bluff, good-natured man in his early fifties with
an unpretentious manner and thinning, caramel-colored hair. He
drives to work in a pickup truck, and wears black cowboy boots
and a large, silver-plated belt buckle. He refers to most women as
either "sweetie" or "babe" and men as "sport." He keeps a cartoon
on his desk blotter which shows a judge glaring at a long-haired
witness and saying, "You better show me the proper respect, sonny.
I kissed a lot of ass to get this job." Next to it is a small statue of
Rodin's "Thinker" mounted on a toilet seat, with the inscription,
"Congratulations on Your New Position."

He is relatively new to the bench—"I'm still scratching around
to find my way." His courtroom is long and low-ceilinged, with ten
rows of upholstered seats—trial-watching is a popular spectator
sport in Texas—a linoleum floor, and a carved wooden bench
painted white. The pace of court business is unhurried and the

89

atmosphere neighborly; he spends two to three hours on the bench in an average day (longer during a trial). Lawyers, prosecutors, clerks, and judge all seem to be old friends and drinking buddies. Aside from a modest "All rise" when he enters in the morning, there is little ceremony. "I'm flying by the seat of my britches in this job," he told me one day. "You know what they say—all it takes is a keen sense of justice and a legal-sounding noise."

We had met in another city, and when I wrote asking if I could visit him on his home ground he replied with characterisic directness, inviting me to come ahead but warning that "my candor will be directly proportionate to how far away from home I am." He greeted me in the same spirit: "Come on in," he said. "I'll try to avoid telling you the truth as much as I can." Judicial candor varies with the judges' position in the hierarchy—the lower the court, as a rule, the greater the candor; the curtain of dignity thickens as they climb. Bryant was far and away the most open and ingenuous judge I interviewed, which is why I can't identify him.

"We ain't got much today, just a few little pleas," he said. "Later in the week we might have us a con-test. And I might be running off now and then. I'll go to any damn meeting I'm invited to if there's gonna be voters there. Hell, I'd go to a dogfight if somebody asked me."

His office was small and windowless. There was a desk, a vinyl couch, and three wooden chairs. A shelf behind the desk contained several lawbooks, including a well-thumbed *Manual of Reversible Errors*. On the wall was a painting of a thoroughbred race horse, courtesy of a distillery, titled "She was Bred in Old Kentucky."

A young prosecutor knocked at the door and poked his head in. "We're all set, Judge," he said. "I think we're gonna con-test maybe Thursday."

"Good," Bryant replied. He put on his robe and strode down a hall into his courtroom, greeting staff and friends as he went. "Whaddaya say, sport?" he said to a bailiff.

The first case involved a heavy-set, middle-aged Mexican woman who was pleading guilty to shoplifting. She stood to enter her plea. Her lawyer remained seated, toying with a pencil.

"Does the prosecution have a recommendation for sentence in this case?" the judge asked.

"The state recommends two years probation and a three-hundred-dollar fine."

"Let me see the jacket," the judge said.

The prosecutor handed up a brown folder containing the police report and the woman's prior record.

"Do you have any source of income, Mrs.—ah—Garcia?"

"I make clothes." She sat down next to her lawyer.

The judge studied the file. His lower lip began to creep upward. "Whose car was it you were in when you were arrested, ma'am?"

She shrugged. "I don't know. They just picked me up and then they left."

"Did you steal seven bags of clothing?"

"I guess so."

"What were you going to do with the men's clothes?"

"I don't know."

"Were the clothes returned to the store?"

The lawyer spread his arms out, palms up. "I don't know," he said.

The woman said they were.

"How many times have you been picked up for shoplifting?"

"This is the first time."

The judge raised his eyebrows. "I have a report that says you were picked up several times before—let's see, one, two, three. It says you served twenty-five days in jail. Is that true?"

She stared at him without replying.

"Mrs. Garcia, what's it going to take to get you to stop stealing?" He thrust his jaw forward as he spoke.

"I'm not gonna steal no more."

"Stand up, please, ma'am."

She stood and pressed her hands together.

"I find you guilty and sentence you to pay a fine of three hundred dollars and serve two years in county jail. Now, do you know what probation is?" She nodded vaguely. "It means somebody's gonna be watching you. If they catch you again, it'll be two years in jail. Okay, sentence is probated for two years. That's all." He nodded as she turned to leave.

The next case was a well-dressed, middle-aged white man who pleaded guilty to drunk driving. He was fined $200 and sentenced to the three days he had already spent in jail. Then came a young Mexican man charged with the same crime. The prosecutor recommended a $200 fine and thirty days probation. The judge agreed.

Bryant was ready to call a recess when about twenty-five high-school students appeared through the swinging door at the back of the courtroom. "What's this, a jailbreak?" he cried in mock alarm. "Bailiff, check the jail and see if there's been a break."

A teacher explained that the students were members of a business-law class. They shuffled uncomfortably to the front of the court. "Well, we don't have any business in this court," the judge said. "We're in the business of putting people in jail."

"What crimes do you—uh—deal with?" a boy asked.

"Pistols, drunks, talking abusively on the telephone—any of y'all talk abusively on the phone?" A few laughed self-consciously. "And we get some shopliftin'. Any of y'all do any shopliftin' while you're downtown?"

He stood and led them to a small jury room. "This is where the business gets done," he said. They glanced inside the door.

"Well, thanks very much, Judge," the teacher said. "Anybody have any questions?"

A girl raised her hand. "What do you think about your job?"

"Like it," he said.

He retreated to his office as the students filed out. A probation officer was waiting for him.

"You know, Judge," he began, "that Mrs. Garcia lives about fifty miles from here. She's plumb in another jurisdiction, and she doesn't have a car—"

" 'Less somebody comes to pick her up," the judge interrupted.

"Well, the thing is that we can't supervise her from here, and they ignore misdemeanor probation cases over there."

Bryant thought a moment. "I probably should have put her in jail," he said. "I'm kind of a slob, you know. She's a goddam professional thief." He looked at the probation man. "No way to supervise her, huh?" The man shook his head. "Well, okay, let's just cut her off, then. Maybe she'll stay out of this county."

Bryant hung his robe on a clothes rack as two prosecutors and a defense attorney came into his office. "Hey, men," he said. "How y'all doin'?"

They exchanged greetings and sat down.

"John, what'd you figure the jury was up to last week in that drug case?" he asked the older of the two prosecutors, a man of perhaps thirty.

"I think they were about half flaky, Judge."

Bryant explained that the jury in a drug-possession case had been unable to agree, forcing a mistrial. "The defendant was a hippie type. He was a no-good little shit," he said. "But the trouble was the police beat the living crap out of him. I think a hang-up is reasonable in a case like that."

"Hey, Judge," the younger prosecutor said, "you remember that guy Diggs, the one we put away for molesting that woman?"

"Was that the black on white?" the judge asked. "Black man and a white woman?"

"Yeah. He tried to grab her purse, and there was nothing in it, so he stuck his hand in her blouse."

The judge leered. "Did she like that?" he asked.

"Well, the trouble was he scratched her when he did it. Anyway, I hear he wants out of prison."

"Is that right?" the other prosecutor said. "Why, I'm right surprised to hear that. I guess they'll be wantin' Saturday-night dances over there next."

The defense attorney remained silent, but the prosecutors' remarks were clearly for his benefit. The younger one turned to him now and said, "What about Harris, Rupe? We'll let him know you bled for him. You wanna plead him guilty?"

"Why?" the lawyer said. "He ain't guilty. Besides, it was just a little ol' hubcap theft."

"Well, Rupe," the other prosecutor said, "we're going to add a charge of receiving and concealing against him and ask for a bond of fifteen hundred dollars."

The lawyer reddened. "There's no point in that," he said, looking at the judge. "He just sold the hubcaps. He says he didn't know they were stolen. He's made every appearance in court. He ought to be on a personal-appearance bond. Judge?"

Bryant picked up the phone. "Sweetie, check the file on Harris, will you, please? Find out if he's made his court appearances." He drummed his fingers on his desk and then lit a pipe while he waited for a reply. "That right?" he said. "Thanks." He turned to the prosecutors. "He's made his appearances, Rupe's right. I'll leave the bail where it's at." The man was free on $250 bond.

"But, Judge," the prosecutor said, "everything points to this dude doing it. It was his car. He sold the hubcaps. It seems unfair that just because he didn't get caught with the goods because of some quirk, that he doesn't get punished."

"Well, that may be," Bryant replied, "but for bond purposes he's been here every time."

The prosecutor turned back to the defense lawyer. "Well, why don't your boy tell us who the thieves are, then?"

"I had a client got himself killed for doin' that not too far back," the lawyer said.

"Hey," the judge said, "we're down on murders this month anyway. We're seven behind last month." The lawyer smiled thinly.

The prosecutors got up and left. "It's not fair to add another charge now, Judge," the lawyer said after they had gone. "The state gets by with things the defense can't."

"Ebb and flow, Rupe, ebb and flow."

The lawyer continued to mutter: "They said they had an eyeball witness, but they never produced him."

"Well, it's all just part of the game, isn't it, Rupe?"

"They play so damn many games I never know what's real and what isn't."

"I've noticed you play a few yourself."

Trial lawyers are an exalted species in Texas. "There's no freer spirit in the world than a Texas trial lawyer," Bryant says. "If you're good with a jury, you can do just about anything." The prospect of a good courtroom scrap lights up lawyers' eyes and warms their blood; they see themselves as twentieth-century gunfighters who shoot it out with words instead of bullets.

Texas juries are likewise exalted: most trials in Texas are jury trials, and the jury often sets the penalty as well. It's all pretty tepid for a two-fisted Texas judge, who has little to do beyond seeing that the rules of combat are obeyed. "I'm just the guy in the black-and-white-striped shirt," Bryant says. "It's not that much fun for a judge—there's too many pleas, for one thing. I thought there'd be more excitement and action than there is. I go along with the plea bargaining because the system couldn't work without it. And I'll just about always take the prosecutor's recommendation for a sentence. I figure it's the result of a bargain and they hit on a balance."

Plea bargaining depends on the judge's acquiescence, either stated or implied. It also relies on a chummy working relationship among judges, prosecutors, and defense attorneys.

"A defense lawyer who isn't one of the boys isn't much help to his clients," a lawyer in Bryant's town told me. "The prosecutors have an edge because they're in there with the judge all the damn time. I have to step over four prosecutors to get to the judge's office. You feel uncomfortable when you go into chambers and they're talking about what they did wrong or what their next play is. We do it too, on a coffee-drinking, story-telling basis, but if you're not in on it you've had it. If I go to some other city and I don't know the judge or what football game he went to that Sunday, I don't know what to talk about when it comes to pleas. And the judge doesn't care because he knows I won't be there next week. It gets to be a buddy-buddy situation where it's embarrassing for a judge to go against a prosecutor."

"Plea bargaining operates on a basis of fair market value," another lawyer said. "The assumption is that a jury will usually be tougher. The going rate for selling marijuana, say, might be three years, and a jury might say seven. So a judge will usually go for three or four years. The prosecutor sets the pattern more than the judge.

"You get penalized for going to trial because you lose credit for time served. That's in the judge's discretion. If you plead guilty, your man will usually get credit, but if you go to trial, he won't."

Many of the folkways of Texas justice operate against a criminal defendant. Not only do prosecutors work closely with judges, but judges themselves frequently betray a bias against the defendants. Texas political scientist Allan K. Butcher, who surveyed the attitudes of Texas municipal judges, found that fully one fourth of them *admitted* to a presumption of guilt. Probation workers rarely make pre-sentence investigations of misdemeanor defendants. "The result," says one probation officer, "is that the prosecutor recommends a sentence without knowing anything about a guy— whether a drug violator, say, is a pusher or a user or a mainliner or what. There's a hell of a lot of backscratching with sentences too— a lawyer who contributes to a district attorney's campaign gets a better break."

Defendants may or may not be advised of their constitutional rights. "It depends on whether the judge thinks he needs it," a lawyer says. "Bryant now, he'll plop along in the regular way unless he thinks a fella needs to know about his rights. It depends on what penalty he thinks he's going to give—if it's probation or a light sentence, he doesn't bother to tell him that he's waiving his right to a jury trial, or that he has a right to appeal, or any of that good stuff. The defendants don't always have lawyers, and the ones who don't can get screwed because they don't know the market value of a bargained plea."

Bail is sometimes used as a bludgeon to force a defendant to hire a lawyer. "They'll raise the bond if he can't afford a lawyer," the same attorney says, "and then throw his ass in jail for failure to make bond. It discriminates against the poor, sure, but it keeps lawyers in business."

"I give 'em their warnings, but I don't hold to any form on it," Bryant says. "I try to be reasonably sure a defendant knows what's going on. If he wants to plead not guilty, I make him get a lawyer. If he pleads guilty and doesn't have a lawyer, I look real close at what the prosecutor recommends. In effect, I become the defense lawyer."

The judge was on the phone in his chambers. "It's twenty-one acres, fenced," he was saying. "Got a well and a house on it. I'm looking to buy it, but I want to get an idea of property values up there." He nodded as he listened. "Well, I'm gonna try and get me a veteran's loan."

As he spoke, two policemen and three prisoners entered the room, the prisoners in overalls and handcuffs. The officers stood near the door and signaled the three to take seats. "Well, I'm gonna have to go now, sweetie," the judge said. "I'd like you to get me some of them appraisals. I'll call you back."

He nodded at the officers and fished in his desk for an arraignment form, then looked up at the prisoners. "Okay, Mr. Grimes, I'm about to read you your constitutional safeguards. You have a right to an attorney. You have a right to remain silent. If you're too poor to afford a lawyer, you can request that one be appointed for you. You may have reasonable time to consult with a lawyer." He turned to one of the policemen. "Burglary, that right?"

The officer nodded.

"You been in the penitentiary before, Mr. Grimes?"

The prisoner, a thin, dark-haired white man with tattooed arms, nodded.

"About how many times?"

"Once. Then I—uh—escaped from there."

"All right." He made a note. "Did you understand the warning I gave you?" The prisoner said he did. "If you'd just sign this form," Bryant said. The man clutched a pen between his manacled hands and signed. "I'm going to set your bond at fifteen thousand dollars."

Bryant turned to a second prisoner. "Mr. Price, did you hear what I just read to Mr. Grimes there?" Price nodded, but Bryant went through it again. "Any questions?" he asked when he finished. He repeated the process with the third prisoner, and they left to return to their cells.

He had started to pick up the phone again when a lawyer came in. "Hey, sport," Bryant said, "I was just thinkin' about you."

The judge asked the lawyer several questions about land values and his prospects for a loan. The lawyer, who seemed to be expert in the subject, glanced uneasily at me. "He's okay," the judge said. "He's just a hatchet man."

"Well," the lawyer said, "the way you do it is you get two acres free and get a vet's loan on the rest. I can maybe set it up for you and go along with you to the office. They got caught rinky-dooin' down there, you know."

The judge raised his eyebrows in surprise.

"Yeah," the attorney went on, "the land commissioner had his hand in. They were buying land for thirty an acre and selling it to vets for three fifty. Trouble was some of the buyers weren't *bona fide* vets."

"Well, we better quit talking about it right now," the judge said. "I'll get back to you."

The judge nodded at the door after the lawyer departed. "Old Whitman there," he said, "he knows a few things."

Bryant's surface is all goodoleboy: he is a beer guzzler, a skirt chaser, a storyteller—"just a red-blooded old country boy," he says of himself. But he is also country shrewd, with a kind of earthy wisdom, and considerably more perceptive than he cares to admit. He is unsure of himself as a judge—"I'm still groping"—and uncomfortable with the moral rigors of his authority. He is neither sensitive nor insensitive to the people who appear before him; he seems to suspend moral judgment, on himself as well as others, and to regard all professions of righteousness with good-natured cynicism. He has the gift, rare among judges, of self-deprecation.

He grew up in a small Texas town. "My people were all truck drivers," he says. "My daddy died when I was two, and my grandparents raised me." He hitchhiked through the West as a youth, driving a sightseeing bus for a time at a national park. He went to college on a music scholarship as a percussionist, then took his law degree at that cradle of Texas judges, the University of Texas. He served four years as an enlisted man in the Navy, worked a year for an oil company, then became an assistant district attorney. He was a prosecutor for more than a dozen years before he made his first political foray as a candidate for the state legislature.

"I ran as a Democrat," he recalls, "but I didn't have any family behind me or much support. I went to the biggest banker in town and asked for his help. He said the incumbent did about everything he asked him to, so he didn't see much point in switching horses. So I ran as a labor candidate and lost."

He won a judgeship appointment on his second try. Texas judges are elected, but most of them reach office through interim appointments; the governor names higher-court judges and the county commissioners appoint judges at Bryant's level. "The way it works is that a judge will be about to retire and he'll quit a little before an election so that his replacement will have a head start when he runs. I thought I had it sewed up the first time, but you know politics—they smile at your face and pee-pee on your leg.

"This job is more politics than law, there's no two ways about it. Hell, you can have all kinds of dandy ideas, but if you don't get yourself elected, you can sell your ideas on a corner somewhere. Politics isn't a dirty word in my mouth."

When another vacancy came up, he organized a careful campaign to win over three of the five commissioners. "He wasn't anybody's first choice," a local politician recalls, "but he had the retiring judge behind him and he was available."

"When I got it, the story in the paper mentioned 'a vigorous behind-the-scenes campaign,'" he recalls. "They just wouldn't believe how vigorous it was." He won the appointment by a 3–2 vote, then had to run in a Democratic primary to keep it.

"I hit the bench running. I started with the grand-jury lists. I knew all those folks from when I was a prosecutor, so I sent 'em all letters asking if they remembered old sweet Frank and how smart I was. It got me a bunch of contributions and invitations. I romanced the county chairman and the businessmen—hell, I was everybody's pal. I hustled votes with the police—I'd show up at their roll calls at three in the morning. I'd talk law and order to the police and I'd stay quiet about drunk driving when I talked to civic clubs—I'd talk to them about shoplifting and property rights.

"It got a little silly. I was out at a café in some little place one morning, shaking hands and passing matchbooks around. This old fella walked in and I stepped up and said, 'I'm Frank Bryant.' He didn't seem to understand, so I pointed to myself and said it again, about three more times. He seemed to like that. Then he pointed to himself and said, 'Cecil Perkins.' " Bryant was elected in the primary by a comfortable margin, and was unopposed in the general election. "The Republicans think I'm one of 'em. I reckon I'm pretty conservative."

I asked whether campaign contributors had sought favors. "Well, it happens," he said. "There's been some lawyers who haven't said a word to me, but others try to push me a bit—asking for a continuance, you know, or a reduced bond for their client. I don't know where the line is. I know the Sunday-school rule, that you take a hard stand and don't do anything special for anybody, but that's a lot of happy horseshit. But it's just as much horseshit when they ask me for a favor. How much do you gut your enemies or help your friends? Nobody's asked me for a break on a sentence, and I can't say what I'd do if they did, if they really leaned on me. I've given continuances in a few cases. I guess I figure if I can help them consistent with my duty, I'll do it. But somebody's gonna make it tough for me sooner or later—they're gonna say, 'Frank, I need you.' I'll probably have a nervous breakdown.

"I don't know if I'm a slob or a hardnose on sentencing," Bryant says, "probably more of a slob. I don't think jail is even the second-best choice a lot of times. I'll go with probation even though I know it's just a shot. I'm tougher on thieves than I am on booze—booze is pretty popular, you know. I try to study the older judges, see what they do. But I figure I'm kind of a pushover. I'll believe stories that really don't warrant belief.

"I don't like to preach at a defendant. I don't figure that's my job. And he's probably got enough trouble without me hollering at him."

The idea of "justice" baffles and obsesses Bryant. "I think everyone has an idea what it is," he says, "and the old man with his Bible just as much as some Ph.D. I trust the people, the jurors—people who are in the 'hurly-burly of life,' bumping into each other and trying to live. They have as good an idea of justice as some college professor who's read all the philosophy of the Western world. The professor—hell, he's probably never been in a fight, hustled ass, or competed for business.

"I'm scared to death of making some goddam intellectual pro-nouncement on what justice is. I don't know what's fair—it's based on experience. The law tries to find so-called immutable principles, but I don't know what they are. People aren't mechanical robots. I'll go with a jury. It's just a way to give some finality to a decision. Some of them are wrong and some right. 'Equal justice' doesn't exist except in heaven. Down here we're just thrashing around. Justice is what my gut says it is."

"Then what qualifies anyone to be a judge?"

"Nothin'. Judges aren't any smarter or better than anybody else. There's probably not a bit of difference between me and that guy I beat in the election. I just happen to be here."

"Why did you run for it?"

"Ego. I think it's in the back of everyone's head in law school. I thought I'd see what it feels like to play God. It ain't bad."

He picked up the phone and asked his secretary to call the loan office. "This is Frank Bryant, *Judge* Frank Bryant," he said when he got through. He asked a few polite questions, then inquired "whether I'd be violating the regulations of the program if I con-tacted an appraiser to get an educated guess on that land." There was some more discussion, then the judge said, "If I can be of any service to you, y'all just let me know, hear?"

He hung up and turned back to me. "That's one reason for bein' a judge right there," he said, grinning. "Hell, if I was just old Frank, he'd probably tell me to run along. But I'm *Judge* Frank."

Later that afternoon, as we were on our way out for a drink, we encountered another judge in the courthouse elevator. "Y'all been litigatin'?" the other judge asked.

"Here and there," Bryant replied.

Bryant mentioned that he had talked to attorney Whitman about getting a veteran's loan. The other judge's brow wrinkled. "But I'm not gonna play any of his little games," Bryant added quickly.

The other judge eyed him. "I hope you know what you're doing," he said.

"The state of Texas versus R. C. Jones," the court clerk called. Jones was a wiry, thirty-year-old black charged with carrying a pistol illegally, a crime punishable by a $500 fine and/or a year in jail. He had pleaded innocent. There was going to be a contest.

Fifteen prospective jurors had assembled in the first two rows of Bryant's court. The two young prosecutors, both wearing blue blazers and red ties, and the older defense attorney turned to study them as Bryant talked about their responsibility.

"The defendant is presumed to be innocent. . . . A reasonable doubt is an honest or substantial doubt, not a capricious doubt. If you have no doubt, it is just as much your duty to find him guilty. . . . The law contemplates fair and attentive jurors. Take your common sense and your reason into the jury room with you. . . ."

The veniremen were seated in order of numbers (1 through 15) they had been given. Two were black, two Mexican-American, and the rest white. At least a half-dozen were under thirty. The men wore sport shirts and slacks, the women either cotton dresses or skirts and blouses. Six would be chosen to hear evidence, make a judgment, and fix the penalty.

The older prosecutor, whose name was Graham, polled the prospective jurors on their opinions of the law. Each agreed that it was a good law. He explained the charge and asked each individually if he thought he could be fair. "There may be some conflicts of testimony," he told them, "but it takes more than that for a finding of 'not guilty'—you must have a substantial doubt."

The defense attorney, a folksy, drawling man, asked if any juror had friends or relatives in the police department. Juror number 9, a trim housewife in her thirties, said she was friendly with an officer who had been wounded. The attorney explained that the prosecution had to do more than prove the defendant was in possession of the pistol—"they have to show that it was *unlawful* possession. There can be times when such possession is lawful."

When the questioning was finished, the two prosecutors followed Bryant to his office. The defendant and his lawyer went into the jury room. Each side was permitted to strike three of the first twelve jurors—13 through 15 were extraneous.

"It's a squirrelly-looking bunch," Graham said as they sat down. He and the younger prosecutor, a broad-shouldered ex-football player named Buford, examined their notes, crossing out some numbers and writing in others.

"I like one, eight, nine, and ten," Buford said. "Three is too flaky. I'm inclined to cross off five and six too." Juror 3 was a

college student, 5 was a laborer who wore a mustache and long
sideburns, and 6 was a middle-aged black.

"I want that little number seven on the jury," Graham said. "I
think she's unhappily married. We have that in common."

The judge, who was idly looking through his mail, glanced up
and smiled.

"Hey, Judge," Buford said, "do we really have to prove it was
unlawful possession?"

" 'Fraid so," Bryant said.

Graham agreed that they would strike jurors 3, 5, and 6. He
beckoned me aside as we started back to the courtroom. "That
panel is so squirrelly that I called downstairs to see if they had any
more standing by," he whispered. "I was going to force a mistrial
to get a new panel. I was going to ask them if they thought it was a
good law if it kept ex-cons from carrying pistols." He grinned
maliciously. "That would have driven old Silver Tongue [the
defense attorney] right up the wall." Jones had a record of several
previous convictions, but the record could not be mentioned in
court unless he testified.

The defense challenged jurors 1, 7, and 9. The six who remained, three women and three men, moved into the jury box. One
of the women was a black high-school teacher and another was a
Mexican-American telephone operator. The third was a young
bank clerk. Two of the men were young factory workers, the third
a middle-aged businessman.

Graham began to read the formal "information" spelling out the
charge. He suddenly stopped and walked rapidly out of the room
and into the judge's chambers. He returned after ten seconds.
Astonishingly, he moved for a dismissal. He had found a trivial
mistake in the document: the wrong district attorney was named.
Bryant declared a recess and bustled out, accompanied by the
prosecutors and a smiling defense attorney. "I like to win 'em any
old way," the lawyer said.

The judge grabbed three lawbooks and began leafing through
them. The lawyers filled coffee cups from an urn and sat down.
"Hey, Joe," Graham said to the defense lawyer, "I hear your client
can speak Spanish. I heard him counting—he said *uno, dos, tres,*
fo' . . ."

Bryant switched on an FM radio. The lawyers chatted amiably
as he reached for another lawbook. "Says here a mistake has to be

prejudicial to the defendant," he said. "I don't see how having the wrong name on the information is prejudicial. I'm inclined to let the state amend it." He looked up quizzically. "Now y'all get out of my office and let me look up some more law." I was permitted to stay.

"Hell, the easy thing to do is call a mistrial," he said. "But all that time would be wasted. I don't know when we'd get all the witnesses and everybody together again." He was talking half to himself. Soft music came from the radio: "*Again, this couldn't happen again. . . .*"

Buford knocked on the door and looked in. "Joe says he'll go for a two-hundred-dollar fine," he said.

Bryant looked up. "I think I'm going to let y'all amend the charge, if that's his leverage," he said. "That's for your information. You do what you want to do."

"I just wanted to feel your pulse on it," the prosecutor said.

Bryant pointed triumphantly to a paragraph in a lawbook. "That's it," he declared. "I'm gonna hang my hat on that. I'm taking the position that it's a matter of form and not substance. We can go on back."

The three lawyers were sitting around a table in the room adjoining the judge's office. "Well, if I had a nice clean feller, I wouldn't offer anything," the defense attorney was saying, "but he ain't nice and clean." They stood up as the judge came in. He led a parade back into court.

With the flawed information disposed of, the trial moved on to the testimony. The first prosecution witness was the arresting officer, a thin young man in a nylon windbreaker.

"I stopped the defendant in his car at approximately 2:10 a.m.," he said. "I checked headquarters and found that he owed money for unpaid traffic tickets. I took him downtown."

Defendant Jones, sitting expressionless at the defense table, jingled coins in his pocket.

"I searched his vehicle and found a twenty-two-caliber pistol in the console between the two front seats."

"Objection," the defense attorney cried. "Move to strike the testimony and ask that the jury be excluded."

Bryant ordered the jury to leave. The attorney then moved to suppress all evidence concerning the gun because the officer had failed to get a search warrant.

"Motion denied," the judge said.

"Thanks, Judge," Graham said.

"Don't thank him," the defense attorney said irritably. "It's a ruling." The jury returned.

On further questioning, the policeman said amid a dust storm of objections that Jones had told him the pistol belonged to his brother. The weapon was introduced in evidence.

"Let me see that," the judge said. The prosecutor handed it up to him. Bryant pulled the trigger five times in quick succession, aiming at the floor. The clicks sounded unnaturally loud. He returned the gun to the prosecutor. "Okay," he said. The state rested.

"Arnold McBean," the defense attorney called.

McBean was a long-legged young black with an Afro. He testified that he owned the car, and that he had loaned it to his friend Jones that night. He said that the pistol belonged to him, that he used it at the service station where he worked, and that Jones had not known it was in the car.

"Where did you keep the pistol?" Graham asked on cross.

"Under the seat," he said.

"The defense calls R. C. Jones," the attorney said. The defendant approached the witness stand with long, slow strides. The jurors stared at him. ("If he puts the defendant on the stand, we've got him," Graham had said earlier. "It's a risk and maybe a mistake," the defense attorney had said, "but I've got to do it.")

Jones was slightly truculent. "I didn't know there was no gun in the car," he testified. "I was going to get a sandwich for my wife when the po-liceman stopped me. The first time I saw the pistol was when the officer showed it to me."

"Have you been in prison before, Mr. Jones?" his attorney asked. He wanted to bring it out before the prosecution did.

"Yes, I was in the penitentiary from 1962 to 1966." The lawyer glared at the prosecutors. The jurors looked nonplused.

Graham practically leaped to the cross-examination. "Is it true you were carrying fourteen hundred dollars on the night you were arrested?" he demanded.

"Yes, but—"

"OBJECTION."

"Sustained. Jury will disregard the question and answer."

"You went to prison for two counts of burglary, is that true?"

"Yes."

"Were you convicted of mail theft in 1958?"

"Yes."

"You've been arrested for burglary eight separate times, isn't that right?"

"No." Jones appeared calm.

"Move for a mistrial," the defense attorney said. "The prosecutor knows perfectly well that his last question was a lie."

"Denied," the judge said.

Jones was excused. "The defense rests, Your Honor," his lawyer said.

"Okay, we'll have a recess and then return for the charge and final arguments," Bryant said.

The defense attorney shook his head as we followed the judge to his office. "You gotta watch that bastard Graham like a hawk," he said. He was smiling as he said it.

"I thought you could have objected a little more, Joe," the judge said. "Did he really have fourteen hundred on him?"

The lawyer nodded.

The judge shook his head. "That nigger juror looks like she's gonna rip the defendant up," he said.

"I thought that other nigger would have been favorable to me," the lawyer said, "the one they knocked off."

"Well, I don't think your witness did too hot, Joe."

"It's not like last week," he said. "I got a guy off with three years probation on a murder charge."

"Ain't no flies on that," said Bryant.

Bryant had instructed his secretary on what he wanted in his jury charge, and she was now ready with the typed copy. He looked it over briefly and returned to court.

"If you find and believe from the evidence, or have a reasonable doubt thereof, that the pistol was left in said automobile by some person other than the defendant, and that defendant did not know that said pistol was in the automobile . . . you will find the defendant not guilty, and so say by your verdict. . . . You are the exclusive judges of the facts proved, of the credibility of the witnesses, and of the weight to be given the evidence. . . ."

"Let's don't guess him into jail," the defense attorney said in his final argument. "The state has not proved that the defendant knew that pistol was in the car."

Graham followed. "The defense witness said the pistol was under the seat," he said. "The policeman said it was in the console. Who do you believe? This was an *ex-convict* out with a pistol at two o'clock in the morning." He pulled a handful of .22 bullets out of his pocket and lined them up on the railing in front of the jury box, a tiny picket line of incrimination. "*These* were in that pistol," he cried. "Now you can hand the pistol back to this ex-con and let him go, or you can say with your verdict that we don't like ex-cons carrying pistols in this county." He lowered his voice dramatically. "It's in your hands." He sat down as if awaiting applause.

"Okay, y'all can retire to your deliberation now," Bryant said. "Just knock on the door when you're ready."

The judge returned to his chambers again. "I don't think they'll be out long," he said. "It'd be even quicker if it was downstairs. They got a little bitty jury room down there. You get a couple of buck niggers in there with some white women and you get some awful fast verdicts."

Graham came in. "I've seen you make better final arguments, John," the judge said, "but that wasn't bad."

The jury was ready in thirty minutes. They looked self-consciously solemn as they entered. The foreman, one of the young factory workers, handed a document to the bailiff, who gave it to the judge.

"Would you stand, please, Mr. Jones?" Jones got slowly to his feet. "The verdict of this jury is that you are guilty as charged." Jones didn't blink. "Now we'll hear arguments on the penalty."

The jury could decide to fine him, jail him for up to a year, or place him on probation. The defense attorney asked for probation. The prosecutor, leaning forward with his hands on the jury railing, said it was a chance "to let other criminals know what our juries think about ex-cons carrying pistols on our streets. Probation is a string, but we need to put a rope on him and not a string." Jones looked at him sharply.

The jury retired for another fifteen minutes. "If he gets anything less than a year, I'll eat my cowboy hat," the defense lawyer said.

" 'We, the jury,' " Bryant read, " 'assess the punishment at one year's confinement in the county jail.' I want to thank each of you. The jury is the backbone of our system—everything else is just mechanics and procedures. I'd like to express the court's appreciation for your work here. The jury is dismissed."

The jurors, looking confused and uncomfortable, started to move out of the jury box. A woman juror whispered something to the bailiff, who rushed over to the judge.

"Oh, excuse me, folks," Bryant said. "I'm sorry, but you'll all have to come back for a minute. I forgot to read the rest of your decision." Several jurors smiled. " 'We do further find,' " he read, " 'that the defendant is eligible for probation and we recommend that he be granted probation in this case.' "

Bryant looked at the defendant. "I'm real sorry, Mr. Jones," he said. "Seems you got probation after all."

The defendant's face creased in a rueful smile.

"That's all, then," the judge said.

Jones wheeled and walked quickly through a gate, his attorney trotting alongside. "You want to appeal?" the lawyer asked. "No way," Jones replied.

The attorney stopped and turned away. "The state offered us six months and four hundred dollars, you know," he told me, "and we would have taken it except he didn't have the money. Hell, he's not going to make probation anyway. He's got three heroin charges against him."

The judge and I adjourned to a tavern. He shook his head as he thought about his gaffe. "If I was a defense lawyer and a judge did that to me," he exclaimed, "I'd punch him in the mouth. I guess I was so surprised that they gave him probation that I couldn't believe it. I read the part I agreed with and not the other part. I'd have given him time in jail, but not the maximum."

We ordered beers. Bryant waved at several friends and flirted with the waitress. He took a long drink. "You want to know why I became a judge?" he asked in a confidential tone. "To get a better parking place.

"Being a judge makes a pantywaist out of you, is what it does. You're supposed to stay out of suspect situations," he said, smacking the table with his beer mug. "Well, I figure that means I can't go to Mexico for a wild party on the weekend." He signaled the waitress for two more.

"Christ, I just about screwed up one time, though. I had a bawdy-house case. There were four girls, and they came back to chambers and I was playin' fun and games, joking with 'em, you know. I told them I was queer for pussy. Well, I left the case pending, I didn't take any action on it, just told them to quit and get out of town, and they said they would. That was a mistake. They got arrested again at another place in town. Now they think they own me."

Bryant is regarded with cheerful tolerance by local lawyers. "He's a hell-raiser," one said, "but he's not a bad judge. I think he's flexible, and he seems to know the difference between being morally guilty and legally innocent and vice versa. He takes it seriously."

"I haven't seen him try to screw anybody," another said. "Most of the judges here are a sight meaner than he is. One of them gave a kid twenty-five years for selling marijuana just because a high-school civics class was in court. Bryant's practical, and he has good sense."

"He's no tougher on blacks," said a third attorney. "The approach here is to be nice to the blacks but make damn sure they know you're being nice to them."

"He stands behind us, but we can't get away with any cheap stuff," a prosecutor said.

"You see that old boy sittin' over there, staring at the girls?" Bryant asked. "I'll bet he knows as much about justice as you and I put together. Some judges think they piss in a boot. It's hard not to get the feeling that your ass is the divinity if it's been gettin' kissed for twenty years. Hell, they all laugh at my goddam jokes. But I know they're salutin' the bars and not me."

Bryant seems almost a textbook example of democratic theory: he seems no better or worse than his constituency, living proof of his own notions of judicial representativeness and moral relativism. He believes that his virtues are those of the plain folks—a willingness to do the job and to try, by his lights, to be fair. And he has no illusions about his vices, which are theirs as well. "I'm a bigot, okay," he says. "I know in my mind that I'm no better than a nigger, but when I shake hands with one, I'm saying 'uk' to myself. The only way to solve the race problem is for everyone to be coffee-colored, but who wants to start it?"

He drained his glass. "It seems like I see nothin' but poor folks in my court sometimes, and it makes me a little, well, lenient. I kind of wonder if there aren't just as many drunks coming home from the country club, but all I see in court are niggers and Mexicans. Hell, I'd probably test out drunk right now."

He is dimly aware of an inequity he can't quite get his emotions to share. It is as if his dawning sensitivity were in a race with the calcification of the robe. "I reckon I'll probably change," he said. "I'll forget about the poor folks. All I know is that I like this job and I'll bust my ass to stay in it."

VI

Soul on the Bench

The singular position of America's black judges

The Honorable Elreta Melton Alexander, judge of the Guilford County, North Carolina, District Court, gazes down at the shy, long-legged, fourteen-year-old black girl who stands before her.

"You know why I sent you to training school, don't you, darlin'?" she says.

The girl stares at the floor of the small courtroom.

"It was because you were getting to be a habitual thief. Was that because you're colored, or black, as you kids like to be called?"

"No, ma'am."

"Why did you steal from someone else's locker?"

The girl is silent.

"Well, what are you going to do about it?"

The girl's eyes brighten as if she has suddenly remembered the answer to a test question. "I'm not gonna steal no more," she says. "Stealin' don't get you nowhere."

The judge smiles. "I'm going to let you go home, sweetheart, but you report to your caseworker every thirty days. And I want to tell you something. Whenever one of you falls, it takes something out of the pot. I sacrificed to open doors for you. Every time I send one of you off, it's hurting me all the way through."

The girl clasps her hands and bows her head as if in prayer.

"But I'm not going to pet you any. If there's one bad apple, they'll say all black kids are thieves. You have a responsibility to *me*. I've sweated my life's blood for you, darlin'. Go home now, but if you come back here, you're going to be in training school a long time."

The judiciary is still one of the most segregated institutions in America. Only in the past dozen years have blacks established a beachhead. When Elreta Alexander was elected in 1968, she became the first black judge popularly elected in the South in this century. Of 136 federal judges in the South, not one is black. Nationally there are 314 blacks out of an estimated 16,700 full-time judges.

Blacks were excluded from the legal establishment for generations. Discrimination by the American Bar Association led black lawyers to form their own organization in 1925. Some Southern bar groups are still segregated. So few blacks were admitted to law schools that even today only 1.3 percent of the nation's lawyers are black. "The low number of both lawyers and judges comes out of the same thing," says Detroit Recorder's Court Judge George Crockett, a leading spokesman for black judges. "There has been a studied effort to exclude blacks and other minorities from the judicial process. The white majority wanted to keep to itself the whole business of interpreting and administering the law, because judges are the most powerful single group in the country. The essence of due process is judgment by a cross-section of the population; that's the reason for juries. But how the hell can you have a cross-section if all the judges are from one group in the society?"

Black judges form a barely visible thread through the fabric of our history. The first was Robert Morris, appointed to Boston Magistrate's Court in 1852. During Reconstruction, black judges appeared on lower courts in Arkansas, Florida, and South Carolina, and one even reached the South Carolina Supreme Court, but they were forced out with the restoration of white supremacy.

It was 1924 before a black was elected to a judgeship in a Northern state, Illinois. The first black judge in New York did not reach the bench until 1930; in California it was 1940, in Ohio 1943, Michigan 1954, and Pennsylvania 1956. Even then they were freakishly rare, and were confined to the lowest courts in the largest cities. It was a fraternity so small that *Time* magazine said they could all meet comfortably in the back of a single bus.

The federal bench was an equally whites-only preserve. President Franklin Roosevelt named William Hastie to the federal District Court in the Virgin Islands in 1937, and twelve years later Harry Truman appointed him to the Third Circuit Court of Appeals in Philadelphia. Except for his successors in the Virgin Islands and two Customs Court judges, Hastie was the sole black federal judge until John Kennedy honored a campaign promise by appointing two in 1961.

One consequence of the segregated bench was a black community that feared and avoided the courthouses, with good reason. Elreta Alexander and George Crockett, growing up in the South, learned to keep a safe distance from the white man's law. Black-on-white crime was dealt with urgently and often viciously; white-on-black and black-on-black offenses were frequently ignored, the latter shucked off as "nigger disorderly."

"A Negro involved in a federal court action in the South," said a 1965 Southern Regional Council report, "can go from the beginning of the case to the end without seeing any black faces unless they are in the court audience, or [unless] he happens to notice the man sweeping the floor." The sea of white, says Crockett, confronted a black defendant "at every stage of the most traumatic experience of his life."

Many blacks believe that equal justice demands an integrated judiciary. "A judge is a product of his own experience and background," Crockett says. "The theory of law and the beauty of it is that it leaves so much to judicial discretion. There are guiding principles such as 'probable cause,' but one judge will find probable cause and another won't with the same set of facts. One judge is afraid of the ghetto and will associate things with it that I as a black man know damn well are not true.

"Out of our varying experience is determined whether what an officer did in a given case was reasonable. I think black judges on the whole, because of our prior history, are more sensitive to constitutional issues. Not necessarily more sensitive to people, but to issues involving human freedom." "We're experts in human relations," a black parole-board member once told me, "because the society made us so."

The notion of ethnic equity on the bench did not originate with blacks. Politicians have traditionally apportioned judgeships with one eye on the quilt of religions and nationalities in their constituency. The "Jewish seat" on the U.S. Supreme Court, a custom begun with Justice Louis Brandeis in 1916 and followed until the resignation of Abe Fortas in 1969, is only the most visible example of what political scientists call "mirror representation."

New York Court of Appeals candidates M. Henry Martuscello and Domenick Gabrielli competed for what had become known as the "Italian seat" on that court in 1972. When a vacancy on the Connecticut federal bench opened up in 1964, Democratic leader Arthur Barbieri demanded, and got, an Italian judge, Robert C. Zampano. As many as a dozen different legal groups help members of Chicago's ethnic and religious minorities who lust after judgeships: the organizations represent Catholics, Italians, Jews, Poles, and even Lithuanians.

Sometimes political blood runs thicker than nationality. Leaders of the Italian division of the Chicago Democratic machine balked in 1966 when it appeared that a non-machine Italian might get "their" seat on the local federal bench. One bluntly told Senator Paul Douglas, "I'd rather have another nigger"—a reference to U.S. District Judge James Parsons of Chicago. He got a more acceptable Italian.

Now blacks are demanding their share. The Negro population is 11.1 percent of the national total, but only 1.9 percent of all judges are black. Political scientist Beverly Blair Cook of the University of Wisconsin-Milwaukee has calculated that if blacks were represented in proportion to their population in the South, there would be twenty-five black federal judges between Maryland and Texas.

The picture is even gloomier for the ten million-plus Americans with Puerto Rican or Mexican backgrounds: there are probably no more than twenty-five judges representing them, the majority concentrated in a belt across the Southwest from California to Texas; the only Mexican-American federal judges are Reynaldo Garza of Brownsville, Texas, another 1961 Kennedy appointment, and Manuel Real of Los Angeles, nominated by Lyndon Johnson in 1966.

"I think that race relations are improving in direct proportion to the number of minority members on the bench," Crockett says. "Our presence alone has an influence on our white colleagues—it makes them more conscious of racism. It makes the failure to employ blacks in clerical and other positions in the judicial system stand out. When I started in Detroit in 1966, about ten percent of the court staff was black. Now it's nearly fifty percent.

"Improvements have come because everyone is more conscious of discrimination, going back to the Supreme Court school-desegregation decision, and even lip-service simmers down to something. But the biggest reason is the growing political consciousness of black people and their increasing use of the ballot."

Like most black judges, Crockett opposes a switch to merit selection as a threat to the vehicle of progress. "Once we get through this historical period and get to something like fair representation, I'd be for it," he says, "but not now. We're in a period where emerging black power is electing judges, and there still aren't enough of us."

The chamber doors began to open in the 1960s. The number of elected black judges increased gradually in Northern cities such as New York, Chicago, Philadelphia, and Detroit where the political clout of the ghettoes was growing. In 1961 President Kennedy appointed Parsons in Chicago and Wade McCree in Detroit to district judgeships (McCree was promoted to the Sixth Circuit Court of Appeals in 1966). In 1964 Spottswood Robinson was appointed to a Washington, D.C., federal judgeship and A. Leon Higgenbotham to a seat on the Philadelphia District Court. Higgenbotham, at thirty-six, became the second-youngest judge on the federal bench.

In the late sixties the South finally began to give way. In 1968, Elreta Alexander was elected in North Carolina and Charles Owens became Oklahoma's first black judge; Israel Augustine, Jr., was appointed to a New Orleans court in 1969; other black judges appeared in South Carolina, Virginia, Georgia, and Tennessee. A 1971 survey by *Ebony* magazine found 23 blacks on Southern state courts, not including the always uncountable JPs.

By 1972, when the city council of Birmingham, Alabama, appointed the city's first black judge, Crockett counted a total of 278 full-time black jurists in the country, 42 of them in the South. Thirty-six more have been elected or appointed since then. Mississippi is the only Southern state without a black judge.

In some instances the appointment of a black was a direct response to the racial explosions of the 1960s. "After the black kids at Texas Southern College rioted," a Texas attorney told me, "the

Houston City Council went to the local NAACP and asked for a list of black lawyers for a municipal judgeship. The NAACP gave the council one name, and they appointed him."

Blacks were deliberately sought out elsewhere as well. A temporary commission set up to nominate judicial candidates in Massachusetts made a special attempt to find qualified blacks. The commission rated only 25 percent of all the candidates it interviewed as fit for the bench, but found 40 percent of black applicants qualified. The result was the appointment of three black judges by Governor Francis Sargent in 1972, upping the black complement on the commonwealth's bench from four to seven.

"It's moving, in both North and South," says Judge Crockett, "but not nearly fast enough. We don't really have a program to encourage blacks to try for the bench. So much depends on the confidence a black judge has in the electorate. If there aren't enough black votes, then he feels he has to play the game with the forces that can put him there. We have a history of getting ahead as a matter of favoritism—somebody says you're a 'good boy' and you get a job. So a black judge has to either have the confidence of the black community or play ball with the politicians."

In 1971 black judges formed their own lobby, the Judicial Council of the National Bar Association. Crockett was the first chairman. One of the council's goals is to increase the black judicial population, which requires persuasion in two directions. "We have to sell the black brother on leaving his private practice and his beautiful home to come to the bench, where his income is limited," says Crockett. "A good black lawyer can get so affluent he's not interested in a judgeship."

The council asked President Nixon, in April 1972, to make "special efforts" to appoint blacks to Southern federal courts. "If, beginning now, a majority of future appointments are black," Crockett said in a letter to the President, "the present imbalance may be corrected in just a few short years."

"I got three replies from the White House saying our request was under 'serious consideration,' but I still don't see any black federal judges in the South. A lot of congressmen didn't even know about the discrimination until we told them."

Crockett is a short, stocky man who wears bright shirts and a tailor-made robe. His manner is at once easy and forceful. A striking mural-like painting on one wall of his courtroom portrays nineteenth-century black activist Frederick Douglass at different periods of his life—the young Douglass breaking the chains of slavery and an elderly Douglass as minister to Haiti. The slave-hunters' dogs snarl in a corner.

Crockett grew up in Jacksonville, Florida, the son of a carpenter. "It wasn't a ghetto, that would be taking on a character that isn't there. We were considered middle-class. But I understand the language of the ghetto. We have a white court reporter, and I remember a case where a black witness was testifying that 'this cat drove up in a deuce and a quarter.' I understood, my black clerk understood, and the black policeman understood. But she asked him to repeat it. I told her it means a Buick 225."

After graduating from Morehouse College in Atlanta and the University of Michigan law school, he returned to Florida to take the bar examination in 1934. "It was given in the chamber of the Florida State Senate," he recalls, "and heaven forbid that a black man should sit in a white senator's seat. . . . So instead they put up a temporary table just outside the door of the chamber in the corridor," and Crockett passed the bar in the back of the legal bus.

He worked for the Department of Labor, the Fair Employment Practices Commission, and the United Auto Workers Union. In 1949 he was among a team of lawyers who defended the leadership of the American Communist Party against conspiracy charges. He drew a four-month sentence in federal prison for contempt of court, an experience that he has come to relish in retrospect.

"I have always favored the underdog in our society, and prison pushed me further into the underdog's camp," he says. "When I tell a man he has so many years in prison, I know what I'm doing because I've been through it. I think it would be wonderful training if we could arrange, as a prerequisite to serving on the bench, that you spend some time in prison. . . . I think our institutions would be altogether different places if judges had that kind of experience."

He sees himself as an instrument of change within the system—"pledged to change it but not ready to overthrow it." "I don't think revolution will help because we can't win," he says. "There are too many guns on the other side, so we must use the Constitution. I am not so sure that the door will always be open for us to use the Constitution. . . . When you interpret the Constitution literally, the Establishment wants to change the rules."

A judge, he believes, should anticipate changes in the majority opinion, gambling on an evolving national conscience. "The judge himself is and must be civilly disobedient," he says, to help in "extending and expanding our social concepts and our law."

Such opinions put Crockett in the vanguard of a tiny minority of outspokenly activist judges, black and white. Judges are reflexive conservers, cherishers of rules. They are uncomfortable with disobedience, civil or otherwise. "Who are we, after all?" Federal Judge Marvin Frankel of New York has written. "The average judge, if he was ever a youth, is no longer. If he was ever a firebrand, he is not discernibly an ember now. If he ever wanted to lick the Establishment, he has long since joined it."

But Crockett's is an unbanked fire. "If you can get one judge who is willing to stick his neck out and say I'm not going to be moved," he contends, "eventually he draws other judges to him."

Black judges in the South, like their white counterparts, tend to be conservative. "I don't consider myself a black judge," says Elreta Alexander. "I think of We, the People. The duty of the judge is to interpret the law fairly, impersonally, and accurately." "Sometimes the idea that you are a rectifier may briefly cross your mind," says General Sessions Judge Adolpho Birch, Jr., of Nashville, "but you realize that you must judge each case on its current merits."

The black judicial firebrands are in the North, and their impulse to rectify has embroiled a few of them, including Crockett, in furious controversies.

¶ Crockett was the duty judge on a weekend in 1969 when two Detroit policemen were shot, one fatally, outside a ghetto church. Witnesses said the assailants ran into the church, where a black separatist group was meeting. Police rounded up 142 men, women, and children at the church and held them incommunicado. Early Sunday morning Crockett set up a courtroom at police headquarters and began holding *habeas corpus* hearings. He dismissed charges against 130 prisoners for insufficient evidence, and released nine others because they were subjected to nitrate tests (which reveal the presence of gunpowder) without being advised of their rights. Two were held on other charges and one was released on bond.

The uproar was immediate. Crockett was accused of foiling the search for the killer. Police picketed the courthouse, and a policemen's association took a newspaper ad to condemn him. Michigan's Judicial Tenure Commission was asked to investigate Crockett's actions with a view toward removal. Both houses of the state legis-

lature passed a resolution criticizing his "allegedly hasty intervention" in the case. His brother judges, both black and white, were
silent.

His "affront to society," Crockett said later, was that "I will not
be a part of the inbred and self-perpetuating 'arrangement' for the
handling of black and poor arrestees," an arrangement he said
condones arrests without evidence, denial of the right to counsel,
brutality, and high bail. "Because a terrible crime was committed,"
he said, "it does not follow that other wrongs be permitted or
condoned."

There were no appeals from Crockett's rulings. The Judicial
Tenure Commission concluded that "no cause for action" against
the judge existed. And, sweetest confirmation of all, within a
month the Supreme Court decided a mass-arrest case the same way
that Crockett had.

¶ "There are only two things that a black man can be today,"
says Judge Harry Alexander of the Washington, D.C., Superior
Court. "He can either be strong or he can be an Uncle Tom. . . .
The black judge must be courageous enough to take chances." A
former bootblack, disc jockey, and federal prosecutor, Alexander is
one of the stormiest judges in the country.

He ordered that the designation of a defendant's race be deleted
from reports of federal officers in his court. He exploded at a policeman for referring to a black woman witness by her first name. He
threatened to jail a social worker, chastised a lawyer for his facial
expression, and accused his fellow judges of racism. In turn, white
prosecutors and policemen called him a black bigot. Senator Robert
Byrd of West Virginia labeled him "petulant, intemperate and
capricious." He was rated "unqualified" in a poll of lawyers conducted by the Washington *Post*.

In 1972 Alexander became the first judge censured by the newly
created District of Columbia Commission on Judicial Disability
and Tenure. The five-member commission (composed of a white
federal judge, two black laymen, and two white lawyers, including
John Wilson, the counsel for former presidential aides John Ehrlichman and H. R. Haldeman) cited nine examples of "unaccept-
able conduct."

Black leaders in Washington defended him. "His only mistake,"
said one, "is being a black man who has been forthright and had
the courage to speak out." More than three hundred attended a
"salute to Judge Alexander." Commission chairman Newell Ellison

replied that Alexander was censured not "because he's a colored man but because he's the worst."

"His trouble is that he blows his cool, he sticks his foot in his mouth," another black judge commented. "You don't do it that way. When you're dealing with a racist cop, you don't scream at him, you continually call attention to the fact of racism and then decide against him. Then there's no appeal."

¶ Judge Bruce McMarion Wright of New York City's Criminal Court describes himself as "a keeper in the black and Hispanic zoo where those crippled by America's sabertoothed racism have given themselves over to narcotics, hard liquor and hopelessness." Wright, appointed by former Mayor John Lindsay, is a Yale law graduate and the author of a book of poetry. He believes that too few black judges are "ferociously devoted to humane realism in the law," and that most of them are "pillars of the black bourgeoisie," too timid to rock the boat, preoccupied with status rather than with black progress.

In December 1972 Judge Wright presided at the initial court appearance of a man accused of the attempted murder of a policeman, felonious assault, robbery, and possession of a dangerous weapon. Wright released the man on $500 cash bail—the equivalent of a $5000 bond.

The low bail provoked cries of protest from the precinct house to the mayor's mansion. "Loosie Brucie," the cops called him. Lindsay pronounced himself "dismayed," Police Commissioner Patrick Murphy called it "a disgrace," Congressman Edward Koch proposed an investigation of Wright's "fitness," and the New York *Daily News* charged him with a "calculated gesture of contempt toward police and prosecutors." Another judge raised the bail to $25,000.

"Bail is not a game of money to be won only by the rich," Wright said. "It is to insure appearance in court, and if the accused has roots in the community, then there is no [high] bail." The defendant owned a driving school and ran an insurance business. Judge Wright, said a Legal Aid attorney, "doesn't use high bail to coerce guilty pleas. He's one of the few judges who really seem to believe in the presumption of innocence."

Would the actions of Crockett, Alexander, and Wright have provoked the same reaction if they were white? Maybe, but probably not. In one sense these were confrontations between "permissive" judges, those described memorably by President Nixon as "softheaded," and the law-and-order boosters in police, press, and public. White judges have been caught in the same wringer. But in another sense these were black men acting out of their own social perceptions, their identification with the underdog, and their racial consciousness.

Harry Alexander was censured, but nothing happened to Judge Alfred Burka of the same court when he told a black defendant that "black is pretty ugly based on my experience." Bruce Wright was denounced, but the reaction was less strident when the judge who overruled him, George Postel, barred the press from the trial of a Mafia hoodlum in 1971.

Crockett may be right when he describes the brouhahas over black judges as signposts of progress. He says the attacks reveal a fretful Establishment afraid that "it no longer will be able to reserve unto itself the exclusive right to . . . exercise undisputed control of the judicial process." The millennium, of course, would be the removal of all judicial criticism from a racial context, and the removal of the context.

But Crockett isn't holding his breath. "We can anticipate that these attacks upon black judges will become more and more frequent," he said, as more blacks attain the bench.

There are 22 black judges in the federal judiciary (Supreme Court Justice Thurgood Marshall, three on the Circuit appellate courts, 13 District judges, and five on special federal courts). The obstacles they had to overcome were formidable. One is the Senate Judiciary Committee, led by Senator James Eastland of Mississippi. Eastland can block or delay an appointment. Half the members of his committee are Southern. The three who sit as a more or less permanent subcommittee on judicial appointments are Eastland, Democrat John McClellan of Arkansas, and Roman Hruska, a Nebraska Republican. Eastland and Hruska are sixty-nine, McClellan is seventy-seven. All three are conservatives who call regularly for law and order.

President Kennedy submitted Marshall's name for a seat on the Second Circuit Court of Appeals in September 1961. Eastland's committee took no action, and Kennedy gave Marshall a recess appointment after Congress adjourned. A subcommittee including McClellan, Hruska, and former Senator Olin Johnston of South Carolina got around to hearings on the Marshall nomination the following May. The subcommittee failed to report. Finally, in September 1962—a year after he was nominated—the full committee bypassed its subcommittee and recommended Marshall's confirmation. The Senate voted 54–16 to confirm, with all 16 "no" votes cast by Southern senators. Marshall later served as Solicitor General in the Johnson administration and was appointed to the Supreme Court in 1967.

A potential federal judge may be torpedoed from a half-dozen directions, and he may or may not know what hit him. The President or the Justice Department, his home-state senators, a powerful party leader or a large contributor, the dons of the American Bar Association's judicial selection committee—the blast can come from any of them, for any reason. A President like Nixon may be seeking an ideological soul brother; a senator is looking for a friendly press back home; service to self inspires them all. Prejudice in this atmosphere is a dark nugget covered with layers of intricate dissembling.

At a minimum, a black candidate needs vigorous support from his home-state U.S. senator of the ruling party and a qualified (the three levels of endorsement are qualified, well qualified, and exceptionally well qualified) rating from the ABA. If the President's men are for him too (or, better yet, the President himself), then he'll probably get by Eastland. If the President or the senators are lukewarm, it is time to rededicate himself to private practice.

One of the subtler elements in the equation is the aversion, particularly in Republican administrations, to a candidate who is closely identified with civil rights. It is not grounds for immediate elimination; it is just another obstacle. The appointers prefer men untainted by the stain of controversial positions; never mind if the best black lawyers and law professors in the South, for example, were involved in the civil-rights struggle; better a safe "political" lawyer of minimal competence than a brilliant crusader, especially a black one. In Northern states a powerful senator can leap this obstacle as well, but in the South the will is absent. When Georgia's Republican leaders met to propose their choices for four District Court vacancies in 1970, no black candidates were suggested—too identified with civil rights.

During his 1960 campaign John Kennedy told the ABA that a Democratic administration would provide "far better representation, on the basis of merit, of persons of all our racial groups, including particularly those who in the past have been excluded on the basis of prejudice."

But Kennedy had to deal with Eastland and company, and talking to them was a different exercise from addressing the ABA. To get Eastland's tacit approval of Marshall, a frequently told story goes, Kennedy had to let the Mississippian name his old college roommate, William Harold Cox, to the District Court down home. Cox, who once described blacks from the bench as "chimpanzees," is widely regarded as the worst of several racist judges appointed to Southern federal courts by Kennedy. "The brothers had to pay a lot of dues to get Marshall," says Rap Brown's brother Ed, who ran a black self-help program in the Mississippi Delta. "If he was Eastland's boy and he was qualified," a Kennedy Justice Department official asked, "wasn't that enough?" The Eisenhower administration had refused to nominate Cox for judgeship when Eastland suggested it in 1955.

Kennedy's only other black appointments (aside from the District of Columbia lower courts) were McCree in Detroit and Parsons in Chicago. McCree, sponsored by liberal Democrats Philip Hart and Pat McNamara, had been the first black state judge in Michigan's history. Parsons was the nominee of the Chicago Democratic organization commanded by Mayor Richard Daley.

Parsons, who had also been a state judge, is rated by Chicago lawyers as low man on a thirteen-man bench. A poll of 362 attorneys by the Chicago Council of Lawyers found that a rousing 67 percent opposed his continued presence on the bench. He was rated low in legal ability, integrity, diligence, and decisiveness. The only Chicago judge who came close to Parsons' dreary showing was Julius Hoffman of the Chicago Seven case, now in semi-retired senior status. Hoffman had a 57-percent unfavorable rating.

Kennedy nominated two other blacks before his assassination, Higgenbotham of Philadelphia and Spottswood Robinson of Washington. Both were confirmed after his death. Higgenbotham, backed by former Senator Joseph Clark, is a socially conscious judge whose views are similar to Crockett's. He is one of seven black federal judges who belong to Crockett's Judicial Council.

Robinson was a professor and dean at Howard University law school who had a hand in the school case that culminated in the Supreme Court's desegregation decision in 1954. Since Robinson sat on a Washington court, President Johnson didn't have to contend with senatorial sensibilities; he elevated him to the D.C. Circuit Court of Appeals in 1966.

Johnson named five other blacks to district judgeships. Constance Baker Motley of New York, sponsored by Senator Robert Kennedy, was one of the legal stars of the NAACP team that carried the school case to the Supreme Court. (Three others are now judges: Thurgood Marshall, New York state judge Edward Dudley, and Nixon federal appointee Robert Carter.) Rated highly by civil libertarians, Mrs. Motley is one of only six women—and the lone black woman—in the federal judiciary. In 1969 she ruled that a black radical held in solitary in a New York prison was being punished for his political views and was entitled to $13,000 damages.

Damon Keith of Detroit, backed by Senator Hart, is the son of a laborer who migrated from Mississippi. He became a major Democratic fund-raiser in Detroit, and was appointed to the bench in 1967. Keith, a member of Crockett's council, ordered busing to desegregate schools in Pontiac, Michigan. In another courageous decision he ruled that government wiretapping of domestic political radicals was unconstitutional.

Johnson's three other black appointments were all in Washington—William Bryant, Aubrey Robinson, and Joseph Waddy. Bryant is widely regarded as an excellent judge who is particularly sensitive to civil-liberties issues. Robinson and Waddy are rated as competent by Washington lawyers. Both had been law-school professors and lower-court judges.

By mid-1973, when his Justice Department was reeling from the effects of the Watergate scandal, President Nixon had picked six blacks for the federal bench, excluding the lower District of Columbia courts. Unlike his two Democratic predecessors, he named no blacks to federal appellate courts. At least one black lawyer, former Howard dean Clarence Ferguson, was rejected for an appellate-court seat because of his judicial philosophy. Ferguson, proposed for the Third Circuit by New Jersey Senator Clifford Case, was regarded by Nixon's men as too "soft" on law and order. The appellate seat was vacant for three years while Case and the administration stood each other off. Case finally withdrew, and Ferguson was selected as ambassador to Uganda.

Lawrence Pierce and Robert Carter were appointed to the District Court in New York City. Pierce, backed by Governor Nelson Rockefeller, had served Rockefeller as chairman of the state Narcotics Control Commission. Carter, a Democrat sponsored by Republican Senator Jacob Javits, had been general counsel of the NAACP Legal Education and Defense Fund. He was also on the commission that criticized New York officials for their handling of the Attica prison uprising. Carter is the only black Nixon appointee with a record of civil-rights activism; Javits was apparently strong enough to override administration reluctance.

David Williams of Los Angeles, another Nixon appointee, was the target of criticism as a municipal judge for denying defendants the right to counsel. He saw things differently from his new aerie: in 1972 he ruled that defendants at military courts-martial are entitled to an attorney.

Almeric Christian, another Democrat, was named to the Virgin Islands judgeship that had traditionally gone to blacks. Barrington Parker was selected for a seat in Washington, where lawyers rate him only so-so. The other Nixon appointment is Clifford Scott Green of Philadelphia, a former Common Pleas judge who was supported by Senators Hugh Scott and Richard Schweiker.

Boston lawyer Herbert Tucker came close to becoming a seventh black Nixon appointment. Proposed by Senator Edward Brooke, Tucker failed to win the blessing of the ABA—a failure regarded as fatal by the Nixon administration. "I think we should have made a special effort and bent the standards a bit in his case," said one ABA man. "He was a kind of Horatio Alger story, he had a tough time coming up. But that doesn't count much in the scales, the fact that he's a deserving man." Tucker was rated unqualified because he had limited federal-court experience. "The question was his ability to deal with the complicated legal questions that arise in a federal court, and there was a real doubt about it."

The concentration of black federal judges in Northern cities—nineteen of the twenty-two sit in Washington, New York, Philadelphia, or Detroit—buttresses Crockett's argument that progress toward an integrated judiciary waits on the success of black power in other governmental arenas. "You find that black judges follow black legislators, congressmen, and senators," he says. Thirteen of the twenty-two were appointed in circumstances where senatorial approval was not a factor.

In the South, a revolution in the political structure must precede major gains by blacks in government. When Mississippi or Alabama has a black senator, as either might within a decade, black federal judges will breach the Confederate lines. Perhaps sooner, but certainly no later. The first salvos of this revolution could be heard in the 1972 elections: Georgia and Texas sent blacks to Congress for the first time in more than sixty years.

"He had a notion he was a-wantin' to go home here these last two or three weeks, Judge," the woman said. Her nephew, a stooped and slack-jawed white youth of fifteen, stood beside her. "He's been a-sneakin' off. I told him to be home at twelve and we seen him six days later." The boy had run away from his aunt's house, where the court had placed him, to visit his mother.

"What do you like to do most?" Judge Elreta Alexander asked him.

"Nothin'."

"What subjects do you like in school?"

"None."

The judge is a matronly, fifty-four-year-old woman with cocoa-colored skin. She was wearing a curly silver wig, Ben Franklin glasses, and an enormous pearl necklace. "Would you like Judge Alexander to tell you how to be happy?" she asked the boy.

He sullenly stared at his fingernails.

"Nobody's happy standin' still," the judge said. "You have to use what you got or it will atrophy and you'll be miserable." The judge, a minister's daughter, lapses easily into sermons. "Life is probably energy," she told the yawning youth, "and if it isn't used con-structively, it's going to be used de-structively. I used to think 'soul brother' was just an ethnic thing, but it isn't. People have to radiate to each other."

She ordered a psychological evaluation of the boy and sent him home with his aunt. He had been in frequent trouble when he lived with his mother and a stepfather he disliked.

"Now, if you run away again, darlin', Judge Alexander's going to have to take you under her wing," she warned. Her smile was broad and easy, but this was a threat of detention. "And I have so *many* children."

The judge walked down the narrow corridor between the court-room and her chambers. The sign on her door said "JUDGE." Behind it was a small room with space enough for a desk and a few chairs. She took off her robe and then put it back on. "Chilly in here," she said.

We were in High Point, North Carolina. The judge divides her time between High Point and her home town of Greensboro, fifteen miles away. Her court hears juvenile and divorce cases, misde-meanors punishable by two years or less, and civil cases up to $5000.

"I wanted to be a minister," she said. "It was a case of father adoration. I went to Columbia law school more or less to pass the time. I was the first Negro woman there, but I didn't want to be a social experiment. I didn't think I'd go all the way through.

"My father was against it." She shifted her voice an octave lower. "He said, 'Bay-uh-by, what can you do with the law in the South?' He thought I'd just work on titles. But I had white clients in my first month. People would come in—I think they figured a black woman lawyer was like a dog walking on his hind legs: she doesn't do it well, but it's surprising she does it at all."

She speaks rapidly in a rich, melodious voice that glides up and down the scale. "We grew up thinking that courts were unfair to Negroes—we were middle-class and sheltered; my father had pride in our identity. I didn't ride in segregated buses. But I felt the prejudice when I started practicing law. They'd do snide things to make me uncomfortable. I'm an Aries—sensitive, fiery, creative; we don't always finish what we start. They'd wink when I tried a case, judges as well as lawyers. There'd be an inflection in their voice when they overruled me—scornful. I didn't let it bother me. I learned how to talk about a judge to a jury and not be in contempt. After a while they had to get three or four lawyers to beat me.

"They'd sneer and say, 'Elreta, howyadoin'?' I wouldn't permit that. They found out I'm a fighter. Even my best friends put a handle on my name. They call me Mrs. Alexander or Judge Alex-ander. That's the way they kept Negroes down in court, kept them in place. I'd wear my mink, and I'd sit next to the blackest and dirtiest person in court.

"I was waiting in a courtroom once and a lawyer came up and

said, 'You got a case here, honey?' I said yes, a larceny case. He said, 'I don't think they'll do much to you.' I said, 'Darlin', it's my client, not me.' "

She became a successful trial lawyer, handling both civil and criminal cases. "I had a rape case involving four black boys and a white girl," she said, "and I think that's about when I started thinking about becoming a judge. They were convicted, but it was like a kangaroo court. The judge called them 'niggers.' We didn't have a chance." In another case she represented Klansmen accused of assault. "I told them that if they had the money, I had the time." ˋ

She switched her party registration from Democrat to Republican when she ran for judge. "I had to decide we were going to open the door. Seems like my whole life I've been opening doors without an organization behind me. All the judges were Democrats. I felt that in a one-party system all I'd get would be the crumbs. And I'm like Pearl Bailey, honey"—her voice descended into Pearl Bailey's range—"I don't like crumbs.

"I ran as a woman, a Republican, a black, and a divorcee." The black population in her district is only 12 percent, but she finished third among seven winners. She was easily reelected in 1972.

Her judicial style is empathetic. "I believe that whom God would use he first makes ready. I've lived through a lot of these problems that people in my court have. I've worked on a farm and I know the ghetto and I've had problems in my own family. I can say, 'Listen, darlin', the judge is divorced.' I believe you cannot teach what you do not know and you cannot lead where you cannot go.

"I try to put myself in the position of the person I'm passing judgment on. My father always said, 'Bay-uh-by, when you have a question, just put yourself in their position and use your common sense.' A judge should let a person know that he loves him. The trouble with the judiciary is that it's narrow. Too many judges are the honor-society, law-review types who review life and never live it."

A white lawyer came in. "This is lawyer Tate," she said. "What do you think I've contributed as a judge, Mr. Tate?"

The lawyer, only slightly nonplussed, sat down to think about it. "Judge A. is the only judge in the county who took a pay cut, and that's significant right there," he said. "She has sense enough to know the law and guts enough to follow it." It sounded like a line he had used before. The judge beamed.

"The only thing wrong with her is her woman's viciousness," he went on. The judicial eyebrows rose. "Once she gets mad at you, you can't say anything because she'll just get madder and meaner. With a man there's usually something you can say to cool him off. With her you just have to pray for a continuance."

"If I feel an injustice has been committed," the judge put in.

Tate's opinion is shared by other local lawyers. "There's no district judge who can touch her on ability," one told me. "If she has a weakness, it's her temperament. She can roar like a lion."

"I have to work twice as hard as other judges," she said. "I have to make myself indispensable to remove the stigma, for the sake of our freedom. I tell people that freedom hasn't been born yet, but it's getting closer. If I were a white woman, this would be just another ball game. It means more because I'm black. But I try to think of color only if it's relevant to anti-social behavior. Some Negroes say I'm ashamed of black people. I don't say the words 'black' or 'white' in court. I think of color as an opportunity, in a sense.

"I think we overcome problems in this life and the next to get back to our original life," she said. "We select the vehicle we come back as." The lawyer looked dubious. "Why, Mr. Tate, I could come back white in my next incarnation. Then I'd be wrong again, because we'll be in charge by then."

She reached under her desk and pulled out a plastic container of salad and a canned diet drink. "Lunchtime," she explained. The lawyer departed.

Judge Alexander is something of a heroine in the local black community, particularly among the older people. "I know what Jackie Kennedy goes through trying to get some privacy," she said. "It takes me an hour to walk a block. They come up to the bench and give me roses."

There was a flurry of speculation in early 1972 that she might be named to a Federal District Court vacancy. She was willing, but Republican leaders submitted the names of three white men. "I think they backed off when they found out how strong Wallace was in North Carolina," she said.

I asked if she felt she was being exploited because of her race and sex.

"Oh, sure, darlin'," she replied, "but you have to catch the rabbit before you can cook the stew. I might not know the reasons I'm picked for something, but I know how good I am. Everybody's used in one way or another, but they can't demean my ability. I defied the custom of limiting Negro lawyers to title work and my parents rode in many big cars because of the money I made. There's an awful lot of window-dressing offers. They asked me if I wanted to run for Congress, but I said, 'Darlin', why should I?' If I don't know myself by now, I never will. I'm like an African whifflebird who flies backward—I can see where I've been."

I asked if whites were respectful in her court. She mulled the question as she ate her salad. "Most of the time," she said. "Actually, there's nothing as fine as a converted bigot. If whites talk liberality, you figure they're expecting something. But if you convince a bigot—by being *just*—you've got him.

"We had a man from South Carolina picked up for a highway violation by one of our black policemen here," she said. "He said no black officer was going to arrest *him*. Well, he came in here and, first thing, he went before a black magistrate. Then he came before me, and he was getting smart, so I gave him some time in jail to meditate. I turned him over to our colored bailiff. He went away muttering he didn't know what was happening to this country."

Mr. and Mrs. Early—a dark-haired, spidery white man and his hollow-cheeked wife—were charged with neglect of their seven children. The state contended that the Earlys' living conditions were so poor that the children were mentally and physically stunted. A finding of neglect would mean moving them to a foster home.

"The furniture and the kids were extremely dirty," a social worker testified. "It was a situation I've never seen before in my life. There was a piece of meat covered with flies—the predominant color was green. There was urine from the front porch all the way through the house."

"You wanted to break up the family, didn't you?" the defense lawyer demanded.

"I wanted to improve conditions so they wouldn't produce sociopaths."

"You didn't want no psychotics and all."

"Sociopaths," the witness repeated.

"You know what a sociologist is?" the lawyer asked.

"I know the difference between a psychotic and a sociopath."

"What is it?"

"A sociopath turns against society because he's denied all opportunities. . . ."

"Your Honor, I'd like to see the records of what help this family was given by this agency."

"You're just shooting wild now," the judge said. "Denied."

Mrs. Early gazed open-mouthed at the lawyer, as if she had just learned that he was wearing the Savior's clothes.

"They were sweet and sensitive children," the social worker went on. "I referred the family to agency after agency, but there was no understanding, no motivation."

"You didn't see anyone nekkid, didja?" the attorney asked.

"I found the baby wearing only a T-shirt in the winter."

"Haven't you found it doesn't take a group of kids long to get dirty?"

"Not like this."

"I even smell myself sometimes," the lawyer said. "Don't you?"

"This was the exception, sir, and not the rule."

The judge asked that the children, who were at home, be brought to the courthouse. The first defense witness was a lay minister in Early's church, the Chapel of Jesus.

"I never found no offense in their home," the witness said. He was a thin man with frightened, fawnlike eyes.

"Did you find dirt in their home?" the young prosecutor asked.

"It wasn't my purpose to examine their worldly articles for dirt. The kids are Christians, they desire to be in the Lord's house." He hesitated. "I don't believe the Lord would be pleased if they were taken away from their parents."

Mr. Early, his expression struggling between fear and defiance, was next.

"Are you the father to these children?" the prosecutor asked.

"I'm the daddy. The Father's in heaven."

The prosecutor asked if he had threatened a social worker who visited them.

"I was worried when that man came. I was skeered." The defiance crumpled. "If I offended, I'm sorry. But these are my young'uns, God's young'uns. I love 'em, I'd die for 'em. . . ." He began to weep. His friends in the audience were crying. The judge looked impassive.

"Why don't you get a second job to help support the family?"

Early earned about eighty dollars a week as a laborer. He tithed 10 percent to his church.

"I'll work any night except Wednesday," he replied. "I go to church meetin' Wednesdays. I cannot deny my God."

The judge asked a bailiff to bring the children in. They ranged in age from three to seventeen, bright-eyed and lank-haired kids with bewildered expressions. Their clothes were clean. All but the oldest were barefoot. The judge invited the four oldest, one by one, to sit in the witness chair.

"How old are you, darlin'?" she asked the first one.

"Fifteen." The girl spoke in a low and halting drawl.

"Can you cook a cake?"

"Yes, ma'am."

"Does it ever fall on you?"

"Yes, ma'am."

"Me too," the judge said.

Mrs. Early smiled.

"Do the kids at school make fun of the way you talk?"

"Sometimes."

"Excuse me, Your Honor," the defense attorney interrupted. "I just want to say that we're prepared to show that these are the same clothes the children were wearing this morning."

"You wouldn't let me forget it, darlin'," Judge Alexander said.

"Do you want to stay at home with your parents?" she asked the girl.

"Yes, ma'am." All four children testified that they loved their parents and wanted to stay with them.

At recess I followed the judge to her chambers. "I wouldn't sit in Juvenile Court all the time for ten million dollars," she said. "These cases break your heart. It's Tobacco Road. What can you do? They'll always be ignorant. We just hope we can keep them halfway clean.

"The mother is lazy and unmotivated. The father uses his church to feel important the way some people use racism to feel important. They have love of a sort, but there's no strength in the home. One or two of the kids seem to be retarded." She rested her chin on her hand. "Lord, I don't believe I can remove them from their home." She closed her eyes. "I'll try to get a housekeeper brought in and keep them under supervision."

The defense attorney came in. "Those people never done nothin' wrong, Judge," he said. "Shucks, *I* smell sometimes."

"I've heard that," the judge said.

"I'm just asking that you keep those kids with their loving parents."

"We'll see," she said.

Back in court, the judge delivered a rambling discourse on love and the law. "The question is does the law censure a person who doesn't exercise proper care within means. . . . You can have sickly children in clean homes, and in the ghetto—not using it that way—they can be healthy. . . . The strongest factor I know in life is love. . . . The parents did neglect their children, but the best solution is to leave them in the home with constant supervision and correction. Religion can be used to deprive children. Faith without works is dead. . . . The only thing I know to do is to require the social-services agency to make an investigation, to continue the matter under supervision, and to have a homemaker sent in."

She looked at the Earlys. "You ain't makin' enough to tithe, darlin'," she said. "Use that money you give to the church to feed your family. Work for God and leave your money home."

The lay minister stood up and started to say something. "You can't deny a man—"

She cut him off. "You ain't tellin' him, preacher, the judge is tellin' him.

"Okay, you check on your kids—go to the school and see how they're doing. Get a part-time job." She peered over her glasses. "I couldn't take your kids away from you."

Later that day I drove to Winston-Salem, twenty miles away, to watch another Judge Alexander. This was District Judge Abner Alexander, a white in his early forties who had been an all-conference tackle in high school. He was dealing with a stream of misdemeanor defendants, most of them black.

Two armed policemen hovered near the bench. "Settle down," one shouted periodically at the spectators. "Take your hands out of your pockets," the other ordered a defendant.

A young black man stood before the judge. "Where do you live when you're not in jail, Fowler?" the judge asked. The man muttered a reply. "You work anywhere?" The atmosphere in the courtroom was oppressive. It was as if the judge were an impatient first-grade teacher dealing with a class of unruly children. The policemen looked around sharply, alert to any show of disrespect. The man was fined for disturbing the peace.

Another black man was called. He had an Afro comb in his hair. The judge stared at it as if it were an exotic tropical snake. "What's that *thing* you got in your hair?" he demanded. The man removed the comb. He pleaded guilty to simple assault and received a fine.

"I want to know why they went in my house without a warrant," another black said. He was accused of selling homemade liquor. "You have a right to take the stand and tell your side if you want to," the judge said. His tone implied that it wouldn't make much difference anyway. The man walked toward the witness chair. "Go back and sit down," a policeman yelled. The defendant retreated.

Two black women had sworn out assault complaints against each other arising from a fight. The judge cut the second one off before she finished testifying—he wasn't interested. "Not guilty both cases," he said.

The accused bootlegger returned. He was found guilty and fined $250 plus costs. A young white girl, accompanied by a lawyer, came forward. She pleaded guilty to shoplifting a dress from a department store. "Fifty dollars," the judge said.

I saw Elreta Alexander once more before I left, at her spacious ranch home in the Greensboro neighborhood she integrated. A sign above her doorbell said, "Please do not stop without a prior appointment. I regret that due to doctor's orders I must rest."

"I had to do that because my former clients kept coming by to ask advice," she explained.

The house was furnished with Oriental screens and cabinets, shelves full of books and statuary, an elaborately carved desk, and expensive sofas and chairs. The walls of one bathroom were covered with leopardskin wallpaper. A statue portrayed a young black boy holding the world, Atlas-like, on his shoulders. "That's it, honey," she said. "I show that to my white friends."

She poured drinks. "My son might come in any minute," she said. "He's twenty-one and very disturbed. He's suffering from having two professional parents—my husband was a doctor. He's going to ask you what race you are." The boy had been under treatment for an emotional disorder.

"When I was in school they used to call me 'Free Issue' because I was fair-skinned," she said. "The dark-skinned kids hated us. You were supposed to be the white man's child and so you were no good, you hadn't suffered. They had a saying, 'If you white you right, if you brown stick around, if you black step back.'

"I have Indian, white, and African blood in me. There are no slaves on my family tree. My mother's father was white, and her mother was white and African and Cherokee. My father was Indian and Negro. I could pass for white when I was younger."

She sipped her bourbon. "I'm a product of the South, darlin'. I have all of it in me. And don't forget the Negro woman is freer. I got breaks because I had the courage to go ahead.

"I don't have any illusions," she went on. "I know I'm the 'good Negro' and there's always one 'good Negro.' That's me. It's for their consciences. I've been taken over by the whites, but I'm not fooled. If the Establishment wanted to, they could have ganged up on me and wrecked my practice, but they didn't. I try to look on the pretty side.

"When I started on the bench, the sheriff didn't assign any bailiff to me. He asked if I knew where he could get a good Negro bailiff. I didn't say anything for four months, then I told the sheriff I'd beat him at the polls—I'd tell my friends to vote against him. That worried him.

"They tried to make it inconvenient for me, that's all. They don't know I'm an Aries and I fight back. I converted it into publicity. What I do is kill 'em with kindness and keep on whippin' 'em."

It was time to go. "Sometimes I fool 'em, though," she said as we walked to the door. "There was a white woman in court one time whose daughter had run away. She came up to the bench and whispered to me, 'The worst thing is that she's running around with colored boys.' I just said, 'Darlin', have you looked at your judge?'"

VII

Broken Reeds
Judicial thieves, tyrants, bigots, and other menaces

NO ONE EVER EXPRESSED the moral commandments of judging better than Sir Francis Bacon, the Elizabethan man of parts who is periodically unveiled as the genius in William Shakespeare's closet. Bacon was essayist, scientist, philosopher, politician, lawyer, and judge. He was "learned counsel" to Elizabeth I and Lord Chancellor, the highest judicial officer in the kingdom, to James I. His writings on equal justice anticipated the "equal protection of the laws" doctrine in the United States Constitution by more than two hundred years. His essay "Of Judicature" is quoted admiringly whenever jurists discuss their craft. "Judges ought to be more learned than witty," he wrote, "more reverend than plausible, and more advised than confident. Above all things, integrity is their portion and proper virtue." He called the courtroom "a hallowed place" where "not only the bench but the footpace and precincts . . . ought to be preserved without scandal and corruption."

In 1621, when his political power and intellectual renown were at a zenith, Bacon was charged with violating his every hallowed principle. The House of Commons presented twenty-eight articles of impeachment against him, each one alleging a separate instance of Bacon merchandising his decisions. The price of Bacon's justice ranged from £50 to £2000, along with gifts of clothes and jewelry.

135

In some cases, like the apocryphal justice of the peace who took $10,000 from the plaintiff and $15,000 from the defendant, Sir Francis had collected from both sides.

Amid the ensuing storm, Bacon conceded that he had accepted money but denied that it had influenced his decisions. At length he gave up and offered the House of Lords an abject confession. "I do plainly and ingenuously confess that I am guilty of corruption," he said. "I beseech your lordships to be merciful to a broken reed." It may have been history's first instance, though it wasn't the last, of a fallen judge citing the distance of his fall as grounds for mercy.

Their lordships fined him £40,000, banned him from public office, and ordered him imprisoned in the Tower "during the king's pleasure." But the king's pleasure was surcease for Bacon, and the learned minister suffered little more than shame. His fine was canceled by James, his stay in the Tower ended after four days, and five months later he received a general pardon. Judicial thieves, then and now, know a different justice than their brothers in crime.

Judicial venality is different in kind from the lay variety. It "poisons the well of justice" and rattles a society's foundations. As Bacon's contemporary up in Stratford put it, "thieves for their robbery have authority when judges steal themselves." To find a modern parallel to Bacon one has to imagine the chief justice of the United States selling his opinions to ITT or Jimmy Hoffa for $100,000 and a case of wine, the story unfolding in lurid detail in the *New York Times*, and the chief justice coming forward to bare his shame before an embarrassed Senate. Or, to ease the strain on the imagination, one can turn to the case of Otto Kerner.

The Kerner story has vivid parallels to Bacon's downfall. As a judge of the U.S. Court of Appeals for the Seventh Circuit since 1968, his eminence lacked the loftiness of Bacon's. And it's true that no one ever accused Otto Kerner of philosophy. Yet his plunge from rectitude and respectability—"hanky-panky was as foreign to him as Zoroastrianism," a stunned observer said—was every bit as precipitous as Bacon's, and even a society gone edgy with cynicism could feel the tremors of his crash.

Like Bacon, Kerner was a courtly patrician and a man of accomplishment. His elegant personal style is the kind that sets scruffier mortals to checking their buttons reflexively. His credentials were, in everybody's word, impeccable, and his observation point was so clearly above the battle that he could spend twenty-five years on the mud-spattered field of Illinois politics and never dirty his boots. He could gaze at his prosecutor-tormentor during his trial and say in earnest condescension, "We obviously didn't go to the same school."

Like Bacon, he admitted that he had profited in office—from racetrack stocks he was invited to buy at below market price while governor of Illinois—but denied any return of favors; it was a *quo* without a *quid*. Why would such a windfall come his way? Kerner's reaction, a witness at his trial said, was, "That's very nice of Marge." Nice Marge was Marjorie Lindheimer Everett, owner of two of Illinois' largest racetracks. In the end Kerner, again like Bacon, wore his tattered honor to the ceremony of judgment. "I have been in many battles in my life where life itself was at stake," he said after he was convicted. "This battle is even more important than life itself because it involves my reputation and honor. . . ."

Kerner's concept of honor is bound up with his *noblesse oblige* approach to politics, a notion that he picked up while doing post-graduate work at Francis Bacon's alma mater, Trinity College, Cambridge. His father was a judge on the same Seventh Circuit court he later attained; young Otto was born, in the folklore of an awed generation of machine pols, "with a golden ballot in his mouth." Square-jawed and kindly-eyed, his portrait is on the walnut-paneled wall of the Seventh's handsome Chicago courtroom, only two floors above the room where he stood trial, and across the room from his father's portrait. It must seem to Kerner that his life's blood is streaked through the marble of that building.

He went to the right schools (Brown, Northwestern Law, Cambridge), joined the right National Guard unit (the "Black Horse troop"—F. Scott Fitzgerald would have loved it), and married the daughter of Anton Cermak, the murdered mayor of Chicago. He toe-danced into a corporate law practice, left to serve with distinction as an artillery officer during World War II, and then commenced his smooth and effortless climb up the greasy pole of Cook County politics. He was U.S. Attorney (1947), county judge (1954), and twice governor (1960 and 1964). Mayor Richard Daley and his clubhouse politicos could only shake their heads and count their blessings: this Brahmin, this *high-class guy* was one of theirs; but not precisely, of course—with them, but not of them. His prosecutor jabbed tellingly at his hauteur: "It [the bribe offer] had to be done delicately and diplomatically. Otto Kerner could read between the lines. It couldn't be crude. That's not how you talk to Otto Kerner." Kerner's "peers" were not Bacon's (nor Kerner's); only one of the twelve jurors had gone beyond high school. How would *they* talk to Otto Kerner?

In 1967 Kerner headed the much-praised "Riot Commission," winning a national name in the process. A year earlier, the government contended, he had made some shrewd stock purchases. He and an associate were offered racing stock worth $300,000 for $50,000. With one quick swipe he cleared $125,000. Other easy profits upped his take to $143,000. In exchange, the prosecution said, he helped Mrs. Everett obtain a longer racing season and expand into harness racing. In all, there were seventeen counts of bribery, conspiracy, perjury, tax evasion, and mail fraud. The jury found Kerner guilty on every one. U.S. District Judge Robert Taylor sentenced him to three years in prison and a fine of $50,000. The sentence contained a provision enabling Kerner to apply for parole as soon as he begins serving his term. The case was still on appeal in January 1974.

Kerner may not have been handled as gently as Bacon was, but his pre-conviction treatment was clearly no bed of nails. His indictment was delivered personally by the U.S. Attorney, a service not available to your average felony defendant. His co-defendants had to submit to arrest and fingerprinting, but not Kerner: he signed a personal-recognizance bond in his chambers. Daniel Ellsberg was not permitted to question his jury panel—nor were his lawyers— but Otto Kerner was.

Kerner suggested in his four days of testimony that he was a dupe, an innocent; indeed, he claimed that he, a federal judge on the second-highest court in America, was "tricked" into dubious testimony before a grand jury. His claim of ignorance does not sound farfetched to many Chicago lawyers, who regard him as a legal flyweight. "He's just plain dumb," one attorney said. "Only someone as dumb as Kerner would have become implicated in the racetrack scandal. He's so dumb he didn't see he was doing anything dishonest."

Judicial corruption did not start with Bacon, nor will it end with Kerner. The form it takes seems to vary with a judge's position in the hierarchy. At the more elevated reaches it is usually a matter of

a cautious shuffling of assets, discreetly managed by an inter-
mediary, with minimal judicial visibility. In the lower depths it
tends to be crude, a payoff made for a service rendered, and the
amenities may disappear with the middleman.

There is no discernible pattern, either of character or of motive.
Joseph Borkin, author of *The Corrupt Judge*, studied thirty-two
federal judges who were subjects of congressional investigations,
impeachment proceedings, or criminal actions. He found that they
came from "the most diverse of environments, varying from theo-
logical seminaries to Tammany politics. Many were honor graduates and became trustees of universities; . . . one entered politics
as a reform candidate; and another was the daily associate of
gangsters and 'ward' politicians."

The straws that broke a judge's resistance to temptation were
similarly diverse. "There are cases when the size of the stakes
seems to have been the compelling or initial factor," Borkin wrote,
"or the payment of political debts, or the entreaties of cleverly
persuasive fixers suggesting a potential 'killing.' Sometimes it was
the carefully planned suggestions of a 'return on investment' by an
executive in the world of commerce, or the result of the judge's
unfortunate investments and subsequent financial discomfort. Not
infrequently it was a favor requested by a son for his law partners,
business associates, or poolroom cronies, or the suggestion of a
decision based on the 'old school tie.' . . . Or it may have been
the simple fascination of money."

A Kerner case—a federal judge tried and convicted of a criminal charge—is one of the rarest spectacles in American law. Borkin
documented 55 cases in U.S. history where federal judges came
under investigation for some form of misconduct. Forty-four were
settled short of either impeachment or criminal trial—8 judges
were censured, 17 resigned, the others were either absolved or
their cases died in committee. Only 8 went to trial on impeachment,
and only 4 were convicted, the most recent, U.S. District Judge
Halsted Ritter of Florida, in 1936. The sole penalty for an im-
peached judge is removal from office.

Three of the 55—J. Warren Davis of the Third Circuit Court
of Appeals (Philadelphia), District Judge Albert W. Johnson of
Pennsylvania, and Martin T. Manton of the Second Circuit appeals
court in New York—were tried for corruption. Davis' jurors twice
failed to agree on a verdict, and the indictment was quashed.

Johnson was acquitted, though four co-defendants were found guilty. The other—the one who didn't get away—was Manton.

Manton was a judicial *wunderkind*. He was thirty-six when President Woodrow Wilson appointed him to the District Court in 1916, the youngest federal judge in the nation. He advanced to the appellate court after only eighteen months; in 1922 he came within a whisker of joining Oliver Wendell Holmes and Louis Brandeis on the Supreme Court. His prestige rivaled theirs; unlike Kerner, he was widely respected as a legal scholar. Universities gave him honorary degrees; Congress invited him to testify on complicated questions of law; as chief judge of the Second Circuit, he was the highest-ranking judge in New York; in one ten-year period he wrote 650 opinions, more than one a week, an output rarely equaled.

Manton's problem was a financial reach that exceeded his grasp. By 1934, when the Depression was swallowing fortunes daily, he was $736,000 in debt. His frantic efforts to recoup snarled him in a web of bribery and more debt. In 1939 Manhattan District Attorney Thomas E. Dewey charged him with taking bribes in exchange for bankruptcy appointments, borrowing from litigants whose cases were before him, and employing a fixer to sell his decisions. He promptly resigned.

At his federal court trial for obstruction of justice and intent to defraud the government, Manton trotted out a glittering lineup of character witnesses including two former presidential candidates, John W. Davis and Al Smith, and Judge Learned Hand, his colleague on the Second Circuit and perhaps America's greatest judge. A jury convicted him after deliberating four hours.

Pleading his own case on appeal to the Supreme Court, Manton made the disingenuous argument that his conviction would harm the judicial image. "From a broad viewpoint," he said, "it serves no public policy for a high judicial officer to be convicted of a judicial crime. It tends to destroy the confidence of the people in the courts." The Supreme Court was unmoved by this plea for absolute judicial immunity, and in 1940 Manton entered Lewisburg, Pennsylvania, federal prison, where he served nineteen months—the only federal judge ever imprisoned for corruption. He died, a broken reed, in 1946.

What gnaws at these implausible felons? Visions of invulnerability? In a society that venerates judges, it is not so deluded a vision at that. A record of one out of fifty-five comes close to invulnerability. Is it simple, dirty greed? But these are men who gave up the big money—or stashed it—when they donned the robe. Some impulse of the strong to test the limits of power? Yet they are rational men, not tilters at windmills; rationality is their religion and their strength. Character, then—but is character carved in marble or clay? And how identify it, or assess it? And how be certain?

Corruption in the federal judiciary is negligible. Manton, Kerner, Ritter, perhaps three dozen others in the history of the republic is not bad. There are tyrants on the federal bench and bigots, but few thieves. In a year of listening I heard serious ethical questions raised about only three active federal judges—William Lynch of Chicago, Mark Costantino of Brooklyn, and Frank Gray of Nashville, Tennessee—and no formal charges were brought against any of them. Lynch, a former law partner of Mayor Daley, was allegedly permitted to buy the same racetrack stock that Kerner was blessed with, at similar cut rates. Costantino and Gray were accused of conflicts of interest for deciding cases involving personal business associates.

The state courts are where the thieves are. "It's a forgotten area," says a Justice Department official with eyebrows raised. "It's full of shadows and vacuums. Judges are bought, sure. I think it's the best-hidden branch of government."

Corruption in state courts is oceanic in comparison to federal courts. Salaries are lower, prestige is lower, and inevitably the quality declines. Most important, the state courts are too often havens for failed politicians and mediocre lawyers. Character, given these limitations, is a sometime thing.

¶ Edward J. DeSaulnier, Jr., was a Republican member of the Massachusetts Senate when he bolted party ranks in 1958 to support a Democratic bill increasing the number of Superior Court judges. His reward was appointment to one of the judgeships, a lifetime job in the commonwealth.

In 1971 a convicted swindler named Michael Raymond told a U.S. Senate subcommittee that DeSaulnier was the fixer who arranged a suspended sentence for him on a fraud case. The payoff was $35,000, which Raymond said was divided among the judge, a bondsman, and the victims of the fraud. Raymond quoted the judge as saying, "I hope we can do business in the future."

Raymond stood by his story under questioning by Massachusetts investigators. DeSaulnier's chief, Judge Walter H. McLaughlin, took the extraordinary step of turning transcripts of the interrogation over to DeSaulnier, with the explanation that it was "only fair." No criminal charges were filed, but Massachusetts' Supreme Judicial Court concluded after an investigation that DeSaulnier was guilty of "grossly improper" conduct and was "unfit to continue either as a judge or as a member of the bar."

Governor Francis W. Sargent demanded DeSaulnier's resignation in January 1972, and within two days he got it, accompanied by a letter sounding the familiar notes of outraged innocence and ravaged honor: "Had I in fact been guilty of such misconduct I would long since have departed from all I hold dear including my family, friends and the profession I have served and loved. . . . I will if necessary devote the balance of my years in attempting to vindicate my honor and the name of my family."

¶ Mitchell Schweitzer, in twenty-six years on the New York City bench, gained a curiously contradictory reputation. He was known as a knowledgeable judge who worked hard, and also as a courtroom bully who "moved the business" with high-handed efficiency. Defense lawyers complained that he frequently frightened their clients into guilty pleas by threats of severe sentences if they pressed for a trial. He sustained his vigorous courtroom pace with thirty-minute midday naps in chambers.

Schweitzer first came under serious suspicion when he was revealed to be a close friend of the late Nathan Voloshen, a convicted influence peddler who worked for former House Speaker John W. McCormack. He was charged with softening sentences after meetings with Voloshen.

In 1971 Schweitzer was named by the ubiquitous Michael Raymond as the recipient of a $25,000 bribe through an intermediary in a sixteen-year-old stock-manipulation case. The currency of exchange on Schweitzer's side was said to be a light sentence and easy probation terms.

New York's antiquated Court on the Judiciary, which creaks into action about once every six years, then authorized an investigation. His attorney said Schweitzer "welcomes the opportunity to appear before an impartial tribunal."

His eagerness faded fast. Schweitzer was charged with conspiring to obstruct justice in his dealings with Voloshen and Raymond, and with running a profitable money-lending business on the side.

After an across-the-board denial of all allegations, the judge announced his plan to retire—at full pension—on the day the Court on the Judiciary hearing was to begin. The publicity, he explained, had "seriously undermined" his health. "My doctor has warned me that exposure to such stress and strain as will arise from the hearings might well affect my health adversely and might result in my complete mental and physical breakdown." It was the cry of a breaking reed.

¶ In 1965 four justices of Oklahoma's nine-man Supreme Court were implicated in one of the most sordid exposés in American judicial history. One, Nelson S. Corn, confessed that he and three colleagues collected $150,000 to reverse a tax decision against an investment company. Asked if there had been any year during his twenty-four years on the court when he failed to take a bribe, Corn could only say, "Well, I don't know."

Corn and Justice Earl Welch, who resigned rather than face impeachment, were convicted of income-tax evasion. A third justice died before the story broke. The fourth, Justice Napoleon Bonaparte Johnson, a part-Cherokee selected as "Indian of the Year" in 1964, fought the charges through a rare impeachment trial. "Johnson was bought," his prosecutor said, "by ten thousand dollars in hundred-dollar bills." The state senate voted 31 to 15, one more than the required two-thirds majority, to remove him.

The scandal led to the adoption of merit selection for appellate judges in Oklahoma, but it didn't end corruption in the state courts. In 1968 Judge Glenn Sharpe of Bryan County was ousted from office for taking more than $13,000 to waive the requirements for marriage licenses.

¶ Unscrupulous lawyers and judges have milked estates, through the assessment of maximum fees for minimum labor, for generations. The judge's power to appoint appraisers and special guardians gives him the opportunity to help his political or personal friends, his family, and—with a little judicial discretion—himself.

Probate Judge Clem McClelland of Harris County, Texas, had discretion enough to set up a dummy corporation as a front. Grateful appointees were advised how much stock to buy in McClelland's Tierra Grande Corporation, which amounted to a donation to his personal wealth and well-being. McClelland was convicted of stealing $2500 from an estate in his court and sentenced to ten years in prison, which he began serving in 1965.

In Oregon, District Judge Edwin L. Jenkins appointed his wife an appraiser in several probate cases and named her an estate administratrix in others. After boasting that he was "immune from any form of discipline," he was found guilty of improper conduct by the state Supreme Court and forced to resign in 1966.

¶ The ties between organized crime and the judiciary are probably not as close as they were thirty years ago when New York Judge Thomas Aurelio thanked Frank Costello for nominating him and promised, "When I tell you something is in the bag, you can rest assured." But there are still judges whose actions help the mob rest easy.

Ralph DeVita was appointed to a county judgeship in Union County, New Jersey, in 1966. He was an ex-prosecutor, a lean, emotional man with many friends in the local legal and business communities.

In 1969 he offered a prosecutor $10,000 to drop a bookmaking case against two Mafia operatives. "The indictment has got to be killed," prosecutor Michael R. Imbriani quoted DeVita as saying. "There are ten big ones in it for you."

A jury convicted DeVita of "obstructing justice," rejecting a more serious bribery charge. His lawyer, claiming that as an ex-prosecutor and ex-judge DeVita's life would be endangered in prison, urged a suspended sentence. But Superior Court Judge Walter Conklin, allowing that it was "the most difficult decision I ever had to make," sentenced a weeping DeVita to one to two years.

In a melodramatic statement to the court, DeVita cried that he had lost "my self-respect, my license to practice law, and my judgeship." After the sentencing, reporters asked him if he had found another job. "You know I have no talent except devoting my life to the law," he replied.

DeVita served eight months at a prison in Leesburg, New Jersey, where guards kept him isolated from other inmates, some of whom he had sentenced. He died of a heart attack shortly after his release. He was fifty-one.

¶ Bail procedures, often scandalous in themselves, present yet another opportunity for covert lining of the judicial pocket. Judge Louis W. Kizas of Chicago attracted more attention than he wanted when he released two men charged with armed robbery on their own recognizance. The subsequent investigation turned up evidence that Kizas had repeatedly granted low bail for a price.

Suddenly afflicted with poor health, Judge Kizas resigned before a scheduled hearing by the Illinois Courts Commission in 1967. Two years later he pleaded guilty to criminal charges of official misconduct and was fined $15,000.

In 1972 a Los Angeles grand jury accused three judges of signing blank prisoner-release orders and dispensing them to favored bail bondsmen. The bondsmen, who bought and sold the orders among themselves, were then free to set bail at whatever figure they chose—or negotiated. A prosecutor said that one pre-signed release order was used to bail a suspected Mafia member out of jail for $1000 when arresting officers had recommended bail of $100,000.

The three judges—Superior Judge Leopoldo G. Sanchez and Municipal Judges Antonio E. Chavez and Morton H. Barker— were charged with "willful and corrupt misconduct," but no criminal indictments were returned. Sanchez and Chavez were formally censured by the state Supreme Court on the recommendation of the California Commission on Judicial Qualifications. Barker, who had retired, was not punished.

¶ Seymour R. Thaler, a theatrical, feisty politician with a reputation as a honey-tongued orator and an abrasive investigator, paid his dues with thirteen years in the New York Senate before he won nomination to the state's Supreme Court (the confusing name given to New York's highest trial court). His nomination came about through machinations refined by generations of New York politicians: a slate of six candidates, three from each party, was agreed upon by Queens party leaders and given bipartisan backing in the 1971 election.

Thaler won easily, and promptly collected his JSC (Justice of the Supreme Court) license plates. But he never reached the bench. A month after his election he was accused of criminally receiving $800,000 in stolen U.S. treasury bills and reaping $93,000 as his share of the profits. An art fancier, Thaler spent part of the swag for an original painting by French artist Jean Corot.

Thaler was a "very wealthy boy," a friend said. "There's just no reason for shenanigans." His wife's family owned a mattress company. At his trial he emotionally denied knowing that the securities were stolen, dissolving frequently in sobs. He testified that he would have "staked my life" that the bills, obtained at 25 percent of their value, were legitimate. He added, "I did stake my life, unfortunately. . . ."

A federal-court jury convicted him of selling and transporting stolen bills, plus one count of perjury. "I have a feeling that I'm in a nightmare," he said to sentencing judge Murray I. Gurfein. "None of this is true. . . . I have lost my dream that I had as a child, to become a member of the judiciary." Tears streaked his taut face, and even courtroom cynics winced at his pain.

Judge Gurfein, calling Thaler's transgression a "unique episode in an otherwise unblemished life," sentenced him to a year and a day in prison and a fine of $10,000.

Thaler suffered a heart attack after his appeal was rejected by the U.S. Court of Appeals for the Second Circuit. He began serving his sentence in late 1973.

A judicial thief, theoretically at least, is subject to arrest and punishment like any other thief. But in a dismaying number of instances corrupt judges manage to avoid criminal judgment. One reason is the lodge, the brotherhood of the robe. Like the rest of us, judges tend to empathize most vividly with their peers; a judge can understand the temptations and torments of another judge, and it is not difficult to move from understanding to sympathy and from sympathy to protection. Judges are no quicker to blow the whistle on one another than policemen or union officers are, and their routes of escape are more accessible. The tendency is to find a seemly and dignified way out—a reprimand, if necessary, or preferably a resignation.

Where judges are under suspicion, the prosecutor's safest course is often a discreet withdrawal. "In the case of judges," says Maurice Nadjari, a special prosecutor assigned to uncover corruption in New York's criminal justice system, "we tended to say that if there is no hard evidence, don't look for it. We go for perjury or contempt with the cops, we go for it with lawyers and we go for it with city commissioners. But we don't do it with judges. . . . There is favoritism that grows out of the fact that most district attorneys want to be judges and most assistant district attorneys want to be district attorneys."

The raw fact of judicial power, and the fear that accompanies it, will cause a lawyer, policeman, or prosecutor to think several times before he makes an accusation against a judge. According to a newspaper report, City Court Judge Charles J. Roskoski of Newburgh, New York, was picked up by police early one morning and arrested for public intoxication and disorderly conduct. Later in the morning the police could find no arrest records, and no charge was filed. District Judge Clyde R. Ashworth of Fort Worth, Texas, spent three hours in jail after his arrest for drunk driving, a newspaper said, but District Attorney Frank Coffey chose not to file charges. "It's discretionary with the district attorney to file or not to file," he explained, "and I used my discretion and decided not to file." Even when a judge is brought to trial, he often has advantages unknown to other defendants.

Judge Joseph P. Pfingst sat erectly in the witness chair, his hands folded. Tall and balding, natty in a brown suit and brown-and-white-striped shirt, he peered over his glasses at the jury as he dealt handily with the prosecutor's questions.

The prosecutor, a blocky man with an Irish profile and a plodding manner, was trying to prove that Pfingst had bought his New York Supreme Court judgeship for $50,000. Pfingst had already been convicted of bankruptcy fraud. Federal District Judge Jack B. Weinstein had postponed sentencing him pending the outcome of this trial.

"As a lawyer of eighteen years' experience," the prosecutor began.

"Twenty-five," Pfingst snapped.

"Pardon me, twenty-five. You didn't know any way to protect yourself when signing receipts for one hundred and eighty-six thousand dollars?"

"I probably know seven hundred thousand ways to protect myself," the judge replied.

"And you didn't use one, did you?"

"That's right."

"Is Mr. Fellman [the Republican leader Pfingst allegedly paid for the judgeship] framing you too?"

Pfingst glared scornfully at the prosecutor. "That's a pretty silly question."

The prosecutor pressed him on Fellman, who had pleaded guilty to accepting a bribe and had testified for the government.

"You gave him the key to the jail," Pfingst declared, "and people will do anything to get out of jail. . . . A prosecutor can go to a man who is a high liver and who is indicted for a crime—it's an old tradition in criminal law. He expects a suspended sentence in exchange for his testimony."

An uninformed spectator would have been startled to learn that Pfingst was the defendant. He scolded the prosecutor. He lectured the jury. He haughtily corrected his interrogator's questions. At times he appeared exasperated with the prosecutor's frailties. He took the offensive and answered questions that were not asked, then shot his own questions back at the prosecutor.

"May I ask that the defendant be treated like any other witness?" the prosecutor asked Judge Weinstein at one point.

"Just ask a question," Weinstein replied.

For a long instant Weinstein on the bench and Pfingst on the witness stand were in the identical posture, heads resting on the backs of their chairs—judicial meditation.

The prosecutor, stretching his neck and jutting his head forward like a turkey, asked about the contributions expected of a judicial candidate.

"After I found out Fellman expected me to raise money from my clients," Pfingst said, "I talked to [a client] and said something like, 'Well, you're one of my clients and—' You don't spell it out, you know. . . . I paid twenty-five hundred dollars made out to a company for printing expenses and got twelve tickets to a dinner. It was a contribution to the party. What I did was illegal, but I didn't know it then. I should have had my wife do it, that would have been legal. It's silly, but that's the way it is."

Pfingst's client had later bragged that he bought him the election. "Were you furious when you heard this?" the prosecutor asked.

"You bet." Pfingst looked at the jury as he spoke. One juror wore sunglasses. Another smiled.

"What did you say to him?"

"Keep your big mouth shut. . . . I said he didn't buy me any election. He said get off your high horse or something like that."

"Did you report it to the district attorney?"

"Oh, come on." Pfingst was appalled at the prosecutor's naïveté.

Pfingst was an expert witness. "Are you suggesting that the state lied?" the prosecutor asked him a few minutes later.

"You lied a number of times. This is a phony prosecution. You've lied repeatedly and suggested lies to this jury."

Judge Weinstein sat impassive. No objection was made. The prosecutor was overmatched. "Is it possible—" he began.

"It's *possible*," Pfingst cut him off, "that the sun will fall down from the heavens and render this trial meaningless."

The jury took eleven hours to find him innocent. The following week Judge Weinstein sentenced Pfingst on the fraud charges, which carry a maximum of fifteen years. He described Pfingst as "basically an honorable man," and gave him four months. The Court on the Judiciary removed Pfingst from office more than a year later.

A judge must do better than simply obey the law; he must exemplify it. "Public confidence in the judiciary" is a constant theme in discussions of judicial ethics. The American Bar Association's Canons of Judicial Ethics, first set to paper in 1924, were inspired by the conduct of U.S. District Judge Kenesaw Mountain Landis of Illinois, who was found to be supplementing his $7500 federal salary with an additional $42,500 earned as commissioner of baseball. There wasn't anything *illegal* about it; it just seemed wrong. And the canons said as much.

The original canons—ornamented with quotations from Sir Francis Bacon, among others—remained the accepted guide of judicial behavior until the actions of another federal judge, Supreme Court Justice Abe Fortas, goaded the ABA into a complete revision, which was approved in 1972.

The new canons forbid a judge to "serve as an officer, director, manager, advisor or employee of any business." He is to report the receipt of any gift worth more than $100, and to decline to serve on government commissions except those dealing with law and justice. In a direct response to the issue raised by Fortas, the canons require judges to file regular reports "of compensation received for quasi-judicial and extra-judicial activities."

Many judges bridled at the new rules. The National Conference of State Trial Judges, composed of judges active in the ABA, voted 60–31 against the provision for disclosure of outside income. "We considered it's probably an unconstitutional invasion of the privacy of judges," said Judge Warren P. Cunningham of Houston. "Judges do not give up their citizenship upon becoming judges." The principal fret of the state judges was electoral. "Financial information spread upon the record," Cunningham said, "could be distorted by political opponents who would not have to file income statements themselves."

"The public has a definite interest in what a judge does with his time and any money he makes from extra-judicial activities," replies Roger J. Traynor, retired chief justice of the California Supreme Court, who headed the committee to revise the canons. "He's not like an ordinary citizen. He is first of all a judge."

What constitutes conflict of interest for a judge is not always clear. The new canons tell a judge "to refrain from financial and business dealings that tend to reflect adversely on his impartiality, interfere with the proper performance of his judicial duties, exploit his judicial position, or involve him in frequent transactions with lawyers or persons likely to come before the court on which he serves." Ambiguities linger in that stricture, and judges may well yearn for a clearer line. In some cases, however, the line is as plainly visible as a cop's badge or a bagman's smile.

¶ Justice Roy J. Solfisburg of the Illinois Supreme Court was among those mentioned in 1969 as a possible nominee to the U.S. Supreme Court. His colleague Justice Ray I. Klingbiel was the first chairman of the Illinois Courts Commission, a five-judge body with power to remove errant jurists.

In June 1969, Sherman Skolnick, an independent court reformer in Chicago, charged that both justices had accepted financial favors from Theodore Isaacs, the defendant in a case before them. (Isaacs, a sort of Midwestern Michael Raymond, was also a co-defendant with Otto Kerner.)

Evidence amassed by a special commission showed that Klingbiel accepted a gift of 100 shares of stock in Chicago's City Bank & Trust Co., which Isaacs served as general counsel, and Solfisburg was permitted to buy 700 shares while the Isaacs case was before their court. Illinois Justice Byron O. House testified that Klingbiel wrote the Isaacs opinion outside of the court's normal rotation schedule. Klingbiel and Solfisburg were among the majority in a 4–2 decision to exonerate Isaacs on charges of defrauding the state. Other testimony indicated that Solfisburg began selling his stock at a 25-percent profit after the decision.

The commission held that the two justices had not only sullied the "appearance" of judicial propriety but committed "positive acts of impropriety," and called for their resignation. Two days later, still denying any misbehavior, Solfisburg and Klingbiel quit.

¶ When Delmar Shelby sued his wife Jean for divorce in St. Louis County Circuit Court in 1967, the judge at the initial hearing was John D. Hasler. Hasler heard evidence at a subsequent hearing, including testimony by Mrs. Shelby, and took the case under advisement.

Four months after the first hearing Shelby found several letters the judge had written to his wife. The letters revealed that Mrs. Shelby had at least one good friend in court. They had romantic overtones, and included a discussion of evidence in the case and advice on how to proceed. Judge Hasler and Mrs. Shelby had dined together and seen each other socially. Shelby's lawyer asked that the judge disqualify himself from the case, and Hasler complied.

Hasler was tried and convicted of "oppression, partiality, misconduct, and abuse of authority." He argued that his relationship with Mrs. Shelby was strictly paternal, arising from his concern for her and her children. A sympathetic jury assessed his punishment at a $1 fine.

Missouri, the state that pioneered merit selection, had no removal commission at the time (one was established in 1972), so the state House of Representatives voted four articles of impeachment against Hasler. He resigned from the bench three days before his scheduled impeachment trial.

¶ Judge Ross L. DiLorenzo of Brooklyn Civil Court has never been celebrated for his courtroom demeanor. "Why don't you get out of here, fella?" he once demanded of a poverty lawyer whose argument in a landlord-and-tenant case displeased him. A few minutes later he said to the same attorney, "Take a walk, will you?" On another occasion he ordered several Jews out of his courtroom for not removing their skullcaps.

Off the bench he was equally direct. In 1971 a former attorney for the New York–New Jersey Waterfront Commission charged that DiLorenzo had approached him in behalf of a friend who was subpoenaed to testify before the commission. The judge's friend was identified as a cousin of Mafia boss Carlo Gambino.

The appellate division of New York's Supreme Court suspended DiLorenzo for seven months while they investigated the charge, then reinstated him after ruling that he "did not act judiciously or properly" but his conduct "was not such as to justify his removal." DiLorenzo shrugged off his censure as "a spiritual punishment." "I never did anything wrong," he told a newsman. "All I did was to put in a good word for an old friend."

Special Prosecutor Nadjari pursued the investigation, and in the summer of 1973 DiLorenzo was indicted on eight counts of perjury and one of obstruction of governmental administration. The indictment charged that he lied eight separate times during his hearing before an appellate-division referee.

Standards for a judge's personal morality are even more difficult to codify than those for conflict of interest. The canons flee from the field under a covering fire of rhetoric: a judge may "engage in the arts, sports, and other social and recreational activities, if such avocational activities do not detract from the dignity of his office or interfere with the performance of his judicial duties."

What *should* guide a judge's personal conduct, other than faithful obedience to morals laws and avoidance of public nudity? Is he forever barred from Harold's Club? Must he avert his eyes when passing a topless bar, swallow his oaths (quaintly alone among American males of my acquaintance, judges frequently say "goldang" and "sonofagun"), and politely reject a third glass of sherry? What good is a judge who hasn't tasted sin anyway? How does he know what he's condemning?

Justice Traynor's views are somewhat more precise than the canons: "The easy answer is that a judge's personal morality is none of the public's business, but that's not the true answer. It doesn't do the judiciary any good if judges do things contrary to the mores of their community. It undermines public confidence. I'm not bothered if a judge shoots crap at a casino, but if it's his constant habit to go to the races and bet heavily, it would harm the judiciary. It's a weasel-worded answer, I know, but it's a question of balance. I don't like the idea of a judge going to a house of prostitution even if it's legal. It's a matter of moral behavior by common-sense standards of propriety."

The following judges need work in this area:

¶ *Judge Gotcha.* Judge Leland Geiler of the Los Angeles

Municipal Court kept a battery-operated "dildo" in his chambers. On one occasion, in the language of a 1972 report recommending his removal, he "appeared from the vicinity of the filing cabinet" holding the dildo "and thrust it into the area of Mr. E's [a public defender] buttocks touching his body. Mr. E. joined the others in Judge Geiler's chambers in general laughter." In the courtroom later that day Geiler threatened to use the dildo on the public defender to speed his questioning.

Another time Geiler came up behind a traffic commissioner in a hallway and "reached under his crotch and grabbed him by the testicles, causing Commissioner M. so much pain that he almost passed out."

Geiler was conferring with several men in his chambers when his court clerk (Mrs. P.) entered the room briefly and then left. "How would you like to eat that?" the judge asked. "His question," the report noted, "referred to Mrs. P." He would frequently ask Mrs. P., "Did you get any last night?"

The California Commission on Judicial Qualifications cited these and other incidents in urging Geiler's removal "for conduct prejudicial to the administration of justice that brings the judicial office into disrepute and for willful misconduct in office." The judge's attorney described the incidents as "friendly horseplay." Geiler was also charged with removing public defenders from nine cases when they refused to plead their clients guilty.

In October 1973, more than a year after the commission urged his ouster, the California Supreme Court unanimously ordered Geiler's removal.

¶ *Judge Fondle.* Judge James H. Edgar of Ingham County, Michigan, was publicly censured in 1972 when the Michigan Supreme Court found that "on numerous occasions [he] slapped, patted or touched in a familiar or suggestive manner" the buttocks of nine different female court employees. Edgar also wrote his name on a woman's undergarment and bumped another's head on a counter hard enough to make her cry.

Chief Justice Thomas M. Kavanagh, citing Edgar for "vulgar misconduct," told him that "you displayed the most crass behavior, so tawdry . . . that you have brought dishonor and public disgrace to the office you hold." Edgar lost his bid for reelection in November 1972 by a vote of nearly two to one.

¶ *Judge Whoopee.* Edward A. Haggerty, Jr., a Criminal District Court judge in New Orleans, presided over one of the most notorious trials in recent years, the assassination-conspiracy trial of Clay Shaw. Although Shaw was acquitted, prosecutor Jim Garrison praised Haggerty for "the most distinguished work on the part of a district judge that I have ever seen since I've been a lawyer."

Nine months after the Shaw trial, Judge Haggerty was arrested while trying to flee a vice raid on a stag party that he had helped to arrange. He was subdued after struggling with two policemen.

Haggerty had contributed to the night's merriment by supplying three prostitutes and pornographic films. The girls performed "lewd and indecent acts," the Louisiana Judiciary Commission found, as well as acts of prostitution. The judge's contention that he was unaware of the girls' professional standing was called "incredible" by the state Supreme Court.

The court also found that Haggerty was a regular customer of a New Orleans bookmaker and a frequent winner at poker parties. With one dissenting vote, the court ordered Haggerty removed from office for "gross disregard of the judicial obligations as set forth in the Canons of Judicial Ethics."

¶ *Judge Gunslinger.* Judge John J. McDonnell of Cook County's Circuit Court bench warmed another bench as a substitute halfback for Notre Dame in the 1950s. He won his judgeship through the sponsorship of former Chicago state's attorney Edward Hanrahan, but he retained his taste for physical combat. He was also given to carrying a .38 caliber pistol.

In November 1972, twenty-seven-year-old Allen Simon was edging his car out of a Chicago parking lot when McDonnell suddenly appeared at his window, rapping on the glass with his pistol. Simon said the judge yelled, "Put that car back or I'll blow your fucking head off." He waved the pistol, shouted a few more obscenities, and finally permitted Simon to leave.

Simon complained to police, and after some delay he was able to get a warrant charging McDonnell with aggravated assault. But another Cook County judge, Maurice D. Pompey, dismissed the case after McDonnell testified that he believed Simon was tampering with his car.

"Simon came to court believing that the odds were stacked against him," prosecutor Thomas Burnham commented, "and it turned out to be true."

The Illinois Courts Commission later suspended McDonnell,

without pay, for four months. He was back on the bench by November 1973.

Bigoted and tyrannical judges are the most widespread menace to our dream of equal justice. The manner and attitude of a trial judge are crucial to everyone concerned. The idea that the sins of a lower-court judge come out in the wash at the appellate-court level is fantasy; a topheavy majority of all cases are not appealed, and an equally imposing number of appealed cases are upheld by the higher court. The trial-court judge is The Man.

"Glaring down from their elevated perches," writes law professor Herman Schwartz of Buffalo, "insulting, abrupt, rude, sarcastic, patronizing, intimidating, vindictive, insisting on not merely respect but almost abject servility . . . Armed with the power to cite for contempt and more, the power to dispose of or influence the outcome of a case by subtle and not so subtle means, as well as the power to sentence, many trial judges daily prove the truth of Acton's dictum"—that absolute power corrupts absolutely.

If the judge is arrogant or abusive, says Professor Harry Jones of Columbia law school, lawyers cannot make their cases, witnesses become resentful, and jurors estranged. "The entire trial process is distorted, and the parties, certainly the losing party and often the winner, leave the courtroom with a distinct impression that their dignity has been assailed and their claims and grievances inadequately heard." Jones believes that "every multi-judge trial court of general jurisdiction has at least one tyrant in residence."

If a hard-eyed observer includes *all* judges, including the thousands whose jurisdiction is limited to misdemeanors, the proportion of autocrats escalates dramatically. "The lower the court, the worse the behavior," Schwartz maintains. My own estimate is that between one fourth and one third of our trial judges are autocratic on the bench.

Judge L. Jackson Embrey of Arlington, Virginia, was suspended briefly after he ordered that an eighteen-year-old girl be beaten by her mother in court. In another case a *Washingtonian* magazine writer reported this dialogue between Judge Embrey and a black youth charged with trespassing:

Embrey: "You say this boy is a friend of yours?"

Defendant: "Yes, sir. He's a friend."

Embrey: "And you don't know how old he is?"

Defendant: "Not exactly. No, sir."

Embrey: "Have you ever had your head examined?"

Defendant: "No, sir."

Embrey: "I think that would be a good idea, don't you?"

Judge Floyd Sarisohn of Suffolk County, New York, who was ultimately removed from the bench on a variety of charges, once candidly told a lawyer, "I'm going to screw you every way I can short of reversible error."

When a lone dissenting juror caused a mistrial in a 1972 airplane-hijacking case, the late U.S. District Court Judge George Rosling of Brooklyn threatened to have the juror investigated by FBI agents to "see whether she was performing her jury functions or some other functions."

Judge Edward Beard of Washington, D.C., Superior Court once sentenced a defendant awaiting trial to thirty days for falling asleep in court. A co-defendant who was awake got the same sentence. When he protested, Judge Beard said, "You are guilty by association. Get them out of here."

This kind of tyranny springs from more than personal arrogance and intolerance. It derives as well from a system of selection that values politics more than professionalism, and often from a warped view of their function by judges themselves. Allan K. Butcher of the University of Texas asked 232 Texas municipal judges how they perceived their role. Twenty-one percent answered that the court's job was to "determine appropriate punishment for people the police say have violated the law," and another 4.3 percent called their court an "agent or extension of the police." This means that a defendant in Texas Municipal Court has a one-in-four chance of drawing a judge who does not understand the purpose of the courts.

The racist judge is an immeasurable but formidable presence in many American courts. "If they want to live like animals," said Maryland Circuit Judge William B. Bowie of a group of black defendants before him, "let them stay in a pen somewhere."

Superior Court Judge Gerald S. Chargin of San Jose, California, was censured after he delivered this remarkable tirade to an eighteen-year-old Mexican-American boy who pleaded guilty to incest:

"Mexican people, after thirteen years of age, it's perfectly all right to go out and act like an animal. . . . We ought to send you out of the country—send you back to Mexico. You belong in prison for the rest of your life for doing things of this kind. You ought to commit suicide. . . . Maybe Hitler was right. The animals in our society probably ought to be destroyed because they have no right to live among human beings."

There is no certain method of finding and disciplining the scores of judges who are guilty not of a crime, not even of a clear violation of the ethical canons, but simply of the human excesses of prejudice, arrogance, or petty despotism. The canons say a judge "should be patient, dignified, and courteous" to everyone in his courtroom, and let it go at that. The most encouraging sign of reform is the development of judicial disciplinary commissions, which have flowered in recent years and now exist in various forms in thirty states. The commissions, usually dominated by judges, have the power to censure a judge or recommend his removal. In the states that still lack them, trying to bring down a judicial tyrant can be a long and disillusioning struggle.

Jerome P. Troy became a Municipal Court judge in Boston's Dorchester district in 1962. Over the years the complaints about him increased: he denied defendants the right to counsel, he forced others to waive their right to appeal, he abused the poor for being on welfare, he denied their right to cross-examine witnesses, he set outrageously high bail. A Dorchester community group gathered ten thousand signatures calling for his removal. Higher-court judges regularly criticized him in overruling his decisions.

But Troy, like all Massachusetts judges, had life tenure. He was a Democratic Party loyalist who had found the politician's velvet cushion. And there was no commission with power to remove him; there was only a hesitant, vacillating Supreme Judicial Court.

A campaign by reformist Boston lawyers finally forced the system to move. A special three-judge panel convened by District Court Chief Justice Franklin Flaschner heard sixty-nine witnesses, including Troy, and concluded, without saying it in so many words, that Troy should be removed. "He was primarily responsible for the bankruptcy of a public institution," Flaschner said.

Flaschner sent his report to the supreme court, and the justices bounced it back to Flaschner, suggesting that he deal with Troy's "irregularities" administratively. Flaschner assigned Troy to different courts and limited his docket to civil cases. "But I couldn't keep him out of his court forever," Flaschner said. And Troy went back to work in Dorchester.

Only after formal misconduct charges were filed with the supreme court by the prestigious Boston Bar Association did the court take a second look at its power to discipline Troy. At last, more than two years after the campaign to sack Troy began, the supreme court disbarred him and ordered him not to hear cases. The state's Executive Council then voted 7–1 to remove Troy from office.

VIII

The Usual Man

Mediocrity on a juvenile court
in Washington

J O H N F. D O Y L E is a name tucked low on a long roster, a face
in the judicial crowd. If all the judges of the Washington, D.C.,
Superior Court were lined up in order of ability, Doyle would
probably be standing a little south of the middle of the line, talking
amiably with his colleagues. If they were told to realign themselves
by seniority, he would scuff around only slightly before winding up
in about the same place—he has been on the job three years. His
professional background is that of a thousand other middle-level
judges: some trial work, a stint or two as a prosecutor, occasional
chores on the fringes of politics. He is reasonably diligent, moderately stuffy, and unassailably earnest. His intellectual attainments
are modest, but so are his pretensions. He has a tendency to speak
in paragraphs instead of sentences and to raise his volume when
befuddled. He will never sit on the U.S. Supreme Court and alter
the course of our history, but neither will he take a bribe and
debase his office. If it were possible to divine an "average" American judge in terms of training, temperament, and skill, I suspect
that Doyle would come close to it.

He is fifty-seven, a moon-faced man with thinning gray hair and
large, expressive eyes that grow larger when he talks. He has a
comfortable look about him—an ample stomach bulges above a
large Western-style belt buckle, which glitters incongruously amid

his otherwise conservative clothes—and a pleasant, agreeable manner. He appears to be a slightly more learned, polished, and guarded version of the goodoleboy JP, a man at ease in the company of other men but just a shade uneasy with their wives or children. One of the aspects of his job he finds troubling is its loneliness—"There's nobody but you. Lawyers can lean on each other, but there's no one a judge can ask for advice. It takes getting used to."

Doyle's face is the kind that looks natural behind a cigar, and he keeps a box on the desk in his spacious chambers. But he chain-smokes Parliaments as we talk about how he happened to become a judge. "It was more a matter of opportunity than anything else," he says. "It was no lifelong ambition of mine. The District Bar Association and some friends of mine initiated it and asked me if I was interested."

The son of a Kansas City lawyer, he came to Washington in 1938 after graduating from Rockhurst College, a Catholic men's school in Missouri. The paneled walls of his chambers hold reminders of his Western origin (a large Charles Russell painting of an Indian war party), his faith (a portrait of Catholic martyr Sir Thomas More), and his Republican politics (a photograph of Richard Nixon).

He attended Georgetown law school, graduating in 1941, and then entered the Marine Corps. "I liked the corps—I was in for almost six years. I thought about staying in." He served in the Pacific for two and a half years and spent a year assigned to naval intelligence. He was discharged as a captain in 1946.

Back in Washington, he joined a firm, but left after two years to become a government prosecutor in misdemeanor cases. He spent a short time on the staff of the House Appropriations Committee, then moved to the United States Attorney's office as an assistant in 1953. Between 1957 and 1961 he headed the office's civil division. Then a Democratic administration came in and Doyle was out.

Washington has two layers of judges. At the higher level is the federal District Court, which deals with constitutional questions, federal crimes, and most of the cases arising out of governmental action. The Superior Court combines the functions of the several strata of lower courts in most other cities, handling most criminal cases, juvenile and domestic-relations matters, and the bulk of the civil business as well. Formerly known as the Court of General Sessions, the lower court was renamed, streamlined, and upgraded in the D.C. crime bill of 1970, which also gave us the "no-knock" law and preventive detention.

There is a wide gap between layers. District judges are appointed for life, superior judges for fifteen years. District judges earn $40,000, superior judges $36,000. But more important than status is the care taken in selection. District judges, in Washington as elsewhere, are traditionally prominent and/or well-qualified political lawyers. They are screened by the Justice Department and the American Bar Association, and usually "sponsored" by a senator—often, in the case of D.C. district judges, by Maryland or Virginia senators.

But Superior Court judges are not so carefully culled. "They're the overflow," says a former Justice Department official. "There's no one pushing them for District Court. The meritorious civil servant can get a job there, maybe a guy with fifteen years in the Department of Justice and no political patron." A man deeply involved in federal judicial selection says "the standards aren't the same. We don't work as hard on Superior Court judges. I guess that's human. There's not as much concern. I don't think those rated 'qualified' for the Superior Court would necessarily be found qualified for the District Court."

Doyle returned to private practice in 1961, specializing in civil law, and became active in the bar association. His clients included the U.S. Catholic Conference and the Council of Bishops. In 1969, with a Republican in the White House, he was appointed ("in one way or another," he says coyly) a United States magistrate, the committing officer in the District Court.

In September 1970 he was on a list of eighteen Superior Court nominees sent to the Senate by the Justice Department. Deputy Attorney General Richard Kleindienst called the group a "composite of whites, blacks, Republicans, Democrats, men, women, and lawyers from the District, Maryland, and Virginia." He added that the list "does not satisfy completely any one critic. It responds partially to the point of view of all critics. . . . All are qualified."

There was indeed something for everyone on the list: it included thirteen Republicans and five Democrats, six blacks, two women, and a former campaign aide to Senator Barry Goldwater. The only grumbles came from a few lawyers who thought professional quality had been subordinated to political suitability. "The administration is rewarding some nominees for long years of civil service or partisan loyalty," one complained.

John Doyle, however, was happy. "I don't know many attorneys who wouldn't want to be a judge," he says, echoing a conviction widely held among judges but disputed by some lawyers, especially the richer ones. He maintains that his politics was a minor factor: "I'm a Republican, but I never worked in campaigns. In the District we didn't have a formal political organization in which a man could work his way up the ladder. I think there's less sheer politics in judicial appointments here than elsewhere."

Doyle is content in the job. "I like it, sure. There's a lot of action, a lot of diversity. I prefer law in the courtroom to law in the abstract. I like cases and controversy. I like seeing a case in the flesh." Married but childless, Doyle won a fifteen-year appointment at age fifty-four; security in his sunset years was assured.

The forty-four Superior Court judges rotate among the court's three divisions—criminal, civil, and family. In a given month some twenty will be assigned to the criminal division and perhaps a dozen each to the civil and family sections. When I visited Judge Doyle, he was sitting in family division, primarily hearing juvenile cases but drawing an occasional divorce or custody hearing. He had served one previous three-month term in family court. Prior to that, he confessed, "I'd never seen a juvenile case in my life."

The courtroom looks like a somewhat gaudy theater-in-the-round. The walls are filled with square soundproofing panels painted chartreuse. The empty jury box has three rows of chartreuse chairs, the rows terraced like a theater and filling a corner of the room. The judge's perch, at the level of the highest row of jury chairs, is behind a curved, paneled half-wall directly opposite the jury box. The witness chair, also elevated, is between judge and jury. A curved railing separates the court from two rows of spectator benches. In the center, on the floor of the arena, four teenage black boys are bunched around a table with four white lawyers. A lone prosecutor, not long out of law school, sits at another table.

In the euphemistic language of juvenile court, this is not a trial but a "fact-finding hearing." The four boys are accused of delinquency, specifically of second-degree burglary and malicious destruction, more specifically of ransacking a construction trailer in a schoolyard. The rhetoric of juvenile court is different—a "petition" is the equivalent of an indictment, a finding of "involved" means guilty—but almost everything else is the same as in adult criminal court. The accused must be represented by a lawyer (all four in this case are court-appointed), the same standards of proof apply, a verdict must be "beyond a reasonable doubt." Pleas are negotiated in the corridors just as they are in grownup court, and liberty is often on the line as well, even though the institutions are called "homes" and not prisons. The one significant difference is that a juvenile in Washington (as in about four fifths of the states) does not have the right to a jury trial.

A black policeman, dressed in civilian clothes, is the first witness. He recounts the incident in the stilted language of a police report: "The juveniles were proceeding in a westerly direction and I joined another officer in pursuit. I apprehended Master Wilson."

"Would you identify Master Wilson, please?"

"The one in the denim jacket, with the short hair."

The boys look dully at the policeman. All four are fifteen, but one is considerably taller than the other three. He seems to be the leader; when one closes his eyes and starts to nod a few minutes later, he pokes him and delivers a whispered reprimand: "Be cool, Ricardo." Ricardo wears red, high-heeled, patent-leather shoes and a corn-row hair style with alternate furrows of skin and hair. He is the flashiest of the four.

Master Wilson stands up to be identified. He is thin and sharp-featured, resembling a fifteen-year-old Stokely Carmichael. The fourth boy is the smallest, with gentle features that edge occasionally into a thin, ironic smile.

A second police witness, white and mustached, testifies that he found rubber gloves and three locks in the possession of the smallest boy, whose name is Ben. Ben looks at his lawyer and shakes his head from side to side. Ricardo raises his eyebrows. The gloves are introduced in evidence. The policeman says Ben stopped running "with a little assistance." He smiles at the prosecutor, who looks down at the table.

Suddenly a short, stout man waving a piece of paper enters the courtroom, talking steadily as he passes through the gate and approaches the judge.

Doyle is startled. "Have you a case?" he shouts. His eyes are bugging out. The man, who resembles George Jessel, is a lawyer representing one of the boys on another charge. He mutters something to the judge.

"ARE YOU IN THIS CASE?" Doyle says in a voice that sounds like a landslide. "Oh, approach the bench," he says impatiently. There is a short, whispered conference and the lawyer leaves, clutching his piece of paper.

Two more policemen testify for the prosecution, and the outlines of the case begin to appear. An anonymous telephone caller had reported that some boys were breaking into the trailer at 1:30 on an August night. Three squad cars of police were dispatched. They seized three of the boys as they ran and found Ricardo hiding under the trailer. They called in a helicopter with a searchlight. ("We had Juno up.") They found the interior of the trailer in disarray and windows broken. Nothing was found on the boys besides the locks and gloves. The police witnesses disagree on how much light was present and which way the boys were running.

Two of the four police witnesses are black. So are the clerk, the court reporter, and most of the spectators—the hearing is closed to the public except for family and those (like me) with special permission to attend. The juvenile docket in Washington is composed almost totally of fourteen- and fifteen-year-old blacks. In a week I saw perhaps thirty cases at one stage or another, and every one involved a black teenager. In Washington, with its 71-percent black population, the lower-court system is probably the most integrated in the country: 15 of the 44 Superior Court judges are black, and so are a large percentage of the court employees, social workers, and policemen. Still, in most cases, as in this one, the judge and prosecutor are white and the defendants are black. A slave market once stood a few blocks away.

The final prosecution witness is the owner of the construction firm. "There was nothing broken the day before. I went there that morning and found three windows broken, the plywood was pried open, aluminum was bent out of shape. Desk drawers were opened and a fire extinguisher had been pumped over the wall." The judge listens intently. Ricardo starts to fall asleep again, but Willie, the leader, gets one of the lawyers to rouse him.

On cross-examination, the owner testifies that the trailer had been broken into four times in the previous week. He says that after this particular night he noticed three chairs were missing.

Doyle calls a recess and goes into the "robing room"—a good-sized room empty save for a small desk, a wooden chair, and a coat rack—to smoke two quick Parliaments. "Juvenile court is the crucible," he says between puffs. "It's where it begins, it's where the great sores are seen. The kids are influenced by their 'peer group,' the manhood thing is important, it's the whole mess of what happens when you have an unsettled society. All this is set before a judge and he's supposed to find solutions."

He shakes his head and looks out a window at some construction equipment. "Solomon couldn't determine some of these cases. You can't reconstruct the family or create a father where there isn't one. We have tremendous powers, but when you boil it down, it's damn limited—institution or probation, foster homes in neglect cases, and that's it."

Out in the corridor the lawyers are dealing. "I'll take a plea to malicious destruction," the prosecutor says. "Two of them have other cases pending." He whispers an aside to me: "The way this one's going, I'll be lucky to get malicious destruction."

"I'm inclined to go along," one lawyer replies. "This is going to go late, it looks like. I've got to be in Spottsylvania tomorrow."

"The cops contradicted themselves," another lawyer says. "They missed that big window altogether."

"No problem," the prosecutor says. "I say let it all come out. There's no question those boys hit that trailer."

"Wait a minute," one of the defense lawyers says. "I'm not so sure. My kid tells me the place was hit earlier and they were just scavenging."

"Bullshit."

"They're not smart enough to pull a job like this. They heard from this girl that the place was hit, and went back to pick up what they could. And what about those chairs? Can you produce them?"

"You want it or not?" the prosecutor says.

"To hell with it," the lawyer says. "I think we can win it."

"Well, it's four o'clock now," the prosecutor says to the lawyer with an out-of-town date the next day. "If you put all four of them on the stand and I cross-examine them for thirty minutes each . . ." It is said half jokingly, half threateningly. The lawyer winces.

The four boys are gathered in a circle about a dozen feet away. Ricardo is entertaining the others. "Come out, Teresa, wherever you are," he chants. Their mothers stand nearby. "Looks like we gonna have night court tonight," one says.

When the hearing resumes, the lawyers move for a directed verdict of acquittal—the euphemisms are abandoned now in the warmth of combat. "There is no evidence of breaking and entering," one argues. "There's no testimony connecting these boys with the destruction." In his reply, the prosecutor concedes that there is no evidence of theft (the locks have been forgotten; no one asked the owner to identify them). "The proof of entry I will admit is circumstantial," he says, "but we have evidence of destruction."

Doyle interrupts to ask for a copy of the criminal code. "I'm concerned with whether a trailer is regarded as a domicile under the burglary statute," he says. He satisfies himself that it is. He seems uncertain about the state of the proof. "Proof of entry *is* missing," he says. "What it boils down to is the disarray, the drawers pulled out—no, I'm going to rule that a *prima facie* case has been made and I'll resolve all inferences in favor of the government. Motion denied."

The judge seemed to be most persuaded by the testimony of the owner—a middle-aged white man and a property owner like himself. "Most judges," says Stanford law professor Anthony Amsterdam, "come out of firms where their clients, like their friends and families, are the sorts of people whom they will always identify as the possible victims of 'crime,' not the possible victims of cops."

Ricardo is sullen and almost inaudible on the witness stand. He tells a story that stretches even his lawyer's credulity: "I went to pick up my sister at her boyfriend's house [she is twenty, he fifteen; it was 1:30 a.m.]. I saw Ben talking to his girlfriend. We started to jive around at the playground."

"Did you take anything from the trailer?"

"No." He looks at his fingernails.

"Did you do any damage to it?"

"No."

"Why did you run when the police came?" the prosecutor asks on cross.

"I had a ten-o'clock curfew."

The lawyer who had interrupted earlier bursts in again, still holding his piece of paper. "Oh, come on, come *on*," the judge groans when he spots him. "But I need a date, Your Honor," the man says. A defense attorney, seizing at anything, is on his feet asking for a mistrial.

"I'm quite capable of distinguishing the matter before the court and otherwise," Doyle huffs. "If I didn't think so, well—I'd be surprised, that's all." The lawyer is given a date by the court clerk and departs.

Ricardo steps down. Ben's lawyer, the one with the appointment in Spottsylvania the next day, says his client will not testify. Master Wilson is next.

"We were just jiving around, throwin' rocks at each other."

"At one thirty in the morning?"

"Yeah. We didn't have nothin' else to do."

"Why did you run?"

"Cuz they did."

"Because the others did?"

"Yeah. Po-lice probably thought someone was breakin' into the place."

"They didn't think someone might just be playing at one thirty in the morning?"

"They never do."

The fourth boy, the leader, testifies for ten tortured minutes in an anxious stutter. The defense rests promptly at five o'clock.

The trial has taken on a certain element of mystery, as trials often do. The air is full of unanswered questions: What happened to the chairs? If the trailer was broken into four times in a week, why was this the first call to the police? Who called the police anyway? (Was it Teresa?) What is the human truth of the incident, setting aside the legal truth? Could they in fact have been just "jiving around" at 1:30 a.m.? Is that perhaps a natural thing to do on a hot summer night in the ghetto? Does the judge know whether it is or not? And what will happen to these boys if they are found guilty? Is this a turning point for them? If convicted, will they be outlaws from this day forward? Are they already? If acquitted, will they go on to hurt someone seriously?

"I ask you, Your Honor," the prosecutor says in his summation, "is it plausible that these boys were at the schoolyard just to 'jive around,' as they say? I say it is incredible. The police found the gloves on the accused, but he denies it. It's a question of whom you choose to believe."

"The evidence is not merely circumstantial, Your Honor, it's thin," a defense attorney replies. "There's no reason to believe a police witness over any other witness—that's a standard jury instruction. I say the government has not made its case."

Doyle looks down at his desk. "May I see the code again?" he asks his clerk. He is quiet for a moment.

"The court is not satisfied beyond a reasonable doubt on the charge of burglary," he says. "But on the charge of malicious destruction of property the court is convinced." He asks if the boys are in custody, and learns that only Ben is—he has another delinquency charge pending against him. The other three are subsequently placed on probation.

Later the judge offers some clues to his reasoning. "They were caught right in that area," he says. "Look at the property damage." What about the missing chairs? "They could have been taken later," he says. "I'm not going to analyze it."

The prosecutor is smiling as he walks back to his office. "Hell, I knew my case was circumstantial," he says. "I was in a quandary about whether to go ahead with it. The police botched up the evidence. How could he find malicious destruction and not burglary? He just took the easy middle ground. Ask me what I would have done if I were the judge."

I do.

"Found them innocent," the prosecutor says.

"I believe in free will," John Doyle says, "that people at bottom have within themselves the power for good or evil, that they are responsible for their actions. Obviously their environment has an influence, but individual responsibility is more important. A kid can grow up in a rough neighborhood, but others in the same neighborhood turn out all right. What makes the difference?"

He mulls the question for a moment as he leans back behind his desk. "Almost every case is a tragic circumstance, really, for both victim and defendant. These delinquencies wouldn't happen if everyone had good family relations and we had a perfect society. We don't possess powers to straighten all that out. What's given to me to create a stable family?" His thought trails off. "One day you get depressed, because you see case after case where nothing at all is accomplished, then once in a while something affirmative happens—just often enough to give you some hope."

I ask whether there are cultural differences between blacks and whites which hinder a judge's understanding and make his job more difficult. He doesn't think so.

"I've lived here a long time," he says. "I know the town and the people. You get a feel. I know the neighborhoods, the streets, the different parts of town. When a kid says he was 'jiving around,' that's not unfamiliar to me. I know it's different from Chevy Chase."

He leans forward, suddenly intense. "The main thing everybody wants is a fair assessment," he says. "No one wants to be treated any differently from anybody else, or to be patronized or to have a different set of rules. I'll tell you something. If you approach the bench with religious fervor, as if you're dispensing bounty, you're making a big mistake. People in this town don't respect anyone who doesn't apply equal justice. People don't believe crime is okay here. They don't believe blacks deserve more probation for social reasons. It's not basically a racial question, it's knowledge of people, and human beings are remarkably similar at bottom. There's not that much difference between black and white. I don't really buy racial distinctions. The feelings and reactions are human and not black and white."

He lights another cigarette. "The decisions don't get any easier with experience," he says. "I haven't noticed that I'm much different in the way I react than I used to be. You seldom find a case that squares on all fours.

"I'm basically a trial lawyer who appeared before a lot of the old masters—Edward Curran, John Sirica, David Pine, men who were really great judges. It's hard to say what they had in common. Some were great legal scholars, and others weren't. Some were strict courtroom disciplinarians, others were more kindly. They had—they all had a great instinct for being right. I guess it's judgment. It's more than strictness or leniency. It's experience with human beings more than just legal experience. You have to have that to assess who's telling the truth.

"I don't know how good at it I am. You take demeanor into consideration, but it's touchy. Some witnesses might be frightened, but they aren't necessarily lying. You measure demeanor against other things. Sullenness can be shyness. Cockiness can be a cover-up too. It's common sense, experience in the everyday affairs of life."

I ask if he has to prepare himself psychologically for a day on the bench. It is an idea he has apparently never considered. His eyes open wide. "How could you?" he asks in reply. "You have to do it every day. It's your business."

"He's comfortable with his authority and confident," Doyle's law clerk says of him. "He doesn't give the appearance of being that bright, but he is. His mind is a lot faster than his voice. He'll ramble and then zap right to the central issue. I think he's as sensitive to young black kids as any white man can be. He's a little absent-minded, but he has a 'conceptual' knowledge of the law, more common sense than case law."

"He has a low boiling point, but he controls the witnesses and keeps the testimony in bounds," a lawyer says.

"He seems to respond to kids," a social worker says, "but he doesn't get too involved."

The more frequently heard opinion of Doyle is that he is, in a word, pedestrian—not especially bad or especially good. He doesn't bring any particular strength or insight to his job. He might be a capable attorney, a respectable prosecutor, or a perfectly suitable insurance executive. But as a judge he belongs to the great fraternity of the ordinary, the judges Herbert Brownell once described as "gray mice."

It is easier to say what he isn't than what he is: he is not lazy, venal, cruel, or bigoted; but neither is he particularly vigorous, insightful, or wise. He is somewhere in between—too earnest to condemn, perhaps, but too muddling to admire. The gray mice of the judiciary, Brownell said, "look on judicial appointment as the reward for their loyalty and devotion to the party, and they look forward to judicial service as socially and financially rewarding. To them the courthouse is a cozy rest home. In other words, they are ordinary, likable people of small talent."

One lawyer recalled arguing the case of a seventeen-year-old boy charged with assaulting a policeman before Judge Doyle. "Doyle was going to release him," the lawyer said, "but the prosecutor said, 'Your Honor, this is a case of an assault on a police officer,' and right away he decides to have a hearing to consider detaining him. The kid's brother had been to Annapolis, he had an exemplary family, everything argued against locking him up. Doyle sent him to the [juvenile] Receiving Home. I came back with a preacher and his teacher as character witnesses and a motion to get him out. Doyle was obviously vexed, you know? He felt intimidated and didn't like it. But he released him, after giving the kid a lecture on how serious it was."

"He gets upset in juvenile court," another lawyer said. "A lot of judges feel insecure in there. There's a big difference between finding fault in an accident case and looking a twelve-year-old kid in the face and finding him guilty of armed robbery. Doyle's just wishy-washy."

A colleague interrupted: "He tries to avoid making decisions. He flies off the handle when he doesn't know what's happening. I think he cares, he's just light. He's nowhere near one of the worst, and nowhere near the best."

Leroy sits with his sister and parents on a spectator bench in the rear of the courtroom. Wearing a fresh white shirt and new pants, he gets up when the prosecutor calls his name, smiles at his parents, and walks to the witness stand. His mother rocks with pride.

Leroy, who is twelve, tells the court that his bicycle disappeared outside a store. He says his sister saw Moo-Moo riding the bike. Later he found the bike, or what was left of it, in a garage behind an apartment house.

Moo-Moo is sitting at the defense table, looking invisible. He is thirteen, but looks eight. With him is Sam-Sam, who is sixteen and looks it. The charge is petty theft.

Leroy's sister, wearing her white dress, is next. She testifies that she saw Moo-Moo on the bike and ran home to tell her mother, who called the police. The police found the bike. "It was all taken apart," she says. Leroy, back with his parents, studies an Afro comb intently, as if searching for its essence.

"We saw Moo-Moo standing behind a tree," the girl says.

"Objection," says defense counsel. "Hearsay."

"What's that?" Judge Doyle says. "Where was Noo-Noo?"

"Behind a tree. It's Moo-Moo."

"Oh, yes. Overruled."

She identifies Moo-Moo, who looks blandly at her.

A black policeman is called. "Each kid said the other one took it," he says. "I followed Sam to the bike. He showed me where it was. It was stripped, there was nothing there but the frame. I took them to the Youth Division and told them they were under arrest."

Sam's lawyer stands up. "Move to strike the statements made prior to the advisory of rights in reference to my client. According to rule one eleven, he is required to advise them. It was not a general investigation."

The judge permits the questioning to continue and then asks for argument on the motion.

"When did you advise my client of his rights?" Sam's lawyer asks the policeman.

"After he said he had the parts and showed me the parts."

"Did you advise him in the car on the way to the station?"

"No, sir." The officer cannot keep the disgust out of his voice.

"So my client had made a statement prior to the advisory?"

The policeman looks at the judge, who shows no expression. "I asked him if he took Leroy's bike. He said Moo-Moo took it."

"You told them their rights after you got to the station?"

"Yes."

The attorney again moves to suppress any testimony prior to the rights advisory.

"Where do you think that leaves the case?" the judge asks. "I mean, assume I agree with you, what portion of the government testimony still stands?"

Leroy's family looks on in perplexity. The smiles are gone. The Constitution has landed, somewhat heavily, amid the case of Leroy's bicycle.

The lawyer says that the *Miranda* ruling should have been given when Moo-Moo was identified. To their astonishment, Leroy and his family are now asked to leave the courtroom. The defense has requested it. The only discernible reason seems to be the system's embarrassment.

The prosecutor argues that "not every question asked of a citizen needs to be preceded by the *Miranda* warnings."

"But don't you think he should have been warned?" the judge asks.

"It might have been better, but—"

"All right," Doyle says. "I'm suppressing everything after the identification of respondent Foster. Everything beyond that is 'fruit of the poisonous tree.' "

The defense then asks for a judgment of acquittal against Sam-Sam, who was picked up after the tree was poisoned, and the judge grants it. He and his lawyer leave the room as Leroy and his family return. Leroy does a double-take as he watches Sam leave, then looks at his father.

Moo-Moo, who missed out on constitutional liberation because he was unlucky enough to be caught first, looks smaller than ever at the defense table. He sucks his fingers as the lawyers make short closing arguments. "There are doubts here," the defense lawyer says.

"*I* have no doubt," the judge says abruptly. "I find him guilty as charged. Now, what's his status?" Moo-Moo is in the care of the Social Rehabilitation Administration, he is told; he has already spent time in Cedar Knoll Juvenile Home (the names sound like housing tracts). The judge permits him to remain free under supervision.

A lecture is welling up in Doyle, inspired by the peculiar twists of the case. "I'm not blind," he tells the boy. "I made a legal decision on a technicality. The lawyer raised the constitutional question as he was obliged to, but a little light must have sifted through. You saw who walked out, didn't you?" Moo-Moo looks evenly at the judge and nods almost imperceptibly; next time he won't be the first one caught. "Now who's holding the sack?" Doyle asks.

His message is the folly of running with older boys. "It's a loser's game," he says. "It's snipe-hunting. You can get into serious trouble. Start thinking about it. The guy that's left is you. Does that give you any idea about things?" Moo-Moo is expressionless. It seems that the accumulated wisdom of law and behavioral science should have provided the perfect question at this point. Has Moo-Moo soured on society? Can he be helped? What can we offer him? Love? But there is no such question; there is only earnest, futile moralizing colliding with a thirteen-year-old's mask. "Am I getting through to you at all?" the judge asks. Moo-Moo nods dutifully. In the corridor outside, his lawyer picks up the sermon. "Next time it'll be different, you know." Moo-Moo stares at the door. Leroy is short one bicycle, Sam-Sam is in the clear, Moo-Moo is taking the rap; but it will be over soon.

"One of those insoluble cases," the judge says afterward. "What do you do with them? Maybe we should have worried more about the kid's bike than the *Miranda* warnings, I don't know. I'm sure the victim's family isn't satisfied, but there's a reason for those warnings. They used to put their little ass in jail without any warnings, but an adult would get out if he wasn't advised of his rights. At least kids have the same protection now. But still . . ."

Doyle's frustration and ambivalence are shared by thousands of judges and social workers. It is an affliction of the times: the theory and practice of juvenile justice in America is mired in uncertainty, confusion, and failure. The goals of juvenile courts are in dispute—should a delinquent be treated as a child who needs love or as a criminal who needs punishment? Facilities are unavailable or cruelly deficient (the juvenile "Receiving Home" in Washington, where children are held prior to trial, was formally pronounced unfit two years ago, but is still used in the absence of a replacement). Children are often punished for their parents' neglect; those innocent of any crime but in need of shelter are placed in the same institutions with delinquents. The original rationale for a separate system of juvenile courts was the promise of help and "rehabilitation" for the youngsters. The idea was that the juvenile-court system would provide the "wise parent" the troubled child had never had. But reality never came close to the promise.

"The whole concept of the juvenile court seems to me to be ridiculous," a Washington prosecutor said, "but I don't know what to replace it with any more than anyone else does. It's not helping anything—everyone knows the recidivism rate is tremendous. It seems like the whole system has failed—the attorneys, probation, the courts, everything. Even if we had better institutions, I doubt if it would help; they don't change a kid's values."

Lawyers impose their rigidities on the process, and social workers impose theirs. I sat in court one day as Judge Doyle and the social workers disposed of two dozen or more juvenile cases, looking up after each one to confront still another sullen black face. They were dusted with the vapid jargon of social work—"immaturity," "adjustment problems," "he does not relate," "her affect is good"—and nudged on to the next stop, to someone else's "in" box, to become another name on another list. One child was held at an institution because the social worker said her mother's apartment was too small; another was sent to a "home" because his father couldn't be found and his mother was in the hospital. It was a soggy drama in which everyone knew his own lines and everyone else's too. Lawyers spoke of the "concerted effort" a boy was making, the "marked improvement" he had shown; the judge nodded and tried to believe it, *did* manage to believe it. To work at all, it seemed to me as I listened, this system depended on an extraordinary combination of breaks: if a child was lucky enough to get a good (sensitive, intelligent) lawyer, then a good (compassionate, insightful) judge, and finally a good (resourceful, loving) social worker, he and society might actually benefit from his tour through the juvenile process. But the odds against that were astronomical; the weight of numbers, as always, worked to banish the graces, and the sodden march of the bureaucratic mind did the rest.

The gap between the rhetoric and reality of juvenile justice became obvious many years ago. The Supreme Court acknowledged it in a series of decisions that gave juveniles most of the rights of an adult criminal defendant. Chief Judge David L. Bazelon of the U.S. Court of Appeals for the District of Columbia wrote that the "only alternative" of a judge facing that gap "is to say, 'If you insist upon treating him as a criminal, at least give the young offender the protections an adult offender receives.' In short, don't give him the worst of both worlds." The worst of one is punishment enough.

Everyone agrees that the treatment of juveniles is enormously important to whatever success we have in dealing with crime. The prisons are packed with the graduates of juvenile "homes." Failure there is even more critical than failure elsewhere in the judicial system. And failure is the rule.

New York Times reporter Lesley Oelsner surveyed New York's juvenile courts and found a system "marked by high recidivism, inefficiency, muddled policies, inadequate resources, and almost total inability to rehabilitate." In Kansas the reformatory where delinquents are held is widely regarded as a tougher institution than the adult prison; the same is true in Connecticut. A West Virginia judge told me, "We have no facility for treatment of drug addicts, insufficient psychiatric counseling help for 'incorrigibles,' no alternative to offer for school systems they cannot adjust to. Our institutions are at best no help; on the contrary, they are often detrimental. . . ." Similar opinions are echoed in state after state.

A sensitive judge, afloat in this tormented sea, can recognize the need and succumb to anguish. Former Family Court Judge Justine Wise Polier of New York has put it better than anyone else: "A child—a human being—reaches out for love. And gets hit. And he reaches out again, and gets hit again. And he keeps reaching out, and every time he's denied. And then finally, defensively, he stops reaching. And in no longer looking for love, he loses the ability to love, and the ability to feel. The capacity to feel for another person is cut off, and he can destroy other people without reaction. And then you get rapes and robberies and murder."

"We have the advice of the social workers," John Doyle says. "We have the child's reaction in court, and the lawyer's suggestions. From that you make a judgment. We can't escape being up to our neck in social work. We can order mental or physical examinations, or special schooling, but there's no wand we can wave to make it right.

"I'll send a kid to the Receiving Home if nothing we've done before has done any good and we can't guarantee his appearance in court any other way. If a permissive approach has failed, then I'll try something else." He puts his feet up on his large desk. "Some kids are contemptuous of the gentle approach—we can at least cure that.

"Sentencing these kids is a calculus," Doyle goes on. "You can't be blind to the idea of punishment, but you give more weight to the social factors in a juvenile case. It's not *supposed* to be a criminal court. But you're not a mercy-dispensing power either. What you do, really, is just hope that perhaps somebody can find something to help the kid."

Coping with the frustrations and contradictions of juvenile court is difficult enough for a gifted judge. A judge like John Doyle can only flounder and hope. Mediocrity on the bench, Columbia law professor Maurice Rosenberg has written, "can be in the long run as bad a pollutant as venality, for it dampens opposition and is more likely to be tolerated." Fairly or unfairly, we expect more of our judges. "Judicial office today demands the best possible men," Rosenberg continued, "not those of merely average ability who were gray and undistinguished as lawyers and who will be just as drab as judges." It is a sort of indictment by default; their only vice is their lack of distinction.

IX

New York Follies

The perils of a judicial system engulfed by politics

JUDGES OF THE New York Court of Appeals, the state's highest court, are customarily selected by arrangement between Republican and Democratic party leaders: when a vacancy occurs, the politicians decide whose turn it is and choose a candidate who is then nominated by both parties and ratified by complaisant voters. The arrangement works nicely for the politicians, since it enables them to reward their own while avoiding the messiness and uncertainty of a legitimate contest. Sometimes a certifiably good judge rises to the seven-judge court by this route—former Supreme Court Justice Benjamin Cardozo was one, the state's recent Chief Judge Stanley Fuld was another. But the system, which also operates at the district level for lower-court judges (with minor exceptions, all New York judges are elected), is regarded as more important than its by-products of justice or injustice and competence or incompetence.

When an appeals-court seat fell vacant in 1969, party leaders drew up a two-stage compact. First, Republican James Gibson was tapped for the 1969 opening. In 1972, when three judges (including Gibson) would reach the mandatory retirement age of seventy, the seats would go to two Democrats and a Republican. Handshakes all around. Order and harmony preserved.

But in early 1972 the deal was torpedoed by Democratic State

177

Chairman Joseph Crangle. Crangle's head was turned by greed; confidently expecting Senator Edmund Muskie to lead the Democratic ticket, he sniffed roses for the whole stable of Democratic candidates. Crangle pulled out of the compact and decided to run three Democrats for the fourteen-year Court of Appeals terms. His decision presaged that rarest spectacle in New York politics, a contested election.

Since politics dictated a balanced slate, the Democratic convention dutifully nominated an upstate Catholic (intermediate appellate Judge Lawrence H. Cooke), an urban Catholic (Brooklyn appellate Judge M. Henry Martuscello), and a suburban Jew (Nassau County Supreme Court Justice Bernard S. Meyer). The Republicans consulted their own ethnic-demographic charts and countered with an upstate Protestant (State Bar Association president Hugh H. Jones), a suburban Jew (Nassau Supreme Court Justice Sol Wachtler), and an urban Catholic (appellate Judge Domenick L. Gabrielli of Rochester), and the race was on.

Well, not quite. Into this neatly ordered field galloped an unauthorized contender, Family Court Judge Nanette Dembitz of Manhattan. Judge Dembitz was urban, Jewish, and—new factor in the equation—a woman. No woman had ever served on the highest court in New York. Backed by a Democratic reform group and women's-rights advocates, she won enough convention votes to force a four-way Democratic primary. To her considerable astonishment, she won it. Judge Martuscello, who had secured the endorsement of New York's Liberal Party as insurance, had to collect on it when he ran fourth.

Seven candidates were now running for the three normally uncontested seats. After the Conservative and Liberal endorsements were lumped atop those of the major parties, the field was finally ready: Meyer was running with Democratic and Liberal backing; Cooke as a Democrat and Conservative; Wachtler was on the Republican and Liberal lines; Jones and Gabrielli had both Republican and Conservative endorsements; Dembitz was on the Democratic slate only; and Martuscello ran as a Liberal.

With the runners in place and their labels pinned on, all the candidates had to do now was figure out how to campaign. They were in an absurd position. The canons of judicial ethics closed off all the normal avenues of politics: they could not attack their opponents; they must not make promises; they were forbidden to give their views on "disputed legal or political issues," which eliminated everything interesting; they were not to endorse other candidates, not even the presidential nominees of their own party. They were limited to winsome smiles, résumés of their legal careers, bland pronouncements on non-controversial subjects, and innuendos. They were unable to answer the legitimate questions of voters who wanted to know their views on abortion, capital punishment, school busing, and local property taxes. They were suspended between their profession and the public, jammed into an impossible corner by a system laboring in transition. The rules of politics made them campaigners, the code of the bench all but precluded campaigning. The canons were highway signs on the interstate to merit selection. But the candidates were down on the county road, taking their meals at the diner and waiting, impatiently, while the freight train passed.

The campaign's built-in contradictions, coupled with the gingery presence of Judge Dembitz, appealed to me. In October I spent three days with her as she campaigned.

"You better take this," the judge's husband said, handing her ten dollars through the car window. "You'll need to get gas."

"Oh, *really*, Alfred," Judge Dembitz said. "Don't you think we can think of anything by ourselves?" Alfred Berman smiled as he stood back on the curb in front of their apartment house on the East Side of Manhattan. The judge did not look at him as we drove off. "Goodbye, Alfred, goodbye," she said to her purse.

"Now, isn't that the most typically male chauvinist attitude?" she asked as we pulled into a gas station three blocks away. Virginia Demmler, a campaign volunteer who was driving, took the ten-dollar bill and asked the attendant to fill the tank. "I mean, the male view is that a woman can't find a gas station by herself," the judge said.

She was a thin, dark-haired woman, small-boned and fragile-looking. Her large mouth was habitually set in a tolerant smile, but her eyes were cool and appraising. She wore an expensive red suit, hemmed judiciously at the knee, and a little hat. Her hair was short and pulled back. She was fifty-nine.

"We're going to Rockland County," Virginia said, "to a meeting of the . . . let's see. Oh, yes, the Building and Construction Trades and the Central Labor Trades Council."

"Am I supposed to talk or say hello or just do nothing?" the judge asked.

"They want to hear about drugs," Virginia said. "You're supposed to speak. They're generally conservatives, hardhat types. The paper isn't covering tonight, but the head of the labor council is a very influential man." The judge nodded.

The labor men were waiting at a union community center in New City. A Little League banquet was in progress in an enormous room next door. An announcer was calling out letters and numbers for a bingo game. Waitresses rushed through the meeting room on their way between the banquet and the kitchen. There were perhaps forty men and five women there to hear the judge.

"Hey, fellas, Judge Dembitz," the leader said as we entered. Two dozen middle-aged men in plain suits and white shirts shuffled self-consciously to their feet like schoolboys standing for company. A group of younger men in sport shirts, some with mustaches and most with long sideburns, stood against one wall. Virginia began piling posters and buttons on a table. The posters said, "Make history with your vote. Judge Nanette Dembitz for Court of Appeals. Elect the first woman to New York's highest court." The buttons said, "Yes Yes Nanette."

The judge smiled steadily as she met a bakery man, a construction worker, a steamfitter, and an electrical contractor. Her small hand disappeared inside the workingmen's grips. Their shirt buttons strained to contain their stomachs. "B nine," came a voice over the microphone next door.

"Fellas, Judge Dembitz is well recommended to us," the leader said from a rostrum. "She's a journeyman in her job. You gals who are with women's lib"—he winked at a table full of gray-haired women—"the judge wants to show alla New York what she can do for all the people."

The judge, who had shed her suit coat, stood up as they applauded. She made a short, low-key talk. "The Court of Appeals is very important. It affects everyone's life. . . . The seven judges have always been men. The idea that a woman ought to sit on the court came from Governor Rockefeller. . . . What a judge does has no connection with a party platform or with anyone else on the ticket. The question is whether that person is qualified to be a judge."

"N thirty-nine," cried the announcer's voice next door.

The union leaders listened politely behind their cigars. The apprentices along the wall folded their arms on their chests. "I'm not an extremist for women's lib," she said, "but I've heard men say it's about time to give women a chance. I think a mix of one woman and six men would be good for the court. A woman judge would bring a particular viewpoint on questions concerning the family, children, consumer matters, and the environment.

"I feel quite, well, *thrilled* to be with union representatives. . . . I began my career as a labor lawyer."

"G fifty-one." A platoon of waitresses bearing empty trays hurried through the room.

"I've been told you're interested in the drug problem. I can tell you that what you've heard about heroin is not exaggerated. As a Family Court judge, I've seen it with boys down to thirteen.

"And I do want you to know that I have the endorsement of the state AFL-CIO," she said. Her voice was soft but sharp-edged, almost raspy. She smiled and said, "Now I'll let you get on with your more important business."

The leader thanked her as the members applauded. "Judge, we want you to know you've been talking to the building trades and central trades and apprentice-training classes of Rockland," he said. "And we found it very enlightening."

Two days later I joined Judge Dembitz and her husband at a storefront Democratic headquarters in Beacon, fifty miles up the Hudson from New York. They had started the day on a bus in the city at 8:45 a.m. A dreary rain was falling.

We drove to McGovern headquarters in Poughkeepsie, where a dozen students were folding letters. "They don't look voting age," Alfred said. The judge asked if they had any questions.

"What about abortion?" a teenager asked.

The judge sighed. "I'm afraid I can't say whether I'm for or against it," she said. "I know that's, well, unappealing, but the canons won't let me. I will say it is a function of the court to decide its constitutionality. And I don't think it's fair if a rich woman can get an abortion and a poor one can't." She smiled helpfully. The kids seemed satisfied.

"How about the state bar association rating you unqualified?"

This was a question she could warm to. "I was interviewed by two elderly men for twenty minutes," she said. "They weren't accustomed to the idea of women lawyers or judges. They asked me if I had experience in commercial law. I told them my experience was mainly with questions of human rights. They asked how I could be a 'homemaker' and sit on the court. I told them my son was married and my husband wasn't objecting."

Alfred nodded in agreement. "They may have a point," he whispered to me, "but it's my point and not theirs. I say just leave me the can-opener."

The state bar had cited her "insufficient judicial experience"— she had been a judge for five years. But Republican candidate Jones, who had no judicial experience, received their highest rating. Jones was a past president of the state bar.

In the evening the judge was the guest of honor at a Democratic dinner in the Wappingers Falls Masonic Lodge. She and Alfred disappeared for an hour's rest before the dinner, and I waited for them in the foyer of the lodge. The room filled up with men in shiny suits and women with teased hair and hostess gowns. The men looked as if they might be small shopowners or bureaucrats, perhaps real-estate salesmen. It could have been a suburban bowling banquet. The atmosphere was congenial, hearty; everyone seemed to know everyone else; the men gathered in little huddles and issued bursts of loud laughter. Posters containing the judge's picture lined the room.

Suddenly she appeared at the door, alone, and looked tentatively inside. No one paid any attention to her. She looked tired and momentarily disoriented, as if drained of confidence and uncertain why she was there at all. She stepped inside, still unnoticed by the two dozen people in the room despite the posters. It was as if her unnatural, political self had been mislaid somewhere, as if Nanette Dembitz the candidate was a skin she had inadvertently shed and she was exposed now for what she was: a fragile, inconspicuous fifty-nine-year-old woman, alone in a strange town among an alien crowd.

Then she caught my eye and smiled, and the moment was past. I went to help with her coat and take her umbrella. Within seconds she was surrounded, the candidate again. "Oh, it's grand to be here," she said.

Downstairs in the main hall a two-piece combo was playing. Some two hundred guests were drinking and forming lines at a buffet table offering cold ham and turkey and potato salad. The judge was taken to a seat at the speakers' table, where Alfred joined her. "This is my husband, Mr. Berman," she said to the master of ceremonies.

"Pleasure, Mr. Brennan," the MC said.

When the guests had settled at tables, the MC stood up and tapped a glass with a spoon. "Folks, we got a wonderful young lady here with us tonight and she'd like to say a few words to you. You heard of the show *No, No, Nanette*. Well, this lady is Yes, Yes, Nanette. She's running for . . . uh." He looked urgently at some notes on the table. "Come on Jerry," someone yelled. "Uh, she's running for the New York Court of Appeals. She has a few things she, uh, wants to say to us. So here she is, Judge Nanette Dembitz."

The judge smiled her candidate's smile and waved a thin arm at the audience. "We're very happy to be here in Dutchess County," she began. "Today reminds me of that old song 'Smilin' in the Rain.' We thought it was a bright day in spite of the rain." She paused, and the outsider's expression raced across her face again. "I suppose I'm the only one here old enough to remember that song."

She went into her standard speech. "The court has always had seven men. . . . They need a woman's perspective. . . . Women should be able to do whatever their talents and tastes lead them to. . . . The bar-association rating was half politics and half sex. . . . My reputation . . . qualified . . . distinction." Alfred smiled contentedly; the day was almost over. "And thanks to whomever for the lovely flowers." She sat down to mild applause.

The MC thanked her. "I hope if I ever come before you I get off with a hug and a kiss," he said. "Now we got a few people here I'd like to introduce. . . ." After the tenth introduction the judge and Alfred got up to leave for a train back to New York.

The last time I saw her was in Schenectady five days later. It was raining again, and she had a cold.

She spoke on "women in politics" to an audience of alert, well-informed women at an elegant Unitarian church. They questioned her on everything from judicial selection ("It should be removed from politics. What a judge does has no relation, and should have none, to any party platform or ticket") to the causes of crime ("Most criminals begin with delinquency, and most delinquency begins with neglect"). Asked about a recent Nixon-administration decision to withhold funds for day-care centers, she passed up a chance to criticize the President.

We got into the car of her local chaperon to drive to the headquarters of a woman legislative candidate. On the way I asked why she hadn't criticized Nixon. She seemed surprised at the question. "It never occurred to me," she said. "That's not what I'm doing. The party's supposed to support me, but I'm not allowed to support them. I can't say something like 'I need your vote.' Can I? I mean, it sounds foolish. Okay, I'll try it." She turned and looked me in the eye. "I need your vote," she said earnestly. She turned back and waved a hand. "See? It's ridiculous. I can't do it."

We dropped in briefly at the candidate's headquarters and then scurried through the rain to the car, where a local reporter climbed in to interview her. He began to talk about the machinations that preceded the Court of Appeals election. The judge was fascinated.

"The deal was made for both parties to cross-endorse Gibson last time," he said, "but Meyer tried to break it at the Democratic convention, and he almost made it."

"Really?" she said. "I mean, I kept hearing things, that Meyer was supposed to get it, but I didn't realize he was *trying* to get it. There's no honor in politics, I suppose. What a lousy business!"

"Yep," the reporter said. "Then Crangle backed out of it this year, but that was before he got stuck with McGovern."

"Crangle doesn't want me either," the judge said. "I'm not one of his."

"What do you think of Wachtler? You think you can sell a judicial candidate on TV?"

"I hope not," she replied. "I can't afford television time."

"Everyone knew Wachtler was going to run a year ahead of time," the man said. "He has money, you know."

The judge stared at him with the expression of an anthropologist studying a member of a particularly exotic tribe. "Well, *I* didn't know he was going to run," she said. "I blush to think he has the Liberal endorsement. But I guess we all know the Liberal Party makes all kinds of deals." She looked intently at him. "You know all these things in your cynical way—oh, my."

"Meyer would have had it this time if the deal went through."

"I really think Meyer has legal stature," she said. "In a way, it's a human tragedy, isn't it?"

The reporter smiled. "He'll be a better man for it," he said. He opened the car door. "How much money are you getting from the state committee?" he asked her.

"Not a cent." He smiled again. "No, I mean it. Not a cent."

"Okay, Judge," he said. "Good luck."

The judge was catching a plane back to New York, so we headed for the airport. I asked if she was enjoying anything about the campaign.

"I hate it," she replied. "I'm the world's least gregarious person. There's nothing about it I look forward to or enjoy. I'll never run again for anything."

I asked how she had happened to run in the first place.

"It was almost a lark," she said. "A friend of mine in a semi-serious way wrote a letter to the *New York Law Journal*. He said that a lot of women were being mentioned for the Court of Appeals and I was more qualified than most of them. I thought it was complete nonsense. I never aspired to the Court of Appeals. It just wasn't part of my range of possibilities. But people took it seriously. So I got into it."

I asked whether any part of the campaign had been useful to her as a judge.

"Not really," she said. "You don't pick up much from people because you don't discuss issues. Maybe you learn something about public speaking, but that's about all. I don't know whether it's undignified or not, but I find it rather unpleasant, having to sell yourself. It's personally disgusting."

"What about the principle of judicial elections?"

"It depends on how perceptive the electorate is, but I think the estimation of judicial qualifications is beyond the capacity of most voters. There's no reason in principle why a judge shouldn't go before the voters and be appraised. But the difficulty is that I don't think the voters can do it. And the people who can impress the electorate aren't necessarily the best judges."

We came in sight of the airport. "You know," she said softly, "it really would be fantastic, wouldn't it?" Her voice was almost wistful.

"What?"

"I mean if I won."

I dropped her at the airport and watched her walk briskly into the terminal, her little hat bobbing as she disappeared into the crowd.

The names of the seven appeals-court candidates were snuggled close to the presidential nominees on New York voting machines. When the electorate spoke on November 7, the winners were

Gabrielli, Jones, and Wachtler, the three Republicans. Cooke ran fourth, Meyer fifth, and Dembitz sixth. "We won because of the Republican landslide," said winner Jones.

"If there's anything constructive at all that emerged from this campaign," said Wachtler, another winner, "it's to illustrate graphically the weakness of our system of electing judges." All seven candidates had urged that Court of Appeals judges be appointed.

Five months later the New York City Bar Association issued new and stiffer guidelines for judicial candidates. They were not to accept large contributions, not to appeal to the "fear, passion or prejudice of the electorate," and not to pose for ads in robes (as Wachtler had done). The ambiguity of judicial campaigning in New York was deeper than ever.

The theory underlying the popular election of judges is that an office so important and powerful demands accountability to the public, that the voters have a vital interest in who settles their disputes and enforces their standards. The theory is tempting, and many political scientists defend it. But if New York City is a laboratory for the empirical study of that theory, it is clearly an idea whose time has gone.

In an overwhelming majority of instances, judicial elections in New York are devoid of choice. The candidates are accountable not to the voters but to the party leaders who bargain their nomination. The voters may endorse the agreed-upon candidate or decline to vote.

Between 1968 and 1972, 104 justices of the Supreme Court (the highest trial court) were elected in New York. Ninety were nominated jointly by Republicans and Democrats, and more than half of those had the additional support of either the Liberal or the Conservative party. The percentage of bipartisan candidates has been declining, but only slightly: a *New York Times* survey reported that 49 of 50 candidates in 1968 had the backing of both major parties; in 1969 it was 20 of 21; in 1970, 6 of 8; in 1971, 9 of 12; and in 1972, 6 of 13.

The most malodorous example of judicial dealing may have been the 1971 election of six Supreme Court justices in Queens. Democratic leader Matthew Troy and GOP chief Sidney Hein worked it out. Two of the seats went to Republican Assemblymen Alfred Lerner and Joseph Kunzeman, who had switched their votes to help Governor Rockefeller pass his state budget. The third Republican was Civil Court Judge Frederic Hammer, who had a reputation for heavy-handed intolerance.

The lucky Democrats were Queens Borough President Sidney Leviss, Civil Court Judge William Giaccio—and State Senator Seymour Thaler, who was ambushed by a criminal indictment on his way to the bench. Congressman Herman Badillo accused the negotiators of showing "absolute contempt for the people of Queens."

The New York City Bar Association rated five of the six—all but Judge Giaccio—"not approved." Hammer's rating was because of his "lack of judicial temperament." The other four had refused to be interviewed by the association's judiciary committee. They could afford to skip it.

The cozy code of judicial "arrangements" demands discretion. Criminal Court Judge Edward Caizzo of Staten Island foolishly revealed that he had lined up a promotion to the Supreme Court, and went on to identify his political benefactors. Caizzo not only lost his chance for elevation, but found that he was being investigated on various charges by the Supreme Court's appellate division. He became seriously ill shortly afterward and retired.

Stories have circulated for decades about the "price" of a New York judgeship. Former Suffolk County Supreme Court Justice Joseph Pfingst, one of the few judges ever directly accused of buying his job, disclosed something of how it works when he said that he was expected to raise money from his legal clients for the party treasury.

In 1960 a scholarly study of New York courts and politics reported that the rumored "going rate" for a judgeship was the equivalent of two years' salary in office—which would be more than $86,000 for current Supreme Court justices in New York City. (Judges in New York are paid more than any other judges in the country except justices of the U.S. Supreme Court.) In 1966 Martin Mayer wrote of the general belief that "a contribution of at least $10,000" was necessary for a judicial nomination.

"It doesn't happen all the time," an anonymous Criminal Court judge told the *Times* in 1970, "and not for standard prices like you always hear. It's more selective and casual, in the form of a big contribution to the party from a grateful worker about to be rewarded with a seat on the bench."

"I'm convinced it goes on," Brooklyn Assemblyman Stephen Solarz told the *Times* man, "because I've heard widespread instances of it from too many people in a position to know. . . . My understanding is it [the price] fluctuates, like stocks."

A more predictable response came from a retired judge: "Young man," he told the reporter, "you must say I never, never talked to you and, if that's clear, I'll say this: you should never deal in rumors with the legal profession. If you don't have evidence, be silent."

Justice Pfingst testified at his trial that the customary way for a judge to conceal contributions to the party was to make them in his wife's name. Thus the New York Democratic Committee was enriched by a $6500 contribution from Claire Silverman, wife of Manhattan Supreme Court candidate Samuel Silverman, in 1970. A brother may also be useful. Dr. Stuart Asch donated $10,000 to the Bronx Democratic Campaign Fund Committee in the year that his brother, Civil Court Judge Sidney H. Asch, won three-party nomination to the Supreme Court.

Another way that judges pay their dues is by appointing party workers to court jobs. The New York Crime Commission discovered in 1953 that 57 of 199 local political leaders held patronage jobs in the courts. The penalty for resisting the party's man was described by a Brooklyn judge in 1970: "For weeks," he said, "all my papers would get lost, and the court bureaucracy kept fouling up my schedule. It all stopped when I took their guy." An investigation by New York's *Village Voice* in 1972 turned up thirty-two party leaders on court payrolls in Manhattan and the Bronx. Their positions ranged from "confidential attendant" to law secretary to chief clerk.

The courts are handy havens for defeated or retiring politicians. Former Democratic Assembly Speaker Anthony Travia moved from the legislature into the judicial big time, a seat on the federal District Court in Brooklyn, but most politicians settle for state judgeships. Party control of judicial elections gets the jobs for them. "The legislators prefer the elective system," says former State Senator Clinton Dominick, who headed a commission on New York courts. "They know that appointments would be less certain. They might be impossible to control."

"Worthy legislators have always looked on the courts as a retirement village," a New York judge told me. "Especially if they are about to be indicted," he added only half facetiously. "They fake the DA out."

Political kinfolk do all right too. Queens Justice Francis X. Smith, whose name came up in one corruption investigation, is the son of a former county leader. Manhattan Justice Oliver Sutton is indebted to his brother Percy, the borough president. Justice Guy Mangano of Brooklyn can thank his father, a district leader and general clerk of the Supreme Court.

Corrupt judges have reached office by both appointment and election, and so have the best men on the bench. There is no convincing evidence for a connection between method of selection and judicial caliber. But the selection system does create an atmosphere—of trust or cynicism, confidence or despair. The smoky atmosphere of judicial selection in New York influences the standards applied to potential judges and the attitudes of the judges themselves. And, court for court, judge for judge, New York's judiciary is second to none by any measure of judicial venality and ineptitude.

The Knapp Commission, which investigated police corruption in New York, turned up evidence that as many as a half-dozen trial judges were susceptible to bribery. The commission surveyed the sentences imposed on policemen convicted of corruption between 1968 and 1972 and found that 49 of 80 convicted officers "were either set free or given suspended sentences." Of the 31 who were jailed, 14 were sentenced to less than a year. "It is clear that the risks of severe punishment for corrupt behavior are slight," the commission concluded. "A dishonest policeman knows that even if he is caught and convicted, he will probably receive a court reprimand, or at most, a fairly short jail sentence."

Another investigative agency, the Joint Legislative Committee on Crime, led by the late State Senator John Hughes, looked into 1762 criminal cases involving Mafia figures between 1960 and 1969. The committee found that 44.7 percent of the indictments against syndicate members were dismissed, as contrasted with an 11.5 rate of dismissal for indictments against all other defendants. Of 193 organized-crime figures who were convicted, judges gave fines or suspended sentences to 46 percent.

Nicholas Gage of the *New York Times*, one of the leading investigative reporters in the country, found case after case where mob members received gentle treatment from the courts. In one, Justice Domenic S. Rinaldi of Brooklyn Supreme Court sentenced mobster Paul Vario to a fine of $250 after he pleaded guilty to bribing a policeman. In another case Justice Rinaldi sentenced six of seven men convicted on swindling charges to prison. The seventh, identified as a Mafia member, was given a suspended sentence. (Rinaldi was indicted on charges of perjury and obstructing governmental administration in November 1973.)

Vincent Decicco, described as a member of the Carlo Gambino Mafia family, was convicted of contempt for refusing to testify before a grand jury after being granted immunity. Justice Joseph R. Corso, also of Brooklyn, threw out the verdict on grounds that the district attorney had not properly explained the immunity. Corso's ruling was reversed on appeal.

Manhattan Supreme Court Justice Gerald P. Culkin, son of a former Tammany Hall leader, dismissed perjury charges against two former detectives charged with lying to a grand jury in an organized-crime case. The appeals court reversed him. Culkin's rulings in corruption and organized-crime cases had been overturned on seven previous occasions.

"There's a handful of good Family Court and Supreme Court judges in the city," one New York judge said to me, "but most of them are a bunch of bums. It's not usually corruption or venality, it's a lot of things. Culkin just likes cops. He gives light sentences for the wrong reasons—he believes blacks and Puerto Ricans are animals and not responsible for what they do.

"Sometimes it's incompetence. With Corso it's more of a hard-hat, crime-in-the-streets reaction. But don't forget that a judge sentences according to the charge in front of him, not on a man's general reputation. A black up on a knife charge is treated differently than a Mafia figure charged with contempt. It's a different category of crime."

New York judges were startled in October 1972 to learn that writer Jack Newfield had picked "the ten worst judges in New York" for a New York magazine article. Rinaldi, Culkin, and eight others, including Edward Dudley, the administrative chief of the Manhattan and Bronx Supreme Courts, found themselves on Newfield's ten-least-wanted list. One of the ten, former Congressman Paul Fino, drew more "negative unanimity," Newfield reported, than any other judge in the city. Fino was rated unqualified by the city bar association, but won bipartisan support anyway.

Newfield's piece set off land mines in the house of justice. Fino reportedly contemplated suing for libel, was advised against it, and quit the bench a month later to return to more active forms of politics. Justice John Monteleone, another on Newfield's list, fought back with testimonials from the Brooklyn Bar Association and the New York State Trial Lawyers Association. "Shame on your false and libelous statements," huffed Civil Court Administrative Judge Edward Thompson, a former city fire commissioner.

"There were four kinds of reactions," one judge told me. "First there were the old-pol judges who figured they were out of the battle and should be left alone, that criticizing them was somehow unconstitutional. Second, the judges whose names end in a vowel were uptight because it looked like Italians were singled out [five of Newfield's ten had Italian names]. Third were those who were neutral, they didn't get involved. And fourth are the few who thought it was a good thing, who feel that judges should be criticized like ballplayers or anybody else and if they're wrongfully maligned, tough titty."

Judges under attack, another judge told me, "tend to draw the wagons in a circle and commence firing." Legal Aid attorney Martin Erdmann felt the force of judicial counterattack after he was quoted in *Life* magazine as saying "the only way you can get [a New York judgeship] is to be in politics or buy it." He described appellate-division judges as "the whores who become madams." The appellate judges, ignoring a bar-association recommendation that no action be taken, censured Erdmann for "professional misconduct," a decision that was reversed by the Court of Appeals.

Another victim of judicial return fire was Mayor John Lindsay. He told an interviewer that the state Supreme Court was "instinctively unproductive and subject to all the possibilities of venality one could possibly imagine," adding that judges were selected "in the most deplorable kind of backroom political deals."

The presiding justices of the city's two appellate divisions immediately branded the mayor's statement a "smear." Brooklyn judges called the charges "reckless." Queens jurists demanded (and received) an apology. Manhattan and Bronx judges, through their public-information committee, called the criticism "scandalous," adding piously that "one of the great injustices done the judiciary of today comes from the presumptuous judgment of the ill-informed."

Lindsay's pulpit was not exactly pristine. "He has participated in the same kind of political deals in making his appointments," City Council member Ruth Lerner said. He had reportedly offered Criminal Court judgeships to councilmen in exchange for support of his budget. In 1972 the wives of Criminal Court judges were invited to a $100-a-plate fund-raising dinner for the mayor's abortive presidential campaign.

The best place to inspect judicial quality is in the bottom-rung courts, where the issues are apt to be non-payment of rent or damages in an accident case. Mark Denbeaux, a young law professor at Seton Hall University, saw the system from this perspective during the two years (1968 to 1970) he spent as a Community Action for Legal Services attorney in the Bronx.

The CALS was a legal division of the federal anti-poverty program. As a poor-people's advocate, Denbeaux was so dismayed by the judges he encountered in landlord-and-tenant court that he compiled a dossier of bad examples, hoping to goad the hierarchy into disciplining the worst offenders. His complaints were generally ignored.

His portfolio is a catalog of small, mean acts: Civil Court Judge Thomas Mirabile of Manhattan, told by a tenant that her bathroom leaked, suggested she "use an umbrella" (Mirabile was nominated for the state Supreme Court in 1973); Judge Ross DiLorenzo of Brooklyn advised a landlord's lawyer, "They have no evidence, you can't lose"; Judge George Abrams of Brooklyn Civil Court repeatedly told a witness he didn't believe her; when her lawyer objected, he said, "Let him make a record, he has to pay for the minutes"; Manhattan Judge Morris Wahl, unhappy with an attorney's refusal to waive his client's rights, said, "You just wait until you come in front of me again"; Bronx Judge William Drohan, amused by a tenant's complaints about rats, told her that an exterminator would come in the morning, so "be sure to wake up the rats." (Drohan was among several new Court of Claims judges appointed by Rockefeller last year to handle cases stemming from New York's tough new narcotics law.)

"Poor people's rights were consistently diminished or denied," Denbeaux said. "The judges invariably found for the landlords. They weren't bigots as such, they were just intolerant, insensitive, biased against welfare recipients. Anything that slowed up collection of the landlord's money was a violation of the code."

"Landlord-and-tenant court makes tremendous demands on a judge's humanity," says Manhattan Civil Court Judge Irving Younger. "The guy in the black bathrobe has to be God, minister, social worker, the local psychiatrist, and everything else. You can tell instantly whether a judge is a good human being."

Younger is a trim and tidy-looking man of forty with a rapid-fire speaking style and a lively wit. Before his election in 1968, he had been successively a newspaperman, advertising copywriter, law student, prosecutor, and law professor at New York University. Running as a reform Democrat in an overwhelmingly Republican district ("the typical voter is, say, Nelson Rockefeller"), he won an upset victory with the help of his law students, who were deployed with campaign placards at strategic intersections. "It was a political accident," he says. He has a gift for showmanship and an idealistic view of the law. The walls of his chambers contain photographs of Supreme Court Justices Oliver Wendell Holmes and Louis Brandeis, the Marx Brothers, Charlie Chaplin, and J. Edgar Hoover. Younger is a bright ray amid the bleakness of the New York judiciary. There are others, but he is among the best.

I sat in court one day as he charged the jury in an accident case. "Your job is an extraordinarily solemn task of citizenship," he told the six jurors. "A lawsuit is imperfect and clumsy, but it's the best device we have for these purposes. You should think about these questions: Did a witness lie? Does he know what he's talking about? Does what he said conform with other evidence? Does it conform with your sense of reality, of how the world really works?" He explained the specific question of law the jury had to decide. The issue boiled down to which of two drivers involved in an accident had had the green light.

After the charge I accompanied him to his chambers. "The defendant is a boob," he said. "The defense lawyer is young and not too bright. The plaintiff's lawyer is pretty good, but I think he went overboard in cross-examining the defendant. He's just a kid and the lawyer made him look bad. I think that had a reverse effect on the jury and they'll punish him for it and find for the defendant.

"You know," he went on, "like all intellectuals, I fancy myself a cynic, but I believe in nothing in the world except juries. It's so magical it sends shivers down my spine. The lawyers can be fools, the evidence can be complicated, and the law bewildering, but it doesn't matter. If I were G. K. Chesterton, I'd say the Holy Ghost is in the jury room with them when the door closes. It is not six times one person or twelve times one person, it's something unique.

"Sometimes you can hear their deliberations through the wall of the jury room. It's eerie. There's an air of extraordinary serious-ness. Personalities don't get in the way. They know what the evidence is, and they know the law, and, best of all, they *know what to do.* They do the right thing. Do they find the truth? I don't know, but they do the right thing. It's scary. Maybe there *is* a God."

Younger's courtroom manner is intense. "It's total concentra-tion," he said. "My mind is open to nothing else while the trial is on. Until twenty minutes ago I could have repeated the testimony in that case to you verbatim. In your mind as a judge you see all the elements as part of an algebraic equation. You hear a piece of testimony and something drops in place and you know that some-thing else will have to move tomorrow or another time. Now this trial is gone, it's all emptied out. I make notes during a trial to keep myself from unintentionally signaling the lawyers. It's not fair to do that, so I take notes to keep my eyes down and my hands busy."

His job engages and satisfies him. "I didn't know if it would, but I found it has great intellectual satisfaction," he said. "With aston-ishing frequency you confront legal questions to which there is no answer, and it's your job to work it out. It sounds soupy to say it, but there's a feeling of being useful. As long as humans live together, there will be disputes, and in settling them in this way to minimize unhappiness and keep a kind of intellectual coherence, you're doing good work. I feel that I can check out with the knowl-edge that I've done something."

The jurors had been out for an hour. Now the judge's law secretary came into the room and said they were ready.

"I think I picked up something about juror psychology," the secretary said. "I overheard some of it. One juror took the plaintiff's side and made all the arguments for his case and then destroyed them one by one."

"Verdict for the defendant?" Younger said. He slapped his palm on the desk. "I knew it. See—they gave it to the plaintiff's lawyer. He turned them off."

* * *

Judges like Irving Younger are too rare in New York court-houses. The generally tepid level of judicial competence, coupled with the traditional intimacy between politics and the bench, have provoked repeated cries for selection reform. "We can't say that all elected judges are worse than all appointed judges," says Gary Sperling of New York's Citizens Union. "But you can also get some good judges just by picking men whose name begins with the letter A. What we need is a system that doesn't just occasionally pick good judges."

Reformers of all ideological persuasions have zeroed in on merit selection as the road to judicial glory in New York. A committee of legal luminaries, including former Appellate Judge Bernard Botein and corruption investigator (now federal Judge) Whitman Knapp, weighed in with a merit-selection proposal in 1972. They described the current selection of New York judges as an "obscenity" and a "charade." Former Mayor Lindsay, who voluntarily used a screening committee in appointing judges of the Criminal and Family courts (including Nanette Dembitz), was a consistent advocate of merit reform. The *New York Times* and other newspapers have regularly endorsed it. The state bar association emerged from ninety-six years of silence on the subject in 1973 to urge merit selection. A month later Governor Rockefeller included the appointment of judges (with confirmation by the state Senate) in the court-reform plan he submitted to the legislature. One after another, the reformers spoke of merit selection as "an idea whose time has come."

Another arrow in the reformers' quiver is the establishment of an effective judicial discipline commission. New York's Court on the Judiciary, a panel of appellate judges empowered to remove jurists "for cause," has convened only five times since it was created in 1948. The appellate division of the Supreme Court, which also may remove judges for misconduct, did so only ten times in 120 years.

Pressure for reform escalated recently with disclosures of corruption and sentencing inequities, especially the relatively lenient treatment of organized-crime figures. But despite the revelations, the pressure, the broad-based support for change, and the backing of leaders like Lindsay and Rockefeller, the prospect of merit selection in New York is still no more than a gleam in the reformers' eyes. The reason is simple: the legislature must pass it (it means a constitutional amendment, which requires the approval of two successive legislatures and a voter referendum); and legislators, like their political patrons, are comfortable with Things As They Are; merit selection might shut off their chances for a judgeship.

The legislative perspective was obvious in the operation of the courts commission led by former Senator Dominick. The commission was composed of eleven members—five named by the governor and six by leaders of the Senate and Assembly. One, a gubernatorial appointment, missed most of the commission's meetings because of illness.

The commission spent more than two years investigating New York courts. In early 1973 it unloaded dozens of recommendations, including elimination of bail, a unified court system, and the establishment of a strong judicial discipline commission. But the commission voted 6–4 to retain judicial elections. The six commissioners voting for elections included five who were appointed by legislative leaders and one Rockefeller appointee. The four favoring merit selection were Dominick (who was named by the Senate majority leader) and three of the governor's choices—a law professor, a League of Women Voters representative, and the former president of the New York Legal Aid Society.

"It wasn't our greatest chapter," Dominick told me. "The only shift from election to appointment we managed to get through was for New York City Civil Court judges. And I think maybe they gave us that one because we lost on the Court of Appeals and the Supreme Court.

"Knowing the legislature as I do," he said, "I'm sure we could have come up with a great scheme which would be praised by the bar association and law-school professors, and the crazy legislature would chop it up and do whatever silly thing they wanted to do anyway. I don't think they're going to change judicial selection. Most of them figure they were elected, so why shouldn't judges be elected?"

The "political thicket," as Supreme Court Justice Felix Frankfurter once described it, is still dense and thorny in New York. It enveloped a contest last year for chief judge of the Court of Appeals.

The post became open with the retirement of Judge Stanley Fuld. Since 1916 the senior associate judge had traditionally moved up when the chief judge retired. He was then elected (as Benjamin Cardozo was in 1926) with bipartisan backing. But in 1973 the senior judge, Adrian Burke, said he was not interested in promotion. Next in line was Republican Charles Breitel, a widely respected jurist who had been considered a candidate for the U.S. Supreme Court. Breitel was promptly endorsed by Rockefeller and the Republican organization.

A deal was made—Democratic support of Breitel in exchange for the next two openings on the court. Then two top Democratic leaders, Matthew Troy of Queens and Meade Esposito of Brooklyn, got into a public shouting match over a labyrinthian network of other endorsements and trades. Both angrily repudiated the agreement to support Breitel.

The immediate effect was to force a contest, first for the Democratic nomination and later for the chief judgeship, which was eventually won by Breitel. But the long-run effect was recognition of the dreary truth that genuine merit has little to do with the selection of New York judges. Even the highest judicial office in the state was deeply snarled in the machinations of self-serving politicians.

X

View from the Middle

A Colorado judge struggles to make the punishment fit the crime

THE DEFENDANT, a tall, tanned, black-haired man in his thirties, stood before Judge Richard Greene with his hands folded. He wore a black blazer, striped slacks, and an expression of contrition.

Greene, a judge of the Colorado District Court (the state's highest trial court) in the Denver suburb of Littleton, stared coldly at the defendant. The man had been convicted of sexually molesting several eleven- and twelve-year-old boys at a summer camp. He was appearing for sentencing.

"He has an affliction, Your Honor," his attorney said. "He is remorseful to the depths of his despair." The defendant let his eyes fall demurely to the gold rug on the courtroom floor. In the spectator seats were several well-to-do friends he had brought along to vouch for his character.

"It's rare that you find a man accused of a criminal charge with friends of this caliber," the attorney went on, gesturing toward the well-dressed spectators. "He is an outstanding citizen. This is a man who helps deprived children."

Judge Greene's eyebrows rose above his glasses. His habitual courtroom expression, a studied impassivity, now seemed about to crack, if only slightly.

"I appreciate that," he told the lawyer. "And I'm not bothered by his affliction. But there are things here that are very troubling to this court. There were several children assaulted. What bothers me is the devastation to these young boys—"

"That's been exaggerated, Your Honor," the lawyer replied. "The defendant is a good citizen. He's already been punished mentally. He put himself under psychiatric care. I'm certain he has the fiber to conquer his problems."

"This court makes no differentiation between a pillar of the community and a poor man," the judge said harshly. "I'm not going to make an exception because he has friends in the community. The crime is the same. I'm considering this case as if his name was Trujillo."

"You're dealing with a good man here, Your Honor," the lawyer said mildly.

The judge's voice climbed half an octave. "The parents of the victims don't think I'm dealing with a good man."

The defendant bit his lip. One parent, a policeman, had told a probation officer that he was "disgusted with the liberal attitude this case has been treated with."

"What's the defendant doing now?" Greene asked.

"Selling real estate, Your Honor. His employer's here today. How often do you find an employer appearing in court in behalf of his employee?" The lawyer glanced around the yellow-walled courtroom in satisfaction.

"Frequently," Judge Greene replied.

The judge looked at the file on his desk. "I see that he continued his homosexual activities even after he started therapy," he said. His voice rose again. "I consider this a vicious and treacherous crime as far as these boys are concerned. The incidents were repeated a dozen times. Why didn't he seek psychiatric treatment when it first happened?"

The lawyer was silent.

"This is a very serious decision," the judge said. "I'm going to continue it for ninety days before I sentence. I want a report from the probation department at that time and I want a psychiatrist here. I won't commit myself on a sentence."

Greene declared a recess and quickly descended the three steps from his bench, disappearing through a door into his chambers. The bench formed one side of a triangle in a corner of the courtroom. The defendant, who was free on bond, walked to the spectator area to thank his friends for coming.

The judge's office was a small, brown-carpeted room shaped like an L. The desk faced windows that looked across an alley to the Arapahoe County Jail; he kept the drapes closed to block the view.

Greene took off his robe, revealing a flowered dress shirt and bellbottoms, and clicked on an FM radio to soft background music. He is forty-eight, a swarthy, stockily built man of medium height, with broad features, a rolling walk, and dark hair cut short.

He sat down at his desk with a sigh. "I just wasn't ready to sentence him this morning," he said. "I wasn't psyched up for it. You go over everything in your mind. It's the classic tug-of-war between the nature of the crime and the argument for probation. I just haven't resolved the debate yet.

"On the one side," he went on, "there's the defendant and his affliction, and on the other is the punitive element, especially since there are kids involved. The parents of the victims say justice is one thing and the parents of the defendant say it's another. I want to give myself time to work it out."

He hunched forward, resting his elbows on the desk. "They should have had the psychiatrist here and on the stand," he said. "I didn't like the attorney saying that all these prominent people in the community had given their support. They came in today figuring probation was going to be a snap, no question about it. It's a fancy day camp; a lot of wealthy people send their kids there."

He said the case had kept him awake late the previous night. "I'm leaning toward sending him to prison at Canon City for a one-to-fourteen-year sentence," he said. "But I need to know more about him. I may be overreacting because I have another sex case I'm worried about. It's a sixty-three-year-old man who molested his eleven-year-old grandson. He used various devices and books; it was *filthy*, just rotten.

"I wish to hell we had some kind of a work program for a man like this. Maybe he could donate a year of his life working at a nursing home, carrying bedpans or something. It wouldn't be an institution, but it would still involve some sacrifice on his part. But I don't have any option like that." (By the time the defendant returned to his court three months later, Greene had found one. He sentenced him to three years probation and ninety days work at a clinic in lieu of jail.)

"We have very little treatment available, and no good mental-health option. The state just authorized a half-million dollars for a computer to register every case that's filed, but we don't have the money for a psychiatrist or psychologist on the court staff. I have no place to send a person for controlled psychiatric therapy, and the worst thing is that there's nothing in the hopper."

Greene believes that part of his function is to protect children. "It's the kids, that's what gets me about this case," he said. "I don't know what permanent damage those kids suffered from this. I have a young son who goes to day camp, I'm sure that influences me too." He views children as fawns in a dangerous forest. "I take a hard stance on aggressive sex crimes involving children. Some of this stuff is just animalistic. God! I remember one where a man had committed a homosexual act with his son. The boy grew up into a rapist to prove his masculinity. I couldn't put this guy who molested the kids at camp into the reformatory—it's full of kids. And I didn't know what might happen to him at the prison.

"Who can a judge talk to about these things?" he asked suddenly. "There's nobody. Other judges don't help—they can give you advice, but then they're wounded if you don't take it. No one can help you."

Richard Greene is a suburban, rootless, middle-class, upwardly mobile, late-twentieth-century American. He seems a creature of his time, a man who could "fit in" and feel at home in any of fifty comfortable and interchangeable suburban milieus. He lives in a ranch house in a development called Cherry Hills, which could as easily be named Woodcliff or Seaview or Manor Park, and which could probably be transplanted *in toto* from Colorado to Connecticut, Wisconsin, or Florida with no more inconvenience to the residents than the bother of transferring schools and finding a new country club. Greene seems to lack a sense of place, an attachment to a physical locale, even in the unmistakable precincts of Colorado, where the setting sun silhouettes the solemn ranks of the Rockies fifty miles beyond his backyard.

His conversation is sprinkled with suburban pieties in the context of law: court disruption is "the kind of thing that happens in the core city," not here; school busing is an example of "federal courts usurping authority"; "I don't believe a judge should be associated with 'extreme elements' or controversial positions." Even the cases that come before him are suburban—drag races instead of knife fights, more marijuana than heroin, very few blacks. "I'm suburbanized, and I have been for years," he says.

He considers himself in the "middle of the road" on most issues, and indeed he hews toward the center of any grouping he's a part of. His tastes are middlebrow; his politics are liberal Republican, with an allowance for shifts across the wavy partisan lines; he seems, in fact, uncomfortable with talk of ideology. When I asked him one day whether he aligned himself with any particular set of political and social values, he said he did not, that he wasn't sure that any of them suited him. "My generation is in the middle," he says. "We're on the fringe of the new and the coattails of the old. We can see the calls for change as good, but we're entrenched enough that change itself seems too dramatic, too precipitous." In court he will frequently compromise the positions of competing advocates—"I did what you should have done," he told the lawyers in a dispute involving child-support payments, "I found a figure in the middle." His court—a general-level state trial court—pins him to the center once again: in the judicial hierarchy, he occupies a point almost precisely midway between Justice of the Peace John D. Herron and Chief Justice Warren Burger.

He was born in Chicago on October 7, 1925—"I'm a Libra. That's the judge's sign." (His date of birth, he points out, makes him "six weeks older than Johnny Carson.") He has no ties to Chicago, though; his father disappeared when he was eleven, and his mother moved to Colorado after World War II.

His childhood in the Franklin Park section of Chicago was poor and scrambling. "It was a big deal to go to the movies," he recalls. His father was the supervisor of a truck depot for Standard Oil of Indiana before he drove off one day, leaving a wife and four children.

"My mother went blind taking care of four kids and working," he says. "She was a Christian Scientist and she always believed that she'd see again, but she didn't. I know what it is to be poor, it's true, and sometimes I think that helps me understand people's problems better. But maybe it doesn't work that way; maybe I'm harder on them because of my background."

He is still bitter about his father's desertion. "I never had a father in those crucial years when we could do things together, father-and-son nights and things like that. When someone makes a pitch to me on the basis of their deprived childhood, it has no influence on me unless he was beaten." Greene and his wife, a thin platinum blonde who is a trained nurse, adopted a son who is now ten.

He attended Cornell College in Mount Vernon, Iowa, graduating in 1948, then came to Denver to join his mother. He spent a few years handling claims for a power company before entering Denver University law school. He dropped out and back in again, finally graduating in 1957. He practiced law in Denver and Littleton, and served for a time as an assistant district attorney. He tinkered around the edges of politics, turning up one year as a delegate to the Arapahoe County Republican assembly (nominating convention) and making an unsuccessful run (as an independent) for the Littleton City Council.

His chance at a judgeship came after Colorado voters approved a constitutional amendment discarding partisan judicial elections in favor of the merit plan in 1966. Under the new method, announcements were printed in newspapers when a judicial vacancy occurred and applications were solicited. His name was submitted by a lawyer friend in 1968, but he didn't make it. He became instead the deputy chief of Colorado's newly formed statewide public-defender office, spending the next two years as the office administrator as well as an attorney for indigent criminal defendants.

In 1970 another judicial vacancy opened up in Littleton, and the commissioners who had interviewed him earlier asked if he wanted to be reconsidered. "I went before them again because they had added new members," he recalls. "They asked me a lot of things—what I'd do if I were assigned to a probate case (I said I'd seek help), how I'd react if there was a longhair-and-sandals-type defendant who had a good defense, what I thought was the most important attribute for a judge. I said it was judicial temperament, that a judge can't shoot from the cuff or lose his temper, and that he should never embarrass lawyers in front of their clients.

"I guess I had becoming a judge in the back of my mind for a long time. I discovered not long ago that I wrote a paper saying I wanted to be a judge when I was in the eighth grade. I know that as a lawyer I used to get infuriated with judges who didn't take the lawyers' problems into consideration, and I'd think about how I'd do it if it were me."

The nominating commission for Greene's district—which contains three largely rural counties in addition to suburban Arapahoe—included his name among three they recommended to Republican Governor John Love, and Love selected him for the post in 1970, effective January 1971.

Colorado's judicial reform was as thoroughgoing as any in the nation, a wholehearted adoption of the principle that judges should be removed from partisan politics.

The new plan established a nominating commission for each of the state's twenty-two judicial districts and another for appellate courts. Each commission is led by a non-voting Supreme Court justice, and includes three attorneys (selected by the chief justice, the attorney general, and the governor) and four laymen named by the governor. In addition, the amendment created a nine-member Commission on Judicial Qualifications (five judges, two lawyers, and two laymen) with authority to recommend to the state Supreme Court that a judge be removed.

The governor must fill a vacancy with one of the names submitted by the nominating commission within fifteen days. Judges are appointed for two-year terms, then run on their record on a yes-no "retention ballot," without opposition. Those at Greene's level are elected for six-year terms. As of 1972, 40 percent of Colorado's judges had reached office by this process.

"A lot of good lawyers wouldn't try for a judgeship under the political system," says Chief Justice Edward Pringle of the state Supreme Court. "I campaigned at every county fair and rodeo in the state. Judges ought to be doing their job and not campaigning. You can't make promises. The only basis for election was whether Republicans or Democrats won the statewide election, and that's the wrong reason for selecting a judge."

The reform plan was controversial from its inception. State legislators made four attempts to repeal it in its first five years. Political leaders fought it as an invasion of their patronage power. Many liberal lawyers feared that it would limit the judiciary to "silk stocking" attorneys approved by the bar association.

Pringle believes that it's been successful. "If a judge is responsible to an electorate, he gets more concerned about the electorate than his duties," he says. "Most of the men selected under the merit plan are able, and we're assured that we won't get incompetents. Oh, we might get one once in a while, but nowhere near as often as with the elective system."

"One of the big bugaboos," says state court administrator Harry Lawson, "was that we were taking selection of judges away from the people, as if it were a sacred right. The fact is that there was very rarely a real contest. Most judges were originally appointed to fill a vacancy anyway, and more than half never had any opposition when they did run."

Applications for vacancies on Denver courts often run as high as fifty for a single post. "The commissioners rank all the candidates in order after interviewing them," Pringle says. "They keep eliminating until there are perhaps seven left, then vote for five of those, then three of the last five." Commissioners are often businessmen, editors, or community leaders. More than thirty have been women, and some effort has been made to include blacks and Mexican-Americans.

Governor Love, who resigned to serve briefly as head of the Nixon administration's energy policy office, is credited by most lawyers with avoiding partisanship in his judicial appointments under the merit plan. "I'm sure he knew what party they belonged to, even though it doesn't say on their application," a Denver attorney says, "and he's paid some political debts. But he's been pretty even-handed about it. He's a good lawyer himself."

Critics have zeroed in on two points, the paucity of choice in some sparsely populated districts and the ineffectiveness of the yes-no retention ballot. "There are some parts of Colorado where there are damn few lawyers," says Dean Robert Yegge of Denver University law school, "and that makes the over-all caliber uneven." Yegge believes, however, that the reform has generally upgraded judicial quality.

Through 1972 only seven judges had been defeated on retention ballots. One was brought down by a campaign charging that he was too "permissive" with juveniles; another had been tried and acquitted (by Judge Greene) of altering a trial transcript; and a third had been accused (and cleared) of accepting a bribe. The great majority sailed through the retention election without challenge. "It's better than life tenure," says Pringle, "but I'm not sure the retention ballot is meaningful."

The qualifications commission received about twenty serious complaints in its first five years. Ten judges resigned or retired under pressure—"most of them were senile and didn't know it," Lawson says—and another three were censured for misconduct. None was removed.

"I think the qualifications commission scares them," says a Denver lawyer. "There was one who wouldn't appoint a public defender, he just refused to do it. He was a heavy drinker. We complained to the commission, and they told him to shape up. They went over transcripts with him. He got religion, quit drinking, and turned into a pretty fair judge."

"If someone could guarantee that the political parties would nominate judicial candidates on the basis of their ability and temperament, the political system wouldn't bother me," Pringle says. "That would be the ideal. We could elect them for life, with a removal commission. But I don't see how you're ever going to get candidates like that under a political system."

One index of improvement is that more than 90 percent of the complaints submitted to the removal commission have involved politically selected judges. "I don't think I'd be a judge if it weren't for the merit system," Greene says. "I wasn't that active politically, I wasn't in the party's graces. It probably would have hurt me that I worked for a Democratic district attorney. And I might not want to get that politically involved. I think there's a lot of judges like me who wouldn't be here under the political system."

Greene learned of his appointment through a telephone call from the governor's administrative assistant. "We knew each other, and we weren't particularly crazy about each other," he recalls. "He got on the phone and said, 'Well, you want to be a judge—I've got your certificate here.' I was on cloud nine. Even he couldn't irritate me." A photograph of Republican Love hangs on a wall of Greene's office, along with a picture of Democratic Chief Justice Pringle. "I'm covered," he says.

He is ambitious, earnest, and conscientious. Like many successful lawyers, he took a pay cut (to $22,500) to go on the bench, but he understands the alternative rewards. "There are three basic types of success," he says, "financial, position, and some combination of the two. When you become a judge, you give up financial success and gain prominence in the community. You can't compete with your peers financially, but you can in prestige, and that becomes important. You get invited to private clubs and restaurant openings. I'm hobnobbing with people I never knew before. I suppose you get more vested and conservative the longer you stay on the bench. But if you resist the temptation to enjoy the prestige and be, you know, part of the Establishment, and you've already given up financial success, what does that leave you with? There's a natural tendency for people to push you toward the Establishment, but it's dangerous too. If you're not careful, you can become part of a narrow little community of ideas, which isn't healthy."

Greene feels himself drifting in that direction—becoming a community pillar—but he takes satisfaction in the job at hand. "It's the idea that people come to you because of your training, experience, and intellect, and you can do something for them. I feel that I'm working at the top of my bent. At the end of a day I usually feel I've accomplished something. Yesterday, for example, I had preliminary hearings, without a jury. It's a comfortable proceeding and I feel in the middle of it, at the heart of it. It can be exciting—sometimes I'll have a case where I'll make law. It's personally fulfilling. The outcome depends on me, it comes out of my head. I'm the only one that the people in the case can look to."

Like a thousand other state judges, he aspires to the federal bench—"but that's a fantasy, it's not a realistic possibility." He would be pleased to be a member of the state Supreme Court. "But my goal is to be a fair judge, that's all, and not a pushover. 'Stern' isn't quite the word, 'firm' maybe. I want to be firm but fair, to run a good ship, and I want people to respect the court and the system."

The burden of the job is sentencing. Greene broods about it constantly, takes it home at night, reads and rereads probation reports, weighs the conflicting imperatives he feels. His eyes will sometimes glaze in the middle of a conversation, as if he has donned invisible sunglasses, when he is thinking about a defendant he has to sentence.

Later that day he gave me a probation report on a convicted narcotics dealer he was due to sentence the next day. The dealer was a twenty-two-year-old man with several previous convictions. He had been arrested after he sold LSD to an undercover policeman. The police considered him a major connection between outside suppliers and Littleton schools, with nine underlings working for him. The probation officer said he was "immature, unstable, and confused."

That evening I accompanied the judge to a cocktail lounge. After we were seated he pulled a letter out of his coat pocket and handed it to me. "Read that," he said. "It's from the dealer I'm supposed to sentence tomorrow." The letter, written in a childish scrawl, asked the judge for "one chance to prove that I can make it and work hard in my life for once." He apologized for trying to be "a big shot" and assured Greene that "I am not a bad guy but just need a friend and to be honest with myself and be a man."

"What do you think of that?" Greene asked. I told him I found it unconvincing. "Me too," he said, sipping a vodka. "It doesn't say anything. He probably got advice on what to write from his cellmates." He looked at me evenly. "Okay," he said, "now you've read the letter and the probation report, you know as much about this guy as I do. What sentence would you give him?" He told me that the range extended from an indeterminate reformatory sentence (with parole eligibility after eight months) to a maximum of fourteen years in state prison.

I protested that I hadn't seen the defendant.

"What good will that do?" he demanded. "That's a cop-out. You can't tell anything from appearance anyway. You can't read their eyes, if that's what you think. What could you tell from that guy in court this morning? I didn't even see his eyes. They can con you with an expression. What would you give him?"

I hesitated, feeling uncomfortable.

"I'd give him three to five at Canon City," he said. "He's a *pusher*. I make a distinction with pushers. He's in it for profit. He'd be eligible for parole after two years and some months. He deserves that time as punishment."

I finally conceded that I was thinking in terms of one or two years.

"Look," he said, "the police did good surveillance work on this case. If I give him a light sentence, they'll be screaming. They have him pegged as the key supplier for Littleton. Don't you believe in supporting your local police?"

I said I didn't think a sentence should be used to reward police.

"But he's a pusher," he repeated. He took another sip of his drink. "I don't know. I'm going to think about it some more tonight."

The judge seemed edgy when I saw him in his chambers the next morning. "This is going to be a bruiser of a day," he said as he zipped up his robe. He walked to the door leading to his bench and stood with his hand on the knob. I realized that a small ceremony was taking place. The bailiff had entered the courtroom and was standing at his desk, gavel in hand. The court reporter stood at another door between the judge's chambers and the courtroom, a position from which she could see both Judge Greene and the bailiff. After a few seconds Greene nodded at the reporter, who in turn nodded at the bailiff. He banged his gavel and Greene bustled through the door and up to his perch.

"Please rise," the bailiff said. "Division Four, District Court of and for the state of Colorado is now in session, the honorable Richard D. Greene, judge, presiding. You may be seated and come to order."

Half a dozen prisoners, wearing jail coveralls and slippers, sat on a bench in the rear of the court. The spectator seats were occupied by perhaps two dozen people, including several policemen. Two young prosecutors sat at a table. The yellow walls gave the small, square courtroom an incongruously festive look. The judge folded his hands on his desk and looked impassive.

"Mrs. Beamish," a prosecutor called.

A plain-faced, dark-haired woman in her forties came forward from the spectator area. She was to be sentenced for writing bad checks.

"She seems to write checks whenever she's under pressure, Judge," the prosecutor said. "She has a long record of bad checks and forgery."

"She did it to buy clothes for her children," her lawyer said. "Her husband wouldn't give her any money." The woman's lips quivered. She seemed close to tears. "She's a good wife and mother in every other respect," the attorney said. "I believe she's turned a corner. They've been to a marriage counselor."

"I'm sure she said she was turning a corner the last time she got probation," the judge said. "Somewhere along the line somebody's going to have to protect the victims. She has a record going back to when she was twenty-one." He was looking down at his desk. "She has no regard for authority or for the consequences of her acts. Probation hasn't made any difference."

"She didn't do it for herself, Judge," the lawyer said. The woman put on an expression of determination. "I'm begging this court to give her a chance."

"She's had chances," the judge said. "At some point we come to the end of the road with compassion. Punishment has to get involved. I'm sure that seventy percent of the inmates at the women's prison are mothers."

The lawyer persisted. "What we're talking about here today is hope for the family," he said. "She was bottled up before. The counselors are convinced that she's not a criminal."

Greene was wavering. He picked up a pencil and tapped his desk distractedly. "I'm not convinced of that," he said after a pause. "But I'll continue it ninety days. I'll give her that much consideration. I don't know what I'll do then." His voice seemed to taper off. "I'm pretty well convinced she should go to prison . . . but maybe I can be . . . convinced . . . otherwise."

The lawyer for the next case had not arrived yet, so Greene called a brief recess. "I intended to slap her a weight today," he said in chambers. "But I gave her ninety days so I could think about it. I frankly don't believe that she's reformed. She's a paperhanger by nature and always will be. You see how limited the court is? If she could get out-patient care from a psychiatrist, or if I could put her on a work-release program . . ." (At the end of the ninety days Greene gave her five years probation and a suspended sentence.)

The bailiff came in and said the lawyer was here. He went back into court and the stenographer went to her post at the door. "Okay, troops," Greene said, and the gavel banged again.

The next case was the one we had talked about the preceding evening. The narcotics dealer looked younger than I had imagined him. He was stooped and pasty-faced, with tiny, frightened eyes. He shuffled to his feet and stood with shoulders slumped. A public defender, a young, nattily dressed man with a soft voice, stood beside him.

The prosecutor summed up the case against him. "There were young children involved," he said. "He had school kids working for him, more than forty at one time or another by his own admission."

The public defender replied that the man had probably confessed to more than he was guilty of. "I think the police wanted to get a suspect for all the drug activity in the county and he was willing to volunteer," the lawyer said. "I think some of it is fantasy. My client says he'd like to say a few words to the court."

The man looked at the ceiling, as if scanning it for cue cards. He clasped and unclasped his hands as he spoke. "What I did was wrong, Your Honor," he said, "but I've learned my lesson. I really did. I thought I could get away with anything I wanted, but now I know I can't." He paused for several seconds, seemingly at a loss, then repeated his last line: "Now I know I can't."

Greene spoke for ten minutes before he finally passed sentence. He said he believed that the defendant was sincerely contrite, but that his actions had "resulted in the near-destruction of young people. Sometime," he said, "your life is going to have to be changed and you are going to have to pay the price.

"I will not minimize the gravity of your offense. On the other hand, I am torn by the idea that if I send you behind the walls of Canon City—I feel that you're immature in many respects—that maybe I would be turning out a monster more than I would be doing a service to society." The defendant's expression had changed during Greene's lecture; he was staring hard at the judge now, no longer contrite and pleading.

"My sentence is that you serve a term at the state reformatory not to exceed ten years. I understand that you would be eligible for parole within a year." The judge looked at him and hesitated a moment. "I'm probably being overly fair," he said, "but somehow I think that maybe you are sincere and conceivably we can make a man out of you. Then you and society will both be served."

The prisoner walked back to the row of coveralled men, where an officer put handcuffs on him for his return to jail. He said something out of the side of his mouth to another prisoner. He was smirking as he walked out of court.

Greene returned to his chambers and shed his robe, pulling on a double-knit jacket. "I was struck by his contrition," he said. "He choked up and couldn't finish his little speech. The hardcore criminal either makes his speech with no trouble or says nothing, but he doesn't choke up—it's humiliating to them.

"I was thinking about it while I was trying to get to sleep last night. I figured maybe we can save him. It's an extremely serious decision to send someone to Canon City, and I wasn't satisfied I had to do it. It's a last resort." He folded his arms on his chest. "I decided maybe I shouldn't go by what the police want. I was going to give him fourteen years indeterminate when I went in, but I lowered it to ten in the courtroom."

The judge had a lunch date at his service club, where he held the office of sergeant-at-arms. "I really look forward to these meetings," he said. "The members are go-getters, live wires, I'll tell you. I'm not a judge there, no, sir. I'm just one of the boys." He hurried happily out the door.

Most of the business of Greene's court is criminal law. District Court jurisdiction covers everything above petty misdemeanors and the violation of municipal ordinances—all serious criminal cases, civil suits, juvenile matters, and domestic-relations cases, including divorces. The five judges of the district annually divide up the work, choosing a particular area on the basis of seniority—two handle criminal cases, two deal with civil suits, and one runs juvenile court. Greene ranks fourth in seniority, but says he prefers criminal work, partly because of his experience as a public defender. Domestic-relations cases are split equally among the five. "It would drive all of us dingy otherwise," he says.

The first case on the afternoon docket was a man up for sentencing on a theft conviction. "Martinez. Joe Martinez," the prosecutor called.

He was a strong, broad-shouldered young man of nineteen or twenty, a young Anthony Quinn. A thin, birdlike woman named Miss Bixford, representing a drug-treatment agency, testified that Martinez had been accepted in the program. He was a heroin addict.

Miss Bixford said he suffered from his "bad environment. It's difficult for people like Martinez to move into a more, uh, suitable neighborhood." Martinez gazed at her from beneath drooping eyelids.

"All right, Joe," the judge said. "Lay it on me. What are your plans and motivations?"

"I think I can make it this time," he said. "The worst part is over." He looked uncertainly at Miss Bixford. "I guess I could move. . . ."

"No, I don't want you to move," Greene said. "I don't want to put an economic burden on you. Besides, it's like cigarettes, it's a question of will power. Moving won't help that much."

"I made a mistake," Martinez said. "I feel I should get one chance, and if I blow it, then I'll know what I have to face."

"That's not bad reasoning, Joe," the judge said. "I'll give you a little more motivation. I'm going to sentence you to Canon City for three to five years, but suspend it and put you on probation to the drug program. If you blow it, you go to Canon City." Martinez nodded. "Good luck with the program.

"I liked him," Greene said later. "I think he was candid. He argued one point with the assistant district attorney and I liked that. He wasn't aggressive, but he wasn't afraid either. He said what was on his mind."

One distinction between a general trial court such as Greene's and the lower criminal courts, which are usually limited to misdemeanors, is the occasional surprise visit by a legal principle. Such principles normally appear in the form of a motion asking that a judgment be granted, or denied, because it violates a defendant's rights. ("Law is motions," a Texas judge explained to me. "Jury is showbiz.") Their rarity in the lower courts is due to the lesser stakes involved (misdemeanor penalties seldom exceed two years), the lower caliber of lawyers, and the rush of court business. But for judges at Greene's level, principles pop up just often enough to keep them interested in their work.

After the Supreme Court's capital-punishment decision, for example, Greene ruled that a defendant charged with a "capital" crime could no longer be denied bail. He reasoned that the elimination of the death penalty also eliminated capital crimes as a category, thus permitting bail. The state Supreme Court overruled him. On another motion he ruled a confession invalid because a defendant was not advised of his *Miranda* rights before he took the lie-detector test that prompted the confession. This time the Supreme Court agreed.

Now, in the final case on the day's docket, another principle swam into view. The attorney for a suspect in a rape case asked Greene to deny the prosecutor's request to take samples of the man's pubic hair. The police had found hair at the crime site and wanted to compare it with that of the suspect. The lawyer argued that taking hair samples without the suspect's consent was an "unreasonable search" prohibited by the Fourth Amendment to the Constitution.

"This does present a novel approach to the Fourth Amendment," Greene said. "I want to do some research and write an opinion on it."

Back in his chambers, Greene switched on his radio and sank heavily into his desk chair. "Jesus, this was a long day," he said. I asked him about the Fourth Amendment issue.

"I generally go along with the Warren Court," he said, "the idea that the end does not justify the means. Sometimes evidence may be suppressed and the truth may not come out, but the truth isn't really an absolute, it's the Bill of Rights that's important. The rights are more important than the truth of a given case. I'm sure all kinds of people confessed to crimes they didn't commit before the *Miranda* ruling. People have to know their rights, and we have to protect individual rights.

"I'm going to look up the law on hair samples. I don't know what I'll do on it. The thing that amazes me is that the police bothered to ask—I think we're getting a new breed of policemen."

He called into an adjacent office where his reporter was typing the motion. "Make sure you get that as 'pubic' and not 'public,' Wyona," he said. He turned back to me. "This will be my short-hair decision," he announced.

Two weeks later he ordered the suspect to permit a physician to take the hair samples.

A conscientious judge is forever questioning himself. He wonders if he acted out of his own mood or weakness, whether he is becoming too egotistical or "judgey," if he explained his decision, whether he is thinking too much about publicity and public opinion. His imperfections have the power to sting. He reaches for certainties that always elude him, slipping away in the night. He clothes his frustration in the "temperament" expected of him. His human frailty collides with his dim conception of justice and sends him rattling once again into his endless internal dialogue.

"The ideal judge, whose mood never changes, does not exist," says Richard Greene. "You get tired, or pressed, and there's not a damn thing you can do about it. A judge is not a machine. What you have to do is realize that you're in a mood. I never sentence out of mood; I deliberately try to get 'up' for sentencing." Lawyers, ever the students of judicial moods, have a phrase for the justice dispensed by a foul-tempered jurist: "gastronomic jurisprudence."

"I think newfound authority is always stern," Greene says. "I notice that new judges regularly set bail at five or ten thousand in cases where a more experienced judge makes it a thousand or fifteen hundred. You come on figuring you'll be stern, but pretty soon you realize you can't equate sternness with justice. Some judges never get beyond that first stage."

Greene worries about the pitfalls of judicial ego. "There's no doubt that your ego is constantly nourished as a judge. It's part of the nature of the job and your place in the community. It's difficult for me to talk about. Too many judges believe it when someone calls them Your Honor. It's embarrassing. There's an FBI agent in my neighborhood who stopped calling me Dick when I went on the bench and started calling me Judge.

"But then you don't want to turn it off either. I like to have my name in the paper, sure. You have to feel that you're somebody, not just one of the boys on the bench. You catch yourself wondering whether this or that decision is going to make the paper.

"I know judges who take themselves so seriously that they leave no room for debate. I try to be myself on the bench, but sometimes you have to rise to the occasion. You'll never get me to admit that I feel superior. I know I'm no better than the man on the street. If somebody tells me I've changed since becoming a judge, it bothers me. I'm sensitive to that.

"I think it gets worse as you get older. I find myself getting more volatile than I should be—it's such an over-and-under position, you're over and they're under. I think you're ahead of the game if you're conscious of it. I think I have a certain amount of humility, and I hope I don't lose it. But I probably will."

He frets also about the public's view of the judiciary, especially charges of corruption. "A case like Kerner or Thaler hurts all judges," he says. "We're more vulnerable because of them. There's no way to defend yourself. It's the one thing that really hurts in this job. I can take accusations that I'm wrong or unfair, but not that I was bought off. I'm sure it happens in the big cities, but I've never been offered a thing, no one ever even intimated it. You make a decision that's unusual or that some people don't like and they tag you as a crook."

Greene's diciest moments came when he was shifted to another Colorado district to hear the case involving a judge charged with altering public records—a trial transcript. "It was a felony charge," he recalls. "Intent was the key. He had deleted statements in the record, but I was convinced that there was no criminal culpability. There wasn't any harm to anyone. His motive was vanity.

"The defense asked for a directed verdict of acquittal, but I denied it. I took a chance on the jury because I was sensitive to the criticism that judges protect each other. Then the jury found him guilty. I was so sure that they were going to acquit him that I started to read it as 'not guilty.' My heart went out to him. It's an emotional moment when a judge is knocked off his perch. The defense asked me to reverse the jury verdict, but I denied that too." Judges usually have the authority—rarely and reluctantly exercised—to set aside a conviction if they are not convinced by the evidence.

"Then I went to Canada on vacation. I was thinking about it the whole time. This was a felony conviction—I felt it would ruin his life. The defense renewed its motion asking me to set aside the verdict. I came back and wrote an opinion reversing my earlier decision and acquitting him. Jesus, I got all kinds of anonymous letters and charges that I'd been bought off. What hurt the most is when my mother mentioned it. She asked if I let anyone influence me.

"The easiest thing would have been to let the jury verdict stand and let the Supreme Court reverse it. I think I went overboard trying not to be biased in his favor. I should have acquitted him before it went to the jury. I feel like I've been tested now, though, like I've been down the hump. I saw the judge at a judicial conference afterwards [he was subsequently voted out of office]. He came up to me, but I deliberately avoided him."

Another charge that offends Greene is the familiar plaint about "permissive" judges. "I hear it everywhere I go," he says. "They say we're not stern enough in sentencing. All you can say is that you judge each case individually. It's obvious that harsh sentences haven't deterred crime or slowed it down. Maybe more probation will. Judges feel defensive about it. One judge here quit the Rotary Club when a speaker attacked the courts as permissive. The public believes that, but you can't determine guilt or punishment by popular vote."

When he suspended the sentence of a young man convicted of cutting down several cottonwood trees, a woman wrote an angry letter complaining about "the kind of permissiveness that is causing disrespect and mistrust of our judicial system." She said such sentences encouraged wrongdoers to "laugh at their prospective sentence, knowing that they'll be put on probation, suspended, or sentenced on a lesser charge."

Greene replied with an even longer letter, observing that citizens who pass judgments "without knowing the facts and background" might be a greater menace than "liberal-minded judges." He said that "it takes more courage not to sentence someone, where there is great public pressure, than to sentence him."

"He's kind of impetuous," a defense attorney says of Greene. "He's high and low. He overreacts sometimes, but he's got balls."

"I like the way he sentences," a prosecutor says. "He digs into their backgrounds, but he's no bleeding heart in any sense of the word—he's not a social-worker type. We prefer his sentences to the other judges in the district."

The most frequent criticism lawyers make of Greene is that he sometimes decides too hastily. "He'll make up his mind without knowing all the facts," one says. "In some cases he puts himself in the position of an advocate instead of a judge." Others accuse him of being "image-conscious." They admire his courage and decisiveness.

"He gets quite upset about sex cases," one attorney says. "There was an incest case in his court, and the prosecution was trying to delay the trial so the defendant could get psychiatric treatment. Greene wouldn't go along, he wanted to bring him to trial right away. The prosecution finally told him that their proof was weak, and he stopped pushing. But his impulse was to go after the guy and get him." "I think that he is controlling an inner rage when it comes to sex cases," another says.

"He's neither prosecution- nor defense-oriented," a defense attorney says. "He has a reputation in the jail for being a tough sentencer, but I think he's just difficult to snow. He's particularly good on illegal-search cases. Some judges will permit illegal evidence if the rest of the facts indicate a man is guilty, but he never does."

"I think he's fair," a prosecutor says. "He doesn't like it much when somebody tells him he's wrong, but he has the ability to change his mind. Hell, he even umpires our softball games." He also umpires Little League games.

"He and I were walking along together one time," a friend recalls, "and he was talking about how much we had in common. He said we'd both come from poor families, and we'd both worked our way through law school, we'd both been in trial practice. Then he mentioned how shocked he was by some pornographic books we saw in a store. I said I was shocked too—I wasn't, but I said it. A few minutes later we passed a girl who was wearing one of those micro skirts that came just a little below the water line. Well, we were both kind of straining to look. So I said, 'You know, Dick, it's true that we have a lot in common, we were both from poor families and all that. And we'll both try like hell to look up a girl's skirt.'"

Greene stood at the door to his court, composing himself before he gave the high sign to his waiting reporter. "I'm ready for this," he said. "I was up three times last night thinking about it." He nodded soberly at the reporter and entered the court.

The defendant got slowly to his feet as the judge came in. He was a gnarly, pale, little old man with a sour mouth and dead eyes. This was a pre-sentencing hearing to take psychiatric testimony before the judge sentenced him. A jury had convicted him on two counts of sexually molesting his eleven-year-old grandson. The convictions carried penalties of one to ten years on each count.

The first witness, a bearded psychiatrist, testified that the man was belligerent and uncooperative. "He says he wants to go to prison," the doctor said. He testified that the prisoner was suffering from "deteriorating impulse control" and a "massive denial" of his acts.

The court gallery was empty, save for a single policeman waiting to take the prisoner back to jail. The old man sat with his legs crossed, looking at his shoes. He seemed oblivious to the testimony.

"Do you have an opinion on the issue of castration, Doctor?" the judge asked. Another Colorado judge had recently given a sex offender the choice of castration or jail. He chose castration.

"I don't believe it's appropriate in this case," the psychiatrist replied. "I mean, it's controversial and, well, irreversible." The judge looked noncommittal.

"Do you have any idea what happens to child-molesters at state prison?" Greene asked him. The psychiatrist said he didn't.

Greene handed him a probation report and asked him to read it. The report detailed a series of homosexual acts that the man had forced on his grandson. "Do you still contend that he has only a mild depressive adjustment to adult life?" he asked.

"The details don't change my diagnosis," he replied.

A second psychiatrist, a younger, bespectacled man, was called to the stand. He testified that the treatment possibilities were remote because the man refused to admit his guilt.

"He is suffering a severe depression," he said. "He hasn't had sex with his wife for three years. He's no longer any good sexually." The old man didn't look up. "I think he might be helped in a closed setting, even though he's uncooperative. He needs hospitalization."

"Can depression be treated?" Greene asked.

"It's the one psychiatric illness that can be," the witness replied.

"What do you think would happen to him at Canon City?"

"I don't know. But it's not the treatment I'd recommend for

depression." The psychiatrist smiled weakly. He did know that child-molesters were unpopular with other inmates. The prisoner closed his eyes.

"These acts," the doctor said, "were a way of trying to deal with impotency."

The judge called a recess. The prisoner muttered as he got to his feet. "That was worthless," Greene said in chambers. "They're just fencing, it's mental gymnastics." He angrily slapped a sheaf of papers in his hand. "Sure, put him in a 'closed setting.' I don't *have* a closed setting."

He sat down at his desk and let the tension drain away. "That poor, pathetic old bastard," he said. "You saw this," he said, pointing to the probation report. "He's an animal, for Christ's sake. His whole family's afraid of him." He leaned back. "Jesus, I was looking at him sitting there. Poor old bastard. He's just withering away. His life's really over. They were talking about his sex life and he didn't even blink."

"Phone for you, Judge," his secretary called. "It's about the golf exhibition."

He picked up the phone. "Hi, Bill," he said. "I think we're all set with Trevino. We've just got to arrange some transportation at the airport." Greene's service club was sponsoring an exhibition by Lee Trevino to raise money for charity. "Okay. I'll be talking to you.

"Let's go back in and get it over with," he said.

The prosecutor argued for a prison sentence. "He can't be tolerated on the streets," he said. "He simply does what he wants to do when he wants to. His behavior was inexcusable. It demands a prison term."

"I don't know how long he'd live in Canon City," the public defender answered. "I don't think this is going to happen again. It won't help his grandson to know his grandfather died in prison."

Finally the man spoke, staring steadily at the floor and talking in a sour snarl. "There were three charges," he said. "The jury found me not guilty on two of 'em. It's supposed to be given in a courtroom." No one asked what he meant.

Greene held his breath and let it out slowly. "The court feels the psychiatric testimony was shallow," he began. "The psychiatrist recommended a closed facility. We have no such facility.

"These offenses were extremely onerous. I can't visualize how you could get involved with a young boy like this. You ruined his life to a great extent." The old man didn't look up. Beads of perspiration appeared on Greene's forehead.

"I can't find any compassion for you. It's unfortunate that this happened at your stage of life, but this is one of the worst types of offense to come before this court since the court, ah, has been on the bench. I can't blind myself to this record of fifteen incidents over three months, and the manner in which they were done. It's treacherous, devastating." The man looked up without curiosity.

"I sentence you to serve four to eight years on each count, to be served consecutively." The judge swallowed. "That's the judgment of the court."

The man got up and extended his arms to be handcuffed.

Greene returned to his chambers. "He'll be eligible for parole in four years," he said. "I figured this way he'd be on parole for the rest of his life." He was perspiring heavily. "Wyona," he called, "bring me some coffee and aspirin, will you, please?

"That bit about depression—that was just something for the psychiatrists to hang their hats on. I was going to give him five to eight on each count, but lowered it to four. I wanted him on parole for life."

He took off his robe. "God, I'm just coming down," he said. "I get butterflies whenever I send someone to Canon City. I feel flushed. It's like when you're going to perform. I don't like to do it. I kept trying to think if there was any alternative, but there wasn't. I just resigned myself to doing what I had to do.

"The poor bastard," he said. "He was talking about the jury verdict—I didn't know what the hell he was talking about."

The secretary arrived with aspirin and coffee. "Jesus," he said, "I'm just getting my breath back."

XI

Justice at the Barricades
The politics of confrontation
and violence invades the courts

THE POLICEMEN ARRIVED EARLY, while the morning fog was still caressing the low hills between San Rafael and the Pacific. They drove up in the patrol cars of a dozen different cities and towns of the San Francisco Bay Area and parked two blocks from the mortuary. They talked quietly as they walked to where the maroon hearse waited.

After a while the pallbearers appeared at the mortuary door. The policemen, aligned in ordered ranks, came to attention as the casket containing the body of Superior Court Judge Harold Haley was carried to the hearse. The officers fell in alongside as the hearse pulled slowly out of the driveway, followed by the other cars in the procession. Clusters of people stood on the sidewalks in front of stores closed for the day. The flags on San Rafael's downtown buildings were at half-mast.

The cortege passed the old Marin County Courthouse, where Judge Haley had spent most of his working life as city attorney, district attorney, municipal judge, and finally superior judge. Not long ago the courts and offices had moved to the meandering, Frank Lloyd Wright–designed civic center, where the judge had been murdered three days earlier.

When the mourners reached the next corner, the police broke ranks and returned to their cars. Red lights flashing, the many-colored police cars—white, black and white, metallic blue, soft green—joined the slow parade to St. Sylvester's Catholic Church, where more than 750 people had gathered for a funeral mass. Archbishop Joseph McGucken was there, Mayor Joseph Alioto of San Francisco, Chief Justice Donald Wright of the California Supreme Court, the Marin County supervisors, and Haley's brother judges. Groups of policemen, priests, and nuns sat together.

"He was a man who was clothed with dignity and strength," Father John Tierney said in his eulogy, a man "who listened attentively to the truth." He mentioned that the judge would not permit prisoners in his courtroom to be shackled. His last recorded words, the priest said, were, "Remember, there are human lives at stake here."

Haley had been presiding at the trial of three black San Quentin inmates. He had ordered their shackles removed. Suddenly the three produced guns, which had been smuggled into court by a seventeen-year-old friend. They seized Haley, a prosecutor, and three women jurors, forcing them outside to a van that was waiting in a parking lot. The kidnappers demanded the immediate release of the "Soledad Brothers," three convicts whose long imprisonment had transformed them into a black rallying cry. An unforgettable photograph showed the captive judge with a loaded shotgun taped to his neck. At the van, shots were fired—who fired first has never been resolved. When it was over, the judge and three of the four fugitives were dead. The fourth, Ruchell Magee, and prosecutor Gary Thomas were wounded.

The murder of Judge Haley was one of those events which focus the fears and tensions of their time and imprint a vivid picture on our tribal memory. It came in the summer of 1970, as the heat of a decade of confrontation seemed finally to be abating, and it seemed simultaneously to cap that decade, to carry it to its ultimate confrontation between law and outlaw, and to puncture the phantom vision of harmony which followed it. Haley was caught—between races, between ins and outs, between rebellion and reaction, between an era of passion aflame and another of passion spent. He was a symbolic victim in every sense of that phrase: he was chosen as a symbol, not for any acts of his own; his murder marked, however imperfectly, a junction in our history; and Haley in death—cruel destiny of martyrs—had a significance far greater than in life.

The impact of his death was profound. It shocked and frightened the legal order as no other event had done. The precarious, uncertain truce between the society's anointed protectors and its rebels was shattered. The vulnerability of the system, the fragile structure of "consent" and "respect" on which it depends, was laid bare. The revolution, generally quiescent since the nightmares of 1968 and before, had surfaced in a courtroom, in the very shrine of the law. On the day of Haley's funeral a judge in San Francisco asked that the upcoming trial of the Soledad Brothers be transferred from a courthouse to San Quentin prison. The vision of the robed and helpless Haley burned in the minds of a thousand judges, haunted them, moved them to question their premises. It would be a long time before they forgot it.

The judge in a political trial occupies one of the thorniest seats a democracy offers. He is embattled within and without. Within himself he has to confront his own loyalties and weigh them: the ideal of justice, the preservation of peace and order as he sees it, the commandments of law, the values of the society he represents, and, tucked away in a curtained corner of his mind, his own well-being, reputation, and ambition. On the outside he must referee a clash of dogmas and find what equity he can amid the smoke of political and social conflict, secure in the knowledge that condemnation awaits him whatever the outcome, and that the revolutionary has already written him off as a slave to the ruling class. It is difficult enough for the most enlightened jurists in their oaken aeries, and considerably more than that for the majority who, like Sam Rayburn, get along by going along.

In the 1920s, when the enemies of the American state included a savory selection of socialists, labor organizers, anarchists, and rum-runners, H. L. Mencken beheld the judiciary and dismissed them as so many "dogberries." "A judicial process before them," he wrote, "is indistinguishable from a bull-fight, with the accused, if he is unpopular enough, as the bull. . . . Judges tend to show . . . decay of the faculties in exaggerated form; they become mere automata, bound by arbitrary rules, precedents, the accumulated imbecilities of generations of bad logic; to their primary lack of sense as lawyers they add the bombastic manner of bureaucrats. It is thus too much to hope for a judge showing any originality or courage; one Holmes in an era of Hardings and Coolidges is probably more than a fair allotment."

Political trials, says Texas law professor Albert Alschuler, "bring out not only the worst in judges, but the worst judges. From Joseph Gary in the Haymarket trial, to Webster Thayer in the Sacco-Vanzetti case, to Julius Hoffman in the trial of the Chicago Seven . . ." Alschuler concludes, rather too generously, that "the luck of the draw has not seemed entirely satisfactory."

Gary presided at the trial of eight anarchist leaders in Chicago in 1886. The anarchists were accused of conspiracy to commit murder as a result of a riot that left seven policemen dead. Gary permitted the seating of jurors who admitted prejudice against the defendants. In his charge, he told the jury that it was enough for a finding of guilt "to believe that there was a conspiracy to overthrow the existing order of society and that the defendants were party to such a conspiracy," which may have been the most sweeping interpretation ever of the always broad conspiracy statute. He sentenced seven of the defendants to death and the eighth to life imprisonment, later reduced to fifteen years. The Supreme Court upheld the verdicts. Four were eventually executed and a fifth died in prison.

Seven years later Illinois Governor John Peter Altgeld granted full pardons to the three survivors. He said his study of the record convinced him that Gary had "conducted the trial with malicious ferocity . . . that every ruling throughout the long trial on any contested point was in favor of the state," and that the eight had not been proven guilty.

D. C. Westenhaver was the judge at the 1918 trial of Socialist leader Eugene Debs in Cleveland federal court. The sixty-three-year-old Debs, a perennial presidential candidate, was charged with violating the Espionage Act by speaking against American participation in World War I, and with obstructing the draft. Mencken said the trial illustrated "the doctrine that, in wartime, the rights guaranteed by the First Amendment cease to have any substance."

Judge Westenhaver, a former law partner of War Secretary Newton Baker, was regarded as honest and industrious, though a man of "narrow sympathies." He ordered the arrest of several spectators for applauding the opening statement of Debs's attorney. During the trial he consistently overruled defense objections to government testimony. Debs, certain that he would be convicted, presented no witnesses.

The judge, pronouncing himself a "conserver of the peace and a defender of the Constitution," sentenced Debs to ten years. He condemned "those persons within our borders who would strike the sword from the hand of this nation while she is engaged in defending herself against a foreign and brutal power." Justice Oliver Wendell Holmes wrote the Supreme Court opinion upholding the verdict.

Debs entered federal prison—"my spirit untamed and my soul unconquerable"—in 1919. He became known as "Little Jesus" to his fellow inmates. President Harding pardoned him on Christmas 1921.

Earlier that year Nicola Sacco and Bartolomeo Vanzetti were tried for murder before Superior Court Judge Webster Thayer in Dedham, Massachusetts. Sacco and Vanzetti, Italian immigrants and anarchists, were accused of killing two men during a payroll robbery. Judge Thayer was widely criticized for his heavy-handed, biased conduct of the trial. The judge's attitude was described years later by Boston attorney Joseph Welch, who became nationally known during the Army-McCarthy hearings in the 1950s.

Thayer "believed Sacco and Vanzetti to be guilty," Welch wrote, a belief that "was not merely an intellectual conclusion on his part, but a passionate dedication to the proposition that the two of them were to die. . . . Judge Thayer was beyond persuasion. He was not to be moved by reason. He was, in this case, incapable of showing mercy." Dartmouth professor James Richardson, who met Thayer after the trial, quoted him as asking, "Did you see what I did with those anarchistic bastards the other day? I guess that will hold them for a while."

In 1925 a man in prison for another murder confessed that he had participated in the payroll killings and said that Sacco and Vanzetti were innocent. The authority to grant a new trial rested with Thayer, but he denied their plea. Thayer sentenced Sacco and Vanzetti to death, and they were executed amid worldwide protest in 1927.

Proposals for posthumous pardons have been debated down to recent years, and regularly rejected by Massachusetts authorities. In 1972 the National Park Service suggested that the Dedham courthouse be made a national landmark, describing the trial as an example of "hostility to radicals, antipathy to foreigners, and a jealous protection of the status quo." But the subject is still sensitive in Massachusetts. Superior Court Chief Justice Walter McLaughlin lambasted the proposal as "a smear upon the administration of justice in this Commonwealth."

Federal Judge Harold Medina was assigned to the 1949 trial of eleven leaders of the American Communist Party accused of conspiring to advocate violent revolution. At the time, Medina confessed some years later, "I really didn't know what a Communist was. I thought of them as sort of roughnecks who wanted to divide up our property and have a good time with it, but that was about all."

The main issue, as Medina saw it, was whether the American system was up to judging Communists. ". . . If they succeeded in knocking me out," he wrote, "or in having some mistrial come about, then they could do it the next time, and the next time, and the next time. And you never, according to our constitutional and traditional methods of administering justice, could convict a Communist."

Medina's court became a political theater. A defendant refused to answer prosecution questions, and the judge promptly gave him thirty days for contempt. "That whole courtroom rose as one man," he recalled. "The yelling and shouting and hullabalooing that went on, you never heard such a thing." The outbursts were repeated, convincing the judge that it was an organized plot "to break me down." He received threats and suggestions that he commit suicide, which unnerved him so that he was afraid to leave his apartment windows open at night for fear that he might want to leap out. He attributed this fear to Communist brainwashing. "The men who thought this up were demons," he said. "And if you remember how many times in Russian history people have jumped out windows . . . I used to think they pushed the people out the window. But they don't need to do that."

In the end his doubts about the system's capacity to deal with Communists were quelled. The jury convicted all eleven defendants and he sentenced them to prison terms of between three and five years. In addition, he sent six defense lawyers, including George Crockett, to jail for between thirty days and six months on contempt charges, sentences that some critics believe deterred first-rate lawyers from defending radicals in succeeding years. Medina's reputation emerged intact, even enhanced: two years later President Truman appointed him to the Second Circuit Court of Appeals.

In the 1960s, political trials in America entered a sort of golden era. First the civil-rights movement, then the anti-war movement, then the explosion of black militance and the escalation of campus protest into generalized rebellion—one after another, the waves of the day washed over the courts. The dissidents turned from seeking vindication in the legal process to challenging its legitimacy. Dr. Benjamin Spock and the Rev. William Sloane Coffin rested their case with the Constitution (with ultimate success). But Tom Hayden and Abbie Hoffman, LeRoi Jones and Angela Davis and the Rev. Daniel Berrigan took theirs to "the people," that sacred if elusive repository of justice and wisdom. "We've learned this," said Chicago Seven defendant Tom Hayden, "that *law serves power* and nothing else." "A fair trial," said black revolutionary Angela Davis after her acquittal, "would have been no trial at all."

The charges varied: sometimes, as with poet-playwright LeRoi Jones (later Imamu Baraka) and Miss Davis, the accusations concerned acts with no apparent political relevance—carrying a weapon, conspiracy to murder; other times, as with Dr. Spock and the Chicago Seven, the "crimes" were directly related to political activity—conspiracy to obstruct the draft law, crossing state lines with intent to riot. It was the difference between the physical and the mental act, between deed and thought, captured neatly by Abbie Hoffman when he testified, "I've never been on trial for my thoughts before." In most cases the political character of the prosecution was clear from the defendants' identities, whatever the charge: they were the leaders of the underground, avatars of the Fifth Column, the loudest voices for change and/or upheaval.

Even American taste in courtroom drama was affected. The national fascination with sensational sex-and-murder cases—the lust-crazed defendant, the purloined letters, the web of deceit, the hint of madness—yielded to a preference for trials-as-political-statements—the "higher law," the oppressed minority, the calls to conscience, the blind violence of authority. As a magazine reporter with a weakness for trials, I was dispatched in the mid-sixties to such spectacles as the Sheppard trial in Cleveland and the Coppolino trial in New Jersey. Indulging the same weakness later in the decade, I found myself present at the Spock trial in Boston and the Bobby Seale trial in New Haven. The news stories abandoned psychological depth in favor of ideological breadth; our interest seemed to shift from Sam Sheppard's tormented psyche to the morality of our foreign policy. Trials did not have names any more, they had places and numbers; the Chicago Seven, the Catonsville Nine, the Harrisburg Seven, the Seattle Seven (the favored number), the Camden Twenty-eight, the Gainesville Eight. The last sex-and-murder trial to seize the public imagination was probably the Manson trial in Los Angeles in 1970, and even that (Manson lunging at the judge with a pencil) borrowed some of its touches from the theater of confrontation.

The era's demands on judicial strength, restraint, and character were not new; they were just more frequent. The other difference, from the judge's perspective, was that retreat behind the curtain of law was more difficult now; a judge who didn't like blacks or longhairs or revolutionaries was easier to recognize; the offending parties could spot his weakness, rub it raw, and exploit it. They talked back.

U.S. Judge Francis Ford was eighty-five, the oldest active judge in the federal judiciary, when he presided at the 1968 trial of Spock, Coffin, and three other anti-war leaders for conspiracy to counsel young men to evade the draft. Ford was a pink-faced, thick-bodied veteran of Boston politics, a onetime holder of the Harvard broad-jump record, and a classmate of Franklin D. Roosevelt, who had given him his job thirty years earlier.

Ford was regarded as tough-minded and knowledgeable, with a record of infrequent reversals. But his conduct of the Spock trial betrayed a consistent prosecution bias. He badgered defense attorneys and indulged the prosecutor. He raised his eyebrows at defense testimony. When Dr. Spock was asked if many Americans agreed with his opposition to the war and replied that they did, the judge ordered the testimony stricken. When Spock conceded that many disagreed with him, the judge said, "Let it stand."

Writer Jessica Mitford reported a whispered comment Ford made to his clerk concerning a statement by the prosecutor. "Tell that son of a bitch to cut it out," the judge said. "He'll blow this case if he keeps it up, and get us all in trouble." After four of the five defendants were found guilty, Ford said at their sentencing that they were convicted of "what amounts to rebellion against the law," quoting an ante-bellum Southern judge's opinion that "rebellion against the law is in the nature of treason." He sentenced the four to two years in prison, but the verdict was overturned by the First Circuit Court of Appeals.

The LeRoi Jones trial grew out of the Newark ghetto riot of 1967. Jones, a militant black leader, was stopped by police during the riot and charged with possession of a pistol. He was tried before County Judge Leon Kapp of suburban East Orange.

During the trial Kapp took over the questioning of witnesses hostile to Jones, ordering them to repeat particularly damaging testimony. His jury charge portrayed the policemen as embattled heroes in blue and Jones as a vicious and dangerous man. The jury found Jones guilty.

Before sentencing Jones, the judge read aloud from an anti-white poem he had written. Kapp looked up from the poem and told Jones, "You are in the vanguard of a group of extreme radicals who advocate the destruction—"

"Of unrighteousness," Jones interrupted.

"If the philosopher can make his own law, so can the fool," the judge said.

"We see that," Jones replied. He was sentenced to two and a half to three years and fined $1000. "You don't represent almighty God," Jones cried, "you represent a crumbling system!"

"Sit down," the judge ordered.

"The black people will judge me," Jones retorted.

Political scientists Kenneth Dolbeare and Joel Grossman, in an analysis of the trial, concluded that the main reason for Jones's conviction was that "he was an 'ungrateful Negro' who refused to humble himself before . . . 'the ship's captain.'" An appellate court ordered a retrial, at which Jones was acquitted.

Not all judges have let their prejudices guide them in dealing with radicals. U.S. District Judge Roszel Thomson of Baltimore presided with an even-handed equilibrium applauded by both sides at the trial of the Catonsville Nine, two of whom were the brothers Berrigan. Superior Court Judge Richard Arnason of California was praised for his handling of the Angela Davis trial.

Judge George Phillips, Jr., of the Oakland Seven trial, a case involving anti-war activity by white radicals, was another who checked his bias, if he had any, at the courtroom door. New York Judge Arnold Fraiman, a sometime contestant in the Boston Marathon and the judge who pronounced a five-to-fifteen-year

sentence on H. Rap Brown for armed robbery and assault, remarked as he did so that Brown had "devoted much of your life to
helping your fellow man."

As the arena of protest shifted from streets to courts, the tactics
of street confrontations infiltrated courthouses. The logic was
inexorable. "We came to Chicago in August 1968 to disrupt the
ritual and sham which is ordinarily put over as the democratic
process," said Chicago Seven defendant Rennie Davis. "Now we are
disrupting the ritual and sham which Judge Hoffman calls the
judicial process."

His co-defendant Tom Hayden called for "a total attack on the
courts. . . . There is no reason," he said, "for us to become submissive at the courtroom door."

Thus the challenge was hurled: revolutionary *macho* v. judicial
macho, best four out of seven. Hayden's "submissiveness" was a
judge's "decorum," a word with layers of special meaning to a
judge. To disdain submissiveness was to violate judicial decorum;
it was to insult the system and to provoke its wrath.

In Tacoma, Washington, radicals on trial for damaging a
federal courthouse tossed a Nazi flag at Federal Judge George
Boldt and screamed invective at him. Later, when they refused to
enter the courtroom, Boldt declared a mistrial and jailed them for
contempt. Spectators at a Black Panther trial in New York became
so disorderly that a policemen's organization asked that the judge
be reprimanded for irresponsibility.

When New York Judge Joseph Martinis sentenced another
Black Panther to life imprisonment for the attempted machine-gun
murder of two policemen, the defendant stalked out and sent word
back that "my appeal will be over the barrel of a gun."

"What?" cried the startled judge. The court clerk glumly repeated the threat.

Courthouses were bombed or damaged in Los Angeles, Oakland,
New York, and even Des Moines, Iowa. Dozens of judges were
threatened, and a few were attacked: an Oklahoma judge was
injured when his home was bombed; explosives were set off at the
homes of judges in Worcester, Massachusetts, and Des Moines.
"All of a sudden I realized how vulnerable I was," one apprehensive
judge told me. Jurors were not exempt. A murder defendant in
Washington threw a bag of human waste at his federal-court
jurors, spattering some of them.

"Some individuals will do as much in a courtroom as they think they can get away with," said Municipal Judge Luther Glanton, Jr., of Des Moines, a Negro. "If someone made a physical attack on me, I'd protect myself by whatever means I considered necessary. If that meant utilizing forces at hand endangering the life of an assailant, then that's what I'd do."

All the strains of political confrontation, disruption, and mutual paranoia came together in the Chicago Seven trial before Judge Julius Hoffman. The long, much-publicized trial shredded any grandeur from its participants, illustrating at once the corruptive cruelty of judicial power gone wrong and the shallow charade of mindless disruption.

The defendants were a cross-section of 1960s dissenters— young radicals Hayden and Davis, yippies Abbie Hoffman and Jerry Rubin, middle-aged pacifist David Dellinger, Black Panther leader Bobby Seale, and teachers Lee Weiner and John Froines. They were charged under a year-old statute forbidding the crossing of state lines for the purpose of inciting a riot, the accusation stemming from the demonstrations during the 1968 Democratic convention in Chicago.

Judge Hoffman was a 1953 Eisenhower appointee, a banty man who had once taught law at Northwestern and had been a state-court judge. Some lawyers referred to him disparagingly as "Julius the Just." "He had always been difficult," a Chicago attorney said. "It just came out more in the conspiracy trial because there were people crazy enough to talk back to him."

The judge's demeanor was irritably hostile to the defendants and their attorneys, and his rulings consistently went against them. He refused to permit the defendants to introduce documents which described their purpose in coming to Chicago that summer. He mocked and ridiculed their arguments. He consistently mispronounced a defense attorney's name. He would not allow testimony by former Attorney General Ramsey Clark and civil-rights leader Ralph Abernathy.

The defendants baited him. They appeared in court in judicial robes, called the judge a pig, a fascist, and a runt, blew kisses to the jury, walked in one day with a birthday cake. "Our strategy was to give Judge Hoffman a heart attack," Rubin said. The flash point of the trial was Hoffman's decision to deny Seale's request to represent himself. The judge dealt with Seale's repeated outbursts first by binding and gagging him, and finally by severing him from the trial.

"Hoffman was not temperamentally suited to the trials of this trial," said Yale law professor Alexander Bickel. "He intruded himself—Julius Hoffman, not the judge—often and imprudently. He was engaged, embattled." Bickel added that defense attorneys William Kunstler and Leonard Weinglass "early destroyed the confidence that normally prevails between a judge and officers of his court." Hoffman's manner reminded reporter J. Anthony Lukas of "a spinster schoolteacher in a classroom of unruly children, forever rapping a ruler for order and sending children to stand in the corner, but stirring more trouble with each new act of discipline."

Near the end of the trial a trembling Kunstler exploded, "There is no meaning in this court, there is no law in this court, and these men are going to jail by virtue of a legal lynching!" Hoffman proceeded to lay down what was probably the heaviest fusillade of contempt sentences in U.S. history, ranging up to four years for Kunstler on twenty-four separate counts. The jury convicted five of the seven on the inciting-to-riot charge.

After the trial Judge Hoffman was invited to the White House, where he attended a prayer breakfast led by Billy Graham. In a speech a few months later President Nixon bewailed the "glorifying [of] those who deliberately disrupt" and said we must recognize "that when a judge necessarily, after intense provocation, must hold individuals in contempt of court, that judge is justified [and] acting in our behalf. . . ."

The Seventh Circuit Court of Appeals disagreed, overturning both the riot convictions and the contempt citations. The appellate court described the judge's courtroom manner as "antagonistic" to the defendants, and declared that "the demeanor of the judge and the prosecutors would require reversal if other errors did not." Earlier Judge Hoffman had told a reporter, "If I had to do it over again, I'd do exactly the same." In 1972 he went on semi-retired senior status, moving to a smaller courtroom several floors below his old one.

"A disruptive trial, gentlemen, is a rare phenomenon. We took a poll of misdemeanor-court judges like yourselves and we couldn't

find one who had had one." The speaker, Judge Tim Murphy of the Washington, D.C., Superior Court, looked out at his audience of seventy-four sport-shirted judges at the Reno judges' school. "But I can tell you this. If you get a political trial, you're between a rock and a hard place."

Murphy's lecture came on the first night of the judges' two-week stay in Reno. Before the week was out, the judges had seen films of disruptive trials in Seattle and Chicago and worried the subject further in discussion groups.

"How many of you anticipate a mass-arrest situation in your town?" Murphy asked.

Between twenty and twenty-five judges raised their hands.

"How many have a plan for it?"

Two hands went up.

"What do you do if you have seven hundred people arrested and they won't tell you their names?" he went on. "That happened at the May Day [1971] demonstrations in Washington. We'd ask their names and they'd say Spiro Agnew, Mickey Mouse, anything. Are they in contempt?

"Contempt is getting tighter all the time," he said. "The appellate courts are looking carefully at it. In 1631 a defendant threw a brickbat at a judge in England. The judge ordered his hand cut off and then had him hanged." Murphy sighed. "But those were the good old days," he said. The judges laughed.

"Disruption won't last without the help of defense counsel," he continued. "Be cautious, keep your cool, and save your big guns for the lawyers, who ought to know better. If you act quickly and cite for contempt right when it happens, you're home free. If you wait, like Hoffman did, you're in a thicket."

The Chicago trial came up again in a discussion group. The judges had just seen the film based on the trial transcript.

"Hoffman was obviously biased for the prosecution," a judge from Michigan observed. "The defense counsel wasn't given a chance. Sometimes the judge gave no reasons for his rulings."

"Wait a minute," a judge from Alaska said. "I think it's a mistake to give your reasons for a ruling anyway. It just gets you into arguments." Judge Alaska had the pale, dry look of a persecuted clerk.

"I thought he was biased," said Judge Rhode Island. "The poor guy was badgered, sure, but he was the old-style, 'I-am-the-law' kind of judge, pompous. He got personally involved."

"A judge can have a legitimate dislike for lawyers or defendants at the end of a trial as long as he starts out unbiased," Alaska declared. *"I mean, that's their problem, isn't it? They created it."*

"He took umbrage at things he should have let pass," Judge Idaho said.

"Well, how much crap are you supposed to let pass?" Alaska replied. *"Are you supposed to let them call you a Nazi and a pig and everything else? If we get in a position where anyone can disrupt a trial if he's unhappy with a ruling . . ."*

"Wasn't the judge contemptuous in not giving the reasons for his rulings?" Judge Washington asked. No one replied.

"Well, it was a weak case," Alaska said at last. *"It never should have come to trial."*

"It was political, for Christ's sake," Idaho said.

The 1973 conspiracy-espionage trial of Dr. Daniel Ellsberg was a different kind of political trial. Ellsberg, who admitted copying and releasing the secret Pentagon Papers, was no radical hotspur, but rather a scholarly intellectual with a background of loyal government service. His judge, William Matthew Byrne, Jr., was one of the few Democrats appointed by the Nixon administration, a diligent, cautious, and ambitious man with a cool courtroom manner.

Byrne's appointment came about through one of the accommodations of power that lubricate politics. The son of a senior federal judge, he was first nominated for a judgeship in the waning weeks of the Johnson administration, then withdrawn from consideration by Nixon. But he had admirers in the Nixon Justice Department, notably former Attorney General Richard Kleindienst. He also benefited from a deal, worked out between the administration and California's Democratic senators, which guaranteed the selection of a modest number of Democrats. He had further enriched his dossier by serving as executive director of President Nixon's Commission on Campus Unrest.

Byrne handled the delicate complexities of the trial with dogged conscientiousness. "He's determined not to make a mistake," a friend said. His even-handed demeanor began to erode only when it became apparent that the prosecution was dawdling in obeying his orders, especially his request to see government reports on whether release of the Pentagon Papers was harmful to the "national interest." Byrne's impatience with the government mounted through subsequent disclosures of federal wiretaps on Ellsberg's telephone and the break-in of his psychiatrist's office by White House "plumbers." He finally dismissed all charges against Ellsberg "with prejudice," declaring that the government's conduct precluded a fair trial.

Questions were raised about the conduct of Byrne himself when it developed that he had discussed a possible appointment as director of the FBI with presidential aide John Ehrlichman while the Ellsberg trial was going on. Ehrlichman told the Senate Watergate Committee that Byrne showed "very strong interest" in the job, a statement later denied by the judge.

The combination of the Chicago Seven trial and the murder of Judge Haley in San Rafael, coming within six months of each other in 1970, sent shock waves through the judiciary and the entire legal Establishment. Judges who blanched at the thought of weapons began carrying sidearms in court. Three out of one group of twelve small-town judges at the Reno school admitted to wearing a pistol under their robes. City judges in Detroit, New York, Los Angeles, and elsewhere did the same. Federal-court judges in Atlanta had their benches armor-plated. Others asked for twenty-four-hour protection. Security tightened in courtrooms across the land—briefcases were searched and identification was demanded in the lobbies of many federal courthouses. Guards at the U.S. Supreme Court searched the purses of women tourists before permitting them to enter the nation's highest palladium of justice.

A conference of Washington state judges was treated to a demonstration of a metal-detecting device which, they were told, had uncovered seven pistols and two thousand knives in the courthouse where Judge Haley was abducted. A policeman showed the attentive jurists a selection of particularly insidious weapons, including a mine detonator concealed in a ballpoint pen and a lawbook wired to explode when opened.

Four sheets of bulletproof laminex were installed between the spectator areas and the courts in San Rafael, and closed-circuit television kept an eye on visitors. Worried judges ordered the laminex shields without waiting for approval by the board of supervisors and without asking for competitive bids. At the first trial of Ruchell Magee for the murder of Judge Haley (which ended in a hung jury), spectators were photographed, assigned to numbered seats in a glassed-off gallery, and searched by platoons of guards. A woman reporter for the San Francisco *Chronicle* described the process:

"I walked behind the partition, routinely went through a light body frisk and waited for one of the two matrons to hand over my purse.

" 'Shake out your bra' was the command. . . . I put my hands under my blouse and shook. I straightened my clothing and started to move over to the exit end of the partition.

" 'Drop your pants.' Completely embarrassed, I stood and stared at her a few seconds in disbelief. . . . I unbuckled my belt, dropped my jeans and saw she was waiting for me to let go of my underpants.

"I dropped them around my knees, she took a quick glance and I jerked my clothes back around my waist—this time positive it was all over.

" 'Take off your shoes,' she said. I looked down at my sandaled feet, shrugged and obliged. She checked out my soles."

The American Bar Association formed a committee of lawyers and architects to study the feasibility of installing plastic chambers or bubbles for defendants, as Israel had done for the trial of Adolf Eichmann. Attorney Louis Nizer suggested leaving an obstreperous defendant in his jail cell and connecting him with his trial by telephone. In addition, he proposed making serious courtroom misconduct a felony, with penalties comparable to those for robbery or assault.

The administrative justice of the Connecticut Supreme Court asked the state legislature for $1 million for more guards and electronic detection devices, thoughtfully including a collection of news stories about courtroom attacks in his memo to legislators. Sessions devoted to "unruly trials" and "expanded courtroom security and personal safety" began to appear on the agendas of judicial conferences and the seminars for fledgling judges at the Federal Judicial Center in Washington.

Patrolling another front, Chief Justice Warren Burger delivered a sonorous attack on what he called the "decline in civility," especially among lawyers.

". . . All too often," he said, "overzealous advocates seem to think the zeal and effectiveness of a lawyer depend on how thoroughly he can disrupt the proceedings or how loud he can shout or how close he can come to insulting all those he encounters—including the judges. . . .

"At the drop of a hat—or less—we find adrenal-fueled lawyers cry out that theirs is a 'political trial.' This seems to mean in today's context—at least to some—that rules of evidence, canons of ethics and codes of professional conduct—the necessity for civility—all become irrelevant."

Finally the overwrought huffing and puffing about "security" and "civility" began to wane, and some signs of perspective returned. A court that excludes or walls off the accused, critics pointed out, tends to threaten such elemental freedoms as the right to confront one's accuser, not to mention the effect such safeguards have on a jury's opinion of the defendant.

Reviewing the chief justice's speech, Yale law professor Fred Rodell found no less than five critical references to the "news media," apparently a particular stone in his craw. Rodell recalled an observation by Justice William Douglas a generation ago that "judges are supposed to be men of fortitude, able to thrive in a hardy climate."

A study of courtroom security commissioned by New York state courts rejected bulletproof shields and armor-plated benches as "inappropriate," commenting that a courthouse is allegedly "a place where justice is dispensed freely and openly." The ABA issued a guide for trial judges containing advice on how to handle disruptions, suggesting that judicial patience and self-restraint might be the place to start.

The New York City Bar Association punched another hole in the fantasies of frightened judges. The group surveyed 1600 judges on their experience with disruption, discovering that only 37 had issued contempt citations and that just 6 of those were administered to uncivil lawyers.

Harvard law professor Arthur Sutherland offered one possible explanation for distress among conservative judges: "You've got a new selection of lawyers, inspired by Ralph Nader," he said, "and they are getting in there and ruffling the hair of a lot of people because they are insisting on poor people getting rights."

Federal Judge A. Leon Higgenbotham of Philadelphia brought

the point home: "When I look at the extraordinary forms and excessive attention given to disruption in trial courts," he told an ABA meeting, "I think we are sort of lost in this country. . . . If we got down to the more important reasons—poverty, racism, injustice—it would do more to limit disruptions in the courtroom."

The main peril to justice, in the view of Stanford law professor Anthony Amsterdam, is not unruly defendants; it is an all too frequent judicial bias against criminal suspects. "A few appellate judges . . . can throw off the fetters of their middle-class backgrounds and identify with the criminal suspect instead of with the policeman or the putative victim," he says. "Trial judges still more, and magistrates beyond all belief, are functionally and psychologically allied with the police, their co-workers in the unending and scarifying work of bringing criminals to book."

Amsterdam lists several reasons for what he considers a widespread judicial bias for the prosecution. "Disproportionately often," he says, judges are ex-prosecutors, and only rarely were they criminal defense attorneys. Most judges seek advancement, and "advancement is usually at the initial will of public authorities with whom the voice of the prosecutor or attorney general is very powerful. . . . Criminals are not nice people," and judges become callous and hard-bitten with experience. And, finally, "power corrupts, but responsibility corrupts more. No one could treat human beings the way our legal system makes cops or judges treat human beings without feeling an enormous weight of guilt, that can be laved away only by the compensatory belief that 'these people' deserve what 'we' are doing to them."

There was a time when William Kunstler worked in a law office with the conventional trappings—floor-to-ceiling bookcases and framed diplomas, swivel chairs and dark rugs. But Kunstler defected from the Establishment to take asylum behind radical lines. Nowadays he is the eminence in residence at the Center for Constitutional Rights, a radical lawyers' group with headquarters one flight up from one of the seediest corners in New York.

Kunstler's current working ambience includes linoleum floors, Black Panther posters, small metal desks, young women in blue denim workshirts, and an amiable dog. I talked with him there one day about judges and revolution.

"All I expect a judge to do is to always opt for the Bill of Rights," he said. "Some do more than others, but I don't know any who will always do so. I think a good judge is one who understands the realities of American life and is consciously doing something to change them, to bring us closer to our professed aims of free speech, due process, and equality. There aren't any like that. Maybe it's an abstract and unreasonable standard—there are judges with great sensibility whom I have respect for—but it's the standard I use.

"The trouble is that they're too concerned with their own advancement and their status. I think the remedy is to give them automatic assurance of advancement. I'd promote all of them by seniority, so that every judge knew he would reach at least the next court up. The Supreme Court would be the nine federal judges with the most seniority. There also ought to be a method of suing a judge for incompetence or bias or incapacity. They're immune from that kind of suit. The public ought to have a way to get an open and fair hearing on a complaint about a judge.

"A judge like Hoffman is afraid of the future and any break in what he considers necessary authoritarianism. He wants to make people toe the line, he fears something he calls 'permissiveness.' Judges won't do anything to threaten themselves or their own view of what the society should be."

Kunstler's colleagues drifted in and out of the room as we talked. He interrupted the conversation to exchange jokes and embrace them warmly. He wore a tweed coat and a wide, colorful tie. The telephone rang constantly. "I've got the Rap [Brown] trial coming up tomorrow," he said. "I've got to do a TV interview this afternoon."

I asked Kunstler whether the judicial system's ultimate vindication of such radicals as Spock, Angela Davis, and the Chicago Seven didn't offer some evidence that it might be working as advertised, that even some of those who challenged the system directly were treated fairly by it. I had asked the same question of other radical critics; some had conceded grudgingly that yes, constitutional liberties were still alive in American courts; others had scorned the idea as a fantasy spun by woolly-headed liberals.

Kunstler is in the latter camp. "The Chicago Seven, Angela Davis, and Dr. Spock all had enormous legal resources and vast publicity," he said. "That doesn't prove that the system is working. If a case involves an unknown black or Puerto Rican with a Legal

Aid lawyer and nobody knows his name, he's always going to get screwed unless a good lawyer or reporter pulls the case out of the miasma."

Beyond the simplistic railing at "pig courts," Kunstler's brothers and sisters in modern American radicalism developed two strategies in pursuit of their demands for equal justice. The first was to circumvent the courts by the creation of alternative tribunals— "citizen courts." The second is even simpler: to work "within the system" for the election of their own to the bench.

When Abbie Hoffman and underground press correspondent Tom Forcade got into a dispute concerning the distribution of Hoffman's book *Steal This Book*, they decided to submit the issues to a panel of three counterculture arbitrators. The panel heard testimony from both Hoffman and Forcade as well as other witnesses. Cross-examination and the introduction of evidence were permitted.

Forcade, who had been hired and later fired by Hoffman, claimed that Hoffman owed him $5000. He spurned Hoffman's offer to settle for $1500. The "people's tribunal" deliberated through three night-long sessions before issuing a "karma alignment": Forcade was to get $1000 and the opportunity to buy ten thousand copies of Hoffman's book at cost, which he could then sell on his own through the methods Hoffman had originally hired him to develop.

One member of the panel, journalist Craig Karpel, described the proceeding as "an explicit rejection of the authority and legitimacy of the courts that create Atticas, George Jacksons [one of the Soledad Brothers] and Panther 21 cases. . . . We think we pointed to a way of settling disputes within the movement by consensual procedure without resorting to official structures. . . .

"We had actually tried to go Alice in Wonderland's 'sentence first, verdict afterwards' one step further: sentence first, verdict *never*. . . . Abbie Hoffman won. Also, Tom Forcade won. But seriously, folks, Abbie lost. Not to mention Tom, who lost too. Like the old saw goes, it ain't whether you win or lose that counts, it's how you smashed the state."

The settlement had to be reconsidered when Grove Press, which had become the distributor of the book, refused to release ten thousand copies for sale to Forcade. But Hoffman was content anyway. "I've been tried by thirty judges," he said. "Twenty-five were businessmen and not one was under sixty. This is the first time that I've felt affection with a panel of judges."

Justin Ravitz is a tall, shambling, dark-haired man of thirty-three who wears aviator glasses, khaki shirts, and high-heeled cowboy boots. He believes that American society is embroiled in "an ongoing class struggle," that its institutions and economic system "create and perpetuate the oppression of the majority," and that a mass movement is necessary for change. It is reasonably certain that no one holding a similar set of beliefs has ever been elected to a judgeship in American history. In November 1972 Ravitz became the first.

"I never aspired to be a judge," he says. "The idea would have been anathema to me. But there was a collective decision that I would run." Supported by an energetic corps of young volunteers and backed by such elements of the straight society as local Democratic clubs, the United Auto Workers Union, and the Detroit *Free Press*, Ravitz finished second in a field of fourteen candidates (seven were elected). He won a ten-year term on the Detroit Recorder's Court, which deals with both felonies and misdemeanors. His salary is $38,000.

"There's only one operative principle," he told me shortly after his election, "and that's building a mass multi-racial movement to take over the institutions and serve the majority. Becoming a judge was a tactical move—I believe it's the best role I can fill as a consciously political person right now.

"There are contradictions, I'll admit," in a revolutionary mounting the bench. "But to be a purist in this society is to be irrelevant. I have an analysis of the society, and I'm part of a movement. That keeps me from feeling the sense of despair that liberals have."

Ravitz ran on a platform attacking every part of the criminal-justice system—police, bail, prisons, court-appointed lawyers, and the judges themselves. "They all function to help each other and violate people's rights," he said. His campaign literature promised reform. His mere presence on the bench, it said, would "provide justice in something like 1,500 cases a year"—justice would be clearly visible to the pure in heart. "Justin will provide a more human atmosphere in at least one courtroom," his brochure said. "Part of having 'our own courts' is not being afraid in them."

As one of Detroit's leading radical lawyers, Ravitz had won a number of impressive victories. He gained acquittal for a Chrysler worker who killed three people, on the grounds that the real killer was "Chrysler's racism." He won a ruling from the Michigan Supreme Court that the state's penalties for marijuana possession were "unduly harsh," enabling 130 prisoners to go free. He earned acquittal for black militants accused of murdering a policeman by arguing that blacks and poor people were illegally excluded from the jury.

Ravitz was up to his boot tops in controversy before he heard his first case. He refused to stand for the recital of the Pledge of Allegiance at his swearing-in ceremony. "There's a phrase in there that I don't much like," he explained. "It says, 'with liberty and justice for all.'"

I saw him again after he had been sitting for three months. "It's going much better than I anticipated," he said. "There's something interesting and deep almost every day."

One of his first crusades was to end the policy of holding criminal suspects up to seventy-two hours without a court appearance. "We worked out a procedure to arraign all suspects within twelve hours of their arrest," he said. "This is institutionalized progress, okay? It doesn't mean the system is going to work or cure itself, but it's a step."

He sent two men to prison during his first ninety days. "Some of my friends on the left wanted me to set everyone free, okay? They said it's a capitalist system, so what difference does it make? I think that's ridiculous. It's real people who are the victims. They're the proletariat, right? Some people are just really dangerous, man, and you can't allow them to rip off real people."

He sentenced a man convicted of armed robbery to one to ten years. Another pleaded guilty to manslaughter and was given a one-to-fifteen-year sentence. "They were both dangerous. I checked them out. It wasn't easy to sentence them, but I didn't wring my hands and cry about it. It was simply an objective job."

Ravitz wears a robe when he thinks the occasion calls for it, but generally shows up on the bench in his boots, a colored shirt, and a loosened tie. "I just suddenly appear," he says. "There's no big to-do when I go in." Members of the court staff refer to him by his nickname of "Chuck." He expresses disinterest in having an American flag in his courtroom.

His judicial restraint was tested almost immediately. He was assigned to preside at the trial of a right-wing activist accused of assaulting a priest at a peace demonstration. The defendant was found guilty by a jury of nine blacks and three whites. The defense attorney praised Ravitz's handling of the case, commenting that he "controlled himself very nicely" and presided fairly.

A prosecutor was also pleasantly surprised. "He knows the law, and he administers it fairly," he said. "He is slow, careful, and methodical."

The only complaints have come from policemen. "When you go in his court," one said, "you feel like you're on trial instead of the defendant." Another said Ravitz demeaned officers in court. "They haven't given me any trouble," Ravitz said. "I've heard about some of them calling me a son of a bitch in the corridor, and if they had a plebiscite on me now, I know I'd lose. But I think they think I'm straight and it might improve."

A young court clerk came into his chambers. "You want your check, Chuck?" the clerk asked.

"Yeah, man," the judge replied. "Hey, I'm going to be around late again tonight. You ready for a little night work?"

The clerk nodded.

"Okay. Stay cool.

"I'll tell you a couple of deep things that have happened," he went on. "There was a hack lawyer in this one case, he hadn't even talked to his client. He just accepted the police version of what happened. So I dismissed him and filed a grievance with the state bar against him. I don't think any judge here has ever done that.

"Then there was a defendant who was in the hospital. He'd been shot in the leg, okay? I went over there to arraign him and his head was all messed up. The police had beaten him. He died the next day. I told his family to get an attorney, and we might indict one of the cops for manslaughter or murder."

He paced his office and fingered his check. "I feel like something is happening. There's some progress." He smiled. "So far it's been a real trip."

Judge George Sullivan has the look and manner of a man for whom the sweet promise of life has turned sour. He has a sad, heavy strength about him, like an ex-athlete living on yesterday's glory. His eyes come to life only rarely, and then with just the tiniest trace of a flicker. His voice is barely audible. His smile is wry, ironic, full of secret cynicism. When emotion rises in him, it comes with a sudden, startling fury and then immediately subsides.

Things started to go wrong for Sullivan when he began to question the Vietnam war. Judges had been conspicuously silent in the national debate on the war: federal courts had consistently ruled that they lacked jurisdiction over its constitutionality; the only judicial role had been the sentencing—sometimes lenient, often harsh—of people who broke the law to protest the war or avoid it. But Sullivan's conscience nagged him. His patriotism teetered. He began to wonder about his own position: was he in effect condoning the war by his silence? The sturdy edifice of his political and moral values, constructed over a lifetime, began to topple. He quietly decided to commit civil disobedience.

The district courthouse in Stoughton, Massachusetts, was strangely serene, almost churchlike. It was almost four in the afternoon and the place was already empty except for Sullivan, who was signing orders at his desk. He is a tall man, broad-shouldered and balding. He was once an All-American tackle at Notre Dame, later a naval officer in World War II and Korea. He became a district judge in 1964 after serving as a state senator.

He talked slowly and uncomfortably about his decision. The words were chewed carefully before he spoke them. "I was sitting unconscious of the war," he began. "I don't think it was any particular thing that triggered my interest—maybe the Berrigans. I began to read about it. My boys were approaching draft age."

He stopped, switched gears. "I was the All-American boy, you know? I thought it was our business to bring freedom to the world. I thought the government must know what they're doing. I'm an idealist, I guess." He twirled a pencil with his thick fingers.

"Anyway, I read about napalm and defoliation, about what was going on in Vietnam. It happened gradually. I began to get more in the bag of asking how was my situation different from the judges in Germany in World War Two. You understand? I didn't want to be in that position."

The tempo of his narrative picked up. "I came to think that it's not a government for the people, it's people serving the government, and anyone who criticized it was called a dirty name. I felt we were dead wrong, and we were causing people's deaths, and with no declaration of war"—he was talking rapidly now—"and the government was lying, lying, *lying*." He released a staccato, snorting laugh. "GODDAM LIARS!" His voice slipped back to its careful pace. "And all this was taking place in the name of patriotism.

"I started to think maybe the judge's responsibility is heavier than that of the average citizen. His business is knowledge of the law, being able to distinguish facts from allegations, that's what the job's about. And we were in a situation where the people carrying this message were long-haired kids, and they were discredited, called misguided. And that made me angry."

He paused, gazed out the window at the autumn sky—football weather—and looked at me for a moment. "It was 'looking good.' It was face, you know? We're always in the business of looking good. My face is not worth one kid's life.

"I went through all the steps—wires to my congressman, petition-gathering. My wife went to Washington with a group. I was acting as a citizen. The idea that this was improper for a judge didn't cross my mind. Propriety! *God*, what a word! If that's the first goal, if that stands ahead of a judge's function of administering justice, then the priorities are wrong.

"Okay." He sighed and paused again. "The demonstration happened to coincide with my growing sense of guilt. Understand? It was pre-announced. Civil disobedience was planned, but it was going to be submissive. They were going to block the Federal Building by sitting down in the street. [The demonstration took place in Boston in May 1971.] I didn't tell anyone I was going. It just fit the way I felt and believed. I didn't agonize about the effect of a judge participating, I did it more personally than that. When I got there I didn't tell anyone I was a judge. That would be too much like 'Look at me,' you know? I suppose I had a hidden desire that the word would get around that I was a judge. I didn't want to be arrested, but I was anticipating it. I wasn't going to make it happen."

His mouth yielded to a small, ironic smile. "I sat there for four hours, and my back started to get sore, so I quit at noon and went home. I wasn't arrested. The funny thing is that a half-hour after I left, the police came zapping down right where I'd been and started belting people with clubs and arresting them."

A newspaperman recognized Sullivan in the crowd, however, and a story about him appeared in a Boston paper. He readily admitted his participation in the demonstration and tried to explain his reasons. "I was willing to take the punishment," he said. "I felt some guilt that I wasn't arrested."

A complaint was made to the Massachusetts Supreme Judicial Court, the state's highest court. Sullivan was invited to a hearing to investigate his presence at the demonstration.

"They asked me if I would do it again. I said it depends on the circumstances. They were asking me to say I wouldn't, but I didn't oblige. If the occasion arose, I would do it again, although I haven't." A few days later Sullivan read in the paper that he had been reprimanded. "I'm embarrassed, but I don't even remember the exact words. Something like 'don't do it again.'" The official report stopped short of censuring Sullivan, but said his conduct "was seriously unwise and reflected poor judgment."

"I thought it was fair enough," he said. "Hypocritical maybe, but fair." The same court had declined to act against judges accused of arbitrary and illegal treatment of the poor.

"The thing that gets me is that all the talk afterwards was about the *propriety* of a judge demonstrating against the war. The injustice of the war disappeared and what's talked about is propriety. Judges hanging on to their cloak at whatever price."

In the weeks after the reprimand, Sullivan's attitude toward his job changed. "I'm a good judge," he says, a little defiantly. "And— well, that's not a big secret. But I don't particularly like the job. You deal with trouble all the time. All you have are winners and losers. You don't accomplish that much." It was an opinion that seemed born in a disillusion not connected with his work. "Maybe you help some people a little bit, but not much. Maybe I ought to get out. The propriety, dignity, all that crap never appealed to me anyway."

I asked if he could reconcile his action with his conception of a judge's duty.

He shrugged. "Maybe it's not reconcilable," he said. "I'm not sure. If it's not, then I probably ought to get out." It sounded like the decision had already been made.

He said he had no regrets. "I feel pride. I wish I did more." But the regrets he feels are deeper—the sorrow of a man betrayed by his own faith, stripped of his confidence in his country. "At least I've done something," he said grimly. "I'm no longer a German judge."

XII

Federal Roulette

The road to the federal bench is paved with good connections

IN THEIR FANTASIES they see it all with vivid clarity: the call from a U.S. senator, the anxious wait through investigations by the FBI and the American Bar Association, the polite questioning by a panel of senators dazzled by their credentials, the sudden deference of their friends, the inaugural inspection of their cool and spacious chambers, the satisfaction of ambition achieved. And then the moment when they ascend the carpeted steps to sit behind the oaken desk, to preside in benign majesty as lesser men argue the gravest issues of the day. Federal district judge! The vision warms the winter nights of state judges, federal prosecutors, and trial lawyers, of loyal party workers and generous contributors. They rehearse it in their imagination: "It is the opinion of this court that the government's action in this instance is not sanctioned by the constitution, and therefore . . ."

The lure of the federal bench is palpable, an attraction felt so strongly that a man can almost taste it on his tongue. The ingredients are power, prestige, importance, independence, and security, along with other, indefinable elements that shade into the mists of lawyers' dreams. It isn't money: $40,000 a year for life is not bad, to be sure, but there are lawyers who spend that much in travel expenses. Nor is it the trappings of office, the rows of books and loungelike chambers, faithful clerks and marble courtrooms. And it

247

certainly isn't the prospect of fame: a football coach has a better-known name.

It is something else, something more than professional accomplishment or raw pride in personal success. It has to do with the clean grandeur of law itself, and with a judge's role as exemplifying the best of our imperfect attempts at government. There is the knowledge that to excel on the federal bench is to better the lot of your contemporaries, to leave behind a richer planet.

"You can tell the difference when you go into a federal court," says law professor Herman Schwartz of Buffalo. "There's a cleanness about it, a sense of fairness. Not so much in the substantive sense, but you know you're not going to be treated like dirt. The grubbiness of the state courts is gone—the impatient clerks, the seedy lawyers, the bored cops sitting around. The whole ambience is different. There's an atmosphere of trust and dignity."

Judges of the federal district bench are members of an elite corps, bound by similar backgrounds, common problems, and a respect for the office and one another. Exclusivity is another of the job's attractions, reinforced regularly at conferences and institutes. The membership roster of 401 is a brotherhood (there are only four women) of power and privilege. "There is really a fraternal feeling among us judges," one reported after only a few weeks of federal service. "We understand each other." A twenty-year veteran felt the same way: "There is a sort of mutual confidence and trust among us."

A seat so comfortable is rarely cold for long. There are between ten and fifty contenders whenever a vacancy occurs, and the competition waits on few amenities. President Harry Truman received a telegram one day in 1948 informing him that "Judge —— died yesterday at his farm. . . . Judge —— would be an excellent man to fill the vacancy."

A state-court judge, scuffling amid the frustrations of long dockets and short budgets, can gaze into the middle distance and envision a brighter day. "The federal bench—now, that's my ballpark," a New York judge told me wistfully. "There's where the prestige, the action, the importance all come together. That, to me, would be making it. I could be happy there forever. Politics is all that matters in our state courts, but in the federal courts, ah . . ." He almost licked his lips. "I don't mind telling you I would sell my soul here and now to be a federal judge. And you know"—he leaned forward excitedly, savoring the thought—"I've heard there might be a chance. A couple of people have spoken to the senator about it, and, well—he didn't say no."

It is a beguiling dream, but any aspirant soon awakens to the realization that it is politics—not his talent, not his wisdom, not even his record, but old-fashioned, backscratching politics—that ultimately defines his chances. There are, as always, the winsome exceptions, but the unappetizing fact is that federal judgeships are gifts to the faithful from grateful senators. To a select number among the faithful, perhaps, but to the faithful nonetheless. "Governors get the highway commission and five hundred other jobs to hand out," a senatorial aide laments, "but a senator gets federal judges and elevator operators, period." The favors-due bill may be for contributions, campaign work, or years of fealty; it may be friendship, or the old school tie; it could be a reward to a crony's son or brother, or a contributor's lawyer. The ABA and senatorial consciences, such as they are, may set a minimum level of qualification. But above that it is who owes what to whom, and let's hope he works out all right on the bench.

This sobering realization can bottle up the ambition of a good state judge and turn him sour and cynical. "The federal system is the epitome of judging, there's no question about it," a Western-state judge told me. "It's the ultimate. But it's political through and through. It's the big contributors and the longtime party workers, and the rest of us can forget it. It's unreachable for me, I don't have those kind of ties. I see who gets it. It's a matter of being in line. You don't aspire to it because it's out of range. You can be the best judge in the world on a state court and not have a chance. It's a rotten shame. It doesn't make for a lot of confidence in the system."

Federal district judges are scattered according to population—Maine and Wyoming have one each, New York and California thirty-five each. In theory they are appointed by the President with the consent of the Senate, but in practice the appointment is normally made on the recommendation of the senator (or senators) from the administration party in the judge's home state. The cases they hear involve the violation of federal laws, suits in which the U.S. government is a party, or issues where there is a federal constitutional question. The power of a federal judge is enormous, the status gilt-edged, the freedom intoxicating. In many ways a district judge, as a trial judge, is more powerful than the appellate courts above him—the Circuit Courts of Appeal and the Supreme Court. With few exceptions, the higher courts can only pass on questions that a district judge has already ruled on; and the overwhelming majority of District Court decisions are not appealed.

"The quality of the District Courts determines to a large extent how law is practiced in the country and, ultimately, whether it is respected or not," says a Chicago lawyer. "It is *the* most powerful chair," adds a United States magistrate in San Francisco. "You sit up there and you can do anything you want to and no one can do anything about it, except for the occasional reversal."

Through their rulings, district judges establish policy on a vast range of legal and social issues. They operate in the zone of tension between traditional legal standards and changing public values. Legislatures can wait, but judges must react to the issue before them. A federal judge "may fashion and sustain the moral principles of the community," says Charles Wyzanski of Boston, one of the most respected of them. "His character and personal distinction, open to daily inspection in his courtroom, constitute the guarantees of due process."

One way or another, every vital question finds its way to a federal court. The most vivid recent examples are the Watergate rulings by Judge John Sirica of Washington and the Ellsberg case, but other illustrations of the sway of federal courts can be found in the newspapers daily:

¶ *School Busing.* District Judges Stephen Roth of Michigan and Robert Merhige of Virginia approved area-wide busing to achieve school integration.

¶ *Environment.* Judge George Hart of the District of Columbia dissolved an injunction blocking construction of the Alaska oil pipeline. Jon Newman of Connecticut held up a federal highway until environmental studies were made. Philip Neville of Minnesota prohibited mining in a national wilderness area.

¶ *Minorities.* Judges John Fullam of Pennsylvania and William Thomas of Ohio ordered city police departments to hire a specified percentage of minority-group members. Samuel Conti of California rejected a similar plan for school administrators in San Francisco.

¶ *Homosexuality.* Judge Sidney Smith of Georgia ruled that homosexual students could not be forbidden to use college facilities. John Pratt of the District of Columbia ordered the Defense Department to restore security clearances to three homosexuals.

¶ *Mental Health.* Judge Frank Johnson of Alabama ordered state hospitals to meet specified standards of treatment for the mentally ill and retarded.

¶ *Wiretaps.* Judge Joseph Lord of Pennsylvania ruled that a 1968 law permitting wiretaps under certain conditions was an unconstitutional invasion of privacy.

¶ *Prisoners' Rights.* Judge Charles Scott of Florida decided that an inmate is entitled to a hearing before being placed in solitary confinement. Robert Merhige of Virginia barred physical abuse, chains, and other practices in Virginia prisons as "cruel and unusual punishment."

The breathtaking vistas of power enjoyed by federal judges can liberate their best or worst impulses, and the quality of federal justice depends in large part on which way they go. Lawyers are forever studying their resistance, or lack of it, to the temptations of office. "It's so easy to turn into a crazy despot in that job," says one attorney. "I mean, a federal judge is really *up there* and you're really *down there.* The normal rules of human exchange don't prevail in a federal court."

The sting of arbitrary power can overturn a principle or punish an innocent man, but lawyers feel it most acutely in the operation of the court. "I was in a federal court in Iowa," a Colorado lawyer recalled, "and we had to ask permission to stand and to approach a witness. We couldn't wear colored shirts because the judge didn't like them. It's an empire. The courtroom is run the way the judge says, with no recourse and no accountability." It is a power that tests the best of men, and it demands the closest scrutiny of whom we give it to and how.

"The federal judiciary is almost a government in exile," one of its members told me. "If a bomb went off in Washington and wiped out the administration and Congress, you could nearly replace it overnight with federal judges—there are enough ex-governors, ex-Cabinet members, ex-mayors, and ex-politicians from all levels."

It was a claim made in pride, and readily provable by the partisan dossiers of most federal judges. But it also touches one of the central controversies of judicial selection: at its simplest, it is elitism versus the arena. Should judges emerge out of the heat and struggle of politics, where public accountability is at least acknowledged if not always honored? Or should they be recruited from the serene reaches of law schools, large firms, and corporate board-rooms a safe distance from public and political vicissitudes? "Political" judges argue that they have learned about human behavior, acquired a talent for compromise, and developed compassion. Elitists reply that they know law, that they are detached, and that—well, frankly, gentlemen—they're smarter. The division cuts through discussions of judicial quality, standards, and selection at every level.

Roughly one out of five federal district judges held an elective office (other than state judge or district attorney) before reaching the bench. Edwin Mechem of New Mexico was both governor and U.S. senator before President Nixon appointed him to a judgeship. John Reynolds is a former Democratic governor of Wisconsin; Republican Raymond Broderick and Democrat John Davis were both lieutenant governors of Pennsylvania; James Battin of Montana, Robert Hemphill of South Carolina, and at least six others are ex-congressmen. Dozens were state legislators, attorneys general, or district attorneys.

Many more were party activists—county or state chairmen, convention delegates, local campaign officers, national committeemen. Kenneth Wangelin of Missouri, a Nixon appointment, identifies himself in *Who's Who* as a "party worker." Another Missouri judge, James Meredith, was Senator Stuart Symington's campaign manager. C. G. Neese of Tennessee, a campaign director for the late Senator Estes Kefauver, survived a "not qualified" rating by the American Bar Association. So did Johnson appointment C. A. Muecke of Arizona, who had been a Democratic county chairman. Political scientist Sheldon Goldman of the University of Massachusetts found that 48 percent of Johnson's District Court appointments were prominent party activists, as were 45 percent of those named in Nixon's first term. Many others were no doubt active, just less visible.

The bench can cushion a loser's fall. Stanley Blair of Maryland, William Steger of Texas, and Hugh Dillin of Indiana all surfaced in federal court after unsuccessful runs for governor. Judicial ambition did not seize Republicans Rhodes Bratcher of Kentucky and Charles Moye of Georgia, or Democrats Frank Wilson of Tennessee and John Fullam of Pennsylvania, until they lost races for Congress.

If the backgrounds of federal judges were patched into a human facsimile, like a police sketch composed of identified features, the result would be a fifty-eight-year-old white male Protestant, a son of the middle-to-upper-middle class who graduated from a good (but not the best) law school, worked as a prosecutor, joined a prominent firm, and contributed regularly to the church and party of his choice.

Women federal judges are still rare enough to startle most lawyers. "It's unsettling and somehow uncomfortable to argue before a woman judge," an unliberated Washington lawyer says. "It's like having a woman referee at a heavyweight fight." There were only 183 women on state courts in 1970 (out of 16,700 judges), and only four sit on the federal district bench—Sarah Hughes in Texas, June Green in the District of Columbia, Constance Baker Motley in New York, and Cornelia Kennedy in Michigan. Shirley Hufstedler, an appellate judge on the Ninth Circuit court in California, is the highest-ranking woman jurist.

The average district judge was appointed at 50 and is now 58. Seventeen were appointed in their thirties—the youngest, at 35, was Robert Zampano of Connecticut. Three current judges—Sam Pointer of Alabama, William Hodges of Florida, and Walter Stapleton of Delaware—were 39 in 1973. The oldest active judge was 81-year-old Allen Hannay of Texas. Thirty were in their seventies.

The ABA rates federal judicial nominees in four categories— exceptionally well qualified, well qualified, qualified, and not qualified. Of the current judges, 23 won the highest rating and 13 were found unqualified; 141 were well qualified and 165 qualified, the lowest passing grade. The ABA's objections were usually either age, lack of "judicial temperament," or inadequate trial experience. Two of the 13 unqualified were Truman appointments, two were named by Eisenhower, six by Kennedy, and three by Johnson. All Nixon appointments have been rated at least qualified.

Lawyers often complain that too many judges are ex-prosecutors. They contend that the result is a judicial inclination to trust a prosecutor more than a defense attorney, if only because of the judges' own experience. "It makes a lot of difference in the general run of cases," says Harvard law professor Alan Dershowitz. "They ought to recruit more from universities and from defense lawyers." F. Lee Bailey believes there should be a law limiting the number of U.S. attorneys elevated to federal judge. "There's a general tendency to be down on the defense," he says. "It's particularly important when a judge has to rely on lawyers rather than evidence. Prosecutors are creatures of politics, and most defense lawyers are the antithesis of it."

Nearly half of all district judges were once prosecutors. Professor Goldman found that 46 percent of Johnson's appointments were onetime prosecutors, as were 42 percent of Nixon's. The U.S. Attorney's office is the most popular steppingstone to the federal bench.

Roughly a third of all federal judges sat on state courts. Twenty percent are Ivy League law graduates; slightly more than 40 percent are products of state schools. Eleven percent won scholastic honors.

Ethnically, federal judges reflect their regions and the political clout of their clansmen. The bulk of those in the South, Midwest, and West are WASPS. A substantial minority in New York are Jewish. Italian judges appear wherever there is a healthy Italian voting bloc—Mark Costantino in Brooklyn, John Cannella and Lee Gagliardi in Manhattan, Frank Battisti in Cleveland, Robert De-Mascio in Detroit, Alfred Luongo in Philadelphia, Alfonso Zirpoli in San Francisco. Reynaldo Garza of Texas is one of only two Chicano judges; by no coincidence, his court in Brownsville, Texas, is the one closest to Mexico. Thirteen, all in Northern cities, are black.

At least twenty-seven once belonged to whites-only Elks lodges. Eight are former FBI agents. Forty-eight have taught at law schools, many specializing in business law. Their credentials are repetitively narrow-channeled—law school, large firm, county chairman, prosecutor, ABA member. The aroma of dusty lawbooks and cracked leather seeps through the bare biographical data. Exotic touches are rare: Charles Carr of California is a big-game hunter; Samuel King of Hawaii was born in China, Stephen Roth of Michigan in Hungary; Joe Fisher of Texas is a "Silver Beaver" in the Boy Scouts; Robert Kelleher of California was captain of the U.S. Davis Cup team; Sidney Smith of Georgia performed with Harvard's Hasty Pudding Society; and Leo Brewster of Texas belongs to something called the Texas Open Shooting Dog Championship Association.

Most federal judges would cheerfully admit to membership in the American Establishment, with no apologies. The system has been good to them; they played by its rules and they won. They are apt to resist suggestions that the rules be changed. They believe in the two-party system, the rule of law, and the American Way.

The backgrounds of most federal judges are sprinkled with corporate connections, if only because so many of them come out of the largest and most prominent law firms, which draw their clienteles from the business community. As lawyers they were advisers to the oilmen, bankers, and other executives who contribute heavily to political campaigns. "Most of the federal judges down here," a Texas lawyer told me, "are business-oriented, with a limited range of legal experience." Leading law firms have always been closely allied with wealth and corporate power, a fact that led Theodore Roosevelt to cherish the judge who can "keep his broad humanity of feeling and his sympathy for the class from which he has not drawn his clients."

They are not, allowing again for the exceptions, the *best* lawyers. They are the best political lawyers, the best of those who have divided their careers between law and politics. It is a crucial distinction, because it excludes many more than it includes; a lawyer with no political connections is, in effect, barred from the federal bench. Many first-rate lawyers, moreover, are not eager to give up their six-figure incomes or the bracing satisfactions of advocacy. Judging may have class and clout, but it's a poky business. Former U.S. Attorney Frederick Lacey of New Jersey, one of the charmed few who earned an "exceptionally well qualified" rating from the ABA, took his seat on the federal bench in 1971. After a year he was reportedly contemplating resigning because the pace was so slow.

Federal judges are an elite, but in a special sense: not an aristocracy of intellect and ability, but rather the cream of the partisans, the best of the political scramblers. "They are the next-best lawyers, and the best political climbers," says Anthony Amsterdam of Stanford. "If it were a genuine elite of quality, it would be different," says Alan Dershowitz, "but we have elitism without quality. We choose them from a relatively narrow group and we don't get the best."

The leap from political lawyer to federal judge leaves many of them short-winded. Texas political scientists Robert Carp and Russell Wheeler interviewed thirty federal judges in Iowa, Louisiana, Oklahoma, Texas, and New Mexico. They found that "ignorance of criminal law" was the judges' most common shortcoming when they assumed the bench, followed closely by an unfamiliarity with civil-liberties issues. The breadth and depth of their new responsibilities staggered them; twenty-eight of the thirty confessed "initial difficulties with matters of both substantive law and legal procedure." The adjustment was handled most easily, Carp and Wheeler reported, by those who had been state judges.

There were psychological hurdles as well—the loneliness of the bench, the anguish of sentencing, the difficulty of finding and maintaining a "judicial bearing," resisting the advice of their neighbors. "You can't go to the places you used to," one complained; "you always have to be careful about what you talk about." "After you become a federal judge some people tend to avoid you," another sighed; "you have to make new friends." A Louisiana judge said that he lived "in a white, middle-class suburb and my neighbors feel pretty strongly against busing. . . . My wife gets 'static' from the neighbors all the time."

They had acquired the robe, the reserved parking place in the courthouse garage, the wall-to-wall lawbooks, and the secret joys of deference, but very little in their background had prepared them for the responsibility. "You sit down and realize that it's all different," one judge said, "that everyone is looking at you and you're supposed to do something." Judging is an elegant art and a demanding science. But becoming a judge is an art of another, less elegant kind.

"We'd been waiting for nineteen years," the administrative assistant of a Western senator was saying. "It had been that long since we had a judge to name. You should have seen the mail. There must have been a hundred lawyers pushing themselves. I could tell where the candidates were by where the mail came from. They'd go down one interstate highway on the west side of the state and I'd get letters from lawyers and chamber-of-commerce presidents in those towns. Then they'd go up the east side and the postmarks would be from there. Factions developed. I had the feeling they had campaign managers. It was fierce.

"They didn't bring up favors they had coming, but they mentioned their loyalty to the party and the contributions they'd made. It was understood that whoever got it had to be a party loyalist.

"We actually looked through the yellow pages for possibilities. We called the state bar association and asked for a list of judges. There weren't many Republicans on the list. The senator took it very seriously. One candidate was the state chairman for Nixon. Others were people that the senator knew. Some were people we were mad at—they had signed Democratic ads. I was arbitrary too, God damn it.

"Finally we decided ten were qualified. The state party organization and the congressmen didn't say anything. It was all ours. We spent a month screening them and then we decided on our man. He was the senator's field assistant, his man back home. He was a corporation lawyer.

"We wrote John Mitchell and told him who we wanted. The senator sent the name down to the Justice Department with a résumé. They sent back the biggest-ass questionnaire you ever saw. Then the FBI started snooping around. They talked to people in his law firm. They even talked to Democrats. The theme of the opposition began to appear—no trial experience. The other candidates found out, and we got more letters. We decided, 'Drive on.'

"The senator had supported the President for years. He even talked to the President about it. He saw John Ehrlichman and Richard Kleindienst [then deputy attorney general]. The trouble was that our man wasn't a bar-association mixer, you know? He wasn't one of the boys. He was just a good old Republican corporate lawyer.

"The ABA rating came back—unqualified because of lack of trial experience. The senator was really pissed. We figured trial experience was something you could learn on the job, like driving a car. It's a mechanical thing, right? It shouldn't be an absolute. We said BS to the bar association. But Kleindienst said no. Guess who won. The senator was bitter. He thought about leaving the whole thing up to the Justice Department. He decided for a while that he didn't care.

"But then we went back to our list. We still had about ten names on it, and a few were sitting judges. We decided not to give it to any of the guys who ran for it—the office seeks the man, you know. We had a couple of letters on this one judge, and he seemed to be a cut above the others. So we picked him. The bar association approved him. I don't even remember his name."

The aide was still angry at the ABA for rejecting their first choice. "When did the ABA get elected?" he demanded. "When did the Nixon administration forfeit its right to choose its own appointments?" He thought for a moment as he played with a paperclip. "I really don't know what kind of judge our man would have made," he said quietly. "I think he'd have been good. Probably."

Federal judges are chosen by a sort of political roulette. The participants in the process are constant—senators, perhaps a congressman, the Justice Department, the President, campaigning candidates, the ABA—but their relative strength varies with the individual cases. Each selection is a fresh spin of the wheel.

The heaviest hand is usually the senator's, but senators approach the responsibility differently. Some are jealous of their prerogative and powerful enough to insist that their man be named. Lyndon Johnson held up the confirmation of thirteen judges in 1959 until President Eisenhower agreed to Johnson's candidate for a Texas vacancy. Johnson retained his influence as Vice President, exercising a veto over Texas nominees.

John McClellan of Arkansas, a key member of the Judiciary Committee, yields no ground once he settles on a name. The late Senator Robert Kerr of Oklahoma bulldozed the appointment of his friend Luther Bohanon, who was appointed by President Kennedy despite a "not qualified" from the ABA.

Other senators—former Senator Frank Lausche of Ohio was one—leave judicial selection to the executive branch. Hugh Scott and Richard Schweiker of Pennsylvania often send a list of four or five to the Justice Department with no preference expressed, thus protecting themselves from the rancor of disappointed runners-up. Still other senators submit a list of names, but follow it with a discreet phone call identifying their real choice. The ABA rating becomes part of the smoke. "They'll send up a name they know will be rejected by the ABA," a Justice Department man says, "just so the candidate back home thinks the senator is looking out for him."

The balance of power shifts with each case; the importance of ideology, professional qualifications, and cronyism ebbs and flows with senatorial attitudes and those of the President's men. If there are two administration-party senators in the same state, they may make the decision jointly (like Scott and Schweiker), or take turns picking judges (like New York Senators Jacob Javits and James Buckley), or divide the state in half (like ex-Senator John Sherman Cooper and Marlow Cook of Kentucky). With no administration-party senator in the state, the Justice Department men will usually have a freer hand, although a powerful congressman, a governor, or a state chairman may fill the vacuum.

"Nobody likes to talk about it," a senatorial aide told me. "They all appoint their guy for personal reasons and they don't want to say that. It's because somewhere, sometime, he did something for the senator or he's a friend of the senator."

An astute judicial candidate knows where the levers of power are, and knows how to play them. Judge J. Sam Perry of Illinois, now semi-retired, is one of the few who have candidly described the machinations.

"I gambled," he said. "I saw a man—Paul Douglas—who looked as though he might be elected to the Senate. I backed him, and as a result I had his support. . . . I tried to obtain the appointment once before and learned that it requires not one but two senators. . . . I was out of politics and they did not need me. I decided I had better get back into politics, which I did. I learned that everyone shoots at the number-one choice, so I told each of the senators not to make me first. . . . That proved to be pretty good strategy because everybody else was shot off and, no use lying about it, I helped to shoot them off. The result was I landed on top."

The process begins when a senator submits a name, or names, to the Justice Department. He may consult powerful politicians back home (Mayor Daley of Chicago had enough influence to get appointments for his close friends Abraham Marovitz and William Lynch), his state bar association, colleagues in Congress, or his list of contributors. The Justice Department turns the names over to the FBI and ABA, both of which commence investigations. A negative FBI report can be fatal, but senators are not permitted to see the reports; a Justice Department man summarizes them for Senator James Eastland, the Judiciary Committee chairman. The FBI is particularly alert to evidence of immorality, skirmishes with the law (one judge had three drunk-driving citations, but was appointed anyway, after he made a vow of abstinence to a Catholic bishop), and any political, business, or social associations (membership in segregated clubs, involvement in left-wing causes) the agents consider significant.

At the same time the ABA judiciary committee checks the nominee out with lawyers, judges, and others to get a bead on his professional qualifications. If the FBI and ABA reports are both positive and the senator agrees with the administration on a single name, the President then announces the nomination and submits it to the Senate. The Senate Judiciary Committee holds a perfunctory hearing, followed by a vote to confirm and congratulations all around. The Senate fulfills its duty of advice and consent, says University of Chicago law professor Philip Kurland, "by paying less attention to the confirmation process of a federal judge than to the price of bean soup in the Senate restaurant." Thirty-two new judges were routinely confirmed within six days in 1970.

John Duffner, executive assistant to the deputy attorney general, briefs judicial nominees on their hearing. "I can write the script for the hearing," he says. "I tell them that the only senators likely to be there are Eastland, McClellan, and Hruska [a Nebraska Republican]. I tell them to volunteer nothing, that it's like the Army—the longer you keep the first sergeant from knowing your last name, the better off you are. I suggest that they answer questions only and don't bring any witnesses.

"The committee will refer to the ABA report, and then they'll recognize the senator or whoever the man's sponsor is. Then Eastland asks if the biographical sketch they have is accurate, and he'll ask the nature of the man's practice—I tell them to hold it down to a minute and emphasize their trial experience. Then McClellan will give a lecture about how judges have to think of protecting society as well as the individual. I tell them to listen politely and to watch for a question at the end of it, but don't volunteer anything unless there's a question. Hruska will ask if he's an officer or director in a profit-making corporation and point out that he's supposed to resign if he is.

"Then Eastland will ask if the candidate has anything to say. I suggest that they say thanks and that they'll do their best. The senators get impatient if a man brings his family and friends along—one did one time and Eastland got irritated. They don't go into the judge's philosophy. It's all over in about ten minutes."

"I have the impression that the Justice Department is juggling so many things that there isn't much deliberate thought given to judicial selection," says Professor Sheldon Goldman, one of the leading students of the federal judiciary. "Even the deputy attorney general doesn't think that much about it; the assistants run the show. There's not much thinking through and consideration of who might be best. The politicians usually take the initiative." Another scholar, political scientist Richard Burke, investigated judicial appointments between 1929 and 1955 and identified the major elements in the selection equation as personal friendship, partisan service, and the system itself. "Professional merit and qualifications," he concluded, "have ranked with other secondary factors such as age, race, religion, philosophy and ideology. Superior judicial temperament and professional qualifications have seldom been the basis for selection."

Presidents will occasionally cross party lines to appoint a judge, but the reasons, again, have more to do with politics than professional ability. Eisenhower's appointments were 95 percent Republican, Kennedy's were 92 percent Democratic, and Johnson's 94 percent Democratic. Nixon's first-term selections were 93 percent Republican. Opposite-party appointments are likely to be low on an administration's priority list.

President Kennedy named Republican Harold Tyler to a seat in New York. "I remember Bobby Kennedy saying we had to appoint a Republican," a member of the Kennedy Justice Department recalled. "Tyler was head of the civil-rights division in the department under Ike, and he stayed on after the Kennedys came in. That really impressed Bob, so he picked him after checking it out with the senators."

The Nixon administration's arrangement with California Democratic Senators John Tunney and Alan Cranston ensures that every fourth California appointment is a Democrat. The *quid pro quo* is said to be the Californians' support of the administration's judicial nominees. Democratic Senator Abraham Ribicoff of Connecticut was able to negotiate the nomination of Jon Newman, his former administrative assistant, through some accommodation of power, perhaps involving Ribicoff's support of ex-FBI director (and Connecticut resident) L. Patrick Gray.

An intense personal campaign may sometimes net a judgeship. Robert Grant of Indiana lined up support from eight congressmen. Myron Gordon of Wisconsin lobbied his senators and the Johnson administration for several months. And once in a while, just often enough to forestall abject cynicism, a judge reaches the bench for no good reason other than his pre-eminent qualifications. New York's Marvin Frankel was sought out by then-Senator Robert Kennedy on the recommendation of law professors. Ex-Senator

Jack Miller of Iowa asked his state bar association to come up with
three names, and he chose William Stuart from their list. Nixon
appointments Thomas Flannery of the District of Columbia and
Philip Tone of Illinois are regarded as non-political lawyers of
proven ability and integrity.

"It always amazes me," a Democratic lawyer in Washington
said, "but you look back and the Eisenhower appointments are
clearly the best. They've held up. Maybe it was because the Republicans had been out of office so long, they were out of practice
politically. Or maybe it was that Ike's men weren't as political to
begin with, they were more like amateurs. And Ike had no personal
interest in the law-and-order idea like Nixon does. Ike left it to his
attorneys general, to [Herbert] Brownell and [William] Rogers,
and they came up with good men."

It is an opinion echoed frequently among lawyers of all political
shadings, particularly when Eisenhower appointments are compared with Kennedy's. "Kennedy ruined the federal courts in the
South for a generation," says William Kunstler. "Eisenhower's
men were infinitely better. Ike appointed Warren and Brennan to
the Supreme Court, don't forget. Kennedy was hypocritical, he
talked liberalism and appointed racists. Nixon is more honest. I
think he honestly believes in a kind of neo-fascism and authoritarianism and thinks that's the way to run the country."

Eisenhower rated "solid common sense" highly in his judicial
nominees, and regarded previous judicial experience as a plus.
Brownell and Rogers, both upper-echelon members of the legal
Establishment, may have given less ground to senatorial sensibilities than their successors. Eisenhower-appointed judges include
several, such as Edward Gignoux of Maine, Frank Johnson of
Alabama, and Edward Devitt of Minnesota, who are widely admired for their courage and intelligence. He also appointed Julius
Hoffman of Illinois and John Sirica of the District of Columbia.

The pre-Watergate John Sirica was generally regarded as a
rigorously honest judge of modest intellectual attainments, notable
chiefly for the tough criminal sentences that had earned him the
nickname "Maximum John." The son of an Italian immigrant, he
was an amateur boxer while working his way through Georgetown
law school. (He accompanied former heavyweight champion Jack
Dempsey, who was best man at his wedding, on a bond-selling tour

during World War II.) Sirica's decisions were reversed more frequently than those of many other judges, often because of carelessness. "He's not the smartest guy in the world," one Washington lawyer said of him. "He has a reputation as a tough government judge and a rugged sentencer." It was Sirica's threat of a heavy sentence, together with his rigid non-partisanship, which propelled James McCord into the disclosures that broke the Watergate case.

"I want for our courts individuals with respected professional skill," John Kennedy said in 1961, "incorruptible character, firm judicial temperament, the rare inner quality to know when to temper justice with mercy, and the intellectual capacity to protect and illuminate the Constitution and our historic values. . . ."

But Kennedy appointments, particularly in the South, have been repeatedly faulted for falling short of that standard. Nicholas Katzenbach, a deputy attorney general under Kennedy and later Johnson's Attorney General, described the Kennedy policy as "play ball with the ABA, play ball with the senator, do the best you can, don't let anyone through who has personally attacked the President." This screen was porous enough to admit at least five Southern judges whose decisions were consistently pro-segregation—William Cox of Mississippi, E. Gordon West of Louisiana, Robert Elliott of Georgia, Clarence Allgood and Walter Gewin of Alabama. Victor Navasky, author of *Kennedy Justice*, wrote that there was an "absence of any deep, abiding and overriding Kennedy commitment to the integrity and quality of the Southern judiciary itself." Navasky found "no aspect of Robert Kennedy's attorney generalship . . . more vulnerable to criticism" than his judicial appointments in the South. Southern senators, of course, share the responsibility: Cox was Eastland's man, West was a protégé of Senator Russell Long, Elliott a close associate of Senator Herman Talmadge.

Kennedy appointed eight judges who were rated unqualified by the ABA. All but one were named in his first year in office. "The general rule is that the appointments in the first year are the worst," says a high-ranking ABA lawyer. "Presidents are more susceptible to political pressure then. They have more debts to be paid."

Political scientist Mary Curzan contends that in racial terms

Eisenhower's record is overrated and Kennedy's underrated. She appraises five of JFK's 16 Southern appointments as segregationists, compared with five of 15 named by Ike. She argues that the racist Kennedy appointments received more publicity, and that the ABA and the press were biased in favor of Eisenhower.

The Kennedy men generally trusted their own judgment of a nominee's character over that of the ABA or others. Sometimes that judgment succumbed to political expediency, but, as Anthony Lewis of the *New York Times* wrote, "the nominees also include a high proportion of the best men." Hubert Will of Illinois, Joseph Lord of Pennsylvania, and William Jones of the District of Columbia rank high among Kennedy appointments.

Lyndon Johnson's career as a judge-maker divides neatly into two periods: before and after Morrissey. Francis X. Morrissey was the Kennedy family retainer backed by Senator Edward Kennedy and nominated to a Massachusetts federal judgeship by Johnson in 1965. Morrissey had received a law degree from a Georgia "diploma mill," then twice failed to pass the bar examination. His pathetically weak credentials inspired the ABA to put up a fight. In a rare breach of the judicial curtain, a sitting federal judge (Chief Judge Charles Wyzanski of the Massachusetts District) publicly opposed his nomination. The Judiciary Committee voted to confirm the nomination, and there were reportedly enough votes in the Senate to get Morrissey through, but Kennedy finally withdrew his name.

Including the Morrissey nomination, six of Johnson's first fifty-six appointments drew gasps of "not qualified" from the ABA. A strong advocate of senatorial courtesy, Johnson preferred to go along with senatorial nominations. After the Morrissey debacle and a long meeting with ABA leaders, however, he changed course. From then on, all his nominees had ABA backing. Morrissey was, in fact, the last judicial nomination made over the objections of the ABA. The Johnson judges remained partisan Democrats, but their intellectual and professional quality rose visibly. Many are among those rated most highly by constitutional lawyers: James Doyle of Wisconsin, Marvin Frankel and Jack Weinstein of New York, Robert Merhige of Virginia, Frederick Heebe of Louisiana, and William Keady of Mississippi, among others. All were named between 1965 and 1968.

Johnson brought his familiar weaving style of political maneuver to the demands of judicial selection. "There were two District Court vacancies in Virginia," a Washington lawyer recalled. "Senator [Harry] Byrd was backing Richard Kellam, Senator [William] Spong was behind John Mackenzie, and Robert Merhige had the support of the Reynolds Metal Company in Virginia, which was a big donor to the Johnson campaign. So he had three men for two spots. Johnson's contribution to the workings of democracy was to elevate Judge John Butzner to the Fourth Circuit Court of Appeals, which gave him three openings in Virginia. Everybody was happy. *Voilà*, eh?"

The twelve members of the ABA committee on the federal judiciary—a chairman and one from each of the eleven federal circuits, chosen by the ABA president—are a cadre of well-established, generally conservative old boys who patrol the summit of their profession. There has never been a black, Spanish-speaking, or female member. Most committeemen are in their fifties or sixties.

The committee moves into action as soon as a candidate for a federal judgeship is proposed. The member for the circuit where the seat is located conducts a series of interviews (often as many as twenty-five) aimed at assessing the potential judge's ability, temperament, and integrity. The choice of whom to see is up to the committeeman, but the list will usually include federal and state judges, the "leading lawyers" in the community ("anyone in the circuit will know who they are," one member says), and attorneys who have opposed the candidate in court. The circuit member also analyzes transcripts of cases the candidate has argued.

"We try to get a fair cross-section of opinion," says Lawrence Walsh of New York, a recent committee chairman and former federal judge. "The standards we apply are is he competent, does he have a 'usable' temperament, and does he have integrity—not whether we like him or not. By temperament we mean is he capable of intellectual detachment, can he hold his mind open? Integrity may be the least subjective area, except perhaps for intellectual integrity. The question is whether he is biased, whether there is crookedness in his reasoning. The lines aren't easy to draw. You approach it as if you're looking for a lawyer for your best client in that neighborhood." The committee rejects District Court candidates over sixty-three, and regards trial experience as essential.

The circuit committeeman writes a report on the candidate and recommends a rating. The full committee then votes, usually in a telephone "conference call," and the result is passed on to the Justice Department. The definitions of the ratings—qualified, well qualified, and exceptionally well qualified—are subjective, as are the committee estimates of a man's qualifications. "We each have the definition in our own minds," Walsh says. "I define qualified as meaning that nothing adverse has been found and he has the qualities to do the job and handle himself adequately. Well qualified means a man of excellence who would be among those one would seek out for the job. Exceptionally well qualified is a brilliant, enormously capable man."

The ABA's influence has oscillated from President to President, rising when Republicans were in the oval office and dipping during Democratic rule. It established a secure foothold during the Eisenhower years, and solidified its position under Nixon, who has refused to appoint candidates who lack ABA approval.

Critics have focused on the committee's secrecy (the ABA refused to release its dossier on Otto Kerner to the Justice Department, for example, even after Kerner was indicted), its conservative orientation (it opposed Louis Brandeis in 1916, but rated G. Harrold Carswell well qualified for the Fifth Circuit Court of Appeals in 1969), and its willingness to accept the marginally qualified.

"Their standards are minimal," says Harvard's Dershowitz. "They don't begin to approach what they should be. There is a strong presumption of suitability. There should be public hearings. The ABA doesn't really get a cross-section—I know of an appointment in Massachusetts where there was all kinds of opposition, but none of the opponents was approached by the ABA." "My impression," adds Stanford's Amsterdam, "is that screening for the lower courts is a matter of asking round over the lunch table at whatever restaurant gets the carriage trade for the local commercial lawyers."

Law professor Herman Schwartz is harsher. "The ABA is dominated by Establishment Republican lawyers who are devoted to the *status quo* in every respect," he charges. "They're no less political than the parties are. I think they're whoring for Nixon."

Walsh concedes that a "presumption of suitability" exists. "If it's a criticism, it's valid," he says. "It's true. It's hard to turn the other way. We have no sanctions except our own powers of persuasion. We can't block a nomination. An opponent of a nomination has the burden of proof."

Walsh and other committeemen deny that ideological bias enters the process. "We avoid passing judgment on a candidate's political views or philosophy," he says. "It may be a factor," another member allows, "but it's unconscious if it is. If you're concerned about built-in prejudices, the whole thing starts to fall apart. I feel strongly that lawyers won't do that, that they'll be efficient and honest. Am I naïve?"

"If there are marginal candidates and clearly superior candidates on the list the ABA gets," says Professor Sheldon Goldman, "they'll try to manipulate the ratings in favor of the superior ones. The committee broadened its contacts in recent years. It's not a conservative, rigid group wanting only upper-class conservatives on the bench. Walsh and [former chairman Bernard] Segal are liberal-establishment Republicans. It's too facile to write the ABA off as conservative fuddy-duddies. They take the job seriously. They want to promote the best men possible, given political realities."

But Goldman concedes that a qualified rating is given "mainly in the absence of any concrete evidence to strike a man down with. There's no doubt that some just marginally qualified, if that, get a qualified rating as the best of a bad bunch—they're dealing with political reality. There's a tendency to go along, because when you go against an administration it's a major battle if it fights back, and the committee's cordial relations with the Justice Department are imperiled. They go along with a borderline nominee in the hope that they can exert more influence in favor of a good one another time."

I asked one member of the committee whether there is any pressure to rate a marginal political candidate as qualified. "I haven't seen it," he replied, "but I can conceive of the chairman calling a circuit member and saying, 'Look, it was close, and for the sake of our ongoing relations with the Justice Department let's give him the benefit of the doubt.' That's how it would happen. But I don't think a committee member is susceptible to that kind of pressure unless he aspires to be a judge. If it were me, I'd have to

relate my decision to what I'd done in other cases, and I couldn't
justify that to myself."

Clinton Dominick is a paunchy, good-natured man who was a
liberal Republican state senator in New York before he was defeated in a primary in 1970. He has spent most of his life in
politics, but since his defeat he has practiced law quietly in the
Hudson Valley town of Newburgh. Dominick has witnessed the
roulette wheel of federal judicial selection from the perspective of
an unlucky number.

"In the summer of 1970 I got a call from an aide to Senator
Javits," he recalls. "He said, 'As you probably know, you're being
considered for an appointment to federal District Court.' I said tell
me about it. He said my name was on the list and I was hanging
right in there.

"Well, I hadn't thought about being a federal judge, but that
has a great appeal. It would be a very interesting job. There were
several vacancies at that time. So in the next few months I went to
Washington five times—once to see Senator [Charles] Goodell
[defeated by Conservative James Buckley later that year], three
times to see Javits, and once to see Buckley. Buckley smiled, you
know politics, and I left. He has a steering committee, and they
interviewed me. They brought up my lack of trial experience and
the fact that I had no experience in federal courts. I said I'd done a
lot of other things and my faults were visible in legislation rather
than court decisions.

"Right in the middle of all this the FBI came around to see me. I
figured they were here in connection with my appointment, but
they were checking on Robert Carter, who was on my state-court
commission. Carter's good [he was later appointed to the federal
bench], but I said I wished I could say something bad about him to
protect myself. But I didn't.

"The bar association had also objected that I didn't have federal
trial experience. But Javits was able to overcome that somehow,
and they were willing to go for me. I was told that Rockefeller was
for me. The interesting thing was that the administration was willing to go along, it was okay with the Justice Department, it was
just Buckley. If the bar association had gone for me early, when
Goodell was still in there, I would have made it. But then Buckley
came on the scene. Javits really stuck to his guns for me, I'll say

that. Finally he called and said Buckley wouldn't go for it. They both have a veto.

"The chairman of Buckley's committee called too. I could have punched him in the mouth, but I admired his guts. He said if they were going to break their rule about trial experience I'd be the one they'd break it for, but they couldn't.

"I don't buy that trial-experience requirement. I have enough confidence in myself to think that I'd be good. I could learn the procedure easily enough. You don't know if a man is going to be a good judge or not. There's no way to tell."

Dominick's office was quiet. There had been no telephone calls for an hour. "The thing that sticks in my mind," he continued, "is a call I got one day. It was Governor Rockefeller calling, and he came on and said, 'Judge . . .' Javits had told Rockefeller that it was going to be me. I don't think they were stringing me along. I'm thick-skinned enough after sixteen years of politics that I'd be aware of that. And I don't believe they'd be that cruel to me. But it still bothers me a bit. It's a little hard to believe that the governor couldn't overcome Buckley if he really wanted to push, you know. It seems to me that even a senator isn't that far removed from the governor's influence."

Dominick shook his large head. "I'm not waiting up nights for it to happen again," he said. "You know, when the appointments were finally made, one of them was Murray Gurfein, and the first case he had was the Pentagon Papers. I couldn't help it, I thought, 'Jesus, what a way to start.' I would have loved it."

If and when he completes eight years in office, Richard Nixon will have appointed more judges to federal courts than any previous President. In his first four years he named 142 District Court and 37 appellate-court judges, plus four Supreme Court justices. In his second term he will pass the record 194 federal-court appointments made by Franklin Roosevelt.

Seventy of Nixon's first-term appointments were to new judgeships added by a 1970 act of Congress. In 1973 a subcommittee of the Senate Judiciary Committee proposed that 27 new district judgeships be created. The Judicial Conference, the policy-making body for the federal judiciary, had recommended 51 new seats on the district bench.

Nixon's selections have brought the partisan lineup of the federal bench close to parity. In 1969, Democratic district judges outnumbered Republicans by more than two to one. By the end of a first term in which he named 132 Republicans and 10 Democrats to District Court seats, Nixon had brought the total to 209 Democrats and 180 Republicans. Unless he pauses to remember his own words of half a generation ago, he is in a position to tilt the balance almost as heavily the other way.

As a presidential candidate in 1960, Nixon endorsed an ABA proposal that both parties pledge to maintain the then-equal political alignment on the bench. "I believe it is essential," he said, "that the best qualified lawyers and judges available be appointed to judicial office, and . . . that the number of judges in federal courts from each of the major political parties be approximately equal." John Kennedy and the Democrats disagreed, and the ensuing imbalance was the result.

Between then and now, however, "law and order" became an important political issue, with Nixon its most ardent advocate. A stout-hearted identification with the "peace forces" as against the "criminal forces" became a Nixonian criterion for judicial appointments at all levels. Judges who dissented from this simplistic interpretation, or who defended the liberal and expansive decisions of the Warren Court, were classified by the President as "softheaded."

"You can't be a federal judge today," says a Washington lawyer with government experience under both parties, "unless you believe the whole hardnosed line. It's like getting ahead in the FBI—you have to be for the death penalty, you have to regard all the criminal decisions of the Warren Court as wrong. I've never seen such stereotypes. Any background of liberalism or orientation toward the Bill of Rights is a disqualifier. Or a philosophical kinship with Learned Hand, say, the idea that better one guilty man go free than an innocent man be hanged—if you feel that way, you don't make it. There are some exceptions, where you have liberal Republican senators like [Charles] Percy or Javits. But if there's no liberal senator, then you get one-hundred-percent law and order.

"The Nixon administration is subjecting nominees to the most intense ideological scrutiny since FDR," says scholar Sheldon Goldman. "They'll appoint law-and-order conservatives wherever they are strong enough to do it."

In California, the three-to-one trade with Democratic senators gave Nixon's men an unchecked hand in the appointment of fourteen other judges in his first term. One was Samuel Conti, a former state judge, who believes that "if judges don't have the intestinal fortitude to send someone to jail, they should get out of the judge business. This is too good a country," he declared in a 1971 interview, "to go down the drain with permissiveness." One of Conti's first acts on the bench was to deny bail to defendants in a Selective Service case, in defiance of the federal bail-reform act.

Another California appointment, Lawrence T. Lydick, is a former Nixon law partner. A third, Spencer Williams, was a losing candidate for state attorney general on the ticket headed by Governor Ronald Reagan. Williams won a qualified rating from the ABA despite minimal legal experience. He dismissed without a hearing charges that San Quentin prisoners were beaten by guards after a shooting at the penitentiary.

"San Francisco had for many years the finest federal district bench in the country," a local law professor said. "Since Nixon the caliber has worsened markedly. Three of his first four appointments were appalling, and the fourth was a hostage to the Democratic senators."

In the South, where there are few Republican senators to impede him (and the few are conservatives like J. Strom Thurmond of South Carolina and John Tower of Texas), Nixon's selections have followed a similar pattern. "The essential requirement seems to be strong services to the conservative wing of the Republican party and an anti-Bill of Rights position," says a Duke University law professor.

Charles Clark, a Nixon appointment to the Fifth Circuit appellate court in the South, once defended former Mississippi Governor Ross Barnett in a case arising out of Barnett's refusal to permit James Meredith to attend the state university. Joe Ingraham compiled a pro-segregation record as a Texas District Court judge before Nixon promoted him to the Fifth Circuit. Robert Varner of Alabama, a friend of former Postmaster General Winton Blount, had been president of a segregated bar association in Montgomery. At one trial Varner asked that blacks be removed from the jury because "white people in the area have not accepted the idea of eating with Negroes." He expressed the view that "a judge should not commit himself one way or the other on segregation. It is a political philosophy, isn't it?"

Friends at the top were helpful to several other Nixon appointees. Ozell Trask of the Ninth Circuit Court of Appeals was a former law partner of Richard Kleindienst. Eugene Wright, also chosen for the Ninth Circuit, is a close friend of John Ehrlichman. Stanley Blair of Maryland was once Spiro Agnew's administrative assistant. Charles Richey of the District of Columbia was another pal of Agnew's.

Richard McLaren's appointment was interesting because of its haste. McLaren, as head of the anti-trust division in the Justice Department, approved the controversial settlement of an anti-trust action against ITT after originally favoring prosecution. A promised $400,000 contribution to the 1972 Republican convention was allegedly related to the settlement. McLaren's appointment to the district bench in Chicago was one of the speediest on record. He was nominated, approved by the Judiciary Committee, and confirmed by the Senate all in one day—December 2, 1971. The process normally takes between a week and a month.

The nomination of William Frey of Arizona followed a bizarre chain of events. Frey was the choice of the state's Republican leaders, but the bar association had doubts about his temperament. Senator Paul Fannin tried to finesse the situation by endorsing another man more acceptable to the bar. He called Frey an outstanding candidate, but said the other man was "even more outstanding." The other man then underwent a physical examination and learned that he had cancer. A short time later he committed suicide. Since Fannin had committed himself to Frey as a second choice, the appointment was his.

"I've heard other lawyers say that Nixon's judges are all law-and-order-minded," says F. Lee Bailey, "but I haven't seen evidence of a general pattern to back that up." Bailey's is a minority view among the dozens of lawyers I spoke with, but it may be related to where he sits—in Massachusetts. Where liberal Republican senators share the appointing power with the administration—in Massachusetts, Illinois, New York, New Jersey, and Oregon, for example—the quality of Nixon's judges has been higher.

"We draw a line here between appointments before and since Percy," says an attorney in Chicago. "His appointments are head and shoulders above what's been done around here before." Percy works with the Chicago Council of Lawyers, a band of liberal-minded young attorneys, in screening candidates. "He tested us by asking what we thought about some liberal judges who were ideologically pure but lousy judges," a council officer says. "He hasn't named any flaming liberals, but they are all solid and capable men." At least two, Frank McGarr and Philip Tone, are ranked among the best on the federal bench.

The highly regarded Levin Campbell of Massachusetts, now on the First Circuit Court of Appeals, was supported by Senator Edward Brooke. Jacob Javits sponsored several highly rated appointments, including Circuit Judge Walter Mansfield and District Judges Arnold Bauman and Murray Gurfein. Frederick Lacey of New Jersey was backed by liberal Senator Clifford Case.

Nixon's appointments across party lines have generally been either Southern Democrats whose ideology is indistinguishable from his, or the beneficiaries of trade-offs with Democratic senators. Eldon Mahon of Texas (a nephew of Congressman George Mahon), Solomon Blatt, Jr., of South Carolina, and James King of Florida are all Nixon's kind of Democrat.

L. Clure Morton of Tennessee, whose brother was a campaign aide to Senator Howard Baker, was considered safely conservative until he surprised the administration by ordering an increase in busing to desegregate Nashville schools. Agnew's friend Charles Richey may have been another surprise. He eschewed the law-and-order line and urged instead that judges become experts in behavioral science. He spent one four-week vacation touring federal prisons to show inmates that "at least one federal judge" considered them "human beings." Richey's name came up in the testimony of Watergate witness John Dean, who said White House aides had covertly pressured the judge to get a delay in the civil trial arising out of the Watergate burglary.

The longest-standing federal-court vacancy as of 1973 was in Wisconsin, where Nixon tried for two years to gain ABA approval for Congressman Glenn Davis. The ABA's rejection was based on his lack of trial experience. A Nixon candidate in Illinois was withdrawn after he was accused of anti-Semitism; another, in South Carolina, was dropped after charges of race prejudice were made.

Estimating the general quality of federal district judges is a feloniously chancy enterprise. No lawyer or law professor knows more than a few dozen of them at most. One's opinion is invariably colored by his own bias, his own success or failure before different judges, and the views of colleagues who think the same way he does.

I have seen perhaps 30 federal judges out of the 401. I have heard opinions, of varying heat and light, on another 75. I am familiar with the background of most of them. I've discussed their over-all quality with perhaps a dozen men with wide experience in federal courts.

My impression is that a few, but only a few, are clearly incompetent. There are many, perhaps a majority, who are competent but not distinguished, not the men of excellence one wishes federal judges to be. The vast majority are unassailably honest. A small percentage—5 percent? 10?—are bigots. A slightly larger percentage—say 15—are everything an idealist could hope for: intelligent, compassionate, fair-minded, courageous, serious, and capable.

Almost everyone agrees that the quality of the federal bench is superior to that of the state courts. "The general level is astronomically higher," says Alan Dershowitz, "but it's not as good as it can be. The range is high mediocrity. There is an unstated tradition that senators will look for a certain level of excellence. There's a kind of minimum floor—a senator just doesn't go to the probate bench of a state court for a federal judge. Not all senators have the same minimum level, but most do. I'd say one out of every three or four district judges turns out to be very good. But the bad ones are still a natural consequence of the system in that other systems would preclude them."

The Chicago Council of Lawyers polled more than 300 attorneys in 1971, asking them to assess the integrity, temperament, ability, and decisiveness of Chicago federal judges. The lawyers were asked if they favored the continued service on the bench of 13 judges; 10 of the 13 got "yes" answers from at least 50 percent of those who replied.

Professor Harold Chase of the University of Minnesota, author of an excellent book on the federal judiciary, concluded that "our present appointment system nets a good but not outstanding array of federal judges." Former Senator Joseph Tydings of Maryland, who has urged that federal judges be chosen by merit selection, finds their quality "very high as a whole." Sheldon Goldman of the University of Massachusetts believes they are "generally high caliber—by and large they're not our wisest, but they're capable."

"Asking whether the quality should be higher," says Tydings, "is like asking whether the quality of U.S. senators should be higher, or whether one should be a better lawyer. You can always be better."

The most persistent complaint about the federal system is that there is no way to remove a senile, disabled, or incompetent judge. Chase estimates that one out of ten federal judges is hobbled by illness or age. There is no mandatory retirement age; a judge who chooses to sit beyond his seventieth birthday sacrifices some fringe benefits, but that's all. Persuading a senile federal jurist to retire is an exercise in finesse which can stymie the most adroit diplomat.

Former Supreme Court Justice John Marshall Harlan once tried to convince the ailing Justice Stephen Field, a Lincoln appointment, that he should retire. When Harlan reminded Field that the old man had once tried to persuade another justice to retire, Field's eyes blazed. "Yes," he cried, "and a dirtier day's work I never did in my life!"

The reason for their reluctance is not hard to find. As one federal judge explained, "When you are an active judge, you are somebody. When you are a retired judge, you are nobody."

Judges of the Sixth Circuit Court of Appeals adopted a secret resolution in 1965 demanding that Ohio District Judge Mell Underwood retire. The appellate jurists felt that he was not doing his share of work. "They have no authority to remove me," Underwood declared when he heard of it, "and they've found that out. I told them to go to hell, and you may quote me on that if you like."

District Judge Stephen Chandler of Oklahoma was ordered by the Judicial Council of the Tenth Circuit to hear no more cases. The action was reportedly inspired by Chandler's erratic behavior. The Supreme Court upheld the council's action, but Chandler retained his office; the court failed to resolve the question of whether the council, the administrative body for the circuit, had the power to remove him.

Nixon appointee Mark Costantino of Brooklyn was accused in a series of newspaper articles of incompetence and conflict of interest. The Second Circuit Judicial Council investigated the allegations and reported, without elaboration, that "no action by the council is warranted."

Senator Hugh Scott, Tydings, and others have suggested the creation of a commission of judges with the authority to receive complaints about federal judges and to order their removal. But no reform plan has breached the black wall of judicial opposition. The bills never got out of committee. Federal judges can be counted on to oppose any reform which they see as a threat to their independence, and they have influential friends in the Senate.

Changes in selection and tenure have fared no better. Governor George Wallace urged popular election of federal judges in his 1972 presidential campaign, and Senator Harry Byrd, Jr., has introduced legislation to make them subject to reconfirmation every eight years. President Eisenhower suggested that they be appointed for twenty-year terms with mandatory retirement at seventy-two. Tydings favors setting up a nominating commission in each state. But the engines of change have remained silent. "It's not going to happen in the foreseeable future," Tydings says. "A major scandal would be necessary—maybe two of them. There would have to be something to convince the public that the present system is intolerable."

"Senators are not going to give up that power," says Sheldon Goldman, "and that's putting it modestly." Goldman and many other critics believe that on balance the present system works about as well as any possible alternative. They distrust as undemocratic any plan which would give the power of judicial selection to commissions of lawyers and judges.

"There's a flexibility and pluralism about the federal process," he contends. "I have faith in pluralism and an active Senate. The politicians and the Justice Department, the ABA and the press are all checking and balancing each other. There's nothing wrong with judges with political backgrounds. It's a way of developing some notion of the desires and expectations of different parts of the electorate and a sense of the country. And even—if we dare—a sense of humility.

"Ultimately the question of what makes a good judge concerns a man's vision, his fitness as a philosopher-king, because that's what our judges are. They have an opportunity to help the country, to resolve our great conflicts. The legal profession trains them to hide their policy views behind legal subterfuge, but the truth is they have enormous areas of discretion. It's their judgment, their opinion of what's good for the country. Even with the inherent antidemocracy of life tenure, we do get judges who are interested in the public good. The present system isn't totally effective, but it may be our saving grace."

XIII

Judge Simpatico

Aggressive compassion in a San Francisco federal court

T H E   C O U R T R O O M has a look of spacious serenity, as if
petty human squabbling is somehow out of place here and the
dissonant sounds of argument might tail off against the rich walnut
walls in sheer embarrassment. The room is perhaps seventy-five
feet long and fifty feet across. Its high, arched ceiling is filled with
light panels. A large, rectangular slab of marble dominates the
wall behind the judge's bench. The walls are paneled with slats of
light and dark wood. The court seems almost a metaphor for
dignity: cool, subdued, clean, solid, bright—no place for frivolity,
clearly, but a place where the law moves with a certain stateliness
and words suitable for transcription are chosen carefully. The
setting seems appropriate for an idea as grand as justice.

"Please rise," the crier calls.

United States District Judge Alfonso J. Zirpoli enters through a
door behind the bench and to the right. He is in a wheelchair,
having injured both legs in a recent accident at home. A dozen
people stand and stare as he wheels in, but from his low vantage
the judge is conscious only of eyes—those of the lawyers nervously
sympathetic, the clerks friendly, the defendant frightened, the few
spectators indifferent.

The judge is lifted one step up and wheels to a point midway
behind the long clerk's desk in front of his bench. He is a trim,

forceful-looking man of medium height, with wavy battleship-gray hair, a large nose and mouth, and warm brown eyes. He is sixty-eight, but looks closer to fifty. He wears a sweater under a dark suit, and no robe. "Please be seated," the crier says.

The defendant, a woman in her early twenties, is accused of embezzling $525 from the federal bank where she worked as a teller. She has decided to withdraw her plea of innocent and plead guilty to a misdemeanor charge of misapplying bank funds.

The judge squints beneath his dark eyebrows and smiles. "Are you prepared to plead?" he asks.

"Yes, Your Honor," she murmurs.

"What is your plea?"

"Guilty."

"Do you understand the charge against you?"

"Yes, sir."

"And it is still your desire to plead guilty?" The judge's manner is gentle, even cordial, though his voice is gruff. He seems totally engaged.

"Yes."

"How old are you?"

"Twenty-four."

"How much education have you had?"

"One year of college, Your Honor." Her voice is barely above a whisper. She squeezes her left index finger with her right hand and stares at a point two feet below the judge's eyes.

"Do you have any children?"

"No, sir."

"Do you understand that you're entitled to a jury trial?"

"Yes, sir."

"And you're waiving that right by pleading guilty?"

"Yes."

"You understand that all it takes is one juror with a reasonable doubt for an acquittal—just one out of twelve. Do you still want to plead guilty?"

"Yes." She looks up quizzically.

"Are you satisfied that you have no defense to the charge against you?"

"Yes." A piece of her fragile reserve cracks. "I told the FBI I would pay the money back."

The judge seems uninterested in this. "Were you warned of your rights?"

"Yes, sir." She has folded her hands behind her back.

"Do you know that you could go to prison for one year and be fined as much as a thousand dollars?"

She swallows. "Now I do."

"Do you still want to plead guilty?"

The response is slower this time. "Yes, sir."

"Do you understand that under the Youthful Offender Act I could sentence you to prison for as long as six years if I choose to?" The judge sees her eyes widen, and adds hastily, "Or of course I could place you on probation, or send you to jail for five days."

She nods.

Zirpoli fixes her with a friendly squint. "Now, knowing that you could be sentenced for as long as six years, do you still want to plead guilty?"

The woman hesitates, half turns toward her lawyer, looks at the floor. Her hands tremble. "No," she says.

"Would you like a trial?" the judge says quickly. The idea seems agreeable to him.

"May we have a few minutes, Your Honor?" the lawyer says.

They walk to a table for a short, whispered conference. The woman holds her eyes on the floor and her hands behind her back. The back of her neck is red. Judge Zirpoli turns to the clerk seated next to him. "I guess I shouldn't scare 'em so much," he says. His eyes, his most striking feature, are alive with humor and sympathy.

The defendant returns to her place before the judge. His voice softens, becomes grandfatherly. "Do you still desire to plead guilty, knowing all the possible consequences?"

She glances quickly at her lawyer. "Yes, Your Honor," she says.

"Were any promises made to you in connection with your plea?"

"No."

"Were any threats made?"

"No."

"Are you pleading guilty because of the nature of the charge, or because you committed the crime?"

The reply is almost inaudible: "I stole the money."

"Are you telling me that you embezzled the money?"

"Yes, sir."

The judge looks at a sheet before him. "All right, I'll permit the defendant to enter a plea."

The judge asks if she prefers to be sentenced now or wants to wait for a probation report. She says she is willing to be sentenced now. "She has no record, Your Honor," her lawyer says. "She has another job. Restitution has been made."

"How much are you earning at your new job?" the judge asks her.

"Four hundred thirty dollars a month."

"Why did you take the money from the bank?"

She looks at her hands. "The money showed up in my account and I just kept it. I had no logical . . . It was just there. When I realized it was there I didn't return it."

Zirpoli looks businesslike now. He has made up his mind. The tang of human contact is just about over. "The court will suspend imposition of sentence and place you on probation for a period of one year. If there are no further charges during that year, your record will be expunged at the termination of probation." He looks up from his desk. "This is an opportunity for you to erase this record and start fresh. Make the most of it, now. Good luck."

The girl sighs, smiles weakly, and nods. Zirpoli turns and begins to wheel out. "It was a privilege to appear before you, Judge," her lawyer says. The judge waves a hand in acknowledgment.

Zirpoli wheels through a short corridor to his chambers, a suite of three rooms on the seventeenth floor of the San Francisco Federal Building. One long wall of his private office is lined from floor to ceiling with lawbooks. A window runs the length of the opposite wall, looking out on the city and the peninsula to the south. The furniture is comfortable and judicial: a large desk, a conference table with six chairs, a sofa and easy chair of dark leather. There is a framed copy of President John Kennedy's inaugural address along with photographs of Earl Warren, Harry Truman, former Supreme Court Justice Tom Clark, and a distinguished-looking Zirpoli ancestor who was a stagecoach driver in Italy. A photograph of President Kennedy is inscribed, "To my fellow sustaining member of the Democratic party. John F. Kennedy." Behind the desk is another bookcase containing family pictures, a bust of Franklin Roosevelt, and several dozen books, among them James Michener's *Hawaii* and *The Source; QB-VII* by Leon Uris; *The Age of Voltaire; The Superlawyers; The Waste Makers* by Vance Packard; Lyndon Johnson's memoirs; *The Crusades;* and Eric Sevareid's *Candidates 1960*, a study of the preconvention presidential candidates of that year.

The judge collects a sheaf of papers from an "in" box—"They reversed you," his law clerk reports, eliciting no response—and wheels his chair to one end of the table. He is still thinking about the woman he has just placed on probation. "It would be ridiculous to send her to jail," he says. "It wouldn't do any good—she has no record, and a year of college—and it might do a lot of harm. It was apparently a one-shot deal. Her husband is a cement finisher."

He shakes his head. "Sometimes they don't quite get it when I tell them the sentence they could get. I hate to scare them like that. But it's a routine we have to go through—they have to understand the consequences of a guilty plea. I never intended to send her to jail."

Zirpoli's judicial style might be described as aggressive compassion. He wants to *absorb*—not only the facts of the cases before him, but the personality and character of the individuals involved. One-to-one justice, a notion severely buffeted by the tides of contemporary caseload pressures, is indispensable to his view of his function. "Letting the job become routine is the biggest curse that can befall a judge," he says. "I try desperately to let every little defendant have his say, to establish a rapport so that the experience carries some meaning and feeling for them. I look them in the eye and start talking. I ask questions because I want to find out the answers. If it becomes a habit, it's like the country priest that [Italian legal scholar] Piero Calamandrei wrote about, who becomes accustomed to saying mass."

The satisfactions of judging, for Zirpoli, are "the feeling that I'm doing a pretty good job in sentencing when I manifest the compassion that a judge should have, and that if the government itself violates the law, I'm here to make dang sure that people aren't hurt by government action."

More than most of us, Zirpoli is a creature of his loyalties. To list them is not to define the man, but rather to paste labels around the edges of his portrait, each one suggesting a different ingredient of his character. In unequal parts and in no special order, Zirpoli is an Italian, an American, a judge, a San Franciscan, and a politician. He is faithful, in one way or another, to all of them.

He sees himself as living validation of the American Dream, as

the confirmation of another generation's faith in an America where
an immigrant's son can elbow-grease and midnight-oil his way to
success and glory. His father was a cavalryman in the Italian Army
before he emigrated to the United States in 1904. His mother, who
"could quote Dante and Tasso stanza after stanza," had come over a
short time earlier. They were married in Connecticut and migrated
west to Denver, where his father took a job with the Italian consulate and where Alfonso, the first of two sons, was born in 1905.

He did well in school, sold newspapers, and worked as a grocery
clerk. In 1918 the family moved to San Francisco, taking an
apartment on Nob Hill, several blocks distant from the predomi-
nantly Italian North Beach district. "We had no luxury," he says.
But young Zirpoli had the kind of alert, eager drive that appeals to
successful, self-made men, and in San Francisco he found a patron.

"I'd often go to the Italian consulate, where my father worked,
and A. P. Giannini's office was in the same building. I used to see
him in the elevator." Giannini's elevator was going up. The
founder of the Bank of America, he was on his way to becoming
one of the richest and most powerful men of his day, as well as a
leader of San Francisco's Italian-American community. "One day I
just asked him for a job," Zirpoli recalls. "I became his personal
messenger boy. It was a hell of an experience. He took a kindly
interest in me.

"I remember attending an SEC hearing with him one time. The
acquisition of a number of branch banks was under consideration.
A.P. rose while one witness was testifying, pointed his finger at the
witness, and shouted, 'That is a goddam lie.' I pulled on his coattails and said, 'But, Mr. A.P., you can't do that,' He looked down at
me and said, 'But I did, son, didn't I?' He got away with it. When
my law clerks tell me I can't prepare a particular order, I tell them
the Giannini story.

"There's an Italian proverb, 'Volere é potere'—it means if you
have will, you can accomplish. I admired A.P. for his strength of
character and his fighting qualities. He was unselfish—he gave
away most of his money. And he was a practical man politically.
He supported those who would help him and his branch-banking
policy."

Zirpoli borrowed money to buy stock in Giannini companies
while a student at the University of California. He later lost his
investment in the market collapse of 1929. By that time he had

graduated from law school in Berkeley and was setting up as an attorney in San Francisco. Two years later Giannini helped him get a job as a prosecutor.

"I wanted to be an assistant district attorney, but I couldn't get in to see the DA, so I went to see A.P. and told him what I wanted. He told his secretary to get Tom Finn on the phone—he was the Republican boss of the city. He said, 'I'm sending a boy over to see you.' I had to tell Finn I was a Democrat. He said, 'A.P. sent you, didn't he?' And that was it. He called the district attorney and I was an assistant DA the next morning."

Zirpoli had plunged into politics as a stump speaker for Democratic presidential candidate Al Smith in 1928. Four years later he represented Giannini, a supporter of Franklin Roosevelt, at a meeting of California Democrats. He was president of the state's Young Democrats in 1935 and a delegate to the national convention in 1936, a year in which Giannini appeared at another intersection in his life.

"I talked to A.P. about becoming president of a federal land bank," he says. "It was a presidential appointment. A.P. asked Senator [William] McAdoo to submit my name, and he did. But then I got to talking about it with a lawyer friend. He asked me why I wanted to do that; he said I had a lot of potential in politics. I went back to see A.P. and said, 'Mr. A.P., I've decided I better stay in the law.' Well, the President had already sent my name to the Senate, but A.P. got it withdrawn. He told me to make up my mind."

His campaigning for FDR had won Zirpoli an appointment as an assistant United States Attorney in 1933. He gained a modest reputation as a crimebuster. His biggest case was the prosecution of a ring of gangsters who harbored the notorious "Baby Face" Nelson, and he knew how to make the most of it. "Shots rang out sharply under the summer moon," began a detective-magazine story on the case co-written by Zirpoli in 1935. "Shots and wild laughter, with the slugs spattering against the white walls of the little schoolhouse until the plaster flew and churned the air with pale, choking dust. . . . Laughter came from their thin lips, hollow and unreal—the humor of madmen. The slugs, peppering the moonlit wall, came from their Tommy guns and the automatics they were using to test a new batch of bullet-proof vests."

Zirpoli and his G-men broke the case when they persuaded a

pudgy Nelson ally named Fatso Negri to become a government witness. Zirpoli relishes the memory. "We had him in jail in Piedmont, across the bay," he says. "He liked it there—he said it was the first jail where they gave him napkins. He was with Dillinger just before he was killed. Fatso and I became quite friendly afterwards. He wanted me to be his best man when he married a madam in Oregon. He later went to sea, and I used to get cards from him."

The job as a federal prosecutor, besides spreading the fame of Zirpoli the gangland nemesis, gave him a close look at federal judges. "I thought a U.S. district judge was the greatest guy in the world. I looked up to them with awe. The respect and power a federal judge commanded was enormous. I began to aspire to a federal judgeship then and there."

He left the U.S. Attorney's office in 1944 to join a leading San Francisco firm as a trial lawyer. "I had in mind becoming a federal judge," he says, "but I didn't really think I'd make it. So many things have to coincide—you have to be with the party, your name goes in through a senator, you need the approval of the Attorney General: it's quite a combination to put together. To get it you have to be politically active, and you have to support a winner for senator and then build your fences with that senator. You also have to do a fair job as a lawyer."

Zirpoli became a highly visible political lawyer, surfacing frequently to offer opinions on issues ranging from capital punishment (he led a group against it) to bomb shelters (he thought the San Francisco hills offered good possibilities). He headed a panel of attorneys who formed a voluntary public-defender program to represent indigents in federal courts. The Italian government decorated him for his contributions to Italian-American relations.

He was a ubiquitous partisan, defecting only marginally in 1948 to urge General Eisenhower to accept the Democratic nomination for President. By 1952 he had overcome this infatuation sufficiently to serve as Adlai Stevenson's Northern California campaign chairman, a task he repeated in 1956. He was elected a member of the San Francisco Board of Supervisors, the city's governing body, in 1957.

By 1960 everything was coming together for Zirpoli. That year and the next were a kind of honeymoon of political bliss for him; the things that had to coincide were coinciding; the offers kept coming in, the fruition of a career of diligent toil in the party vineyards, a carefully honed public visibility, and the talent and energy to make him a leading candidate for any of a half-dozen major offices.

His friend George Christopher, the liberal Republican mayor of San Francisco, wanted to appoint him district attorney. A group of Democrats inquired whether he was interested in running for Congress. There was considerable support for a Zirpoli candidacy for mayor. But he was gambling on a federal judgeship.

Zirpoli had met John Kennedy in 1959 and enthusiastically boarded his bandwagon. He became, along with JFK's old Navy buddy Paul Fay, co-chairman of the Kennedy "volunteers" in San Francisco. With Kennedy's victory in the 1960 election the gamble paid off—but it still took some maneuvering.

"After the election I wrote a letter to the President and to Bob Kennedy with a copy to Senator Clair Engle. I described my experience and expressed my interest in a federal judgeship. About a month later I got a call from Bob. He asked me if I wanted to be U.S. Attorney for this district. I said the only job I was interested in was the judgeship. Later one of his deputies called and suggested I reconsider. He said we'll consider the judgeship later. I still said no.

"The problem was that Governor Pat Brown's brother Harold was in the running too. Well, the California congressional delegation decided to back me, but Engle was leaning toward Harold Brown. The governor tactfully suggested that I withdraw my name. I went to Washington and saw 'Whizzer' White—he was deputy attorney general at that time. He told me to hang in there and I'd get it. They needed a little time to get Engle to withdraw Brown's name. My bar-association rating was higher than his. Engle called me and said he was getting a lot of telegrams from the *paesani* supporting me. I said, 'Clair, I don't believe I can call them off.'

"White told me that Brown would be withdrawn, and finally he was. I got the phone call to appear at the Judiciary Committee hearing. The only question I remember their asking was whether I understood that I couldn't engage in politics any longer. I said I understood."

He was sworn in on October 4, 1961. A few years later he reflected on his appointment in a speech to a group of lawyers:

"The practical political fact of my judicial birth," he said, "will, I am sure, deter me from ever taking myself too seriously. . . . I doubt if federal judges ever will be appointed solely on the basis of merit. That would be the millennium. But . . . as long as we get qualified Democrats during a Democratic administration, we are doing about as well as can be expected. When my appointment was announced," he added, "one lawyer, probably bespeaking the sentiments of the profession, observed that my appointment would undoubtedly result in an improvement in the quality of both the bench and the bar."

Zirpoli went on to describe the awkwardness of his early days as a judge. At the end of his first day on the bench, he said, "The crier again rapped with his gavel and everyone stood up to await the departure of the judge. I, too, stood there for several seconds until it suddenly occurred to me that I was the judge."

"There was a time several years ago when Orlando Cepeda—he was with the Giants then—had to go to court for a lawsuit," the veteran San Francisco reporter was saying. "So a couple of sportswriters came around to the press room in the Federal Building and asked us which judge would be the best one for Cepeda to draw— you know, who would give him the fairest hearing. Well, there were nine reporters there, and we'd never really talked about who we thought was the best judge. But every damn one of us said 'Zirpoli' at almost the same instant, and then we looked around at each other in amazement. It was the first thing we were ever unanimous about."

Judge Zirpoli is at an age where warm tributes wash over the public man, and the anxious scuffling of one's past may seem to the edited memory to have occupied some dimly remembered colleague. He is in that rare circle of men who enjoy their work, and his pleasure is visible. He is rare also in that he achieved precisely what he wanted to achieve, and singular again in the near-unanimity of praise with which lawyers greet his name.

"I enjoy it," he declares, "because my whole life has been the law. I don't have any hobbies to speak of—oh, I like to walk, and I'll watch an occasional football game. But it's been a life of contact with people and pleasure in law. I feel some pressures—the amount of work is one, and sometimes you get the feeling that too dang many people scream like crazy about their rights and say nothing about their responsibilities. But I wanted this job, and I got it, and it's still exciting to me. A patent suit can be exciting, or an admiralty case. You hear a lot of conflicting technical evidence and pretty soon you're saying, well, how the hell *did* it happen? Everyone has a theory—your crier, the clerks. And eventually you have to come up with an answer. The excitement is in finding the truth, in finding what the hell the answer is. The satisfaction comes with two or three well-drawn questions to get at it, and almost any case has that potential."

He is comfortable with his authority, yet careful with it. What sets him apart from many judges is the perspective he has retained about himself. He bears no illusion of infallibility in a position where the temptation to do so is absolute and constant. He likes to quote Calamandrei that "a judge is what remains after there has been removed from the lawyer all the exterior virtues which the crowd admires." The contrast between lawyer and judge, he said on one occasion, "is apparent even in their vices, which are only the distorted images of their virtues. The lawyer, in a fury of activity, may make such a disturbance that he is asked to leave the courtroom. The judge, in an excess of concentration, may simply fall asleep."

"He seems to enjoy what he does more than any other judge on the district bench here," a former prosecutor says. "He's a very activist fella. He'll take cases the others try to get out of. He's always on time, always prepared. If a motion is coming up, he'll have read it and will have a grasp of the issues. Most other judges in the same situation will take the bench with no idea of what's in the file. There's something called 'federalitis,' you know. It happens to men when they become federal judges. They get feisty, temperamental, or arrogant. But he's never had it. The atmosphere in his court is always pleasant and relaxed. You know he doesn't consider his courtroom some kind of shrine. You never have the feeling you're walking on eggshells. If he chews you out, he does it in such a way that you don't feel insulted. There's a tremendous warmth and a feeling of empathy for everyone. He's—what's the word?— *simpatico.*"

Unlike many judges, Zirpoli never reins in his humanity on the bench. When several hippies shuffled forth to place two daffodils

on his desk at the start of a draft-evasion trial, he left the flowers
there throughout the day. Another longhaired, barefoot defendant,
obviously high on drugs, repeatedly referred to him in court as
"Love." "Zirpoli played along with him," an attorney recalled, "and
they had this tremendous dialogue. When he left, Judge Zirpoli
said to him, 'You've made my morning much brighter.'" Zirpoli
once acted the part of a hippie in a judicial-conference skit.

At another draft trial a four-year-old girl walked up the aisle of
the spectator section and passed through the gate clutching a spray
of flowers. "She behaved with great poise and dignity," the judge
says. "She came right up the steps and handed me the flowers. I
thanked her and patted her on the cheek, then she went back to her
mother and got spanked. She was supposed to give the flowers to
the defendants."

His personality is even more effective in chambers. Several years
ago he ruled that California's welfare payments had to be increased
to reflect the escalating cost of living, a decision that provoked a
bitter attack from Governor Ronald Reagan and inspired an acri-
monious meeting in his chambers between state officials and lawyers representing welfare recipients. After two hours in Zirpoli's
office, both sides emerged smiling. "We were shouting back and
forth," one participant said. "We were screaming at the top of our
lungs, calling each other names, and Zirpoli loved it, he loved
it."

He gets along well with court buffs, the fraternity of lonely,
retired men who show up regularly at interesting trials in federal
courts around the country. Zirpoli greets them in elevators, nods at
them in his courtroom. "You can tell how they want you to rule on
a lawyer's objection," he says. "You just watch the buff and he'll
shake his head side to side or up and down. Once I ran into a buff
in an elevator after a case and he looked at me very solemnly and
said, 'An historic decision, Your Honor.' They even turn up at bar-
association luncheons."

Zirpoli works most Saturdays, but Sundays he and his wife like
to drive to nearby towns and walk for hours. His injuries, which
were slow to heal, occurred when he was locked in his garage by an
electronically operated door. He lowered himself out a window and
dropped fifteen feet onto pavement, breaking both heels and an
ankle. "It was a serious error in judgment," he says, "unfortunately
not reversible by the appeals court." Prior to the injury he once

raced his young secretary around the courthouse block, and beat her. In the evenings he frequently walked down from his Russian Hill apartment to Ghiradelli Square to drink coffee and speak Italian with his friends. There has long been an Italian Establishment in San Francisco—Giannini, Ghiradelli, and Rossi are a few of the more prominent names—and Zirpoli has been among its leaders for a generation. He regularly spends his vacations in Italy.

"Zirpoli has a sense of justice in the true, old-fashioned, Solomon sense of the word," says Martin Glick, an attorney for California's rural poor. "It's not just what's the proper procedure—he has a concept of justice, he makes a decision as to what justice is. And he wants to get to the root of things. I saw him once at the sentencing of a kid who pleaded guilty to opening letters while he was working at the post office at Christmas. The judge couldn't figure out what it was all about. He talked to the kid for twenty minutes and finally he got it—the kid didn't take any money, but he was terrified of being drafted. The prosecutor hadn't caught on, but Zirpoli did—he was committing a felony to get out of the draft. Zirpoli treated it as a juvenile case and expunged his record."

Glick regards Zirpoli as "a genius. We had a suit against the state farm-labor agency," he recalls. "We contended that the agency was being run solely for the growers, with no consideration for the workers. We settled it in a series of meetings with Zirpoli. He pushed them into reforms and pushed us the same way. It was very painful—he really made us re-analyze the facts. We each gave up a lot. And he did it all without inspiring any resentment or imposing his own order or abusing his discretion." Zirpoli ruled that health and sanitation regulations were not being enforced and that farm workers should serve as advisers to the agency.

"He's the only judge I appear before where I don't plan out an argument in the regular one-two-three sequence," Glick adds. "I have to be prepared for anything, because he knows the facts and understands the issues and he's going to ask what he wants to know. He directs it all the way." "He runs a tight court—you always know where you stand with him," another San Francisco lawyer says. Still another credits him with "an inhuman acuity to spot a skunk."

"A judge ought to have a good legal mind and strength enough to be in control of the situation," Zirpoli believes, "plus compassion. I didn't fully understand how important compassion was until I got on the bench. Then the lives of individuals, what happens to them, became *my* responsibility. You try to learn about their lives, but so few people really know the life of another.

"I think that compassion can be developed. You get a feeling, an understanding through dealing with people. You discover people with no sense of belonging, with no affection in their lives, no one taking any interest in them. I think I have a greater feeling for them now than I did when I started."

Zirpoli has never had to sentence a man to death, but he has been forced to deny stays of execution. "It was an awful position to be in. There was nothing I could do." He was the final ray of hope for Aaron Mitchell, one of the last prisoners to be executed in America, in 1967. "His mother was in my chambers. I had to tell her. I had the impression that she had some small understanding." Later he granted stays to several condemned men pending the Supreme Court decision on the death penalty.

"I don't know that anyone needs to be punished," he says. "Some people need to be confined, distasteful as it is, to protect society and themselves. I don't believe a man should go to jail unless he has committed a crime of violence, or unless his conduct is so aggravating that society needs to be protected from him."

Zirpoli will take a chance more often than not. "I had one guy before me who'd spent most of his life in prison. He was forty-four and looked about sixty. Convicted of forgery. I asked him what he would say if I released him on his own recognizance and loaned him twenty dollars from the judges' loan fund. He said it would be the first break he ever got. So I put him on probation. He's been out for six or seven years now and has a job as a psychiatric aide."

His hunches have also backfired. "I had a hotel bellboy convicted of forging stolen government checks. I took a chance and gave him probation. He was all right for two years, working as the assistant manager of a hotel. Then one day he absconded with the hotel's money."

He believes that there is a "saturation point" in sentencing, beyond which prison has no deterrent or rehabilitative value. "It's probably between five and seven years, regardless of the crime," he says. "There is also the factor of 'community acceptance.' The community has to accept the court's rulings, and sometimes you send people to prison for that reason—an income-tax evader, maybe, or sometimes a draft violator."

His leniency has drawn criticism from policemen, prosecutors, and legislators. "He does his homework," one officer told me, "but he's a bleeding heart. He'll bend over—if there's any possible way to let a man loose, he'll do it. We can bust our ass getting a guy and then he puts him on probation or gives him a short sentence. Sometimes the investigation takes longer than the sentence does."

Zirpoli doesn't deny the charge, but he hates to give up on anyone; it is as if his own view of mankind were under challenge. Failure is almost a personal affront. "There was one man who was just a genuinely mean SOB. If he had a gun, he probably would have shot up the dang courtroom. He didn't stand when I came in. I said, 'Do you know where you are?' He said, 'Who the hell are you?' I sent him for a psychiatric examination and gave him a prison term for attempted bank robbery. I know there are a few like that. But I think probation is a risk worth taking with a lot of others. Probation is meaningless without some risk."

He opposes any attempt to reduce sentencing to formulas, to mandatory maximums or minimums—anything that diminishes the human involvement of the judge. "There are some things that can't be codified," he says. "Some decisions have to be made by human beings reacting as human beings."

The defendant, a tall, stringy man in his early thirties, pulls nervously at his mustache. He wears slacks and a sport shirt. His eyes are soft and watery. Judge Zirpoli glances from the paper on his desk to the defendant and back to the paper.

"You're pleading guilty to smuggling hashish into the United States, is that correct?" the judge asks.

"Yes, Your Honor," the man replies. He speaks with a British accent.

"And I understand you're willing to waive a probation report and submit to sentencing today?"

"Yes."

"Well, I have a few questions," Zirpoli says.

Zirpoli learns that the man was born in India, where his father served with the British colonial force. He was one of seven children, educated by officers' wives, and "at some stage almost all of us got in trouble."

"What kind of trouble?"

"I stole—oh, the first time I guess was when I stole a hundred eighty-six dollars to get out of what I considered a rut. I got a month in an 'open prison' in England."

"What kind of prison?"

"It was called an 'open' prison. There were no bars. It was experimental."

"Interesting. What happened after that?"

"Lots of things."

"Yes?" Zirpoli appears to be fascinated. He is resting his chin on his hand, gazing steadily at the man.

"I went to Kuwait and met some people who had some hashish they wanted to sell. I was twenty-one. I got four months. . . ."

"You had a pretty long history before you were twenty-one, is that right?"

"Yes, Your Honor. Then I went in the Navy for five years."

"Did you get an honorable discharge?"

"Yes."

"Continue."

"I can't think of anything else I did wrong until this."

"What is your occupation?"

"I'm a writer."

Zirpoli is interested. "What type?"

"Serious writing. Honest. Mostly poetry, some prose."

"Do you make a living at it?" Zirpoli has known a writer or two.

"I have so far."

"Have you saved any money?"

"I'm not the sort who saves." He sounds proud of it.

"Are you married?"

"No."

"Have you ever been under psychiatric care?"

"Once—to learn first-hand the facts of mental hospitals."

"What's your experience with drugs—hashish, LSD, marijuana, and so forth?"

"I've tried something called the 'magic mushroom,' " the man replies.

"Did it damage you?"

"I choose to live on the razor's edge, Judge. I'm glad I did it."

Zirpoli is unfazed. "What do you think of young people who experiment with LSD?"

"I think they need supervision."

"Do you think LSD causes brain damage?"

"I think it's psychological more than physical."

"I get some people in here who are dancing on moonbeams," the judge says. "Why'd you bring hashish into the country?" The question is almost casual, as if they were two friends chatting at a picnic.

"I met two Americans. We all got friendly under the influence of drugs. They suggested I bring it in. I was interested in the story, not the monetary side."

Zirpoli's eyes swing around the courtroom, taking in everybody. "Do you have any religion?"

"I just know my Father is up there—I'm in the most unified church of all."

"What are your future plans?"

"To go back to England."

"When?"

"As soon as possible."

The room is quiet for thirty seconds. "The whole thing is incredible," the man adds. "I want to put it all down while it's fresh in my mind."

His lawyer interrupts. "The immigration people have plans for him, Judge. They have asked him to submit to voluntary deportation."

"Are you ready for judgment?"

"Yes, sir."

"All right. The court will suspend sentence and place you on probation for thirty days on condition that you return to England immediately." Zirpoli looks around again. "You report to a probation officer and he'll tell you what to do for the next thirty days."

The man pivots and walks away, one hand on his hip.

Back in chambers, I ask Zirpoli why the sentence was so light.

"He was of major assistance to the government," he replies. "He helped them arrest a number of smugglers. I couldn't say that in court."

I ask what will happen now.

"He'll be ordered deported, and he'll have to get permission from the Attorney General before he can come back to the country." He raises one leg, still in a cast, and rests it on a chair. "Punishment wouldn't have served any dang purpose anyway," he says. "He's not violent. He's already spent a couple nights in jail, and that's all that was called for."

"Do you think he'll get in trouble again?"

"Yep. He was willing to bring the drugs in here. He says he lives at the razor's edge. If you live that way, you take chances until you get it in the neck." Not, however, from this judge.

Zirpoli squints at me. "I knew intuitively," he says, "that he wrote poetry. I was about to say it before he did."

"When I came on the bench I wasn't particularly thinking of improving the social and economic lot of people," says Zirpoli. "I was thinking of law and justice, you know? Social questions like welfare, prisoners' rights, and school busing weren't in the courts then. The courts dealt more with economic issues. But there's been a reawakening. I changed and the courts' menu changed. I've come to think that if democracy is to mean anything, people are entitled to be protected from tyrannical action on the part of the state. Most people know no more about their constitutional freedoms than they do about the marital customs of the Watusis. They don't know what their rights are. I can't initiate change, but I can react to what's brought before me. If I see something is wrong and I have the authority to change it, then I will. I agree with Calamandrei— that injustice is not a homeopathic drug that can be taken beneficially in minute quantities. If something outrages my conscience, then I say to hell with it. There's no such thing as a little bit of injustice."

He classifies himself as "moderately activist," but most lawyers rate his activism a notch or two above moderate. "I'm not trying to impose any personal views," he insists. "I'm just making constitutional interpretations. They may be new interpretations, but not a complete change. I interpret the Constitution and the statutes in the light of changing times."

One Zirpoli interpretation was his 1968 decision that the Selective Service Act was unconstitutional in its denial of judicial review of draft classifications until after a criminal trial. In 1970 he ruled that a young man could qualify as a conscientious objector if he opposed the Vietnam war though not all wars. "The law said a religious belief or the equivalent is necessary for conscientious-objector status. I decided that a man could object to those wars he deems immoral. Pope John said some wars were immoral, so there was pretty high religious authority." His decision was overturned by the Supreme Court.

"The hardest part of the job is the enforcement of laws of tremendous social and political significance which you feel are not right. The Selective Service law was an example. If you don't feel it's a just war, it's pretty dang tough to answer a kid who says it's immoral and why should I go? Maybe I should have stepped down in cases like that. But if I did, who would have sentenced them in my place? Maybe someone with the opposite opinion." Zirpoli's treatment of draft violators was generally lenient, as was that of most of his judicial colleagues in traditionally tolerant, permissive San Francisco.

Zirpoli is a zestful, aggressive man—even his doodles, harsh lines and circles, are aggressive. He is a product of the work ethic, a striver, a smart kid who always ran hard and kept running. He likes the smack of conflict and the warmth of contact. He is temperamentally incapable of withdrawing demurely from the combat of his times and wrapping himself in the robe. He prefers to work at maximum velocity, all senses tuned up high, thrusting forward to the limit of his capacity. "I believe it's better to understand than to be understood," he says. Philosophical reticence is not his style.

His daughter was a student at the University of California when the "free-speech movement" of 1964 fired one of the first salvos of student activism of the 1960s. "She and I talked about the student movement," he recalls, "and I offered to go to a rally in Berkeley and make a speech against civil disobedience. She said, 'Oh, Daddy, don't do that.' That night they had a sit-in at Sproul Hall. I went over to see what was going on, but I stayed on the edge of the crowd because I didn't want to embarrass her. She called me the next day and said she was sitting in with the others when a policeman asked her to leave. She said she thought of me and got up and left. I told her I appreciated that. My conscience still bothers me a little about that—because she got up for my sake."

He rejects the radicals' charge that injustice stalks American courts. "The true revolutionary won't accept our justice at all," he says. "I feel sometimes they're disappointed when they find justice in our courts; it deprives them of the chance to suffer. I've had Panthers and radicals in court, and some have been convicted and others haven't. I believe the system works." He concedes that political trials have taken place, but "their number has been insignificant."

Zirpoli's decisions have consistently buttressed the First Amendment guarantees of free speech and press. His best-known decision came in the case of *New York Times* reporter Earl Caldwell, who was subpoenaed by a federal grand jury investigating the Black Panthers. Zirpoli ordered him to testify only to corroborate articles he had written. He ruled that Caldwell had a right to protect confidential sources unless the government established an "overriding and compelling national interest" requiring their disclosure. The Supreme Court reversed him, deciding by a 5–4 vote that Caldwell had no right to withhold confidential information from the grand jury. Several reporters have since gone to jail rather than reveal their sources.

In 1964 Zirpoli and two other judges found that a post-office practice of intercepting "Communist propaganda" mailed from abroad was an unconstitutional violation of free speech. In 1971 he had to decide whether human waste included in an art work was a "filthy substance." "The thing was a design on a gold plaque showing three people seated on a bowl and including a vial containing human feces. A man mailed it to an art critic to protest some grievance he had against the media. The critic testified that he thought it was 'conceptual art.' I found it reprehensible, but since the critic was the only government witness, I had a reasonable doubt that it was filthy. I can't say what art is or isn't." Zirpoli, hearing the case without a jury, acquitted the man on the charge of mailing a filthy substance.

Zirpoli's ideology, like his view of his own success, is tied directly to the American creed. "I'm supposed to be liberal and to the left," he says, "and I guess I am in the civil-rights area. But with economic problems I'm still a believer in the free-enterprise system. I think it made this country what it is. Maybe some form of socialism might make it even better, I don't know. But I still believe in the capacity of the individual, in his courage and will and industry.

"It's obvious that we're moving toward socialism in some areas, in transportation and electrification and in welfare, areas where free enterprise hasn't been able to cope with people's needs. But if we're on the road, it's a slow journey, and I don't welcome it. I think free enterprise and rugged individualism create a far preferable society. I believe in competition, and I always had confidence in my ability to compete. Maybe I'd feel differently if I didn't have that confidence. My preference for individualism is both emotional and intellectual, though I think that when there's a conflict the emotions usually outweigh the intellect." His decisions on anti-trust cases have gone both ways—"I go case by case." In one he upheld a merger of the Crocker-Anglo Bank and the Citizens National Bank against a government anti-trust action. He decided against the Sierra Club in a suit brought to halt logging operations in a Northern California wilderness area.

Reversals by a higher court, he says, do not trouble him. "I think that eventually they'll catch up with me," he says. "It's happened before. But in the short run I come around to their way of thinking. I bite the bullet. I can't put myself above the higher court. I do my best and my conscience doesn't trouble me. Once in a while I have the satisfaction of seeing my ideas prevail."

In 1968 he had a chance to become an appellate judge, but turned it down. The Johnson Justice Department wanted to promote him to the Ninth Circuit. He replied that he felt he could "better serve my country, the administration of justice, and myself" as a trial judge.

"I'm the kind of judge who can actively conduct and participate in a trial," he explains. "I live in the court. I'm part of the courtroom scene. I'm just a garden-variety scholar. A trial judge makes a ruling based on his senses as well as his mind. An appellate judge has so little *contact*—he gets a transcript and the briefs and hears arguments. You don't see more than two or three people watching in an appellate courtroom. My personality is suited to trial work, and I can accomplish more there."

His somewhat raspy voice softens when he thinks about the only inducement that might have changed his decision. "If I thought it carried with it any hope of appointment to the Supreme Court, well . . . But I was sixty-three. I knew I was disqualified on grounds of age alone." He lets the thought linger a moment in his mind. "That's the greatest achievement for anyone in the law."

One morning in 1971 Zirpoli appeared unannounced at the Santa Rita "rehabilitation center," a compound of dusty, low-slung buildings where Alameda County detains prisoners awaiting trial. The judge's inspection was prompted by a suit in his court claiming that conditions at Santa Rita amounted to "cruel and unusual punishment."

"I'd been to a lot of prisons," he recalls, "but what I saw there shocked me. There were men confined in seven-by-seven cells with mesh ceilings and poor lighting and ventilation. I saw naked men just staring into space, completely oblivious—it was a startling thing. They were in there twenty-four hours a day. Once a week they'd let them out for two hours. The conditions would have driven anyone insane. And these were men who hadn't been convicted, mind you.

"The next day I made a rather angry ruling. I said that the punishment at Santa Rita was cruel and unusual for both man and beast." He described the conditions as "debased, shameful, and barbaric." He said that the Greystone section, where pre-trial prisoners were held, "should be razed to the ground," observing that San Quentin and Alcatraz were "paradises by comparison." Zirpoli ordered federal prisoners held at Santa Rita to be transferred elsewhere and wrote an opinion outlining how conditions might be improved.

"I thought I'd better write it out," he explained, "so that when they built a new jail they wouldn't spend their money on quarters that violated the law. All I could do was point out where conditions were unconstitutionally cruel and unusual. I can't tell them how to run the place. I can just tell them what's wrong. The courts are a last resort in cases like this where administrators and legislators haven't reacted to problems."

Zirpoli's ruling was strong medicine: "If the state cannot obtain the resources to detain persons awaiting trial in accordance with minimum constitutional standards," he wrote, "then the state simply will not be permitted to detain such persons." There were angry grumbles from Alameda County officials who charged "federal interference." But under Zirpoli's prodding they gradually improved conditions and developed plans for a new facility to replace Santa Rita. His technique, which was vintage Zirpoli, was to invite them all into his chambers at periodic intervals to talk about it.

"This is our county counsel, Judge," the county administrator says, "and I think you know the supervisor here, and the public defender." Zirpoli shakes hands cordially with the six men who have assembled in his office. He beckons them to sit down as he eases off his crutches and onto a couch. They sit in a semi-circle around him.

"I thought we'd just have a little bull session about this," he begins. "I know you're about to build a new jail, and I might be able to help a bit in planning it. I'm satisfied that you're proceeding in good faith, and up to this point I'm pleased with your progress." They smile tentatively. "But you know there's always room for improvement—maybe even on this court."

The administrator describes a new policy for visiting privileges at Santa Rita. "It's just that we're reluctant to spend much money on more guards and all, now that we're probably going to abandon Santa Rita for pre-trial detainees," he says.

Zirpoli nods. "Are you continuing to try to get as many pre-trial prisoners released as you can?" he asks.

The counsel says they are.

"I'm not trying to tell you what to do, you understand," the judge says, "but—I'm wondering if you might be in danger of building too big a facility."

They assure him that the center will not be too large.

Zirpoli scrunches forward on the couch and squints. "Did the board of supervisors get a little sore when I came out with this?" he asks.

They laugh stiffly. "Rather," the supervisor says.

"I get a lot of people sore at me," he says. "But, you know, I've been to a lot of prisons, and this really shocked me. What got me was that they were in those cells twenty-four hours a day, they got so little recreation." The officials nod sympathetically. "That struck me as pretty rough."

The officials describe other plans in the works—a new center for first offenders ("You ought to see the plans for the new federal detention center in San Francisco," Zirpoli interrupts), a library, liberalized rules on mail, the hiring of a "corrections consultant."

"My present reaction is that you've made a good beginning," the judge says. "These are tough problems. I can't run the jails, that's an administrative problem; I know that. The court isn't equipped to deal with these problems."

Zirpoli looks at the young public defender, who had initiated the suit that led to his ruling. "Maybe you ought to raise the salary of the public defender," he suggests. The young man grins.

He turns to the supervisor. "How long have you been on the board?" he asks. The supervisor tells him. "Have you brought the tax rate down?" The man nods quickly. Zirpoli, the former supervisor, smiles knowingly. "Did you actually reduce it or did you just increase the appraisals?"

"We increased the appraisals," he replies sheepishly.

Zirpoli gets to his feet by pushing off the arm of the couch, signaling the end of the conference. "Why don't you all come back in about three months and we'll talk some more?" he suggests. They say they will.

"What happened to your legs?" one of them asks.

"I tried to drop out of my garage," he explains. "Gol-dangedest thing I ever did in my life." The judge's clerk comes in. "Frank wouldn't do a thing like that," he says, indicating the clerk. "He's smarter than I am." They laugh as they file out.

The public defender remains behind for a moment. "You know, we've received an award for this," he tells the judge. "But it's our feeling that the award ought to go to you."

Zirpoli smiles and puts a hand on the man's shoulder. "That's very diplomatic of you," he says. "All I did was wait until the day before the hearing to visit Santa Rita."

The judge, maneuvering haltingly on his crutches, walks him to the door. "I think we're getting somewhere, don't you?" he asks.

The young man nods, one hand on the doorknob. "The only sad part," the lawyer says, "was that it took the federal government to do it."

The qualities of a good judge are the qualities of a good man. There are additional demands on a judge, to be sure—knowledge of the law, a willingness to suspend judgment until all the evidence is in. But at last it must be the depth and texture of his humanity that qualify and define the judge. "The law suffers from being thought of as an intellectual profession," Curtis Bok wrote. "It is intellectual, of course. . . . But it is not scientific in the sense of a science whose rules are impersonal and beyond the reach of human emotions or behavior. Emotion and behavior are the raw materials from which the law is distilled in one way or another. . . . There is no plea to be made except to keep the law personal."

To find a judge like Zirpoli is to feel a rush of discovery, a desire to trumpet the news, to proclaim that justice is alive and well and living in San Francisco. But sobering second thoughts intervene. The existence of one Zirpoli on the federal bench (there are more, but not many) does not validate a system of selection which relies on maneuver, influence, and political clout. The fact that Zirpoli came up that way does not justify the method. He would be an ornament to any system. That he serves ours is more a glorious accident than a reassuring confirmation. Another system—more professional, less political—might produce more Zirpolis, or it might not. His presence on the bench, in the final analysis, is evidence only that a good man can survive in any climate.

"I'm inclined," the judge is saying, "to give them the relief they seek."

The case concerns an effort by the government to prevent two women sharing a house from receiving federal food stamps. The government prosecutor contends that since one of the women is not qualified, the other is ineligible.

"You take some elements in our society," Zirpoli says, "Chinatown, for example, where there's hundreds of people living in a common structure and several sharing the same kitchen. An order like that would bar a lot of them from receiving food stamps."

"Our position is that the regulation forbids it where they share cooking facilities," the government man says. Both judge and lawyers are aware that the real target is hippie communes, but no one says so.

"The only people affected," says the opposing lawyer, "are two women getting ninety dollars a month from the government. They need it. This order would take that money away from them. They have small children to feed."

"I've got a pretty good idea what I'm going to do," the judge says to the prosecutor, "unless you can change my mind."

The prosecutor shrugs. "I'm beginning to get a defeatist attitude," he says.

"Don't," Zirpoli says quickly. "Remember that you're the attorney for the government. You have an obligation to see that justice is done." He looks at the petition before him. "I say what's the harm? It's forty-five dollars a month for each of them. They both have medical and food bills. It seems to me that it would cause them injury if I granted your request. The country will only be out ninety dollars a month."

The prosecutor subsides.

"You have to make a motion," the judge tells him, "or else they'll kick hell out of me in the Court of Appeals." He smiles. "And even you don't want that to happen."

"You know, Judge," the prosecutor says, "it reminds me of a sign I saw somewhere in Washington one time. It may have been in the Justice Department. It said, 'When the government loses, justice is served.'"

Zirpoli smiles broadly. "I'll get you the full quote," he says.

XIV

The Cardinals

The hushed and solemn reaches
of the appellate courts

> "A judge's life, like every other, has in it much of
> drudgery, senseless bickerings, stupid obstinacies,
> captious pettifogging, all disguising and obstruct-
> ing the only sane purpose which can justify the
> whole endeavor. These take an inordinate part of
> his time; they harass and befog the unhappy wretch,
> and at times almost drive him from that bench
> where like any other workman he must do his work.
> If that were all, his life would be mere misery, and
> he a distracted arbiter between irreconcilable ex-
> tremes. But there is something else that makes it
> —anyway to those curious creatures who persist in
> it—a delectable calling. For when the case is all in,
> and the turmoil stops, and after he is left alone,
> things begin to take form. From his pen or in his
> head, slowly or swiftly as his capacities admit, out
> of the murk the pattern emerges, his pattern, the
> expression of what he has seen and what he has
> therefor made, the impress of his self upon the not-
> self, upon the hitherto formless material of which
> he was once but a part and over which he has now
> become the master. That is a pleasure which no-
> body who has felt it will be likely to underrate."
> LEARNED HAND, *The Spirit of Liberty*

THE BEAUTY of the judge's craft, "the expression of what he
has seen and what he has therefor made, the impress of his self

303

upon the not-self," is a grace that few of them ever know. For most judges, each day's work is another lesson in the petty meanness and misery of man, and the disillusion that ensnares the rectifier-judge. Far from the calm and quiet chamber where "things begin to take form," most judges work in an atmosphere where they must scurry down well-worn short-cuts to keep up, where they strain to glimpse a piece of the truth they don't have time to seek, where the dull weight of numbers and habit makes them little more than doormen at a revolving door.

Yet beauty exists in judging, and even romance: the sublime pleasure of finding and forming a fair resolution of human differences; the accidental discovery of justice, which Hand called "the tolerable accommodation of the conflicting interests of society"; the satisfaction of giving life to the dry promise of the United States Constitution. A judge may get no closer to this beauty than a pilgrim does to paradise, but it's there nonetheless.

It is no accident that the judge who best described this judicial nirvana, Learned Hand, was for most of his career a member of an appellate court. Hand, regarded by many as the finest judge in our history, sat for twenty-seven years on the U.S. Court of Appeals for the Second Circuit in New York City. Appellate judges live in a world that trial judges can barely recognize. They work in a bubble of serene dignity where a voice raised in anger echoes with the alien crudity of a barbarian's oath shouted in a cathedral. Thick rugs and thicker walls cushion the pleaders' arguments, and bright-eyed clerks pad among their masters bearing summary and precedent. Almost alone among the fraternity, appellate judges enjoy the luxury of contemplation. No one can tell them when to start or stop, when a case must be decided or an opinion written. Appellate judges are the law-givers, the scholars, the aristocrats of the bench; they are the cardinals to the trial-court bishops.

The central reality of appellate judging is its collective nature. Like cardinals, appellate judges are members of a college, and their decisions are collegial. The sensibilities, idiosyncrasies, and follies of the individual, the personality of the judge, count for less here because he is one among several. The bold innovator and the small-minded tyrant both are lesser as part of a group than they were alone. The excesses of ego afforded by the trial bench seem to subside on an appellate court. Personalities soften; appellate judges invariably seem to be gentler men, more congenial, less willful.

"Appellate judges are more modest," says Professor Delmar Karlen of New York University's law school. Karlen until recently was director of NYU's Institute for Judicial Administration, which sponsors annual seminars for state and federal appeals-court judges. "They're used to working together, and they have to live with other people and listen to them. Their work makes them scholarly and reflective—their personalities and the job interact. It's a job of research and writing. Trial judges have a tendency to become little tin gods."

The only effective strictures on appellate judges are the reactions and opinions of their brothers, but they can be formidable. "The peer pressure is enormous," Karlen says, having witnessed it at dozens of gatherings in and out of classrooms. "One doesn't want to be known as a goof-off among his colleagues." It is an example of a "law" once enunciated by Lenny Bruce: "Doctors doctor for other doctors, writers write for other writers, salesmen sell for other salesmen"—and so with judges, especially appellate judges.

Another blessing enjoyed by the collegial judge is the confirmation implicit in a concurring opinion. One judge of a federal appellate court, where decisions are generally made by three-judge panels, tried to explain it:

"The trial judge wonders more, he has more self-doubt. He's got to say singly what the decision is. If two of you come to the same decision, or, better yet, three of you, you don't feel so . . . I don't want to say alone, it's more that you're reassured. That's it, you're reassured as to the result you reached. The reasons for the decision have been developed by someone else as well as you. It's reassuring if you believe the result is right and the logic compatible, and it comports with your sense of justice—there is some kind of a sense of justice. I don't want to say the trial judge is lonelier, but there's more solitude, let's say. It's just that when he debates he has to do it with himself. There's some of that in the collegial process too— each judge has to meet his own standards of conscience, whatever he has. But he shares the ultimate result with somebody. Two people can't think together, but to come to the same conclusion and share it is reassuring, comforting."

Decisions of an appellate court, in the felicitous phrase of one federal opinion, "are not solos but concertos." The harmony may sometimes be contrapuntal, but the final performance demands a spirit of accommodation. Appellate judges will usually bend to achieve agreement. Unanimity, though rarely a stated goal, is in many courts (the current U.S. Supreme Court is an exception) a consummation devoutly sought. "We seek to arrive at unanimity if we can, without anyone swallowing a principle," says Judge George C. Edwards, Jr., of the U.S. Sixth Circuit Court of Appeals. "We function on a basis of good personal relations. Any harsh, biting, personally oriented comment is not part of our tradition, and it would be resented. We try to avoid personalities or any argument that verges on them." Political scientist Sheldon Goldman, surveying the decisions of the eleven U.S. appellate courts for two years in the 1960s, found that the highest percentage of split decisions was 15.5 percent, on the District of Columbia Circuit Court. The lowest, 2.8 percent, occurred on Edwards' Sixth Circuit Court.

Appellate judges operate in an ambience of courtesy and hush. Seniority, always important to judges, dictates the protocol. Junior judges defer to their seniors; the senior man sits in the middle of a three-judge panel, leads the questioning, and assigns the writing of opinions. When U.S. Supreme Court justices confer, a ceremony that no outsider, not even a clerk, has ever witnessed, the justices give their votes beginning with the junior man and proceeding to the chief justice. The newest justice (currently William Rehnquist) is responsible for opening the conference-room door for whatever minimal communication with the world outside is necessary.

The code of the conference room and the relative invisibility of appellate judges have helped create the lingering mystique that surrounds them. Arguments in an appeals court rarely draw an audience, and the few spectators who do show up are likely to be disappointed by the murmuring tempo and the total absence of legal pyrotechnics: no passionate pitches to the jury, no lawyers bouncing out of their chairs to object, no squirming witnesses, nothing, in fact, but the soft voices of well-behaved attorneys earning large fees, and the occasional polite question from the bench. Sitting in the Seventh Circuit courtroom in Chicago one day, I noticed that one of the two other spectators had dozed off. Judge Wilbur Pell, on the bench, stared at the sleeper with an expression of amused fascination.

The advantages of mystery are not lost on the judges. "It's difficult to describe the appellate process," says Judge Edwards with a small smile. "We're appropriately concerned about the mystique because we know that behind the robe is an ordinary human being. Talking about it is a risk." Edwards, who admits to being both a "liberal" and a "reformer," still confesses a disinclination to "foul the nest I inhabit" by talking about it too explicitly.

The business of an appellate-court judge is hearing arguments, reading briefs, conferring, researching, and writing opinions. Most of his time is spent in research and writing. It is a reclusive life, removed from what Justice Oliver Wendell Holmes called "the action and passion of the times." It can engender a certain remoteness from the people and events that underlie legal conflict. Edwards believes that the best judges are close to human currents. "I would argue against peopling the bench with law professors and office lawyers," he says. "They're too sheltered, too wedded to legal logic. Life is not always that logical. You can pursue logic to the point where it reaches a result contrary to your common sense and experience. This can happen in the law. Logic can take you to one conclusion and your humanity to another."

The rewards are collegial—the esteem of one's brethren, the formulation of a precise and neatly constructed opinion. "The payoff is the opinion," says University of Michigan psychiatrist Andrew Watson. "The satisfaction comes if your colleagues like it." The trial judge's gratifications—the innocent defendant exonerated, the satisfied smile of the justly treated—are denied the appellate judge.

The appellate brotherhood consists of fewer than a thousand judges—704 on state supreme courts and intermediate appellate courts (which exist in twenty-three states), 97 on the eleven federal Circuit Courts of Appeal, plus another 26 on special-purpose federal courts (like the Court of Military Appeals) and the U.S. Supreme Court. In general, the state appellate courts are the courts of last resort for all cases brought under the criminal statutes of the state and all civil cases initiated in state courts. Federal appellate courts review the decisions of federal District Courts. A case with a federal constitutional issue—the lines become hazy here, but one example would be a violation of the "cruel and unusual punishment" clause of the Eighth Amendment—may be shifted from state to federal court.

The process begins with the lawyers' submission of briefs, which the judges usually read before courtroom argument, the next step. At the hearing, opposing counsel are usually granted something like thirty minutes to make their arguments. The judges will generally hear several cases at a sitting, then retire to a conference room to discuss them. One judge is frequently assigned to summarize the facts of the case and the preliminary discussion. They will then disperse to their libraries (or send their clerks there) to research points of law, following which another conference is held, a vote is taken, and the writing of majority and (if necessary) minority opinions is assigned.

Most cases in appellate courts are readily resolved—"cases where one route and only one is possible," Justice Benjamin Cardozo wrote, "make up in bulk what they lack in interest." But a significant minority, particularly in federal courts, confront judges with difficult choices on the most intricate questions of law and public policy. "It is when the colors do not match, when the references in the index fail, when there is no decisive precedent," Cardozo said, "that the serious business of the judge begins. He must then fashion law for the litigants before him. In fashioning it for them, he will be fashioning it for others."

The reach of appellate decisions extends to the warmest and most contested issues. In recent years, different courts of appeal have struggled with the constitutionality of the Vietnam war (the Third Circuit ruled it was not the court's prerogative to pass on it), the limits and guidelines for electronic surveillance (the Sixth Circuit sharply restricted it), the President's ability to "impound" authorized funds (the Eighth Circuit declared it illegal), the Watergate tapes (the District of Columbia Circuit ordered the President to disclose them), and dozens of other questions with social and political reverberations: school busing, welfare, prisoners' rights, environment, federal aid to private and parochial schools. In each case appellate judges were not just resolving a particular case, but establishing "the law" in those areas.

The most important skill for an appellate judge is the ability to write clear and concise prose. They learn with difficulty the writer's curse, that it is often more time-consuming to compose a short piece (or opinion) than a long one. "It takes me longer to write six pages than fourteen," Edwards says. "Deciding what to eliminate requires value judgments it takes hours to make." Attorney John Frank once identified the categories of prose style among Supreme Court justices as "legal lumpy, legal massive, rock-bottom contemporary, and legal lucid."

They work at it and worry it (one federal appellate judge showed me a two-foot-long shelf of writers' reference books; he called them his "tools"), but few attain Frank's category four— Holmes and Cardozo are the most glorious exceptions. Lamentably, too many judges write like the author of the following:

"This is one of an apparently growing class of cases involving the claim of interference with constitutional rights, usually multiple, arising out of authoritative discouragement or outright prohibition of the manner and style in which one would adorn himself whether by raiment or natural exploitation."

The question was whether a National Guardsman could be punished for his long hair.

"A well-written product is one of the real satisfactions of the job," says Edwards. "You really have to like bookwork to enjoy it. There aren't many ego satisfactions in the normal use of that phrase; we're mostly an anonymous court in the judiciary, and the judiciary is pretty anonymous anyway. I enjoy the cerebration and research. Trial work is fun like tennis is fun: it's competition, measuring yourself against other lawyers. This is different. The challenge here comes from the problem of the case, to find just solutions which seem to be consistent with the Constitution and law, and to express them."

Appellate judges may occupy the upper floors in the house of justice, but most of them are selected as politically as their brothers below. State appeals judges are chosen by partisan (12 states) or non-partisan (13) ballot, by gubernatorial or legislative appointment (11), or by merit selection (14). As with trial judges, the popularity of various selection methods varies geographically—the partisan ballot flourishes in the South, the appointive system in the East, while the West and Midwest are divided between non-partisan ballots and the merit plan. Six states use merit selection for appellate judges and another method for lower-court judges. Their salaries range from $22,000 in North Dakota to $49,665 in New York; tenure varies from two years in Vermont to life in neighboring New Hampshire and Massachusetts; the average term is eight to ten years.

Judges of the federal Circuit Courts of Appeals serve for life at a salary of $42,500. They are named by the President with the consent of the Senate. In practice the President and his Justice Department have more influence in the selection of circuit judges than they do at the District Court level, but the opinions of individual senators are still important, buttressed by the custom of sharing the seats on many Circuit Courts among the states in the circuit. In the Tenth Circuit, for example, which covers six mountain and prairie states, there are two judges from Colorado and one each from Utah, New Mexico, Kansas, Wyoming, and Oklahoma. A federal appellate judgeship is the creamiest patronage a senator possesses.

The backgrounds of federal appellate judges are just as political as those of district judges. Sheldon Goldman reports that 81 percent of Kennedy's appellate appointees were active political partisans in their pre-judicial careers, as were 53 percent of Johnson's appointees and 56 percent of Nixon's first-term choices. "I spent a day one time with the chief judges of two federal circuits," a veteran lawyer told me. "They passed the time discussing the intimate details of Democratic party politics throughout the country. Their knowledge of the names and numbers flabbergasted me—and this was many years after they had come to the bench."

A profile of state supreme-court justices compiled by political scientist Bradley Canon showed that the vast majority were white Protestants with small-town or rural backgrounds—only 30 percent came from cities with a population of more than 100,000. Canon found that half were ex-prosecutors and 58 percent had been judges previously; the average age was sixty-two; only four (between 1961 and 1968) were women; and a meager three in those years had suffered the indignity of being defeated for reelection. Other researchers have shown that a disproportionately high number of appellate judges were raised in comfortable economic circumstances.

In 1960 Stuart Nagel, now a political scientist at the University of Illinois, devised a questionnaire to study the social and political attitudes of state supreme-court justices. He mailed the questionnaire to 313 judges and drew replies from 118, giving him a sample far short of comprehensive. The relevance of the survey, in addition, has probably diminished with the passage of time and changes in social and moral values. Nevertheless it is interesting for the attitudes it reveals.

The format was a series of statements with which the justices were asked to agree or disagree. Here are some of them and the judicial responses:

¶ Colored people are innately inferior to white people (41 percent said yes, 59 percent no).

¶ Present laws favor the rich as against the poor (10 percent yes, 90 percent no).

¶ Our treatment of criminals is too harsh; we should try to cure, not to punish them (22–78).

¶ Sunday observance is old-fashioned, and should cease to govern our behavior (12–88).

¶ Men should be permitted greater sexual freedom than women by society (14–86).

¶ Unrestricted freedom of discussion on every topic is desirable in the press, in literature, and on the stage (54–46).

¶ More collectivism, like the TVA, should be introduced into our society (13–87).

¶ Only by going back to religion can civilization hope to survive (73–27).

¶ Marriages between white and colored people should be greatly discouraged (97–3).

¶ There should be far more controversial and political discussion over radio and television (70–30).

¶ Nationalization in any industry is likely to lead to inefficiency (95–5).

¶ Men and women have the right to find out whether they are sexually suited before marriage (17–83).

¶ The principle "Spare the rod and spoil the child" has much truth in it, and should govern our methods of bringing up children (76–24).

¶ The Jews have too much power and influence in this country (10–90).

¶ Differences in pay between men and women doing the same work should be abolished (76–24).

¶ The death penalty is barbaric, and should be abolished (37–63).

¶ Only people with a definite minimum of intelligence and education should be allowed to vote (41–59).

The replies showed that the judges endorsed women's rights but were less committed to racial equality. They were conservative on religious and moral values and law enforcement, foursquare for American capitalism, and divided on free speech. Casting about for a group to compare them with, Nagel found their attitudes comparable to "an average middle-class member of the British Conservative party of 1948."

The prestige and importance of the federal circuit bench attracts high-caliber barristers. Its 97-judge roster (one woman, Shirley Hufstedler of Los Angeles, and 96 men) is an elite even more exclusive than the U.S. Senate, and among the elite are a dozen or so, of varying ideological colors, who command wide admiration among the country's lawyers and legal scholars—David Bazelon of Washington, D.C., Henry Friendly and Irving Kaufman of New York, John Minor Wisdom of New Orleans, Luther Swygert and Walter Cummings of Chicago, Arlin Adams of Philadelphia. They are selected with more care than District Court judges; a higher percentage attended first-rate law schools and won membership in the Order of the Coif, the legal honorary (as Richard Nixon did at Duke), or Phi Beta Kappa; only two were appointed despite a "not qualified" rating from the ABA.

"Most are men of attainment who have proven themselves," says Sheldon Goldman. "There are a few who aren't 'magnas' or 'summas,' but no lemons. It seems to me that it's possible to slip in a barely qualified judge on the trial-court level, but much more difficult on the appellate court. The senator and the Justice Department realize they're really in the big leagues, that these are regional supreme courts. Justice Department attorneys have to practice before them. The ABA takes more care in screening them. Nobody wants hacks at that level." Delmar Karlen of New York University describes them as men of "personal, political, and intellectual force."

Yet the political obstacle course they have to run can eliminate many of the best and reward the mediocre who survive it. Even the "summas" have to hustle for the job. Friendly and Kaufman both aspired to a vacancy on New York's Second Circuit in 1959, and both campaigned for it. Friendly won, but Kaufman got the next opening two years later. James Coleman of Mississippi, Donald Russell of South Carolina, and Otto Kerner of Illinois are all ex-governors. Anthony Celebrezze of Ohio was Secretary of Health, Education and Welfare in the Johnson administration. Kennedy wanted to appoint the liberal J. Skelly Wright of Louisiana to a seat on the Fifth Circuit in the Deep South, but Senator Russell

Long protested that Wright's appointment would fatally wound him with his Louisiana constituents. Kennedy finessed Long by naming Wright to the neutral-ground District of Columbia Circuit.

Nixon selected thirty-seven appellate judges during his first four years—more than a third of the total complement. In comparison with the nominees of his Democratic predecessors, Nixon's men were drawn more from large "white-shoe" law firms (like the New York firm he worked in) and less from government posts. He named more Protestants, fewer Catholics and Jews.

Nixon's appointments have been a peculiar mixture. The majority are the "strict constructionist" conservatives he favors, but their credentials have oscillated wildly between the poles of established professional excellence and pedestrian partisanship. Donald Ross of Nebraska was a longtime Republican national committeeman. James Barrett of Wyoming is the son of a former Republican senator. Malcolm Wilkey of the District of Columbia was a Nixon campaign worker in Texas.

Several of his Southern nominees have records of hostility to civil rights. G. Harrold Carswell of Florida (who resigned after his failure to achieve the Supreme Court) repeatedly insulted civil-rights lawyers. Joe Ingraham of Texas was notable chiefly for the five-year draft-evasion sentence he imposed on Muhammad Ali (the conviction was overturned). The late Henry Brooks of Kentucky once angrily asked a civil-rights attorney, from the bench, if his politics were "the same as your client's."

George Mackinnon of the District of Columbia, who continued advising the mutual-fund company he represented even after his confirmation, is described by one Washington lawyer as "so far right he makes Goldwater look like George McGovern." Two other Nixon appointees to the D.C. court, Malcolm Wilkey and Roger Robb, are regarded as more formidable intellectually but similarly conservative. Robb was Goldwater's attorney in his libel suit against publisher Ralph Ginzburg. William Timbers of Connecticut once complained that his district courtroom was "infiltrated with hard-core subversives" at a draft trial.

But other Nixon appointments have been indisputably first-rate. Walter Mansfield of New York, as a District Court judge, ordered a men-only saloon to admit women, and once ornamented an order protecting the endangered crocodile with the comment that "extinct animals, like lost time, can never be brought back." James Oakes of

Vermont has shown a particular sensitivity to environmental issues. John Paul Stevens of Chicago is described by lawyers in that city as "Supreme Court caliber," as is Arlin Adams of Philadelphia. Robert Sprecher of Chicago is also rated highly. Alfred Goodwin of Oregon, William Miller of Tennessee, and Levin Campbell of Massachusetts are other Nixon appellate judges who have earned high marks from their professional peers.

The pattern appears similar to Nixon's appointments to the District Court: where there is a liberal Republican senator to leaven the administration's law-and-order obsession, the nominees have been superior; Stevens and Sprecher were sponsored by Senator Charles Percy, Campbell by Senator Edward Brooke, Mansfield by Jacob Javits, Goodwin by Senators Mark Hatfield and Robert Packwood. In the South and much of the Midwest, where liberal Republicans are about as common as the passenger pigeon, the caliber has been lower.

Senatorial vanity remains a delicate variable in the appointment equation. Senator Hiram Fong of Hawaii, peeved when the administration ignored his long-standing desire for a Hawaiian on the Ninth Circuit Court, blocked the appointment of three other nominees for two months. When another vacancy arose a year and a half later, Fong got his man, Herbert Choy. Choy is Fong's former law partner.

Judge George C. Edwards, Jr., welcomed me to his cavernous office in the Detroit federal courthouse. In a few days he was due to leave for Cincinnati to join the eight other judges of the Sixth Circuit Court of Appeals for three weeks of hearing arguments. Circuit judges gather for such sessions periodically, working in their home cities the rest of the time. The research for the cases assigned to him was stacked in a dozen neatly separated piles of books and papers, some of them two feet high, completely covering a long conference table. Atop each pile was a short memorandum summarizing the facts and issues of the case.

Edwards is a white-haired, thin-faced man of medium height with bushy eyebrows that flick upward at the ends, giving him a resemblance to Ray Walston as the devil in *Damn Yankees*. A table behind his desk held a row of looseleaf binders containing opinions he has written in his ten years as a federal appellate judge. A framed letter on one wall expressed the thanks of Robert and Ethel Kennedy for his sympathy at the time of President Kennedy's death. He took off his suit coat and offered me a leather chair. "I don't know if I'm happy to see you or not," he said. He had agreed to talk with me for a few hours (which stretched into two days) about himself and his job. "I guess the first thing to say is that I enjoy the job, I live with it comfortably," he began.

Edwards is a vigorous man of fifty-nine who plays tennis regularly, winter and summer, and snorkels on his annual vacations in the Virgin Islands. His complexion is pink, and his frame shows only the faintest bulge at the belt. His clothes are conservative and well tailored, his posture is erect, and his eyes are a cool blue. There is something natty about him, and his personality suggests a once-abrasive man who has mellowed in middle age. One suspects that he would be a feisty and effective foe in an argument, and he's had his share of them.

He was born in Dallas, the son of a prominent attorney and the grandson of a justice of the peace. His father was a lifelong radical, the publisher of Texas's first labor newspaper and a frequent candidate for governor of Texas on the Socialist ticket. "He was an active Socialist until the party was destroyed by World War Two," Edwards said. "He was known as a poor man's lawyer, the civil-liberties–NAACP-type lawyer of those days. He was the best-known Socialist in Texas, though it was not a position with intense competition."

As a boy he accompanied his father on his legal rounds, gaining an eye-opening acquaintance with Texas justice. "When I was about sixteen I drove him downtown one night to get some clients out of jail. They had advocated integrating labor unions, an act which was clearly illegal in the mind of the police. I dropped him off and went to park the car. When I got to the City Hall he was gone—he'd been kidnaped on the steps. For the next three or four hours I tried to get someone to do something about it. Finally a police sergeant took pity on me and said, 'Go on home, no one's gonna hurt your daddy.' He said it in a way that convinced me he knew what he was talking about. They hadn't harmed him, they'd just driven him out of town and let him go."

His father's first criminal client was lynched by a Dallas mob. "He told me about it, it happened before I was born. He was assigned to defend an old black man charged with molesting a white child. This was in the early 1900s. He asked for a continuance to consult with his client, and the judge gave him a half-hour. He went to talk to the prisoner in the jury room, but the mob broke through police lines and grabbed the man before my father's eyes. They threw him out of a second-story window and hanged him at the Elks Temple arch."

Young Edwards grew up in a middle-class neighborhood in north Dallas. "My father's practice wasn't lucrative, but he made a living." He attended segregated schools and developed an interest in writing. By the time he was seventeen he was majoring in English at Southern Methodist University. "I was interested in Upton Sinclair, Theodore Dreiser, the social realists." His experiences with his father had killed any ambition then for a career in law. He recalled one more in particular:

"I went with him to see a client in jail. We were in a large room off the jail office. I began to hear screams and groans coming from a small room next door. I had seen several men lead a red-headed prisoner into that room.

"People came and went from the room and I could see what was going on. The prisoner was spread-eagled over the end of a heavy table, his ankles shackled to the table legs. One man stood behind him with a rubber hose. A man on each side had his arms twisted so he was bent forward over the table. The man was stripped to the waist and there were red welts crisscrossing his back. Once in a while they reached down and twisted his testicles.

"The most macabre memory was seeing the jail staff and other prisoners going about their routine without ever looking in that direction. Seeing this and the cases I'd seen tried didn't give me a high opinion of the law as practiced in Texas."

Edwards came north to take a master's degree in English at Harvard, which he acquired at age nineteen. He wanted to write a novel, and decided that the place to do it was Detroit—"the capital of American industry." With that in mind, he took a job as a laborer in a factory. "But I didn't write the first chapter of the novel and haven't yet. From then on, it was like the cub reporter sent to cover a five-alarm fire who calls the desk and says, 'I can't tell you about it now, there's too much going on.' "

What was going on was the struggle to establish the United Auto Workers union. "I was working at a wheel company, dipping brake plates in a vat of paint," he said. "I was gathering material for a novel. But within a few weeks there was a strike for recognition of the union and a minimum wage. I was getting paid thirty-seven and a half cents an hour. I joined the union and before I knew it I was an organizer." He became a full-time union worker and a close associate of Walter Reuther. "Reuther was president of my local at the time. I became an international representative, then director of the union's welfare department. Reuther impressed me, I think he was one of the great men of the century—he had a very innovative mind and great organizational capacity. He never drank or played poker with the boys.

"I was accused of being an agent of John L. Lewis. They said I was imported to help organize. But it was pure chance that I got a job at that plant just before the strike. The truth was that the industry had treated human beings as material for so long that nobody needed to organize, all we had to do was convince them that they had some chance. Also the National Labor Relations Act had been passed by Roosevelt's New Deal, and the atmosphere for labor had improved." Edwards credits the labor movement with achieving "the greatest net gain for the have-nots in this country since the Civil War." He occasionally twits a wealthy financier friend by urging him to build a monument to Reuther on Wall Street. "It's not so silly an idea," he said. "The establishment of collective bargaining made the economy more secure and viable even for those at the top."

Edwards toyed with a metal letter-opener as he talked, biting on it at one point, running it through his hair at another. "I believe I've lived more vividly than most judges have," he said. "I'm sure I'm one of the few judges who ever walked a picket line, and I doubt if any other federal judge has been in jail." His experience on the wrong side of the bars came when he was held in contempt of court for violating an injunction against a UAW strike in 1938 and sentenced to thirty days. It wasn't the *pièce de résistance* of my life," he said, "but I suppose it has to be mentioned."

He moved from union work into politics, serving first as director of the Detroit Housing Commission and then as a four-term member of the city's Common Council. Having by then shed his youthful prejudice against a law career, he began attending law school at night. He broke off to enter the Army as an infantry officer during World War II. "I was with an invasion force that was supposed to land in Japan on October 15, 1945"—two months after the bomb was dropped on Hiroshima. He practiced law for half a dozen years after the war, specializing in negligence and workmen's-compensation cases.

He ran for mayor in 1949, at the age of thirty-five, losing by a 3–2 margin. "I probably would have stayed in politics if I won." Instead he was appointed a probate judge in 1951 and assigned to Juvenile Court. After four years he moved up to the Circuit Court, Michigan's general-jurisdiction trial court, and after two more years to the state Supreme Court.

"My father came to my swearing-in at the Supreme Court. The chief justice introduced him and asked him to speak. I was wondering what he was going to say. He stood up and said, 'His mother and I are honored by this opportunity for our son, and pray that he will do justly, love mercy, and walk humbly with his God.' Everything that came after that seemed irrelevant." Still an aspiring writer, Edwards is working on a book about his own life and his father's—"his life through my eyes."

The judge suggested we recess for lunch at the Detroit Press Club, several blocks from the courthouse. We walked past a construction site where a large building was going up. "It's going to be named after the man responsible for my being a federal judge," he said. The man was the late Democratic Senator Pat McNamara, like Edwards a product of the Michigan labor movement.

"In a sense, I originated McNamara's political career," he said, "and he never forgot it. He was vice president of the Building Trades Union, and I recommended to the mayor that he be appointed director of rent control." McNamara became an important political leader in Detroit, and eventually a senator.

"When he ran in the Democratic primary, I was committed to his opponent, Blair Moody, but Moody died before the primary and I supported McNamara. In 1961 I left the Supreme Court to become Detroit Police Commissioner—those were my most interesting years. McNamara had asked me when I was still on the Supreme Court if I was interested in a federal district judgeship, but I said no, the Supreme Court was more important. I decided that I'd take the police job for two years and then go back to practicing law.

"Pat came around in 1962 and said there was a vacancy on the Circuit Court coming up and he wanted to send my name in. I said no, that I wanted to stay until the end of 1963. He was a tough guy, you didn't say 'maybe' to him. Turning him down was like what I've heard about turning LBJ down. He said he wasn't sure he could hold the job that long. I said I wasn't asking him to hold it. He asked if I'd be available in late 1963 and I said I didn't know.

"Well, a few months passed and one day we were both at the airport waiting for the President to arrive. I was full of security, responsible for it. McNamara asked me if I was ready to take the federal-court job. I asked when it was effective. He said in six months. I asked if I could have it if I wanted it and he said, 'Yep.' I asked if he could get me through the Senate—I was thinking about my labor background—and he said he could. I still wasn't sure he could get it for me, but I thought about it for a couple of weeks and said okay. He helped get me through, too. He was with me at the hearing."

Edwards had declined to order a drink. He greeted several friends at the Press Club. A dark-haired young man stopped by our table and reported the latest on a municipal political dispute. "This is my son, George Clifton Edwards III," the judge said. "He's city clerk." He turned back to his son. "Stay on 'em, George," he said. Another son is an assistant state attorney general in Lansing, the state capital.

Edwards' confirmation hearing before the Senate Judiciary Committee was one of the longest and most contentious for any nominee below the U.S. Supreme Court. The senators quizzed him about his father's career as a Socialist, his membership in the American Student Union, his record as a labor organizer, his jail term, and a decision he wrote as a Supreme Court justice favoring the UAW.

"The committee included Eastland, Sam Ervin, Everett Dirksen, Roman Hruska, Olin Johnston of South Carolina, and Phil Hart of Michigan," he recalled. "I think the real cutting issues were my record on equal treatment of blacks first, my labor record and the jail term second, and my father. I wasn't asked to renounce my father, and I never would. I think it was legitimate to bring out the questions about me that they did. If I were a senator, I'd want to know it. They could conclude that I'd follow my father, or reject him, or modify his principles, but in any case it's not irrelevant.

"Ervin did a lot of the questioning, and he'd done his homework.

I have a lot of respect for him. He'd read my opinions. He asked about my father and my days in the union. Dirksen read a statement by the judge who had sentenced me to jail, saying he had a duty to enforce his order. Dirksen asked what I thought of it. I told him I might not subscribe to the adjectives he used, but essentially he was right. Dirksen looked surprised, and he lost interest after that. By the way, when I went on the Circuit Court I sent word that I'd be honored if that judge would hold my robe at my swearing in, and he did."

Edwards had the backing of Michigan's Democratic congressional delegation as well as the state bar association. He had won a "qualified" rating, albeit with dissenting votes, from the ABA judiciary committee. The Senate committee recommended his confirmation, the Senate approved him, and he became a member of the Sixth Circuit (covering Michigan, Ohio, Kentucky, and Tennessee) on December 19, 1963—his nomination was pending when President Kennedy was assassinated.

He believes strongly in drawing judges from the political stage. "The strength of the federal judiciary is that judges come out of the American political process at the highest level. I don't think judges should be monks or foreign to the life of the people. I think our contact with ordinary life gives us an understanding of people's problems which creates qualities of compassion and social wisdom. There are a lot of judges who believe that the way they grew up, in prep school and an Ivy League college and their country club, is the only way of life. They reject what they don't understand as evil. They have no street wisdom. They don't think about how criminals get that way, they just regard them as distasteful." He is militantly opposed to the selection of judges from nominations by blue-ribbon bar-association panels. "That's like letting the fox in the chicken coop," he said. "Bar politics is just as fierce as public politics, and less open. I'm against high-level bar control of judicial selection. The bar in most states is under a strong corporate influence, for very good economic reasons"—that's where the money is.

"Judges are a fraternity to some degree," he said, "but it's not us against the world. The issues that divide the country also divide judges. About the only time we draw together is when the authority of the courts is attacked. And judges are unanimously in favor of reasonable salaries for judges, which is always higher than whatever they're getting."

Edwards excused himself to fetch a piece of pie from the restaurant's dessert buffet. He stopped to talk with a friend. "He said he thinks the only things that are any fun are dangerous," he said as he returned. "I think a lot of them are, but not all of them."

We walked back to the courthouse through a neighborhood of debris-littered empty lots awaiting new construction, which give downtown Detroit a bombed-out look. "I love Detroit," he said, "even though I was born and raised in the South. I consider myself a citizen of the world first, of the United States second, of Michigan third, and Texas fourth. I'm still Southern enough that I'd give a lady my seat on a streetcar if there were any streetcars. I believe in Southern courtesy and friendliness, but bigotry has no more value there than it does here."

His North-South background makes him peculiarly well fitted to sit on the Sixth Circuit, a court with jurisdiction in both Northern and Southern states and with its headquarters on the border, in Cincinnati. The judges convene in Cincinnati for three-week sessions five times a year. He plays tennis regularly in both Cincinnati and Detroit, with some skill. "You're looking at the co-holder of the elderly lawyers' doubles title in the state bar tournament," he advised.

"All the judges get together regularly, in Cincinnati," he said. "We have lunch together every day. I think we're closer than we would be if we were all in the same place year-round." He derives pleasure from his job, despite a caseload pressure so severe that "I would travel (and have traveled) miles to listen to anyone who might tell me how to save five minutes a day." But he laments the distance between an appellate judge and "the movement and life and pathos and humor of human existence."

"There's more loneliness on an appellate court than a trial court," he declared, "and I've been on both." He put his feet on his desk and picked up the letter-opener. "Decision-making is lonely wherever you do it. I'll concede the trial judges their complaint about sentencing. For a man with sensitivity, it's awesome and lonely. But there's movement in a trial court. An appellate judge has to people his world, to realize that these are people he's dealing with and not just cases. You have to envision the circumstances, events, and locales. In the end, on the critical issues, you have to make up your own mind, and it's still a solitary obligation.

"The collegial court has great value. I go into conference time after time and find points of view I hadn't seriously taken into account at all, and sometimes they're persuasive. I tend to be impatient with procedural niceties when they get in the way of the merits of a case. It's good for me to sit with judges who are more procedure-minded because procedure has a great relationship to due process and justice.

"You know, there are a lot of controls on judicial decision-making," he continued. "We don't decide a case on the basis of our own individual beliefs, no matter how deeply they're held. There is a body of law to which any conscientious judge must relate his decision—the Constitution and statutes and Supreme Court decisions. Any of them are absolutely controlling if applicable, and precedents also have great weight.

" 'Strict construction' and 'judicial restraint' seem to be popular phrases these days. I think of myself as a strict constructionist, even though others don't regard me that way. I don't try to avoid the intent of a statute or a Supreme Court decision even if I disagree with it. And asking if I exercise judicial restraint is like asking when I stopped beating my mother. We *always* exercise judicial restraint."

His secretary—"Miss I"—made her third appearance in fifteen minutes, and the judge allowed that he would have to get back to his solitary toil. Before I left, though, he handed me a large black briefcase filled with several lawbooks, instructing me to read a number of his opinions, which he selected, before I returned the next morning.

I obediently read the opinions that night. The best-known was Edwards' dissent when the Sixth Circuit Court declined to reverse the conviction of Dr. Sam Sheppard for the murder of his wife. His opinion endeared Edwards to Sheppard's lawyer, F. Lee Bailey, who regards him as an occupant of "the top shelf" of the federal judiciary and "his own man." Edwards wrote that the bias of Cleveland's news media deprived Sheppard of a fair trial, an opinion later endorsed by the U.S. Supreme Court, enabling Sheppard to win acquittal at a second trial after ten years in prison. "If ever flagrant and tolerated interference of the news media in a criminal trial served to deprive a defendant of his constitutional rights to due process and a fair trial," his dissenting opinion said, "this surely must be such a case." He wrote that the conduct of the first Sheppard trial was a "shock to [my] conscience."

In another opinion, this time writing for the majority, Edwards rejected the Nixon administration's claim that the Attorney General was empowered to wiretap without a warrant in the interest of "internal security." "The sweep of the assertion of presidential power is both eloquent and breathtaking," he wrote. "We find in the government's brief no suggestion of limitations on such presidential power, nor indeed any recognition that the governmental power of this nation is by constitution distributed among three coordinate branches of government." He concluded by expressing a libertarian creed, declaring that what "has distinguished the United States in the history of the world has been its constitutional protection of individual liberty. The First Amendment is the cornerstone of American freedom. The Fourth Amendment stands as guardian of the first. . . . The nature of our government requires us to defend our nation with the tools a free society has created and proclaimed and which are indeed the justification for its existence."

An opinion he wrote as a Michigan Supreme Court justice illustrated his view that a judge's personal opinion cannot lead him to overrule the explicit purpose of a legislative statute. The case concerned a foundry worker who died of silicosis incurred on the job. A state statute limited his survivor's benefits to $6000, and his family contended that the payment was inadequate. "The facts are brief and bitter," Edwards wrote, but he concluded that the statute was constitutional and the family's claim invalid. "Changes would require an obvious violation of legislative intent and the substitution of judicial judgment," he wrote.

Other decisions he had assigned me to read included a denial of a plea for legislative reapportionment (prior to a Supreme Court decision ordering it) and his endorsement of the principle of busing to integrate a Tennessee school district.

"The Sheppard opinion," he said when we met the following day, "may be as vigorous a dissent as I ever wrote. The danger to the First Amendment made the dad-gum thing hard to write. The legal issues were whether the trial itself was a violation of due process, and whether the proof was sufficient for a finding of guilty. I voted to reverse on the first point and never got to the second, but I had doubts there too."

The decision on the foundry worker, he said, was the most difficult. "I wouldn't have voted that way if I were a legislator, but I couldn't hold that the legislature didn't have the power to enact such a law. The decision still bothers me sometimes, but legislatures have to have the freedom to deal with problems as best they can. If you have to write bad law to do justice in a single case, that's too high a price to pay for the result. Our main concern on an appellate court is whether the rule of law that flows from a case will do justice generally."

The wiretap opinion was easier. "The spookiest legal argument I ever heard," he said, "is the 'inherent power of the sovereign' to wiretap."

Edwards is less "judgey" than most judges. He is not modest, but neither is he pompous. He appears comfortable with his job. "I worry about a decision in advance, but I don't wake up worrying about it afterwards," he said. "It's like Cardozo said—he said everything best: 'We give our most prejudiced consideration to a motion for rehearing.' The trouble with Cardozo is that he used up most of the best lines in the law." Books by Cardozo, Frankfurter, and Holmes are in his library, plus an eclectic selection including *Oswald: Assassin or Fall Guy?*, *The Conservative Mind*, *Anatomy of a Riot*, the Bible, *Death and the Supreme Court*, Ernest Gann's *Of Good and Evil*, and something called *Image of Hell*. "I have no idea what that might be," he said.

"In some ways we're like doctors," he said. "We deal with life-and-death decisions. You have to find a way to live with the burdens of the job. If you can stand it at all, you have to develop a method. My confidence in the Constitution helps. I regard it as an astonishingly inspired document, and I don't use that language lightly. When I feel I'm abiding by it, I can live with the burdens."

Like Alfonso Zirpoli, Edwards is a passionate believer in American justice. "If you can believe in our system of government, which I do, without qualms, and believe in your ability to serve it, then you can serve with comfort. The system offers an opportunity for good results if we have the intelligence and good will as a people to achieve them. The young people of the burn-'em-up, tear-'em-down persuasion, who want to destroy the whole substance because there are so many existing evils, have very little understanding of history and how people in other countries live under other systems. We somehow gave some of our young people the impression that man could cure death, disease, and taxes, but no such rose garden was ever promised. I believe in living as if life is worthwhile and has meaning and a man can contribute to it. I've tried to live like that and to preserve the possibility of human betterment."

It was getting on toward lunchtime again, and he suggested we send out for sandwiches. "You're smoking a lot," he told me. The corners of his small mouth edged upward. "It must be some guilt you feel when you're around judges." He ordered a hamburger, a cup of soup, and buttermilk.

The principal message he wanted to leave with me is that judges cannot indulge their own prejudices. "You have opinions, of course," he said, "but you don't make your mind up as a judge until you approach the matter in the context of the case. You don't decide your personal view, you decide what is or should be the law, and that is a very different decision. The court process itself tends to make you impartial. You have to compare your thought with other thoughts. I agree with Cardozo that we don't have a 'roving commission to do justice,' and I'm not sure I'd like it if I had it. It might be one way to live, but it's not judging.

"I'm certainly a liberal in political and social policy, but in law I identify with the values—I'm hesitating over which one to say first—of 'ordered liberty.' I identify with the Bill of Rights of the Constitution strongly, and recognize also that any government must be the guarantor of the people's welfare, including the opportunity to live in peace."

Lunch arrived, and he leaned back in his chair to enjoy it. "Does that blur the conflict enough?" he asked.

XV

Portrait in Ermine

The hundred justices of the
U.S. Supreme Court

> "*No matther whether th' constitution follows th'
> flag or not, th' supreme coort follows th' iliction
> returns.*"
>
> FINLEY PETER DUNNE,
> *Mr. Dooley's Opinions*

THE VISITORS QUEUE UP in the marble corridor out-
side the courtroom. Guards inspect women's purses with a flashlight
and ask men to check their briefcases. At intervals a few spectators
emerge through a wooden door and a few in line are permitted to
enter, the quiet comings and goings reminiscent of a theater with
continuous performances, which in a sense this is. Inside, an usher
guides the visitor through plush dark drapes into the rich, marble-
columned chamber and silently indicates a vacant seat on a bench
lined with a pink upholstered cushion. The room is boxy, high-
ceilinged, grand rather than elegant. It manages to suggest majesty without demanding obeisance.

The justices of the Supreme Court of the United States sit at a
long mahogany bench between marble pillars and in front of a red
velour curtain along which pages scurry like military messengers.
The bench is in three sections, the left and right sides canted
slightly forward to enable the justices to see each other. Their
places on the bench, like so many other details of Supreme Court

326

operation, are prescribed by protocol and seniority. Chief Justice Burger sits in the middle, his broad shoulders squared and his elbows on the desk, a pen in his hand. To his left is Brennan, rubber-faced and sunk in his high-backed swivel chair, his hand to his chin. Douglas, briskly leafing through a lawbook and jotting notes he hands to a page without looking up, is to Burger's right. Down the line to the chief's left, in descending order of seniority, are White, granite-faced and stern-looking; Blackmun, who rocks in his chair and looks like a country druggist; and Rehnquist, dark-haired, almost bug-eyed, the only justice not yet fifty. At Douglas' right are Stewart, more animated than the rest, his eyes alive with humor; then Marshall, who looks drowsy and immobile; and finally the long-faced Powell, the corners of his lips turned down as if in courtly distaste.

Directly in front of the chief justice is a lectern at which lawyers argue the republic's most vexing issues. A small light on the stand glows when a lawyer reaches the end of his allotted time. Counsel's argument invariably becomes a dialogue; justices interrupt with questions and commentary; at times a lawyer may be besieged by three or four justices in succession. Attorneys have fainted from the pressure of a Supreme Court appearance; others have been reduced, like figures in a lawyer's nightmare, to incoherent murmurs. These are the mightiest judges in the land, nine mortals with a collective power unmatched by any other court on earth, interpreters of the Constitution, guardians of the form and content of American democracy. It is impossible to overstate the Supreme Court's importance; one writer described it as "the nation's ultimate repository of impartiality, logic, reason, and experience; its conscience, soul, and sense of history and destiny."

Yet the sweep of rhetoric can obscure the fact that they are still only nine flesh-and-blood humans, each an idiosyncratic blend of perceptions, vanities, memories, loyalties, prejudices, and values. They are our philosopher-kings, dwellers at the top of the pyramid of law, but each is still an individual who sees the world through his own eyes, no one else's, and who orders his universe by his own star.

I listened to the justices pepper a lawyer with questions one afternoon, and the impression that struck first was their voices. With the exception of Marshall, each justice who spoke—Burger,

Rehnquist, Stewart, White, and Blackmun—declaimed in firm, full-bodied tones, deep and authoritative. Marshall's voice was weak and high-pitched, an old man's voice (though at sixty-five he is ten years younger than Douglas, the senior justice). Power was so much a part of the others, of their personalities perhaps, that you could hear it in the timbre as well as the content of their words. For a fugitive moment I entertained the absurd notion that they were required to pass some entrance examination in elocution, the way it sometimes seems as though governors must meet some established standard of rugged, American-style handsomeness.

At precisely three o'clock Chief Justice Burger broke into the middle of a lawyer's sentence to announce that the court day was over and they would resume at ten the next morning. (Former Chief Justice Charles Evans Hughes, the story goes, was so rigidly punctual that he once interrupted a lawyer in the middle of the word "if.") The justices rose, their robes swaying gently, and chatted easily among themselves. All but Douglas, who bustled offstage with a book under his arm.

From John Jay in 1789 to William Rehnquist in 1971, an even hundred men have sat on the U.S. Supreme Court. They have been, with few exceptions, the cream of America's legal and political Establishment. Some, like Chief Justice John Marshall, Oliver Wendell Holmes, and Felix Frankfurter, were men of enormous intellectual gifts, among the finest minds of their day. Others, like the succession of corporation lawyers appointed in the late nineteenth century, were distinguished chiefly by their fealty to the barons of American capitalism. Most were members of the privileged classes—the landed gentry (and slaveowners) in the early years, the business and professional plutocracy afterward. Only a few justices (Chief Justices Earl Warren and Warren Burger among them) have known hardship and struggle. The majority were WASPs of comfortable means and genteel manners, well connected and trained to lead. The imperatives of conscience they carried to the highest tribunal were those of their class and profession—conservatism in the broadest sense, individual responsibility, devotion to "the law."

From the beginning, the character of the Supreme Court has

been a reflection of the political currents in the country. Presidents appoint justices for good reasons and bad, noble and petty, but preeminently for their *own* reasons. The history of Supreme Court decisions may be read in one sense as the legacy of the appointing Presidents—the great Federalist Marshall, selected by John Adams; the Southern Democrat Roger Taney, the choice of Andrew Jackson; the flexible conservative Charles Evans Hughes, named by Herbert Hoover. But the liberation of the bench and the longevity of its occupants complicate the theory: Earl Warren's social philosophy was a generous distance from Dwight Eisenhower's; the justices at Lincoln's inauguration and Franklin Roosevelt's were defenders of dying dogmas. The court is, above all, dynamic, an institution in motion; its character at any given time is an amalgam of static philosophy, the society's direction, and judicial reaction to change.

George Washington loaded the first court with men of his own Federalist Party, choosing three Southerners and three Northerners for the then six-man bench. John Jay of New York was balanced by John Rutledge of South Carolina for the same reason that William Rehnquist of Arizona, two centuries later, was coupled with Lewis Powell of Virginia.

Thomas Jefferson and James Madison tried to reverse the court's nationalist direction under Marshall by selecting men of their own ideological hue, only to see their best appointment, Joseph Story, move to Marshall's position. Marshall, like the majority of justices in the court's history, was an experienced politician (he had been Adams' Secretary of State). He guided the court in a series of sweeping decisions (notably *Marbury v. Madison*, which established the Supreme Court's power to declare an act of Congress unconstitutional) through force of personality and a talent for negotiation. Justice William Johnson, a Jefferson appointee, grumbled to his patron about Marshall's dominance. Wondering why Marshall invariably wrote the court's opinions, Johnson reported to Jefferson that he had "found out the real cause. [William] Cushing was incompetent. [Samuel] Chase could not be got to think or write. [William] Paterson was a slow man and willingly declined the trouble, and the other two judges [Marshall and Bushrod Washington] you know are commonly estimated as one judge."

Even the court's size was a recurrent political issue. The original six-man court gained one more justice under Jefferson in 1807, and grew to nine during the tenure of Andrew Jackson thirty years later. The Civil War Congress increased the membership to ten in 1863 (giving Abraham Lincoln the chance to appoint five justices in three years), but Reconstruction legislators cut it back to seven in 1866 in a spiteful swipe at Andrew Johnson. The court finally stabilized at nine members in 1869.

Justices come and go, but politics endures. Andrew Jackson named John McLean to the court because McLean, a non-partisan Postmaster General who had served previous administrations, bridled at Jackson's use of postal appointments for patronage. He found another place on the court for John Catron, an old friend from Tennessee. But his greatest opportunity came with the death of Marshall in 1835. To succeed him as chief justice, Jackson named Roger Taney of Maryland, an intimate presidential adviser who had been both Attorney General and Secretary of the Treasury. Jackson's selection of his confidant Taney has parallels in dozens of later appointments: Holmes was an adviser to Theodore Roosevelt and a frequent visitor at the White House; Louis Brandeis was often consulted by Woodrow Wilson; Tom Clark and Harry Truman were close friends, as were Felix Frankfurter and Franklin Roosevelt, and Abe Fortas and Lyndon Johnson.

The Supreme Court's reputation for independent, disinterested judgment, its stature in the public mind as an institution well above the *Sturm and Drang* of partisanship, developed in an atmosphere of persistent political acrimony. The New York *American* greeted the news of Taney's selection with an editorial lamenting that "the pure ermine of the Supreme Court has been sullied by the appointment of that political hack." As always with such criticism, the real point was not the ermine of the court but the political cloth of the justice: Taney was no threat to the court's grandeur, he was a threat to the political beliefs of his critic. A rhetorical wooliness has frequently characterized criticism of the court. Political and ideological animosity is constantly embroidered with grander language. Franklin Roosevelt's assault on the "nine old men" in 1937 was a political broadside in the guise of a retirement plan; Southern senators, aghast at the desegregation decision of the Warren Court, disguised their objection in the form of legislation requiring that all justices have judicial experience; Richard Nixon hid his differences with the Warren Court's criminal-rights decisions behind a call for an elusive "strict constructionism."

Yet the court does transcend politics—not always, perhaps, but often enough to give some legitimacy to the prestige it enjoys. The reason is that political philosophy and judicial philosophy are different. A man like Felix Frankfurter may incense his friends and baffle his enemies by being at once a political liberal and a judicial conservative. Political and social values depend on a man's perceptions and loyalties about his society, but judicial values rely on different criteria: adherence to the rule of law, precedent, the language of the Constitution, a careful obedience to the principle of separation of powers. Every Supreme Court justice, regardless of his political beliefs, delivers at least one opinion in which he plumps for the right of legislatures to do their job, to experiment in meeting social problems without judicial interference. The "self-restraint" advocated by Frankfurter, Holmes, Benjamin Cardozo, and others was simply their conviction that judges should not substitute their personal views for those of the people's elected representatives.

It is not a clear line, of course, and even the best judges leap back and forth across it. One justice's deference to legislative power is a "shock to the conscience" of another. One's self-restraint is another's abdication of responsibility. "Some justices," Harvard's Alan Dershowitz says, "those with political programs rather than judicial philosophies, are entirely predictable in their decisions." But others are not, and the facile labels of "liberal" or "conservative" cannot describe them any more than their approach to their responsibilities can be conveniently categorized as judicial activism or strict constructionism.

Another, equally perilous way of separating judicial philosophies is to divide them into those which elevate "justice" and those exalting "law." The judge, Cardozo said, "is not a knight-errant, roaming at will in pursuit of his own ideal of beauty or goodness. He is to draw his inspiration from consecrated principles. He is not to yield to spasmodic sentiment, to vague and unregulated benevolence." Law in this sense is the written and accepted body of rules that guide the society; justice is whatever is morally right. But justice is then a subjective determination, dependent on the morality of the beholder, whereas law is objective and codified. "I hate justice," Holmes said, staking out his own position with characteristic cogency.

Learned Hand, the greatest judge who never sat on the Supreme Court, explained what Holmes meant. "I remember once I was with him," he recalled. "It was a Saturday when the court was to confer. It was before he had a motorcar, and we jogged along in an old coupé. When we got down to the Capitol, I wanted to provoke a response, so as he walked off I said to him, 'Well, sir, goodbye. Do justice!' He turned quite sharply and he said, 'Come here, come here.' I answered, 'Oh, I know, I know.' He replied, 'That is not my job. My job is to play the game according to the rules.' "

Constitutional lawyers like to identify periods of Supreme Court history by the name of the chief justice of the day—the Marshall Court, the Warren Court, the Taft Court, etc. The labels, though useful, are mildly deceptive. They seem to suggest, for example, that court membership is constant during the tenure of the chief, which is never the case. In fact the turnover on the court has averaged one new justice every twenty-two months; each President in the twentieth century has had at least one vacancy to fill. The labels also ignore the fierce independence of individual justices and overrate the influence of the chief justice. The chief may be pre-eminent and possess administrative powers that the others lack (the power to assign opinions, for example), but his is still only one vote among nine. Charles Evans Hughes, one of the most domineering chief justices, once sent a messenger to inform Justice James McReynolds that the other justices were ready to enter court. McReynolds sent word back to Hughes that "Mr. Justice McReynolds says he doesn't work for you." Supreme Court justices may be the most independent public servants extant, and even the strongest chief justice cannot make them do what they don't want to do. The umbrella labeled "Warren Court" attempts to cover such proud, disparate, and forceful men as Frankfurter, Hugo Black, John Marshall Harlan, Robert Jackson, and William Douglas.

What the labels really identify are cycles of action, reaction, or synthesis in the court's history, the great cumulative shifts in national policy on which the court has stamped its seal. The Warren Court was more a cycle of action, which happened to fall when it did for a half-dozen reasons, than the creation of a single man. The Burger Court gives every indication of being a reaction to the Warren Court. Another cyclical junction took place when the Taney Court replaced the Marshall Court in 1836.

Roger Taney was regarded as a "radical" in Jackson's Cabinet, a vociferous opponent of entrenched corporate power. A hostile Senate rejected him for both associate justice of the court and Secretary of the Treasury (Jackson gave him a recess appointment anyway) before reluctantly confirming his nomination as chief justice. A member of a slaveholding family, Taney led the court during the anguished years of increasing bitterness which preceded the Civil War. His court turned away from the assertions of federal power of the Marshall era and listened more sympathetically to pleas for state's rights. At the same time the Taney Court expanded federal power to regulate corporations, an issue that was to ebb and flow in the court for the next hundred years.

Taney's court ultimately foundered on the question of slavery. The *Dred Scott* decision, which Taney wrote in 1857, declared that slaves were property and that the Missouri Compromise of 1820, which had outlawed slavery in the frontier territories, was unconstitutional. Five Southern justices joined with two from the North in rejecting the plea of former slave Dred Scott. Justice Catron, Jackson's old crony from Tennessee, went so far as to ask President James Buchanan's help in persuading one reluctant justice to go along with Taney. The President obliged, and the justice came around. John McLean of Ohio, the ex-Postmaster General who had resisted Jackson's bullying, was one of the two dissenters. The other was Benjamin Curtis of Massachusetts. (The commonwealth has produced a disproportionate share of brilliant and courageous justices. The seven besides Curtis include Story, Holmes, Frankfurter, and Louis Brandeis.)

The *Dred Scott* decision intensified the polarization that led to war, and signaled a deterioration in the court's prestige and influence so pronounced that Taney was virtually invisible during the war. He died at eighty-seven in 1864, disgraced and forgotten.

The bonanza of court appointments which fell to Abraham Lincoln enabled him to staff the court with men he could count on to uphold the constitutionality of his war measures. One of his nominees was David Davis, a friend from Lincoln's days as a circuit-riding lawyer in Illinois. Two others, Stephen Field and Samuel Miller, compiled long and generally distinguished records. Lincoln's choice to succeed Taney as chief justice was Salmon Chase, Secretary of the Treasury in the wartime Cabinet. Chase's presidential ambition was so widely known that Lincoln sought assurances that he would not use the court as a campaign platform.

Chase was neither the first nor the last justice to see himself as presidential timber. Hughes resigned from the court in 1916 to run against Wilson (he returned as chief justice in 1930). John McLean was a candidate for the 1860 Republican nomination, which went to Lincoln. Warren was the Republican nominee for Vice President in 1948. Brandeis and Douglas, among others, were considered vice-presidential possibilities at different times. William Howard Taft was the only man in our history who achieved both the Presidency and the court; he became chief justice eight years after he left the White House.

In the late nineteenth and early twentieth centuries the *leitmotif* of the court became the protection and expansion of free enterprise. A succession of business-minded justices, many of whom had served the burgeoning corporations before their ascent to the bench, seized on the "due process" clause of the Fourteenth Amendment as a guarantee of unrestricted business freedom. The amendment declares that no state shall "deprive any person of life, liberty, or property without due process of law; nor deny to any person within its jurisdiction the equal protection of the laws." To courts composed of former railroad and oil-company attorneys, a corporation qualified as a "person" under the amendment, and economic regulation of corporations was thus unconstitutional.

It was the age of robber barons, the accumulation of vast fortunes, and the creation of an American industrial empire. The business of America was business, and the business of the court was to uphold property rights above all others. In 1895 a court now led by Chief Justice Melville Fuller invalidated a federal income-tax law. The *Plessy v. Ferguson* decision a year later upheld racially segregated facilities as "separate but equal." A 1905 decision held that a New York law limiting the working day of bakers to ten hours was an unconstitutional denial of due process. It took thirty more years before Holmes's eloquent dissent was accepted by a majority of the court.

Holmes had been appointed by Theodore Roosevelt in 1902. Roosevelt believed that the Boston aristocrat was "his kind" of Republican and would support his trust-busting efforts. But Holmes was too detached to ally himself with any doctrine or presidential policy, and his relations with the White House grew strained.

Holmes was a philosophical skeptic who believed in the "free trade of ideas—that the best test of truth is the power of the thought to get itself accepted in the competition of the market." His lofty reputation derives not from his identification with any set of principles—he distrusted all dogma—but rather from the clarity of his thought and the luminescence of his prose. "His judicial philosophy of leaving the legislature alone," Max Lerner wrote, "came from a deeper philosophy of leaving the cosmos alone." "Certainty generally is illusion," Holmes wrote, "and repose is not the destiny of man." He defended the right of legislatures to do their best in an imperfect world.

He found himself dissenting frequently from colleagues who read their own *laissez-faire* beliefs into the Constitution. When Louis Brandeis was appointed to the court in 1916, over the objections of seven former presidents of the American Bar Association, Holmes had a partner in dissent. Brandeis was the first Jewish justice (though Judah Benjamin had declined a nomination as far back as 1853), a passionate supporter of humanitarian causes, and a proponent of social and economic reform. "I told him long ago," Holmes said of Brandeis, "that he was really an advocate rather than a judge. He is affected by his interest in a cause, and if he feels it he is not detached." Holmes allowed, however, that Brandeis' "interests are noble, and . . . his insights profound."

Holmes and Brandeis rank among the "twelve great justices of all time" in the opinion of sixty-five law professors, historians, and political scientists polled in 1971. The poll takers, wisely leaving the criteria for greatness up to the individual scholars, categorized justices as great, near-great, average, below average, and failures. The twelve "greats," besides Holmes and Brandeis, were Marshall, Story, Taney, John Marshall Harlan (the earlier of two justices with that name), Hughes, Harlan Stone, Cardozo, Black, Frankfurter, and Warren.

By the professors' standards, 1880 to 1920 was the era of the average. Only 4 of the 33 justices who served during those years were rated great (Holmes, Brandeis, Hughes, and Harlan), and 4 others were called near-great (Miller, Field, Morrison Waite, and Joseph Bradley). The other 25 were classified as average or worse. By contrast, 15 of the 35 justices who sat between 1920 and 1960 were ranked great or near-great.

The court's devotion to the *status quo* persisted despite the addition of Holmes and Brandeis. The conservatives found a new leader when Taft became chief justice in 1921. Taft was a portly political whirlwind of a chief justice. He sponsored wide-ranging reforms in the federal judicial structure, advised President Warren Harding on a variety of issues, and successfully promoted his own favorites for Supreme Court vacancies. He opposed liberals such as Cardozo and Learned Hand, advising Harding that they would be apt to "herd with Brandeis."

Personal relations among the justices, always a delicate balance of formidable egos, began to sour during the Taft years. Taft was a diplomatic and conciliatory leader, anxious to present a unified court and minimize dissent. The trouble stemmed from Justice James McReynolds, a cantankerous Tennessean who had been Wilson's Attorney General before he reached the court in 1914.

McReynolds disdained the court amenities—the praise of a brother's opinion, the willingness to swallow a mild disagreement in the interest of unanimity. An intellectually able conservative, he was curt and sarcastic in manner. On the margin of one "slip opinion," the preliminary draft of an opinion which is circulated among the justices, McReynolds wrote, "This statement makes me sick." Taft described him as "selfish to the last degree . . . fuller of prejudice than any man I have ever known, and one who seems to delight in making others uncomfortable."

Outspokenly anti-Semitic, he feuded constantly with Brandeis, and later extended his vendetta to include Cardozo and Frankfurter. He carped at Justice John Clarke so relentlessly that Taft held McReynolds responsible when Clarke resigned after only six years, contending lamely that he was bored with "the trifling character of judicial work."

"McReynolds was a strange creature," Frankfurter wrote in his reminiscence. "He is a good illustration of my deep conviction that on the whole as good a dividing line as any between men is those who love and those who hate, with varying degrees. McReynolds was a hater. He had a very good head. He was also primitive. He had barbaric streaks in him. He was rude beyond words to that gentle, saintlike Cardozo. He had primitive anti-Semitism. A tough-skinned fellow like me could deal with him because I could be just as rude as he could be. Rude isn't the exact word. He was not rude really, but indifferent, which is worse than being rude. . . ."

The routine of the Supreme Court's work, like all appellate procedure, demands accommodation. The justices gather in conference each Friday of their October-to-June term to decide which cases they will accept. Protocol and custom are important. The justices shake hands all around before the session begins. They speak in order of seniority, the chief first. The chief justice sets the pace and sometimes guides the discussion. McReynolds violated the code by occasionally passing up conferences in favor of hunting trips. Similarly, Chief Justice Burger has complained about Justice Douglas' habit of departing for his retreat in the Northwest before the term is over.

Any suggestion of acrimony at the conference is quickly discouraged. Holmes reacted to a statement by John Marshall Harlan once by commenting, "That won't wash." Harlan reddened. Chief Justice Melville Fuller broke the strained silence that followed by remarking, "But I keep scrubbing away, scrubbing away," pretending to be washing clothes on a washboard.

Justices try to present a serene public face even when intramural rancor runs deep. There is a lot of give and take in the shaping of opinions—a justice will add or delete a paragraph to satisfy another's objection (and secure his vote). The chief justice often assigns opinions for strategic reasons, asking the most moderate member of the majority, for example, to write the court's decision. Assignments have been withheld from senile justices as a subtle means of encouraging them to retire. (Justices have a remarkable record for longevity. No less than forty-six have served past their seventieth birthday, many into their eighties. Holmes was ninety-one when he retired, Black eighty-five, Marshall eighty.)

The dispute between McReynolds and Brandeis was one of the few to break into the open. McReynolds' final act of pettiness was to refuse to join in the collective letter of farewell when the eighty-three-year-old Brandeis retired. Hostility between Justices Black and Jackson flared in the 1940s when Jackson, ambitious for the chief-justiceship, accused Black of lobbying against his elevation (the job went to Fred Vinson). Jackson, who had taken a leave from the court to serve as U.S. prosecutor at the Nuremberg war-crimes trials, charged in a wire to President Truman that Black had threatened to resign if Jackson were named chief justice. The philosophical differences between Frankfurter, the advocate of judicial restraint, and the activist Warren spilled over into a testy courtroom exchange during the formal reading of an opinion in 1961.

Taft's court generally remained kindly disposed toward corporate power and skeptical of governmental interference. The justices blazed no new trails of constitutional liberties. Hughes, Herbert Hoover's selection to succeed Taft in 1930, was only slightly less conservative. But the Depression, just beginning to be felt in the nation, was to turn the court around before the decade was out.

Harvard law professor Lance Liebman has described a Supreme Court decision as "a calculus that considers the clarity of the Constitution's statement, the importance of the alteration that is proposed, the direction and strength of public feeling, the likely real-world outcome five years into the future, and the symbolic significance of court action or inaction." The operative variable in the 1930s was public opinion, the direction and strength of which were clearly visible in the election of Franklin Roosevelt and the implementation of his New Deal. It was Mr. Dooley's Law—"Th' supreme coort follows th' iliction returns."

The liberal wing of the court had gained a new recruit when Hoover appointed Cardozo to replace Holmes in 1932, violating every political rule in the process. Cardozo was a liberal, a Democrat, a Jew, and a New Yorker. He was also, with the possible exception of Learned Hand, the finest judge available. Politicians pointed out that there was already one Jew (Brandeis) on the court, and two justices from New York (Hughes and Harlan Stone). The remainder of the court, as FDR entered office, consisted of a conservative full house—McReynolds, Owen Roberts, Willis Van Devanter, George Sutherland, and Pierce Butler.

Stone, a Coolidge appointee, had slowly, to Taft's horror, come around to the Brandeis viewpoint on the constitutionality of governmental regulation of business. The addition of Cardozo meant three probable votes for the administration's most radical New Deal programs. But three was not enough, and after several setbacks Roosevelt vented his frustration with his "court-packing" plan of 1937, railing at the "nine old men" (the youngest was sixty-two, their average age seventy-two) who blocked the path of progress.

FDR lost his campaign to pack the court, but won the war. Justices Hughes and Roberts joined the liberals in 1937 in voting to uphold federal authority over collective bargaining in industries engaged in interstate commerce. That same year Roosevelt made his first court appointment, Hugo Black of Alabama, and the victory was solidified. Black's selection drew bitter liberal criticism when his Ku Klux Klan background was disclosed, but his subsequent record banished all apprehension.

"American presidents have been most attentive to the work and personnel of the Supreme Court in periods of extreme national tension," James Simon writes in a recent book on the court. In the three stressful years from 1938 to 1940, Roosevelt showed his attentiveness by appointing Frankfurter, Douglas, the moderate Stanley Reed of Kentucky, and Frank Murphy of Michigan, who was probably the most militant liberal in the court's history. When Hughes retired in 1941, FDR elevated Stone to chief justice.

Douglas was only forty at the time of his appointment, the youngest justice since Joseph Story. He grew up in the generous spaces of the Northwest. When he headed east for New York and Columbia law school, he stopped en route to deliver a load of sheep to the Chicago stockyards. Douglas was a non-conformist—"an unpolished gem of irregular design," one admirer said—a prolific writer, and a peripatetic traveler. He was also the most-married justice in the court's history. Along with Black, Douglas came to be the court's most vigorous defender of individual liberties.

Presidents have shown distinctive tastes in their Supreme Court nominees. Ulysses S. Grant was partial to railroad lawyers. Jefferson leaned to men in their thirties and forties; William Johnson, at thirty-three, was the second-youngest ever appointed (Madison's man Story, only thirty-two, was the youngest). Dwight Eisenhower favored sitting judges (Warren was the sole exception). Lyndon Johnson's two appointments (Abe Fortas and Thurgood Marshall) were both members of ethnic minorities. FDR was the only President who recruited law professors. Stone, his chief justice, had been dean of Columbia law school. Wiley Rutledge was a former dean of the University of Iowa law school. Frankfurter was a Harvard professor, and Douglas had taught at Yale before moving to the Securities and Exchange Commission. Political scientist John Schmidhauser found that 49 of the first 91 Supreme Court justices were "lawyers who were primarily politicians." Twenty-four were primarily judges, 11 were corporation lawyers, and 3 were non-corporate attorneys. Only 4—Roosevelt's 4—were professional teachers.

For more than a century the principal battleground of the court had been economics and property rights, but with the arrival of Roosevelt's men the center of action gradually began to shift to social change and human rights. The "due process" clause, invoked by generations of lawyers and justices in defense of corporate freedom, began to reappear in the context of individual liberties.

The dominant question was no longer whether federal or state authority was supreme, or whether (and how) the government could regulate corporate activity—these issues were largely settled. The court was back, in a sense, to first principles—the Bill of Rights and individual liberty. Its landmark cases now turned on questions of civil liberties that had been either denied or eroded.

The labels were no more help than they had ever been. If an "activist" was a justice who believed the court should set moral standards, then Hugo Black was indisputably an activist. But Black argued that he was merely following standards set forth in the Constitution, not promoting his personal philosophy; in his own opinion, he was the strictest of "strict constructionists." Douglas and Warren were activists without qualification. Warren expressed their position as clearly as anyone has when he equated justice with a simple sense of fairness. "A legal system," he wrote, "is simply a mature and sophisticated attempt, never perfected, to institutionalize this sense of justice and to free men from the terror and unpredictability of arbitrary force."

This view of the court's function had been consistently rejected by earlier justices, even those, like Brandeis and Cardozo, with liberal social philosophies. It remained a minority opinion during the 1940s and 1950s, and gained ascendance only briefly during the flowering of the Warren Court in the 1960s.

Harry Truman's first court appointment was a Republican senator from Ohio, Harold Burton—the only Republican ever selected by a Democratic President. His three other nominees were high-ranking Democratic politicians—Chief Justice Fred Vinson had been his Secretary of the Treasury, Tom Clark had served as Attorney General, and Sherman Minton was an Indiana senator. Truman's men generally held to the modest "judicial restraint" defended so brilliantly by Frankfurter, the court's intellectual eminence. Three of Truman's appointments—Vinson, Burton, and Minton—were among eight justices rated as "failures" in the 1971 poll of professors.

Dwight Eisenhower, asked once whether he had made any mistakes as President, reportedly replied that "two of them are on the Supreme Court." The "mistakes" he ruefully alluded to were undoubtedly Earl Warren and William Brennan, who joined with Black and Douglas to increase the court's activist minority to four. The background of Warren's appointment was the Republican nominating convention of 1952, where the California governor supported Ike in a credentials battle with backers of Senator Robert Taft. One frequently repeated story is that Eisenhower promised Warren the first vacancy on the court, then tried to renege when the first vacancy turned out to be the chief-justiceship.

Warren had been a prosecutor during his early years—he was one of the few justices with experience in criminal law—then served three terms as a progressive and hugely popular governor. A warm and amiable man, he was an unknown quantity as a judge when he was sworn in to replace Vinson in 1953.

Warren approached his new responsibilities cautiously, allying himself with neither Frankfurter nor Black at the outset. Gradually the depth of his compassion began to emerge in his opinions. "I always knew that Earl Warren believed that the law is made for the people, not the people for the law," a friend observed. He became the court's most eloquent exponent of judicial activism. His courtroom style was memorably described by Martin Mayer, who watched in fascination as Warren delivered an opinion:

"He told the story of a company which had stalled off negotiations with the union that represented its maintenance employees until three days before the expiration of their contract—and had then informed the union that the work was being contracted out to a third party who could do it cheaper, and all the union members were out of jobs. The company had, of course, secured competent opinion that its course of action violated no laws. . . .

"Warren, his massive head shaking as he spoke, summarized the facts in his earnest, rather heavy way; and what he was saying, really, was 'They shouldn't have done this.' As he neared the decision itself, his tone changed to 'They shouldn't be *allowed* to do this.' And when he came to the end, what he was saying was, 'Dammit, they're *not* allowed to do this.' The union members were reinstated with back pay."

Brennan, the fourth activist vote, was a Democrat (the seventh appointed by Republican Presidents), the son of an Irish immigrant, and a specialist in labor law. Named to replace Minton, he had been a trial judge and later a Supreme Court justice in New Jersey. The death of Robert Jackson and the retirements of Burton and Stanley Reed during Eisenhower's tenure opened up three more vacancies, all of which the President filled with appellate judges. The first was John Marshall Harlan, a skilled corporation lawyer whom Ike had named to the Second Circuit Court of

Appeals only nine months earlier. Charles Whittaker, the son of a Kansas farmer, joined the court in 1957. He had been named to a district judgeship by Ike in 1954 and promoted to the Eighth Circuit appellate court two years later. Potter Stewart, the final Eisenhower appointment, was only forty-three when he was elevated from the Sixth Circuit court.

Stewart and Harlan had the traditional pedigrees of high-court justices. Both were Ivy League educated and members of well-to-do families, with histories of active participation in Republican politics (roughly two thirds of all justices have come from politically active families). Stewart, like eleven justices before him, was the son of a prominent jurist—his father was a member of the Ohio Supreme Court. Harlan was one step removed; his grandfather and namesake graced the U.S. Supreme Court for thirty-four years, where his most memorable opinion was his dissent from the "separate but equal" *Plessy v. Ferguson* decision. A surprising number of justices, like Stewart and Harlan, had judicial limbs on their family trees. Schmidhauser found that 11 of the first 91 (not counting Stewart) were sons of judges; 6 had married daughters of jurists; and 14 more had a judge somewhere in the family.

Harlan and Whittaker joined the Frankfurter-led conservative faction on the court, while Stewart became a "swing man," a justice whose vote was not readily predictable. He has occupied the same middle ground through the Warren years and down to the present.

Whittaker found the pressure of the job so remorseless that he suffered a nervous collapse and retired after five years. By that time John Kennedy was in the White House. Kennedy's advisers suggested six possible successors: state Supreme Court justices Roger Traynor of California and Walter Schaefer of Illinois, Harvard professor Paul Freund, Secretary of Labor Arthur Goldberg, Deputy Attorney General Byron White, and William Hastie, a federal appellate judge in Philadelphia and the country's highest-ranking black judge.

Robert Kennedy raised Hastie's name, but the consensus among the Kennedy advisers was that the appointment of a black would be criticized as a blatant attempt to win Negro votes. Freund was supported by some senior staff members and opposed by others. Traynor and Schaefer, both widely admired in the legal community, were not well known to the Kennedys. White and Goldberg were.

Robert Kennedy later explained their criteria: "You wanted someone who generally agreed with you on what role government should play in American life, what role the individual in society should have. You didn't think about how he would vote in a reapportionment case or a criminal case. You wanted someone who, in the long run, you could believe would be doing what you thought was best. You wanted someone who agreed generally with your views of the country."

They settled on White, a former All-American football player who had known John Kennedy as a college student in England and again in the Navy during World War II. White had grown up in a small town on the Colorado prairie, won a Rhodes Scholarship to Oxford, and clerked for Chief Justice Vinson after graduating from Yale law school. He was a major organizer in Kennedy's presidential campaign, and collected his reward when Robert Kennedy made him his deputy in the Justice Department.

Goldberg arrived six months later, following Frankfurter's retirement at the age of eighty. Goldberg's background was similar to Brennan's. His father was a Russian Jew who emigrated to Chicago, where he sold vegetables from a pushcart. Goldberg had become the nation's leading labor lawyer by the time Kennedy named him Secretary of Labor.

With the addition of Goldberg, the activists finally took command. White had brought to the bench a pragmatic case-by-case approach that allied him most frequently with Stewart. Harlan had succeeded Frankfurter as the spokesman for judicial restraint. Goldberg's views, however, placed him in the activist wing with Black, Warren, Douglas, and Brennan. His appointment also continued the custom of a "Jewish seat," since he was inheriting the chair previously occupied by Frankfurter and Cardozo. He was to be replaced three years later by another Jewish justice, Abe Fortas, but the custom died with Nixon's appointment of Harry Blackmun after Fortas' resignation.

The Warren Court philosophy was demonstrated in a sunburst of decisions that consistently upheld individual rights against property interests or governmental power. The earliest and most dramatic was the unanimous 1954 decision to outlaw school segregation, overruling the "separate but equal" doctrine on grounds that separate schools for black and white children were inherently unequal. In 1962 the Warren Court redrew the lines of state legislative districts with its "one man, one vote" reapportionment ruling. The *Gideon v. Wainwright* case required states to furnish attorneys for indigent defendants charged with serious crimes. The *Escobedo* and *Miranda* decisions expanded the rights of criminal suspects, excluding confessions when a suspect had not been told of his right to counsel. The *Sullivan v. New York Times* opinion broadened the right of the press to publish criticism of public officials.

The Supreme Court had always been controversial, and the court's decisions had provoked outrage at irregular intervals throughout its history. But the rulings of the Warren Court, particularly in the desegregation decision, the criminal-rights cases, and a decision forbidding compulsory school prayers, unleashed storms of public and political protest that dwarfed earlier complaints. Denunciations of the court became politically profitable; the court was blamed for increases in crime and a widely perceived decline in public morality; demands for the impeachment of Warren were so common that the right-wing John Birch Society was happy to furnish an "Impeach Earl Warren" kit to anyone with a dollar.

Goldberg resigned in 1965, at the request of President Johnson, to become the chief U.S. delegate to the United Nations. Johnson replaced him with Fortas, a brilliant liberal who had successfully argued the *Gideon* case before the court. When Tom Clark retired two years later, activists picked up another vote and blacks gained their first Supreme Court justice with the appointment of Thurgood Marshall. Marshall, the son of a country-club steward, had spent twenty-three years as an attorney for the National Association for the Advancement of Colored People, crowning his work by winning the school-desegregation case. He had served three years as a federal appellate judge and two more as the U.S. Solicitor General.

The years 1967 to 1969, from the appointment of Marshall to the departure of Warren and Fortas, were the high-water mark of the Warren Court and of activism on the Supreme Court. The Warren era ended miserably with the resignation under pressure of Abe Fortas, the first such incident in the life of the court. Fortas was charged with accepting a $20,000 fee from the family foundation of financier Louis Wolfson, who was subsequently imprisoned for stock fraud. Fortas had returned the fee eleven months later, following Wolfson's indictment. He denied any impropriety, but submitted his resignation amid public clamor in May of 1969. By then there was a new President, a new chief justice was about to be appointed, and a new court day was dawning.

Warren Earl Burger became the nation's fifteenth chief justice a month after Fortas resigned. Like his predecessor, Burger is a large, white-maned bear of a man, courteous to lawyers and affable. His questions from behind the bench are delivered in a mellifluous baritone. He has the kind of easy dignity and presence that command attention and respect.

From President Nixon's perspective, Burger was the perfect chief justice. Like Nixon, he grew up in a family of modest means and worked his way through college. The family lived for a time on a truck farm outside St. Paul, Minnesota. His father worked as a railway cargo inspector and a traveling salesman.

He attended law school at night, joining a prominent St. Paul firm on graduation. He entered Minnesota politics as a supporter of gubernatorial candidate Harold Stassen in 1938. Ten years later he was Stassen's chief of staff during the first of his many campaigns for the Republican presidential nomination. At the 1952 GOP convention, Stassen delegate Burger backed Eisenhower during the same credentials fight in which Warren earned Ike's gratitude. Burger's reward was a Justice Department appointment as assistant attorney general in charge of the civil division. In 1956 Eisenhower named him to the U.S. Court of Appeals for the District of Columbia Circuit. He moved into an old farmhouse on six acres in Arlington, Virginia, which he filled with French Provincial furniture and a connoisseur's collection of wines.

Nixon wanted a chief justice, he explained, who believed in a "strict interpretation" of the Constitution; he had campaigned against the Warren Court's liberal activism. Burger was his man. In his thirteen years on the D.C. Circuit Court he had distinguished himself as a conservative "law and order" judge notable for his frequent clashes with the leader of the court's liberal wing, David Bazelon. He had also been a consistent advocate of court and prison reform, citing the failure of courts to handle their business promptly and the failure of prisons to rehabilitate criminals.

In a 1968 talk he had contended that American criminal justice "puts all the emphasis on techniques, devices, mechanisms." Overstating for the sake of argument, he said, "It is the most elaborate system ever devised . . . so elaborate that in many places it is breaking down." Among the "mechanisms" he cited were such fundamental protections as the presumption of innocence, a defendant's right to remain silent, the jury system, and the placing of the burden of proof on the prosecution. He obviously shared Nixon's view that the scales had been tipped in favor of the "criminal forces."

As chief justice, he was again the leader of a conservative faction on a deeply divided court. He displayed the suspicious peevishness about the press shared by the Nixon high command; when two reporters appeared at his home late one evening, he answered the door with a pistol in his hand. His administrative style was reminiscent of Taft's: he asserted his prerogative to lobby for or against legislation affecting the courts, and used his office as a platform from which he crusaded for more efficient, better "managed" courts and prisons.

On a Saturday in April 1970 I spent most of a day with Chief Justice Burger as he visited the Maryland State Penitentiary in Baltimore. I was along as a representative of *Life* magazine. The chief justice had invited Hedley Donovan, editor-in-chief of Time-Life publications, to designate a reporter to accompany him and James Bennett, the former director of the U.S. Bureau of Prisons.

We rode through a shabby district of Baltimore's inner city in the chief justice's chauffeured black limousine, stopping in front of the main gate of the 160-year-old prison. The warden, who was expecting us, ushered us into his office. He told Burger that the prison was four hundred over its capacity, and that 70 percent of the inmates were repeaters. The assistant warden, a young, mustached man, said that there was no research under way in the state to help them improve the institutions.

"That's probably true in thirty-five or forty states," Burger said. "We tend to write people off in prison. It's almost a psychic block—we block them out of our minds."

Accompanied by several members of the prison staff, we set off on a tour of the cellblocks. A guard at the end of a long cement corridor pulled a switch opening all the cell doors. The cells were small and damp.

The chief justice stopped at one cell and asked a lean, unshaven man in his forties how many terms he had served.

"This is my fourth," the man muttered.

Burger shook his head. "It's not a good place to spend your time, is it?" he said.

The man made a desultory nod.

"Do you know that seven out of ten of the men here will be coming back?" Burger asked.

"No, sir," the prisoner replied.

Burger glanced around the tiny, airless cell. A chorus of shouts came from the tier above. "Do you care about the inmates?" a voice cried.

"Well, good luck and don't come back," Burger said.

The assistant warden explained that inmates were allowed to exercise for twenty-five minutes a day. "Wouldn't it be better to let them out more?" Burger inquired.

"Our facilities are limited, Judge," the man said. He added that there were two psychiatrists who worked part-time at the prison.

"In Denmark," the chief justice said, "they have psychiatrists on the prison staff where they're needed." He had visited prisons in England and Scandinavia on several occasions.

We walked quickly through the segregation block, where the toughest inmates were lodged. Angry shouts came from behind the cell doors. We did not stop.

"They have a more philosophical attitude in Europe," Burger said. "They admit that some men can't be rehabilitated."

"I think most can, with the right resources available," the assistant warden said. "But I don't think we're getting to more than twenty percent with what we have now."

"I think we can change the public mind about prisons," Burger said. "Institutions like the American Bar Association can make a difference. We can stop pollution, and we can do better with prisoners. Suppose lawyers and judges regularly toured prisons. Lawyers are problem-solvers, and they'd do something about it. They can influence legislatures. If we were talking about pollution and there was a seventy-percent failure rate, then something would happen."

We walked through the metal shop and then into a woodworking shop, both empty. "I think people can be changed," he said, "but mostly we don't know because 'rehabilitation' has never been tried in any meaningful way in this country. I think we need a commission to sell a package of some kind. Get men like Roger Blough [the former president of U.S. Steel], Thomas Watson of

IBM, McNamara—men who can say what needs to be done and who carry weight with the business community, labor, and Congress. You need men who can't be written off as do-gooders."

The assistant warden nodded enthusiastically.

"Two things strike me," Burger continued. "First, the lack of recreation facilities to let them work off steam, and, second, the lack of anything useful to do. The judicial system doesn't encourage deterrence either. People have no confidence in the criminal courts and no fear of the law. Criminals have the impression that they can beat the charge. Prisons and courts are suffering from a hundred years of deferred maintenance."

The official led us into a solitary-confinement cell. The room was bare of furnishings. The only light came from a peephole in the door. A small drain in the middle of the floor served as a toilet. Burger looked around the room and slowly shook his head. I asked if he thought there was any justification for a cell of this kind. "None at all," he said.

Back in the corridor, he was the problem-solver again. "The public has to be persuaded that the system we have now is costing us money, short-changing us. We can sell it on a commercial basis—it would be cheaper to improve prisons. But the public climate at the moment makes it even harder. All we can say for certain is that our present method hasn't been successful."

He looked into another cell, nodding at a middle-aged black inmate. "Are you learning a trade here?" he asked.

"I'm having my leg operated on," the man said.

"How long have you been here?"

The man looked past Burger to a high window in the corridor. "Four and a half years."

The chief justice was silent. He turned to leave. I stayed behind for a minute and asked the prisoner if he knew whom he'd been talking to.

"No," he said. "Who was that dude? Some senator or somethin'?"

Burger seemed more interested in making his case for reform than in learning the details of prison operation. He asked few questions of either prisoners or staff, and frequently interrupted the replies with general observations of his own. He moved at a brisk, businesslike clip, and looked straight ahead when prisoners called out from their cells.

After lunch in the staff dining room we got back into the waiting limousine for the ride to Washington. On the way I gingerly brought up the controversy that was then bubbling over the nomination of G. Harrold Carswell.

Burger said that he believed the Nixon administration had been aware of the backgrounds of both Carswell and Clement Haynsworth, but had not anticipated the reaction that developed. "It might just be poor staff work," he said. He added that he was "disappointed" in the hundreds of law-school deans who had written a letter opposing Carswell's nomination, and hotly denied a published claim that he had lobbied on Capitol Hill in Carswell's behalf.

The limousine pulled into the garage beneath the Supreme Court building. A tall, balding man in glasses was emerging from a car, toting a large briefcase. "Hello, Byron," the chief justice called cheerfully, then introduced us to Justice White. "I see you have some homework."

Burger walked to an elevator marked "Justices Only" and bade us goodbye. "I have a little work to do," he said, "then I'm going to a white-tie dinner at the White House for the Duke of Windsor."

The substitution of Burger for Warren, coupled with the departure of Fortas, erased the activist majority and left the court divided, like ancient Gaul, in three parts—the liberals (Black, Douglas, Brennan, and Marshall), conservatives (Harlan and Burger), and broken-field runners (White and Stewart), who dodged the traditional (and imprecise) categories.

Nixon's choice to succeed Fortas was Clement Haynsworth, Jr., of South Carolina, a conservative Southern Brahmin who was chief judge of the U.S. Fourth Circuit Court of Appeals. Haynsworth was quickly opposed by civil-rights and labor leaders, who claimed that his decisions were biased against their causes. More formidable opposition developed when Haynsworth was accused of conflicts of interest involving decisions he had participated in on the appeals court. He was charged with voting on cases in which he had a financial interest.

Haynsworth's chances for Senate confirmation suffered from the timing of his nomination. The Fortas affair was still fresh in the public memory. Haynsworth's designation "came at a time," a

Nixon administration official said, "when Christ himself would have drawn at least one 'no' vote on principle alone." Earlier investigations, including one by Robert Kennedy, had absolved Haynsworth of ethical impropriety. The *New York Times* concluded that his alleged breaches were "an imperceptive man's neglect in which there was neither profit nor, it would seem, expectation of profit." But the appearance of judicial sin, combined with opposition to his conservatism, was enough to defeat Haynsworth, which the Senate did in November 1969 by a vote of 55 to 45.

Foraging through the Southern courts for another name, Nixon came up with G. Harrold Carswell of Florida, a member of the Fifth Circuit Court of Appeals. (Geographical breadth has remained an honored political imperative on the court. The eight justices waiting to learn the identity of the ninth included Westerners Douglas and White, Midwesterners Stewart and Burger, Easterners Harlan, Brennan, and Marshall, and Alabama's Black.) The ideological objections raised against Haynsworth were immediately repeated in Carswell's case, only this time with more ammunition.

As a candidate for the Georgia legislature in 1948, Carswell had avowed that "segregation of the races is proper and the only practical and correct way of life in our states. I have always so believed and I shall always so act." Carswell had seemed consistent with this pledge when he participated in the formation of a whites-only college boosters' club in 1953, and still later when he took part in a scheme to avoid integration of a public golf course by turning it into a private club. Carswell renounced his racist remarks, but the evidence that made Hugo Black's renunciation convincing was lacking in his case. Civil-rights attorneys charged that he was consistently hostile and insulting to them as a federal district judge.

Other critics focused on Carswell's high rate of reversals and generally mediocre judicial reputation. Yale law school Dean Louis Pollak said that he had "the most slender credentials of any man put forward in this century." But mediocrity didn't bother Senator Roman Hruska of Nebraska. "Even if he were mediocre," Hruska said, "there are a lot of mediocre judges and people and lawyers and they are entitled to a little representation, aren't they, and a little chance? We can't have all Brandeises and Frankfurters and

Cardozos and stuff like that there." A majority of the Senate rejected this plaintive argument, and Carswell's nomination was defeated by a 51-to-45 vote. "Hruska was joking," Burger had said to me. "He has a very droll wit."

A disgruntled Nixon viewed the two rejections as a threat to his constitutional authority. "The question arises," he wrote to Senator William Saxbe of Ohio, "whether I as President of the United States, shall be accorded the same right of choice in naming Supreme Court justices which has been freely accorded to my predecessors of both parties." Nixon's position was both constitutionally unsound and historically inaccurate. The Constitution specifically requires that the Senate advise and consent in presidential appointments. And on twenty-three occasions prior to Nixon's election the Senate had withheld its consent from Supreme Court nominees. Even George Washington had to accept rejection: the Senate turned down his man John Rutledge for chief justice in 1795. President Grover Cleveland may have come up with the most ingenious solution: when the Senate rejected his nomination of Wheeler Peckham, he countered by nominating Wheeler's brother Rufus, who was confirmed.

Nixon concluded glumly that he could not get a Southerner through the Senate (he changed his mind when he proposed Lewis Powell a year later). He turned instead to the Midwest and Judge Harry Blackmun of the Eighth Circuit Court of Appeals in Minnesota, a lifelong friend (and reportedly the recommendation) of Chief Justice Burger. Blackmun, sixty-two at his appointment, grew up just six blocks from Burger in St. Paul, where the two boys met at Methodist Sunday school. Blackmun was best man at Burger's wedding. He spent nine years as general counsel for the Mayo Clinic in Rochester, Minnesota, before Eisenhower appointed him to the Circuit Court. He was a quiet, hard-working conservative who wrote long and exhaustive opinions. His integrity and qualifications were unassailable, and a relieved Senate confirmed him by a vote of 94 to 0.

The similar outlooks of Burger and Blackmun inspired legal wits to dub them the "Minnesota Twins." Each was both politically and judicially conservative, more devoted to law and order than to the individual liberties exalted during the Warren years. Nixon was delivering on his campaign promises. In 1971 he had an even greater opportunity, when Hugo Black and John Marshall Harlan, two of the strongest and most influential members of the court, retired within a week of each other.

Their departure marked a historic turning point. Each had been a respected spokesman for his judicial philosophy. Black had developed an original position that was likely to have a permanent effect on the court. Harlan had come to replace Frankfurter as the court's finest legal mind. But both were pre-eminently students of the court and its place in government. "Both men reached their results," Alan Dershowitz wrote, "not because of any political program, not because they desired a particular outcome in a particular case, but because of the role they thought the Supreme Court should play in the American scheme of things."

The sudden appearance of two vacancies propelled the administration into an extended selection shuffle. Before it culminated in the nominations of Lewis Powell and William Rehnquist, the White House had alienated almost every segment of public and political opinion.

The first step was the submission of six names to the ABA judiciary committee. The list included attorney Herschel Friday of Arkansas, Judge Mildred Lillie of the California Court of Appeals, Senator Robert Byrd of West Virginia, Judge Sylvia Bacon of the District of Columbia Superior Court, and Fifth Circuit appellate judges Paul Roney and Charles Clark. The administration told the ABA to focus its investigation on Friday and Lillie.

The candidates' names surfaced in the press, provoking howls from several directions. Friday, a friend of Attorney General John Mitchell, was a bond lawyer who had helped the Little Rock school board in its attempts to resist desegregation. Clark had played a similar role in Mississippi. Senator Byrd was a onetime Ku Klux Klansman who had never practiced law. Judge Lillie's credentials were widely disparaged as unimpressive at best. Judges Roney and Bacon (who was nicknamed "The Dragon" for her courtroom demeanor by Washington prosecutors) were little known beyond their own jurisdictions.

Senator Edward Kennedy said the President was trying "to undermine one of the basic and vital institutions of our nation." Alan Dershowitz wondered about the absence of Jews among the six as well as a list of eight others who had been mentioned as possible candidates. "In view of the status of the profession today," he said, "any list of fourteen supposedly distinguished lawyers without a Jewish name is suspect. It may not be deliberate, but it shows it's not a neutral list." Half the Harvard law faculty signed a protest statement.

Lawrence Walsh's ABA committee assigned a series of hasty interviews on Lillie and Friday. The committee found Lillie unqualified by an 11–1 vote and divided 6–6 (between "not qualified" and "not opposed") on Friday. After the result of the ABA vote appeared in the Washington *Post*, Mitchell told the association that the administration would no longer submit the names of Supreme Court nominees for ABA clearance.

Even before the ABA committee vote, however, the President had called Powell and offered him one of the seats. Powell, who was sixty-four, thought he might be too old, but Nixon urged him to accept. Rehnquist, who had been busily defending Judge Lillie's record to dubious senators, got word of his nomination shortly before the President announced his choices on television. He had responded to earlier rumors that he might be named by commenting, "You've got the wrong man. I'm not a woman, I'm not a Southerner, and I'm not mediocre."

Powell was a Virginia patrician who had moved easily from finishing first in his law-school class to the state's most prestigious firm. A courtly man of conservative instincts, he had been criticized by both segregationists and civil-rights partisans during eight years as chairman of the Richmond school board. A former president of the ABA, he opened one window to his ideas during a talk at the 1972 ABA convention, deploring what he called the "unanchored individualism in the new mores of our time." What bothered Powell was "excessively tolerant views toward personal conduct: sexual morality, use of drugs, and disobedience of laws believed by the individual to be unjust. Even the concept of honor is now widely questioned."

Rehnquist, forty-nine, the son of a medical-supplies salesman, had been assistant attorney general in charge of the office of legal counsel. He had been first in his law-school class at Stanford, a clerk for Justice Robert Jackson, and a successful attorney in Phoenix, where he was a strong supporter of Senator Barry Goldwater. He came under criticism on the court for taking part in a military-surveillance case on which he had previously testified for the government.

Powell and Rehnquist were clearly qualified for the court, but

Nixon's heavy-footed preliminary shuffle had offended many. The real quarrel with Nixon was not his selection of justices for political or ideological purposes—no President had resisted that temptation—but the level on which he operated. Frankfurter once described constitutional law as "applied politics, using the word in its noblest sense." "It is Mr. Nixon's failure to comprehend the noble potential of politics," the *New York Times* editorialized, "that so consistently leads him to use political manipulation as a divisive tool to gain short-term advantages. This is precisely how he has dealt with the Supreme Court." Nixon used vacancies on the court to help his own chances for reelection. If vacancies recur at the same rate as in the past, he will appoint two more justices.

The addition of Powell and Rehnquist changed the ideological face of the court once again. The conservatives now had a solid four votes—the four Nixon appointees—and the liberals a sturdy three. The balance of power increasingly rested with swing men White and Stewart. The Nixon justices voted as a unit 70 percent of the time during the 1972–73 term. Douglas, Brennan, and Marshall voted together on almost exactly the same number of cases. Both White and Stewart sided with the conservatives more often than not during the term, White in 94 percent of the cases and Stewart in 75 percent.

Factional divisions, of course, are nothing new on the Supreme Court, but the cleavage on the Burger Court seems to many judges and lawyers to be as deep as any in the court's history. It is difficult to imagine any two sitting justices, for example, with views more divergent than those held by Douglas and Rehnquist. Douglas, who set a record for Supreme Court seniority in October 1973, remains the knight-errant, seeking individual and social "justice" with every opinion. Rehnquist seems a throwback to the turn-of-the-century justices, a radical individualist who believes that the best government is the least government.

The cleavage is seen most vividly in the plenitude of 5–4 decisions, but it has extended to the court's internal business as well. Douglas reportedly protested in one case that the chief justice overstepped his authority by assigning a majority opinion when he was in the minority; traditionally, the senior justice on the majority side (Douglas in this instance) makes the assignment in such cases. Justice Blackmun was reported to be "shocked and appalled" when Stewart invited anti-war activist John Kerry to sit in the court's guest box.

The most serious incident involved race. Justice Marshall had asked that a conference be rescheduled so he could attend a relative's funeral. Burger reset the conference, then switched it back to the original date when he learned that it conflicted with the funeral of former Justice James Byrnes, which Burger felt obliged to attend. Marshall was not told about the change. When he found out about it, according to a *National Observer* report, he filed a memo of protest and said privately that "apparently the funeral of a white man is more important than the funeral of a black man." The justices held the conference again with Marshall present.

Marshall later told a *Time* reporter that he had never felt "any racism on the part of my colleagues. I never use the word black anyway," he added. "I use Negro." He did not deny sending the memo, however, granting that "there are tensions. There are bound to be."

The justices even disagree on the mechanics of their working routine. Until 1972 each justice and his clerks reviewed every arriving petition seeking Supreme Court review. The court denies about 70 percent of the petitions without discussing them in conference; many others are dismissed after brief discussion. At the suggestion of Justice Powell, a single law clerk now prepares a pool memo on the petitions. The memo goes to Burger (a consistent advocate of streamlining the court's workload), White, Rehnquist, Powell, and Blackmun. The other four justices prefer to read every petition or a memo on it prepared by their own clerks.

Burger commissioned a panel of high-level lawyers and law professors to study ways of reducing the volume of cases which annually descends on the justices. The panel's recommendation that a new seven-member court be created to screen all petitions for review became still another point of contention. Douglas, Stewart, and Brennan declared that they were not oppressed by the court's burdens—"We are, if anything, underworked," Douglas said. Earl Warren attacked the idea as harmful to the court's stature. Burger, Powell, and Rehnquist, on the other hand, seemed hospitable to the plan.

The court divided 5–4 on several of its most momentous decisions. Stewart and White joined the three liberals in the decision to abolish the death penalty. The vote was 5–4 to preserve the property-tax method of school financing, to uphold the validity of verdicts by non-unanimous juries in some instances, to broaden the definition of obscenity, and to deny a journalist's "privilege" to protect his sources. The lineup was identical on each of the four landmark rulings—White and the Nixon justices were in the majority, Stewart and the liberals were the minority. The pattern was broken in two other critical decisions. The justices voted 8–0 (with Rehnquist not participating) to outlaw warrantless government wiretapping of domestic radicals for purposes of "national security." And seven of the nine justices (White and Rehnquist dissenting) agreed that state laws restricting a woman's right to obtain an abortion in the first three months of pregnancy were unconstitutional.

The deep schism on the court has drawn criticism from some state supreme-court justices, who understand the dynamics of appellate decision-making but believe that a strong consensus is necessary to inspire confidence in judicial law. "They're going off in different directions," one state justice complained to me. "It makes it difficult to tell what the law is. On our court we each give ground and we come up with a rule. But the Supreme Court is getting to be an exercise in egoism. We have blood on the floor after our conferences, but we apply a higher duty than the duty to ourselves. Whatever one thinks of Warren, he held the court together. Burger doesn't."

"I think the Supreme Court should be able to agree on ninety percent of its cases," says another state supreme-court justice. "There's a sense of drift with this court. The court as an institution suffers because of the public's attitude that they're a quarrelsome bunch who can't agree. A justice 'concurs with compulsion' plenty of times. I do, and they should too." A cartoon under the glass on one appellate-court conference table shows a judge leaning forward and saying to his colleagues, "If all you smart cookies agree, who am I to dissent?"

Yet Burger shows little taste for conciliation. Assuming office in an era of clamorous national dissension, much of it traceable to the Vietnam war, and widespread criticism of the court, he may have one ear cocked in the direction identified by Mr. Dooley—the election returns. "Burger seemed prepared to split the court internally," Simon wrote, "in an effort to heal what he saw as the more damaging division between the court and the public."

The court has unquestionably backed off from the commitment to social justice and individual liberty so evident in the Warren years. The court's decisions consistently show a greater trust in the wisdom and correctness of government action as opposed to the complaints of individuals about government infringement on their rights. Warren's determination "to free men from the terror and unpredictability of arbitrary force," though not absent from the Burger Court, has clearly been overshadowed in the rush for law and order.

The Burger Court is not given to large statements of national purpose or public morality, except for the occasional scolding lecture. Nor has it expanded our liberties in the way the Warren Court did. "The new conservative majority," Simon writes, "has cut back on the rights of criminal suspects, largely ignored the constitutional demands of the poor, and held firmly but narrowly to the desegregation line that the Warren Court drew in 1954. The court has been transformed from a tribunal of unprecedented legal daring to one of modest aims and self-limiting accomplishments." He concludes that the Supreme Court is "no longer the nation's ombudsman. Not only [are] the justices less anxious to solve America's most pressing problems, but they [are] even reluctant to identify them for others to work on." It is an achievement that Richard Nixon may well be proud of. The rest of us have to live with it.

It is some comfort to remember that the Supreme Court, for all the sweep and majesty of its authority, is only one of the republic's repositories of power. A Supreme Court decision is "the law of the land" for only so long as Congress permits it to be. An act of Congress or a constitutional amendment may negate a court ruling. In addition, one of the glories of constitutional government is that *no* interpretation of the Constitution is definitive; every Supreme Court has the freedom, even the duty, to reinterpret that grand and mysterious document by the light of its own times. Justice and even law are in the end no more than the best impulses of conscientious men. Holmes was right, as he usually was: certainty *is* an illusion. So is finality.

XVI

Agony and Essence

A journey through the uncharted wilderness of sentencing

"I sentence you to three years' penal servitude, in the firm and God-given conviction that what you really require is three weeks at the sea-side."
G. K. CHESTERTON
The Club of Queer Trades

"I HAD A CASE involving an alcoholic," said District Judge Richard Greene of Littleton, Colorado. "He pleaded guilty to two felony charges of causing death while driving. He hit a car that was stopped at a light. There were four people in it—a mother, a grandmother, and two kids. It was two nights before Christmas. The mother and grandmother were killed and the kids were injured. They were screaming for their mother.

"The man was twenty-eight, a carpenter. He's not an outright 'criminal type,' yet he destroyed innocent lives, two nights before Christmas, with immeasurable harm to those kids. Now, how do you face that at sentencing? We have no special facilities for alcoholics. What do you do?

"There's something punitive involved here. They were *innocent* —they were on their way home to celebrate Christmas. The thought in my mind was what about the kids, what about their

358

feeling about the man who killed their mother? What the hell do you do? He admitted he's an alcoholic and that he blacked out. He was contrite. The statute says one to fourteen years on each count. I gave him four and a half to ten, concurrent. I've thought and thought about it. The kids have to grow up with some sense of justice. Does it involve this element of punishment? It's there; you can't escape it. I don't consciously try to suppress it or elevate it, I just know it's there.

"There had to be some *impact* on his life for what he did, and yet he's not a hardcore criminal. As soon as I sentenced him I called the deputy warden at the prison and told him I didn't think the man was a criminal but I had to do what I did, and I asked him what he could do for him. He said they could send him to a medium-security facility where they could use carpenters.

"I got a contrite letter from the man saying he felt the sentence was severe and asking me to lower it. What do you do? Do you put the punitive element out of your mind? But you can't ignore it. As a judge, you're the guardian of the precepts of criminal justice in the community. The element of punishment is ingrained. A lot of judges give lip-service to the idea of satisfying the community's opinion, and it would be folly to say I didn't think of that.

"But I still wasn't sure I did the right thing. The alternative was an indeterminate sentence to a reformatory, and he'd have a chance to get out in nine months. I didn't think that was sufficient because of the nature of the crime. You decide within yourself, you can't go by some precedent that's twenty years old. I found out he'd be eligible for parole in two years and three months, and then he'd have eight years of parole.

"The kids will want to know later what the judicial system did with the person who killed their mom. Won't they? Won't they want to know what happens to someone who kills an innocent person? If all I did was slap his wrist, they'd grow up thinking nothing happens to someone like that. I have to satisfy, I have to prove something to those kids, that the system does indeed deal with people who kill, with the person who killed their mother. I'm trying to prove the system is worth their faith and trust.

"Judges always wonder. I kept thinking about it. I've been to the prison many times. I know what it's like—drugs, homosexuality, cynicism. He could be screwed up at prison.

"Then he came up for reconsideration of sentence. I released him on probation with three conditions—no drinking for five years, no driving for five years, and he has to contribute one fifth of his monthly income to the support of those two kids.

"It was one of the toughest things I've ever had to do. It's tough for any judge. It tears you up."

Sentencing is the agony and the essence of judging. Every good judge knows the torment and uncertainty Judge Greene describes, and knows too that there is no way to avoid it: it is an occupational hazard.

It is one of the transcendent ironies of our system of criminal justice that at sentencing, precisely the point where most is at stake, the judge is unceremoniously out adrift from all the moorings of law and principle that restrict him at every other point in the process. He is afloat in the dark, with little to guide him, no codified set of criteria, nothing to help him with the most important decision he has to make. His conduct of a trial is circumscribed by dozens of rules, precedents, and statutes. He may comment on evidence only in carefully specified circumstances, and only in jurisdictions (such as federal courts) that permit it. He rules on the admissibility of evidence in accordance with a body of law refined through centuries of courtroom combat. His charge to a jury must hew to limits prescribed by the nature of the offense, the available options, and hallowed precedent. But in sentencing, nothing—one to fourteen, five to life, thirty days to two years, and only his mind and heart to go on.

Sentencing is a judge's greatest, most unfettered power. In other countries, judges have more leeway—"discretion" is the judicial word—in the operation of a trial, and less in sentencing. The maximum penalties in many European countries are less than half what they are in America for the same crimes, and in every other Western country the sentence of the trial judge is subject to review by a higher court. But in most American trial courts the sentence is final; only rarely do appellate courts have the authority and inclination to overrule it.

In addition, sentencing is a dilemma made constant by the press of numbers; the great majority of cases result in guilty pleas. "By any quantitative standard," says Columbia law professor Harry

Jones, "the trial judge's exercise of his sentencing authority far outweighs everything else he does. . . ."

The burden falls most heavily on the most conscientious, the judges who strive to do "the right thing." "Not only do you not know if you're doing right," says New York Judge Sidney Asch, "you know you're never doing right." "It's a puzzle and a torment," says Connecticut Judge David Jacobs. "It's the easiest thing in the world to send a guy away, and people will say you're doing a great job. But they don't see the defendant with his problems, his broken home, having to claw and struggle, the things that went into making his personality."

Some judges find formulas for sentencing—five years for embezzlement, a year for non-support, ninety days for drunk driving. "But this way of easing the strain is barred to the thoughtful judge," says Jones, ". . . who cannot help seeing the patterns of human tragedy in the cases that come before him.

"There is respectable authority, tracing back at least to Thomas Hobbes," Jones adds "that charity and compassion are no part of legal justice and that the sentencing judge must learn to steel himself against humanitarian impulses. ["We have to be like surgeons," a Washington judge told me.] But would we be content with a trial bench of judges who, by personality and character, find no burden or psychic strain in the sentencing task?"

The first job of a sentencing judge is to pick his way through the thicket of conflicting purposes that sentences are supposed to serve. Municipal Judge Philip Saeta of Los Angeles lists them: (1) retribution, (2) deterrence, to others and to the offender himself, (3) incapacitation—he won't hurt anyone while he's locked up, (4) rehabilitation, (5) financial recoupment—"making the victim whole."

But which comes first? And how does a judge weigh them when the purposes (rehabilitation and incapacitation, say) clash? And what if a judge doesn't buy all those purposes, or adds others of his own—filling the local treasury, keeping families off welfare? "Nothing tells us," says U.S. District Judge Marvin Frankel of New York, one of the most thoughtful students of the subject, "when or whether any of these several goals are to be sought, or how to resolve [the] evident conflicts. . . . It has for some time been part of our proclaimed virtue that vengeance or retribution is a disfavored motive for punishment. But there is reason to doubt that either judges or the public are effectively abreast of this advanced position."

The American Bar Association reduces the issue to a pithy statement that leaves everyone plenty of room: "The sentence . . . should call for the minimum amount of custody or confinement which is consistent with the protection of the public, the gravity of the offense and the rehabilitative needs of the defendant."

But, as Frankel complains, "we have no structure of rules, or even guidelines, affecting other elements arguably pertinent to the nature or severity of the sentence. Should it be a mitigating factor that the defendant is being sentenced upon a plea of guilty rather than a verdict against him? Should it count in his favor that he spared the public 'trouble' and expense by waiving a jury? Should the sentence be more severe because the judge is convinced that the defendant perjured himself on the witness stand? Should churchgoing be considered to reflect favorably?"

"I'm considered a judge who has been pretty stern," said New York Judge Paul Fino after he sentenced a narcotics addict to thirty years for the sale of one seventy-third of an ounce of heroin. The severe sentence provoked differing judicial reactions. "An addict is a sick man," one New York judge commented; "he needs help, and he isn't going to get it in prison." But Judge Sidney Asch would not rule anything out: "By God, what I'm doing isn't solving the problem. Maybe what Fino's doing will."

"Solving the problem"—it is a favorite phrase of lawyers, born in the belief that no "problem" can fail to yield to their formidable resources of intelligence, logic, energy, and concentration. Lawyers —and judges—are offended by the problem unsolved, like doctors by the wound unhealed. It unsteadies them professionally, it insults their discipline. Their anguish is palpable. The purposes of sentencing, cried New York Judge Irwin Brownstein, are "deterrence, getting the guy off the street, and respect for the law—and we don't have any of that now."

Brownstein's despairing conclusion reflects the most somber fact of all: nothing "works," nothing "prevents" crime, nothing "solves the problem." At least, nothing we've tried so far.

Judge Saeta, who led a seminar in sentencing at the Reno judges' school, reported the results of the most exhaustive studies on the subject: there is no evidence that any alternative available to a judge is more successful than any other in preventing recidivism—repeated offenses by the same person. The rate of recidivism was stubbornly unaffected by jail or no jail, by length of sentence, attempts at rehabilitation, or close parole supervision. In one study concentrating on drunk drivers, there was no hint that any method of punishment was more effective than any other in preventing accidents. "Basically," Saeta concluded cheerlessly, "we do not know what we are achieving by our sentences. All we know is that we do not know."

Little wonder, then, that a sentencing judge is a man vexed and fumbling for a handhold. Little wonder that disparities in sentences are so wide. And to trouble his repose even further, the pressures on a sentencing judge have never been as great as they are today.

There are two reasons. One is that a measurable segment of the public, brought up on judicious doses of modern behavioral science, has come to question the efficacy of any punishment, or at least punishment as it has been traditionally imposed. "We are divided," says Harvard government professor James Q. Wilson, "between a majority that believes crime is a serious problem but thinks the solution is to be found in more police, more arrests, or more rehabilitation; and a minority that feels crime is either not a grave problem, or is the symptom of something more important, or is beyond the reach of society at all."

The second reason is the reaction of an increasingly enlightened public to the periodic revelation of vast sentencing disparities; it offends our sense of fairness. Judges, thrown on the defensive, reply that individual variation is at the heart of judging, that the guilty should be treated separately, not as so many holes in a computer print-out dictating some arbitrary "equality." Judges shuffle between the poles of this argument, now seeking the punishment that fits the criminal, now striving for a golden mean of equity and predictability. Their ambivalence mirrors our own.

Sentencing was the subject as eight lower-court judges gathered one day at the National College of the State Judiciary in Reno. Judge North Carolina was a tall, easy-mannered man in his early thirties, with a quick wit and perhaps the longest hair in the class. He liked to tell a story about a longhaired young defendant whom he sentenced on a drug charge. After the sentence, the youth was heard to say, "That dude looks cool, but he's just like the rest."

Judges Ohio and Iowa were plain-faced, small-town Midwesterners, earnest Rotarians, officers of their local charity fund drives. Nevada was stiff and touchy about his dignity. South Dakota, the group leader, was one of the few who read widely. He quoted from The Greening of America and Future Shock, among other books, and startled his colleagues by referring to the present age as the "post-Christian era."

Judge Virginia was a wiry, loose-limbed man with a talent for a deadpan put-on. Nebraska and North Dakota were both dark and quiet, their faces weathered by the prairie. The best of them— North Carolina, South Dakota, Ohio, and perhaps Nebraska— were the kind of men the college faculty saw as advertisements for the New Judiciary. They were relatively young, interested in learning, articulate, and ambitious.

South Dakota tossed out a hypothetical problem. "Let's say you have three people convicted of drunk driving. The facts are basically the same and the charge the same for all three. One is the wife of the local bank president, another is a teacher, and the third is a migrant worker."

"I'd give 'em all the same sentence," Nevada said immediately.

"Not me," said Ohio. "The rich woman would get three times the fine in my court."

"That's discriminating, Judge," said Nevada.

"Sure it is. I don't deny it."

"I think there'd be less chance of repeating with the bank president's wife," Virginia said tentatively.

"Not necessarily," South Dakota said. "The migrant is probably used to jail. Jail would punish the banker's wife more, but a fine would punish the migrant more."

"The fact of the arrest would probably punish the teacher more than any of them," Nevada said, "just getting her name in the paper. The migrant wouldn't give a damn, he probably can't read anyway."

"In Sweden," said North Carolina, "the range of fines is relative to income. But if I did that at home, they'd accuse me of being a Socialist. I'd fine them and give them time to pay it. I'd give the migrant all the time he wants."

"He'd probably leave town," said Iowa.

"I don't know if people in my county are ready for discriminatory sentencing," Nebraska said. "I'm afraid to try it."

"I've never done anything else," said Ohio. "If I don't have the discretion to get the result I want, I'll quit. I'd probably fine the bank president's wife five hundred dollars and the others a hundred and fifty. It's discriminating, but it's making the same point to both."

"Do we sentence to please the community or our own conscience?" South Dakota asked.

"Well, we have to face election," said Nebraska.

"I'd say it's half and half," North Dakota said.

"Your banker's wife is going to call the legislator, you know," said Ohio. "She needs her license, and I'm not so naïve that I believe the motor-vehicle department is going to turn down a legislator."

"I would," steamed Nevada. "I don't give a damn who he is."

"I'd give the wife maybe a two-hundred- to five-hundred-dollar fine and thirty days suspended," Iowa said, "then I'd give the teacher the same, only a smaller fine. With the migrant there'd be no use fining him. Jail is probably a way of life for him, so what do you do with him? I don't know. You can't punish him. Maybe send him to a halfway house. I think publicity would be a club over the head of the banker's wife."

"Just don't ask for another loan too quickly," said North Carolina.

"We have to be careful asking for loans anyway," Ohio said soberly. "You don't ever stop being a judge, you know, whatever you're doing."

"I don't even go to bars in my hometown," Nevada declared.

"You don't know what you're missing," Virginia said.

The range of punishments that different judges mete out to similar defendants for similar crimes is staggering. The disparities reflect differences in philosophy among judges, but they also reflect judicial biases. The only certain consequence is the cynical disillusionment of the criminal who compares his sentence with that of the prisoner three cells down the cement corridor.

In Reno, Judge Saeta gave each of thirty-seven judges a set of identical fact sheets on hypothetical cases, and asked the judges to pass sentence. He included details of the offense, the defendant's prior record and physical appearance, and the maximum permissible penalities—in each case this was one year in jail and a $500 fine. The maximum probation was three years.

In some instances he also included a probation report with more details on the defendant's background and personality. In others he identified a defendant as black on half the fact sheets and white on the other half, changing no other details.

¶ "Joe Cut," 27, pleaded guilty to battery. He slashed his common-law wife on the arms with a switchblade. His record showed convictions for disturbing the peace, drunkenness, and hit-run driving. He told a probation officer that he acted in self-defense after his wife attacked him with a broom handle. The prosecutor recommended not more than five days in jail or a $100 fine.

The judges' penalities ranged from a minimum of a $50 fine and six months probation to a maximum of six months in jail and a $250 fine. The sentences were harsher when there was no probation report. When Joe was identified as white and a probation report was included, probation was more likely and jail sentences varied from 3 to 10 days. When he was black, the range was 5 to 30 days in jail.

¶ "Harriet Swing," 20, was found guilty of prostitution by a jury. Vice officers arrested her with a customer in a motel room. She had one prior conviction for prostitution and another for possession of drugs. The fact sheet described her as "a young female Caucasian, very well dressed and quite attractive and articulate."

Harriet's mildest penalty was a 30-day suspended sentence; the most severe was six months in jail and a $500 fine. In all, 15 judges sentenced her to jail (five included a fine as well), 13 fined her, 8 put her on probation, and one suspended her sentence.

¶ "John Weed," 21, pleaded guilty to possession of marijuana after police seized him in a park. One previous charge had been dismissed and another, for being "under the influence of drugs," resulted in a $25 fine. He lived with his parents and attended college part-time. "He appears casually dressed and not showing much concern," the fact sheet said.

Fourteen judges sent Weed to jail and 14 others placed him on probation. Seven imposed a fine. The lightest sentence was six months summary probation (with no terms), the harshest was ninety days in jail.

Sentencing inequities have been documented in dozens of surveys, for every manner of crime, at every level of the judiciary. The causes, Judge Frankel believes, are clear: "Judges vary widely in their explicit views and 'principles' affecting sentencing; they vary, too, in the accidents of birth and biography generating the guilts, the fears, and the rages that affect almost all of us at times and in ways we often cannot know."

Judges are generally rougher on the poor, the non-white, those with court-assigned lawyers or no lawyers at all, and those who go to trial rather than plead guilty. There are often wide differences between rural and urban courts. "White-collar" crime is treated more leniently.

A survey by Boston lawyers divided defendants into those who earned less than $75 a week and those earning more than $100. The poorer defendants went to jail 25 percent of the time and the others 13 percent. A 1972 federal-court study found that 28 percent of white defendants convicted of interstate theft received prison sentences while 48 percent of blacks convicted of the same crime went to prison. The average sentence for blacks convicted of major felonies in seven Southern states in 1968 was 16.8 years; for whites it was 12.1.

Whitney North Seymour, Jr., former United States Attorney in New York City, reported that white-collar defendants are usually handled with more care. The average sentence for securities *theft*, for example, during a six-month span in 1972 in New York, was two years and eight months. The average term for the cleaner-fingernails crime of securities *fraud* was one year and seven months. Embezzlers went to prison only 23 percent of the time, bank robbers at a rate of 83 percent. Seymour found striking differences among judges in the same courthouse: one Manhattan federal judge sent 10 out of 10 Selective Service violators to prison; another imprisoned 2 out of 13, and a third none of 6.

A man found guilty of a $7.50 armed robbery in northern Wyoming was sentenced to 10 to 12 years. Another who netted $124 from a similar crime in southern Wyoming got a sentence of two to three years. A *New York Times* survey found that courts in upstate New York were consistently sterner than New York City courts with defendants convicted of the same crime. Another study showed that federal-court defendants who were convicted after trial received sentences more than twice as severe as those who pleaded guilty.

The evidence suggests that in sentencing, "equal justice" is nothing more than a pretty phrase carved in marble. Judicial prejudices intervene, and so do the lodge rules—reduce the charge, plead guilty, move the business. Many judges, insulated by narrow experience and orthodox values, echo the scorn of the Nevada judge who said, "The migrant wouldn't give a damn, he probably can't read anyway." They punish most those they least resemble. Half the federal judges in one survey sentenced a hypothetical fifty-one-year-old tax evader to probation; nearly all of them imprisoned a young bank robber whose profit was actually smaller.

Judges as a group, says Frankel, are "somewhat elderly . . . almost totally unencumbered by learning or experience relevant to sentencing, and inclined by temperament and circumstance toward the major orthodoxies. . . . Probably a large majority had no contact, or trivial contact, with criminal proceedings of any kind during their years of practice. Those who had such exposure worked preponderantly on the prosecution side."

In narcotics cases, judges are frequently easier on the middle-echelon dealer than they are on street addicts. On a single day in 1972, one federal judge in Pittsburgh sentenced two addicts to five-year terms for possession of heroin while another granted probation to a member of a drug import ring.

At its most bizarre extremes, sentencing loses all relation to sense as well as justice. One Colorado judge won't send anyone to prison; he believes that a prison sentence is in effect a death sentence, which helps neither society, the victim, nor the offender. Opposite urges prevail in Dallas, by common consent the worst place in the country to come up for sentencing. Juries often do the sentencing in Texas trials: in 1973 a Dallas jury sentenced two kidnapers to 5005 years each; the murderer of a stockbroker was given 3000 years by another Big D jury; a third panel sent a narcotics offender away for 1605 years. San Antonio Judge Archie Brown holds the current judicial record: he sentenced the killer of a policeman to 10,000 years, complaining all the while that the Supreme Court had eliminated the "only appropriate sentence"— death. Texas inmates are generally eligible for parole after serving twenty years or one third of their sentence, but the parole board has promised to consider sentence length in determining eligibility; hence the astronomical sentences.

Judges are often repelled by one variety of crime more than

others, but their obsessions vary. Many share the aversion to sex crimes felt by Judge Greene of Colorado. "I suppose I shouldn't," he says, "but I can't help thinking of my family in cases like that." Judge Saeta of Los Angeles is most offended by knifing cases. Rodney Eielson of Connecticut is least tolerant in non-support cases. U.S. District Judge Jack Weinstein of Brooklyn remarked as he sentenced a "fence" to five years that receivers of stolen goods should be treated "more forcefully" than the thieves.

A judge may also be unnerved by his family's experience with crime. One Texas judge "sort of lost his balance," a lawyer told me, after his daughter was murdered. Superior Court Judge Alfred Burka of Washington, D.C., "changed considerably," an attorney said, "after the death of his father [in a liquor-store hold-up], and after the accused killers were acquitted . . . I think he [became] emotionally unfit to handle criminal cases."

The sentencing power is a public podium, and judges use it to spread the word that well-publicized misdeeds of the moment will be firmly dealt with. The heat of the judicial gaze shifts with the drifting fronts of public opinion. In the 1930s it focused on kidnaping, later on treason and subversion, at other times on organized crime and bank robbery.

During the Vietnam war the glare fell on draft resisters and evaders, and in 1966 and 1967 they were commonly sentenced to the five-year maximum, especially in such states as Texas, Kentucky, and Mississippi. As public opinion turned against the war, sentences to draft violators became more lenient; judges began to grant probation and order substitute service in hospitals, drug centers, and the like. In 1967 more than three fourths of all draft cases resulted in convictions, and 90 percent of the convicted went to prison. By 1971 the conviction rate had dipped to 35 percent, and nearly two thirds of those received probation.

But by then there was a new *crime célèbre:* airplane hijacking. "You have to serve notice," a federal judge told me. "That's one of the purposes of sentencing. If the public is afraid of hijacking, then all hijackers go to prison." Fourteen hijackers were convicted in 1972: three were sentenced to life and the others to terms between twenty and forty-five years. Sentences in many other countries were considerably lighter. Hijacker Raffaele Minichiello was released after serving two and a half years in Italy; two others convicted in Argentina were given terms of three and five years.

The next spasm may have been inaugurated by U.S. District Judge Mitchell Cohen of New Jersey in May 1973. Cohen sentenced six former officials of Atlantic City to terms ranging from two to six years on corruption charges. He observed that "the mood of the country today" will not accept "improper or immoral conduct by public officials."

What goes on inside a judge's mind when he sentences? The defendant is young and sullen. He wears workclothes or jail denims. Or he is cooperative and contrite, neatly bedecked in coat and tie. The judge is tired, or hungry, or angry, or he feels fine. He is strong or weak, bright or dull. A bell rings somewhere in his subconscious. Does he hear it? What does it signal? What influences are working on him? Where do they come from? Can he recognize them? The mind balances, the senses absorb, the emotions weave and slide.

The psychological roots of a judge's sentence reach into a bog where most judges fear to tread. To trespass there is to risk unsettling discoveries, to confront demons they would sooner avoid. Hesitation may be wise.

"Sentencing churns very much into their past," says Dr. Andrew Watson, a University of Michigan psychiatrist. "No one in our culture ever gets rid of his belief in the retributive scale of punishment, the idea that that's the way life is. Your conscious attitude may change, but the desire to be retributive and punitive is always latent. It's the childhood conscience. We don't think judges are supposed to behave that way, to believe that if you do something bad you must be punished. But you can't emancipate yourself from that childhood view very easily."

Watson is a heavy, bearded man. He knows hundreds of judges, having conducted courses and seminars on the judicial psyche for more than a decade. He has pushed deeper into the bog than anyone else.

"There's a tremendous strain on judges," he says, "because they have so much trouble acknowledging their own impulses and lusts. They have all kinds of explicit rationales for not thinking about their own involvement. They turn their feelings around so they become a 'reaction formation.' The lure of sin makes you crusade against it, to deny it in yourself. They won't look at a whore and say, 'Jesus, I'd like to screw her.' They'll condemn her as disgusting or talk about social pathology."

Watson believes that the callousness of many judges—"the usual man in the usual place"—is a veneer, a disguise to protect themselves from failure. "It's impotence covered up," he says, "because they *do* care about the people before them, but they don't know what to do. They give a man a light sentence and he's back in court six months later. They feel they've failed. But they're bound to fail, because people don't change that fast. The idealistic judge is screwed again and again until he gets bitter. I've seen it with welfare people, cops, correction workers—they'll become either bitter or callous. Judicial training ought to help them cope with that failure, because they *will* fail.

"They want to be fair, but they're not equipped to deal with their human reactions. I'll bet Hoffman wanted to be fair, but he couldn't face the fact that he had to sit there and be 'objective' while he was in fact hating those guys. You can't get rid of such emotions, so you have to deal with them. If a judge can't comfortably dislike the defendants, then he ought to get off the case. He has to learn to be comfortably uncomfortable. Good judges can do it."

Lawyers become judges, in Watson's opinion, out of conscious or unconscious desires for power, status, and security. "The power to decide about other people's lives is the most significant aspect of the job, and they have to be comfortable with that power. Some exercise it with glee and others with hesitation. Deference and status are very important to many of them. I knew one appeals court where all the judges had their own valets."

At the sessions he conducts with judges, Watson urges them to "learn a theory of human behavior, because willy-nilly they're going to have one anyway. They insist that they know as much about people as I do. I just suggest they learn some theory as a means to understanding themselves." He tries to "show them their feelings so they can cope with them."

His success, by his own standards, has been indifferent. At one seminar for federal judges, his discussion of judicial impulses was cut short when the director "started to ramrod me into yes or no answers. He wanted to shift the focus from judges to defendants." The same thing happened at the Reno school. "They wanted me to talk about criminal behavior instead of judicial behavior.

"I have no illusions about any big positive gains in judicial self-knowledge," he says. "The human mind is essentially conservative. There's a beginning awareness, but that's all."

John Hogarth, a Canadian law professor and criminologist, interviewed seventy-one magistrates in the province of Ontario to analyze their sentencing attitudes and practices. In a careful and exhaustively documented book he showed that the key to sentencing lies in the judge's attitudes and not the facts of a case.

Sentencing, he found, is anything but a neutral, "objective" decision. It touches on "each magistrate's values, sentiments, and commitments; in short, the very material out of which his self-identity is composed." He found that judges "interpret the law, the expectations of others, and the facts of the cases in selective ways which maximize concordance with their concept of self.

"They rearrange the facts," Hogarth said, "to fit the type of sentences they use habitually." They might be inconsistent with each other, but not within themselves. The facts and law of each case "are interpreted, assimilated, and made sense of in ways compatible with the attitudes of the magistrate concerned." He found that most sentencing variations had little to do with the details of crimes, and everything to do with the judges' perceptions.

The angle of that perception colors everything a judge sees. "The magistrates holding strong views about the necessity of deterrence and punishment," for example, "did not see offenders as having serious problems in their family or personal lives. At the same time they tended to perceive offenders as having negative attitudes towards authority and little remorse for their crimes." Judges more disposed to treatment saw the offenders through the other end of the glass. For all the talk about "rehabilitation," retribution and punishment were more important in the judges' minds.

"Sentencing," Hogarth concluded, "is not a rational, mechanical process. It is a human process and subject to all the frailties of the human mind."

"He's in prison now, being punished," [said the White Queen] *"and the trial doesn't even begin till next Wednesday: and of course the crime comes last of all."*

"Suppose he never commits the crime?" said Alice.

"That would be all the better, wouldn't it?" the Queen said.

* * *

The three judges took seats around a conference table covered with a red-and-orange plastic tablecloth. The table was decorated with flowers and spread with sandwiches, soft drinks, pickles, and plastic knives and forks. The three were all judges in the Bronx, and they had gathered for the first meeting of a "sentencing panel," where they would discuss the sentences that they would separately have to impose.

The case under discussion belonged to Justice Arnold Fein, who opened the proceedings by handing out a one-page synopsis of the case and the defendant's background. The defendant, a twenty-seven-year-old Puerto Rican, had pleaded guilty to attempted robbery in the second degree, a felony with a maximum penalty of seven years. He had originally been charged with second-degree kidnaping, second-degree burglary, first-degree robbery, and two other offenses. Fein pointed out that the prosecutor had recommended a sentence of four years, but that he, Fein, had promised nothing.

"Tell us the facts," said Justice Joseph Brust.

Fein recited the details: The defendant had gone to the victim's apartment with three others and demanded money. The victim, who had only twenty dollars, suggested they go to another place where they could get more, which they did. The three other robbers entered the second apartment while the defendant waited outside to guard the victim's car.

"Who were the victims? How old were they?" Justice Brust asked.

Fein didn't know. Neither did a probation officer who was sitting in.

Fein then read the defendant's record—there were several convictions—and reported that intelligence tests showed he had a "retardation of six to seven years."

After fifteen minutes they got around to the sentence. The probation officer, asked his opinion, replied that the defendant had violated probation in the past. "I thought something between five and seven years," he said.

"That's my number," said Justice William Kapelman. "Obviously, four years isn't sufficient."

It was pointed out that the defendant's guilty plea was probably tied to the prosecutor's recommendation of a four-year sentence. Kapelman suggested five.

Justice Brust asked why, if the prosecutor wanted a four-year term, he didn't permit the defendant to plead to a lesser felony with a four-year maximum. "I would give a sentence of five years," he decided.

Justice Fein, who had sole responsibility for the final decision, said that he had never imposed a sentence greater than a prosecutor's recommendation. "My own current view," he said, "with due respect to both of you—and I don't think a year makes a difference—is four years."

Sentencing panels were initiated in the Bronx in October 1972, shortly after a series of articles by *New York Times* reporter Lesley Oelsner revealed wide sentencing disparities in New York courts. Such panels, used in only a few jurisdictions around the country, are one of many tentative attempts at sentencing reform now being tried or studied.

Judicial unhappiness with sentencing is so widespread that many judges believe some change is necessary. But as yet no reform has been widely adopted, mainly because the attempts have been half-hearted. In addition, the principle of sharing or diluting the sentencing authority threatens a judge's cherished "independence."

Out of frustration with the failure of jails and prisons, many judges have come up with creative alternatives of their own. Circuit Judge Alfonso Sepe of Miami gave two teenagers a choice of jail or teaching illiterate inmates to read; he sentenced eight men convicted of marijuana possession to spend one day a week cleaning up a polluted river. Michigan Judge John Roskopp ordered a boy found guilty of shooting a protected swan to work two weeks at a state game preserve. Federal Judge Philip Neville of Minneapolis sentenced a physician convicted of tax evasion to probation with a proviso that he perform "charitable medical services, teaching or an equivalent allied activity" for six months.

State judges in Portland, Oregon, may call on an experimental "diagnostic center" staffed by psychologists, probation officers, and social workers for sentencing recommendations. Judge Stanley Fuld, former chief judge of the New York Court of Appeals, and others have suggested that sentencing be turned over to a superagency composed of judges, correction officials, and laymen. Professor Leonard Orland of the University of Connecticut law school proposes sentencing "referees" comparable to referees in bankruptcy, with responsibility for sentencing, confinement, and parole.

Appellate review of sentencing, now permitted by statute in thirteen states, is warmly endorsed by the American Bar Association and many judges, not including Chief Justice Burger. Federal judges now attend periodic sentencing "institutes," where they are supposed to air their differences and discuss criteria. But Judge Frankel, for one, finds their impact "quaintly inconclusive." The two afternoons he spent at such institutes in six years on the bench persuaded him that "for the most part the judges tend to record their differences, reassure each other of their independence, and go home to do their disparate things as before."

Frankel has little confidence that any of the currently discussed reforms will offer an escape from the wilderness of sentencing. He is particularly unimpressed by "indeterminate sentences" in California and elsewhere, which leave the length of a sentence up to a parole board or an equivalent. "Indeterminacy in its most enthusiastic forms," he writes, "takes on its literal dictionary quality of vagueness."

He believes that sentencing "calls, above all, for regulation by law. There is an excess of discretion given to officials whose entitlement to such power is established by neither professional credentials nor performance." He suggests a permanent national commission which would study sentencing, prisons, and parole with a view toward forming and enacting rules. "I envision a highly prestigious commission," he says, composed of "philosopher-statesmen."

Short of a visitation by the angel of justice, who hasn't been seen recently, Frankel's idea seems as good as any. The wilderness may or may not be hospitable to philosopher-statesmen, but it certainly hasn't yielded to any lesser explorers.

"One of our judges here had to sentence a man to death this one time. It was a jury sentence, he didn't have any choice." The speaker was Texas Judge Frank Bryant. "Well, this old boy, he'd stop and take these long pauses, you know? He'd have to get himself under control every few minutes. It was cuttin' a hole in him, you could tell. He had no heart for it at all. He stayed in his chambers for an hour afterwards.

"Well, then I got on the bench and I went around to this older judge and found out the kind of sentences he'd been giving. I didn't want to get 'way low or high. I wanted to see what he thought quote justice unquote was. I told my prosecutor I wasn't tryin' to set any records, just to follow the example of others. I don't know what justice is, hell, and that old boy probably didn't either. He'd just been looking around for it for twenty years or so, and I'm only a beginner at it.

"So I had this shoplifter in court the other day. I know he would have whacked her in the ass something fierce. She was a thief, you know, and you ain't gonna change that. But still I hated to be the one to send her to jail. I put her on probation. Hell. I'm a slob, I guess. It ought to be more mechanical. If you break the law, you ought to get put in jail, that's what the whole system is for. They don't do no shoplifting in jail.

"I'm just floating with the breeze, trying to figure out what I think. I don't know if I'm a slob or a hardnose, probably more of a slob. It's something that's part of you, I guess—you don't change that much when you become a judge. Seems like sentencing winds up being a committee action a lot of the time—the defense lawyer and prosecutor and I figure it out. Sometimes I figure if I piss them both off I must be getting close to justice."

Sentencing is the judicial obsession, and no judge feels truly comfortable with its demands. Piero Calamandrei quoted the deathbed prayer of an old magistrate who said it best: "O Lord, I would that all men I have sentenced should die before me, because I would fain not think of leaving men who were imprisoned on my order. . . . Not a single time in sentencing a man has my conscience not been disturbed, trembling before an office which ultimately can belong to none but Thee."

XVII

In Search of the Perfect Judge

*"There are, obviously, good judges and magistrates
and exceptionally good judges and magistrates and
what we might call not-so-good judges and magistrates. But good—apart from the fact that we all
know a clear-minded, fair and able man when we
see one and are delighted with what we see—good
in relation to what, good to what end? A judge on
the criminal bench is a man who administers the
law which he has not made; he may do worse or he
may do better, but he cannot do very much better
than this law; and the rule of law itself is not an
absolute, not a mystique, but a contract between
men. It is an instrument of society: our instrument.
What then do we think we want? Maintenance of
our present fabric of living, standardization, protection, certainly; but we do not all agree on the extent,
the means or the price. Moreover this straightfor-
ward matter of expediency is immensely complicated by our simultaneous concept of justice—which
may well be a mystique, by our impulse towards
a disinterested sorting out of right and wrong.
The common law is unentangleable from the moral
law. . . .*

*"The good magistrate, one might say, must be a
good man. And possibly a contented one. He ought
not to be too high-strung; a man with a Dostoevsky
view of life would wear himself to a frazzle in six
months. . . . As a barrister put it, 'Oh, a happily
married chap, you know; garden, kind heart, good
health and not too much out for himself.' Another*

377

> *magistrate named the qualities, in that order: 'Hu-*
> *manity; common sense; humility; a little law, a very*
> *clever chap would be wasted; a sense of humour.'*
> *To which one might add, imagination, some experi-*
> *ence of life and an ability to absorb the unexpected."*
>   S Y B I L L E   B E D F O R D
>   *The Faces of Justice*

H U M A N I T Y ,   C O M M O N   S E N S E ,   H U M I L I T Y . . .
we want good human beings. Humanity is properly first: the
capacity to feel and thus to understand; to know about human
frailty, including one's own; to care. We ask this and much more of
our judges, perhaps too much, and we sentence ourselves to permanent disillusion.

Something in us—our uncertainty, our deep respect for law, our
adolescence—wants to revere judges, and wants judges worthy of
our reverence. It is part of our national character, an impulse in the
American breast. We act like lovers: our reactions to good or bad
judges are gloriously excessive; the love so ardently bestowed is
ferociously withdrawn; hell hath no fury like a believer betrayed.
Hyperbole is lodged in our tribal archives: "There is no character on
earth more elevated and pure than that of a learned and upright
judge," said Daniel Webster, flicking away a tear. "He exerts an
influence like the dews of heaven falling without observation."
Chief Justice John Marshall, glancing in the same direction,
thundered the corollary: "The greatest scourge an angry heaven
ever inflicted upon an ungrateful and sinning people was an
ignorant, a corrupt, or a dependent judiciary."

Such feverish rhetoric obscures a calm assessment of the American judiciary. The subject is unrelentingly emotional; great clouds
of bias are forever overhead; a good judge inspires veneration, a
bad one provokes contempt. Mediocrity is plainly unbearable.

American judges are not all they ought to be. They are too often
greedy, too often weak, too often tyrannical; they are far too often
callously insensitive to human weakness; far too many are pedestrian, "gray mice," devoid of distinction. All this and more: their
means of ascension almost guarantees a sodden mediocrity; judicial
insensitivity may be the least offensive consequence of a selection
system that puts a premium on cronyism and self-promotion. The
nature of their work, especially in the lower courts, is not calculated to attract the best—"It's chopping wood, you're just another

bureaucrat," a law professor says. And finally they are insulated, caressed, and protected by the brotherhood of the robe, the dusty deference that walls them off and chokes their humanness. Measured against what we expect of them, they fall pathetically short.

In rebuttal, judges ask why they must be measured by such a standard. They are, after all, flesh of our flesh, no more touched by divinity than you or I. Short of an assemblage of saints, who could meet the demands we make of them? "It isn't fair," a judge complained after he heard a lawyer's speech cataloging complaints against judges. "Why can't we be judged like everyone else?" The lawyer's reply was swift: "Because you're not like everyone else. *You have more power.*"

How do judges rate, then, by the standards they are stuck with? There is, of course, no answer. But there are at least the subjective, impressionistic estimates of reasonably well-informed journalists, whose trade compels the generalizations judges eschew. One such journalist is Howard James. "If my sampling is a fair indication," he wrote in *Crisis in the Courts,* "perhaps half of the trial judges are, for one reason or another, unfit to sit on the bench." James added that "probably not more than one in 10 lower-court magistrates is, in most states, really qualified to dispense justice." His survey was made in 1966 and 1967.

Mine was made in 1972 and 1973, and my estimate is slightly more generous than his, perhaps because of reforms that have come in the years between—improvement and expansion of judicial education, an increase in merit selection, and, most notably, the tremendous flowering of commissions with power to investigate judges and recommend disciplinary action (22 states introduced such commissions in the past five years; 30 now have them).

My impression is that between 30 and 40 percent of state trial-court judges are unfit to sit. On the federal trial bench, I would estimate the figure to be about 10 percent. At the magistrate's level, perhaps two thirds are unqualified for the responsibilities they hold. Their failures include intellectual inadequacy, corruption, bigotry, tyranny, temperamental instability, and physical or mental disabilities.

I believe that judges, as a class, are no more or less honest, industrious, or moral than any other group of comparably educated professional American men—dentists, say, or engineers, or corporate vice presidents. "Our judges are as honest as other men and not more so," said Abraham Lincoln. "They have, with others, the same passions for party, for power, and the privilege of their corps." The rub is, as ever, that their weaknesses, prejudices, and vanities are compounded by their power.

Whether this estimate of the quality of our bench is cause for pointing with pride or viewing with alarm depends on the disposition of the beholder. The Pollyanna perspective, which is shared by a high percentage of judges and politicians, is that we ought to be thankful they are as good as they are. They argue that, given the obstacles to excellence—relatively low pay (at least, compared to private attorneys), the tedium and frustration of lower-court work, the necessity for political scrambling—the bench attracts a surprisingly high number of dedicated and idealistic men. Maybe so. There are indisputably conscientious, honorable, and sensitive judges at all levels of the judiciary, and the very best of them may well be the finest public servants the republic produces; a celestial hunting party could bag no better men.

But restless pessimists, inevitably including most journalists, view the same scene through a darker glass. There are good men, granted, but why so few? And why isn't the system designed to get the best? Why should justice be a gamble? Judges should be better than other men. Why aren't they?

Generations of lawyers and legislators have sought the answer amid the various forms of judicial selection. The underlying conflict is one of the oldest debates in government: aristocracy versus democracy, translated into judicial terms as "professionalism" versus "representativeness." The American public's attitude has ebbed and flowed in reaction to the excesses of one system or another: our first judges were an appointive elite; dissatisfaction with their aristocratic detachment led to successful demands for elected judges, presumably "closer to the people." But closer still to their patrons, the political power brokers, as eventually became apparent. Back we went to elitism, this time wearing the colors of "merit selection"; since politicians heeded the people's wishes no more than aristocrats did, why not go after the best-qualified, the most "professional"? Merit selection is the direction of the moment; six states adopted it in the past decade (Florida and Wyoming in

1972), and more will probably follow. But the absence of consensus has left us with a fairly even split between elective and appointive systems. The split exemplifies the dilemma: there are (to the optimist) valid arguments in favor of both methods; the pessimist sees pitfalls in both.

The premise of those who tinker with selection systems is that judicial quality is directly related to selection. But scholars who have probed this connection have come up dry. What they *have* shown is that there is some relation between the liberalism or conservatism of judicial decisions and selection systems: political scientist Stuart Nagel discovered that elected appeals-court judges were generally more liberal on economic issues, while appointed judges were more liberal on civil-liberties issues. But Nagel also found that "there was virtually no difference between the elected and appointed courts on . . . the esteem in which they are held by law professors, the frequency their opinions are used in case-books, or the extent they are cited favorably by other courts," all valid criteria of quality.

Many judge-watchers see the roots of the trouble elsewhere—in the caliber of lawyers, for example. "The problem is not who the judges are and how they are selected from the lawyers," says Stanford Professor Anthony Amsterdam. "The problem is who the lawyers are, and how they are self-selected from the people. They are disproportionately scions of the privileged classes; they are unduly motivated by the desire to do well rather than to do good; they are affected by the timorousness and tunnel vision one might expect from those who select a profession long dedicated to making the rich richer and the poor poorer; and all of their worst proclivities in these directions are reinforced by the structure of legal education and the legal profession. No judicial-selection system can touch that problem; and, until it is exposed and cured, we are going to have bad courts, bad judges, bad law and bad lawyers."

Others feel slightly cheerier about lawyers, but believe that the way to improve judges is through close public scrutiny of their behavior combined with strong sanctions for misconduct. This idea is bursting out all over, and I'll return to it later.

Despite the disagreement on root causes, the search for the perfect judge has been primarily a search for the perfect means of selection. Selection has the virtue of being relatively easy to change; all it requires, in most cases, is a constitutional amendment adopted either by voters or by a state legislature. Improvement in the caliber of legal education and the profession itself, though doubtless desirable, is a grander, infinitely more difficult enterprise.

Proponents of merit selection present an impressive array of arguments and a vivid gallery of horror stories: elected judges sacrifice their independence, their freedom to be as good as they're able, if they have to return periodically to the voters for approval. Voters are often ignorant of the relative merits of judicial candidates, apathetic about marking judicial ballots, and inclined to vote for the party instead of the man. In a 1952 special election for the Florida Supreme Court, less than 13,000 of an eligible 1.1 million voters bothered to cast ballots. That same year only 88 of 45,000 voters turned out for a judicial election in Evanston, Illinois. In states with a relative parity of Republican and Democratic voters, a winning governor frequently carries statewide judicial candidates along with him.

Moreover, voters are inclined to choose on the basis of unexamined impulses or slogans—law and order, permissiveness, crime in the streets—and not because of a candidate's qualifications of temperament, ability, and judgment. The electoral choice is seldom a real choice at all; in New York and other states, judicial slates are often determined in bipartisan arrangements that leave no room for opposition; voters merely ratify the bosses' selections.

In recent years the popularity of television campaigning has added another dimension to the debate. A judicial candidate with more money can obviously reach more voters via television, which in turn raises questions about the sources of campaign money and the obligations that may be attached to it. "The popular vote," says Judge John Paul Stevens of the U.S. Court of Appeals for the Seventh Circuit, "is much too blunt an instrument" for judicial selection.

Just how blunt an instrument it can be was discovered by Judge Douglas Loeffler of Clearwater, Florida, in 1970. Loeffler, a Republican elected to a four-year term on the County Court in 1966, refused to raise money for the party by selling tickets to fund-raising events. He bought tickets for his wife and himself, but returned the others he was sent, in accord with the canons of judicial ethics.

In the 1970 primary the party distributed a brochure describing

Loeffler's opponent as "one of the bright new stars of the Republican party." Loeffler received a single anonymous line: "Opponent has been grave disappointment to the Republican party." Loeffler lost by 1500 out of 50,000 votes. An unsympathetic local party leader explained that Judge Loeffler "just forgot he was a Republican once he got in."

Politicos and reformers collided in a 1973 primary to choose candidates for forty-one trial-court judgeships in Philadelphia. A non-partisan reform group urged the defeat of several incumbent judges and supported others the bar association had rated qualified. With only a 20-percent voter turnout, reform candidates were summarily thumped by nominees of the Republican and Democratic organizations. Nine candidates were nominated despite the reformers' active opposition. A month later Governor Milton Shapp signed an executive order pledging to fill judicial vacancies from a list submitted by a merit commission.

The main ingredients of the merit plan were devised sixty years ago by Albert Kales, a law professor at Northwestern University. The plan was adopted and promoted by the American Judicature Society, an organization Kales helped to create, and endorsed by the American Bar Association in 1937. It became a part of the ABA's model judicial article in 1962.

The plan has three major features: (1) the formation of a non-partisan judicial nominating commission composed of judges, lawyers, and laymen; (2) when a vacancy arises, the commission presents a list of names (usually three) to the governor, who is obliged to select one of the designated names; (3) after a specified period, the judge runs unopposed for reelection on a "retention" (yes or no) ballot. As of 1973, this basic scheme had been adopted by nine states. Another six states used the merit method for selecting a minority of their judges, and nine others had voluntary versions operating under executive orders.

The chief supporters of the merit plan are state and national bar groups, which base their argument on professionalism. Glenn Winters, executive director of the American Judicature Society and a lifelong advocate of the plan, has compared the selection of judges to that of teachers. "There is probably no community in the world where high-school teachers are elected by popular vote," he writes, "and yet the determination of the professional qualifications of a judge requires as much care and professional skill in the chooser as does the selection of a teacher of mathematics or biology."

Leaders of the organized bar are frequently ideological conservatives, but merit selection is not a clear-cut liberal-conservative issue. Its backers include liberals such as ex-Mayor John Lindsay of New York and conservatives like California Governor Ronald Reagan. Its critics are no easier to pigeonhole.

"The trouble with the merit system," says a Connecticut attorney, "is that it assumes one can define the qualities of a good judge and that there are a series of tests to determine whether those qualities are present or not. It goes on to assume that there is a group of people who are without bias themselves and can act independently to produce the desired result."

Other critics are offended by its inherent anti-democracy. "So long as we pretend to be a 'self-governing' people," says Texas lawyer Warren Burnett, "efforts to dilute the role of the electing public in the governing process should be carefully studied." Burnett dismisses judicial objections to the "uncertainty, inconvenience, and sacrifice" of elections with the argument that "no citizen has reason to be assured that their removal guarantees, or even suggests, dramatic improvement in public service or public servants." Most black lawyers and judges oppose the plan because they have more confidence in electoral politics than in blue-ribbon commissions.

Martin Mayer's objection is grounded in judicial reality. "The trial judge's job today," he writes, "is mostly to mediate between the parties in an accident case, assess the correct value of property seized by the state, control the behavior of the police through rulings to exclude evidence in criminal cases, and sentence convicted criminals. It is hard to see why removal from concern with public opinion should improve a man's performance in these tasks. . . ."

Merit selection's weakest point is the retention election. In theory it is supposed to give voters a chance to reject an unfit judge by a simple majority vote. But in practice, in the one thousand–plus retention votes that have been held in states using the plan, only ten judges have been voted out—seven in Colorado and one each in Nebraska, Alaska, and Missouri. In most cases the judge's defeat was the result of a public campaign focused on charges of corruption or "permissiveness." That adds up to a judicial survival rate of 99-plus percent, and to argue that all the survivors were adequate judges is unalloyed fantasy. The natural law at work here is that a sitting judge tends to remain sitting. Warren Burnett observes that "in political combat, as in speed contests among horses, the outcome becomes doubtful only after the entry of the second contestant."

There has been only one thorough, unbiased investigation of the merit plan—a study by University of Missouri political scientists Richard Watson and Rondal Downing of its operation in Missouri over twenty-five years. Their discoveries confounded both defenders and critics.

Their most important finding was that the advertised non-partisanship was a chimera. Nominating commissions turned out to be just another political instrument. Their lists of nominees were frequently stacked: the three names included one gubernatorial favorite and two others added for window dressing. Commissioners bartered their support for each other's candidates. The great majority of judges selected were political allies, often cronies, of the governor who appointed them. The chief difference was that ward leaders and local committeemen had yielded their power over judicial selection to the governor.

Watson and Downing also found evidence that merit-selection judges were not the conservative bluebloods of the bar that many skeptics had expected. They tended to be slightly older than elected judges, heavily Democratic (as the governors were), locally born and educated, and no more pro-business than elected judges. But there were no wild hairs. "The Missouri Plan will not produce a maverick," a lawyer told them. "[U]nder the elective system you may get all kinds of wacky characters going on the bench, who will frequently dissent from the views of their colleagues . . . and thus let a little ventilation into the process of justice." The one black judge selected between 1941 and 1963 was the result, according to one nominating commissioner, of gubernatorial spite. His colleagues asked the commissioner what he thought the governor would do if a Negro's name appeared on a panel. "I told them that . . . if he thought the commission was trying to put him on the spot by sending down the name of a Negro, he would respond by appointing the Negro. And this is precisely what he did."

The two professors polled lawyers on the quality of merit-plan judges. Seventy-three percent said they thought the plan had recruited better judges than the elective system which preceded it. Thirteen percent felt it had not. They also found that the plan "tended to eliminate highly incompetent persons," supporting a claim of its advocates. The fools were apparently gone with the mavericks.

Watson's and Downing's research left merit-selection supporters with one pat on the head and one kick in the premise. It also revealed that the political hand is quicker than the legal eye. "Every system so far has turned out differently from the way it looked on paper," says Sheldon Goldman. "Non-partisan elections didn't eliminate partisanship. The Missouri Plan was supposed to be a great step forward, but the commission membership is manipulated, panels are stacked, the governor still operates politically. Reformers never foresee these things." Reformers sometimes forget that politics will out.

The arguments for both popular election and merit selection are ultimately unconvincing. Neither system can guarantee good judges, especially when one identifies the chief ingredient of a good judge as his humanity, his human perception and compassion. In their ardor, defenders of each method ignore large holes in their own arguments. Boosters of the elective system, invoking the democratic piety that "the people" should be the fount of judgment, blind themselves to the ugly reality that politicians long ago usurped the people's right to choose, that judicial elections are commonly no more than charades dressed up in a pretense of democracy. Merit reformers are similarly deceptive. Their contention that merit judges are decided on non-partisan, professional grounds endows both commissioners and the appointing governor with a saintly, above-the-battle character they do not deserve. The claim that retention ballots enable voters to remove a bad judge can withstand neither statistical scrutiny nor logical analysis.

It is arguably true that merit judges are no more conservative, insensitive, or insulated from life than elected judges are. The experience in both Colorado and Missouri seems to buttress this contention. It may even be that merit judges, on the whole, are an improvement over elective judges, as lawyers in both those states believe. But it is clear that merit judges are blessed with no greater resistance to the temptations of office, notably tyranny and corruption, than their elective brethren. It also seems likely that the bureaucratic impulses of a committee, relentlessly steering the middle way, serve to eliminate not only the hopelessly inept but also the gifted eccentric.

As with so many other issues of public policy, the question finally becomes subjective, digging down to the values and assumptions of the individual: Whose ox is going to be gored? Where do you place your faith—in the electorate or the elite? Are you cynical or idealistic about your fellow man?

The experience of other countries offers little guidance. Many American lawyers and judges pay homage to the British system, which may indeed produce the best-qualified judges anywhere. Judges in the mother country are appointed by the crown from a narrow cadre of barristers trained in trial work. It is a system built around an elite, and it depends on a tradition of an aristocracy that enjoys an implicit public trust. No such Eden blooms on these shores: the aristocracy perhaps, but not the trust.

In France and other countries on the continent, judges are civil servants who work their way up the judicial ladder in the hallowed bureaucratic way—they don't rattle the rungs. Two New York University scholars who analyzed the continental method concluded that "European judges as a group are affected by a civil-service attitude of a certain monotony and regularity." Anyone who has spent fifteen minutes with a government clerk can feel a twitch of recognition.

"Picking judges is putting your hand in the sand," says law professor Herman Schwartz. "You're always going to get glass, rough ones and fine ones out of any group. The advantage of judges with political backgrounds is that they won't delude themselves into thinking they're not dealing with social issues; they know them for what they are. The disadvantage is that the politician plays it safe and can be swayed by the mob. On the other side is the ivory tower, the priesthood. There's no guarantee either way."

The relatively high quality of federal judges suggests that the founding fathers, abetted by latter-day refinements, may have been on to something. Federal judges are admittedly political appointments. Still the ABA, despite its inclination to go along with the marginally qualified, screens out the worst and promotes the best. Life tenure guarantees independence, if not feistiness, and frees a judge to listen to his conscience. But, alas, the federal system depends on other inducements—prestige, the high importance of the court's business, a tradition of craft—that are rarely visible on state courts. The stars of the bar lust after federal judgeships; but offer them a state-court seat, particularly if they have to run for it, and you will receive a carefully reasoned letter in which active distaste seeps between the lines. "The state courts can drive a man crazy," says a prominent New York attorney. "There's so much frustration and so little stimulation. There's so little you can do. It gives you a dreadful feeling of sadness."

The genius of the federal system may be its pluralism. The Justice Department, the senator, the ABA, special-interest groups, and the press are all permitted a voice. And therein lies what solution there is: maximize, don't minimize, the participants in the process. Let everyone be heard and do it as openly as possible. Establish the best possible method for monitoring judicial performance.

The most encouraging developments in judicial selection I found were in Massachusetts and Illinois, traditionally among the more desolate reaches of the judiciary. Progress in both states involved active participation in the selection process by young, liberal lawyers, acting on impulses of public service but making no pretense of ideological neutrality.

In Massachusetts, where judges are appointed by the governor for life, the potential for reform surfaced in 1972 when the electorate approved a measure requiring judicial retirement at age seventy, known locally as the "old curmudgeon amendment." The result was thirty-eight vacancies on state courts. Governor Francis Sargent named an *ad hoc* committee to interview and assess candidates for the vacancies. The committee included businessmen, members of civic groups, a man from the state bar association, and a minority of liberal reformers from the activist Massachusetts Law Reform Institute. The reformers dominated the committee. "We found that work is power," one told me. "We worked the hardest and we had the loudest voice."

The committee drew up an elaborate questionnaire for potential judges. In addition to the customary inquiries about experience, education, and business interests, it included such questions as "Do you believe that minority and ethnic group members are prone to commit certain crimes more often than others?" and "What involvement have you had with minority and ethnic group members either socially, in business, in civic affairs, or as employer-employee?"

They made a particular effort to recruit younger candidates, blacks, and women. In all, they interviewed 550 aspirants in two months. Roughly one fourth were found qualified and recommended to Sargent. The governor made no promise to confine his appointments to the committee list, but in fact did so.

Massachusetts was fertile ground for such an experiment. Corruption pops up in the commonwealth's courts with the regularity of coups in Latin America, and for years judicial quality mirrored the caliber of the governor's friends and political creditors. The question of whether the new judges will elevate Massachusetts justice awaits a future reckoning, but there is no argument about whether they broadened its base; 10 of the 38 appointees were under forty; 3 were black and 3 were women; several were Democrats who had campaigned against Sargent. Appraising the committee's work, two young Harvard law graduates congratulated the group for "assuring that political considerations affect only qualified individuals—which is the most that we can expect of judicial selection."

The 1500-member Chicago Council of Lawyers was founded in 1969 as a liberal counterpoint to the city's bar association. Since 1970 the council has published reports on candidates in judicial elections, rating their competence on the basis of interviews with lawyers of all political persuasions. Its most devastating broadside came when 107 Cook County magistrates were nominated for elevation to Circuit Court in 1971. The council itemized the failings—bigotry, laziness, incompetence, arrogance—of dozens of magistrates. Their report concluded that only 2 of the 107 were fully qualified for promotion. Fourteen more were rated passable, and a staggering 82 were described as "clearly unqualified for any judicial position."

The council charged that Cook County judgeships were traditionally "outright rewards" for partisanship. Working through a committee on judicial selection, it published assessments of Cook County judges running on a retention ballot in 1972, rating 8 outstanding, 16 qualified, and 19 unqualified. All of the judges were reelected anyway, as were the magistrates the year before, but many received lower pluralities than they had in previous elections. "We haven't beaten any of them yet," says one member, "but the organization is less likely to pick a gangster or a crook now because of pressure from us. We constitute a loud obstacle to them." "I think we've provoked a growing sensitivity in judicial selectors," says another. "We're flicking away at them."

The council has also compiled a detailed evaluation of Chicago's federal judges, the only document of its kind ever produced, and regularly screens candidates for federal judgeships on behalf of Illinois Senator Charles Percy.

The common denominator of progress in Massachusetts and Illinois is a disposition to open the process of selecting and evaluating judges to public view, to liberate it from the narrow and self-serving perspectives of either partisan politics or bar associations. The Massachusetts *ad hoc* committee held a series of public meetings throughout the state, inviting opinions on the qualities to be sought in judges, and encouraging people to make recommendations. The Chicago council releases its reports publicly, itemizing and explaining the basis for its evaluations and documenting its method. The rites of judicial selection, as with the judicial process itself, suffer from inadequate ventilation, and I applaud any idea that promises to increase it.

It seems to me that both popular election and merit selection founder on just that reef, their failure to open the process to the kind of public awareness on which democracy depends. The judiciary is too insulated from its customers by its nature; remoteness is almost built in. It may also be that judges, politicians, and the bar itself have a stake in preserving the mystique, in the belief that respect and trust would topple if the truth were known, that illusion is necessary for the sake of the institution.

The irony of popular election is that it fails precisely because it denies the public the accountability it claims to provide; its pretensions of democratic choice conceal the reality that politicians have already abrogated choice. Merit selection at least has the grace to abandon any pretense of democracy, but it substitutes a pretense of non-partisanship.

Any information that might conceivably be useful in the assessment of judges ought to be made known. Most merit-selection states hold their hearings in private to spare the losers embarrassment (Nebraska is the sole exception). But embarrassment is a pale consideration compared to the public's right to know who its judges are and how they are selected. A potential judge's political background and allegiance are officially discounted as irrelevant by merit selectors, but why should they be? If a candidate accepts what he believes to be the principles of the Democratic, Republican, or Bull Moose party, why should that fidelity be shielded behind a pretense of irrelevance? It is indisputably relevant—it conditions and helps determine the attitudes he brings to the bench, which in turn weigh heavily in his decisions. "When the human elements in the judging process are covered up," Judge Jerome Frank wrote, "justice operates darklingly."

Merit selection, in my opinion, is potentially an avenue for genuine and significant improvement of the judiciary. If I were fallen upon by six obese judges and forced to declare a position, I would opt for merit selection over popular election. But not as it presently operates.

The virtue of merit selection is that it pays attention to what really counts in a judge—his heart and mind, not his smile, his available cash, or his slogans. Merit commissioners are no better than anyone else at trying to estimate qualities of heart and mind, but at least they try. Bar associations and law professors are forever talking about guidelines to help them recognize what they're looking for, but such perceptions are and ever shall be subjective, the results of one's own experience and values, one's trust in his own sudden or painful insights.

Merit selection fails in its devotion to the mystique and in its overprotectiveness. Judges, like all other public servants and maybe more so, ought to be watched—before they don the robe and after. Selection commissions ought to hold public hearings; they ought to state the reasons a candidate is or is not acceptable; they ought to be accountable for their decisions. The candidate himself ought to step before the public gaze to present his qualifications, to reveal his previously expressed positions on public issues, and to defend himself against criticism. The electoral system is supposed to do all that, but it doesn't.

There ought to be public watchdog commissions, apart from the nominating panels, to keep an eye on judicial performance and to release reports, as the Chicago lawyers do, at election time. Such commissions ought to include representatives of all shades of public opinion, not just liberal hotspurs or conservative fossils. Judges should be excluded from membership.

"If merit selection is done properly with a good governor and sound procedures, then it's the answer," says Allan Ashman of the

American Judicature Society. "But it's all a totality. All the parts of the package have to be there. You've got to assure that the nominating commission is fair and representative, that the commission has some set of criteria, and there must be a strong discipline-and-removal commission and a code of judicial conduct."

Ashman wonders about the efficacy of the retention ballot, and well he might. "My feeling," he says, "is that it's useful only if coupled with a strong removal commission. It is not yet the vehicle for removing judges, and it's a mistake to tell people it is." I would preserve the retention ballot, but make it more of a real test, first by publishing a watchdog commission's reports on contending judges and second by requiring a vote of approval of 75 percent.

The press ought to devote more attention to judicial selection and not cynically abandon it to politicians and lawyers. My point is that everyone ought to be heard and that public exposure ought to be maximized. It seems to me at least possible that such openness would produce better judges and better justice.

Boosters of merit selection are prone to extol the plan as "an idea whose time has come," and it may be, although, if so, its arrival has been remarkably slow and drawn-out. But well to this side of the judicial bend is another reform whose time is unarguably upon us—the judicial discipline commission.

The need for a commission with the authority to accept complaints about judges, investigate their conduct, and make recommendations (usually to a state supreme court) for discipline arose when it became obvious to everyone that the traditional, constitutionally sanctioned method of judicial discipline—impeachment—simply didn't work.

Impeachment, still the only means of discipline for federal judges, is a casualty of the age. It is too cumbersome and time-consuming to be useful. State legislatures are disinclined to go to the trouble of drawing up articles of impeachment and then sitting as a jury to hear evidence and pronounce judgment. Only three impeachments were attempted (all three judges were acquitted) by state legislatures between 1928 and 1948. In the years since, only five states—Alabama, Florida, Missouri, Tennessee, and Oklahoma—have tried impeachment, and the only significant case was the conviction of an Oklahoma Supreme Court justice who was accused of accepting bribes.

The swing to discipline commissions began with the establishment of California's Judicial Qualifications Commission in 1960. Suggested by former state chief justice Phil Gibson, the California panel included five judges, two lawyers, and two laymen. They now receive some two hundred complaints a year from aggrieved lawyers and laymen. Most turn out to be the grumbles of sore losers, but in more serious cases the commission can recommend removal or censure. The idea so captivated the legal-judicial Establishment that by 1973 no fewer than twenty-nine states, plus the District of Columbia and Puerto Rico, had launched similar commissions.

The principal grounds for action, as specified in the California constitution, are a "disability that seriously interferes with the performance of [a judge's] duties and is or is likely to become permanent" and "wilful misconduct in office, wilful and persistent failure to perform his duties, habitual intemperance, or conduct prejudicial to the administration of justice that brings the judicial office into disrepute."

In practice the greatest asset of the disciplinary commission has been what former California chief justice Roger Traynor calls its "prophylactic value." The California panel has recommended removal of a judge only twice in its thirteen-year history (the Supreme Court agreed in one case and disagreed in the other), but fifty-six judges have resigned or retired while under investigation. In many other instances, according to Jack Frankel, the commission's executive officer, the shock of finding themselves under scrutiny inspired erring judges to improve their conduct. "Sometimes," Frankel says, "there may be reason to accept the plea 'I didn't do it, but I'll see it doesn't happen again.' "

Frankel does the commission's spadework: he receives complaints, checks them out, and decides whether further investigation is warranted. Between a fourth and a third of the complaints are taken up by the commission itself, and most of those end with a letter to the judge. "We have to make a massive case before the Supreme Court will censure or remove a judge," Frankel says. "The evidence has to be flagrant, overwhelming, perhaps scandalous."

Incompetence is not enough. "It's not within our scope," he says.

"It's sometimes hard to distinguish between judicial incompetence and a lawyer's disagreement with a decision. There are some judges who shouldn't be on the bench whom we can't touch. If a guy leaves to play golf at three o'clock every day, that would give us a tangible cause for action, but if he does one hour's work in eight hours at the courthouse, it wouldn't." He is hopeful that some standards of competence will be added to the commission's mandate.

Another limitation on commission effectiveness is its cozy, within-the-family character. Texas law professor Albert Alschuler admits to an "uneasy feeling about a regime that emphasizes confidentiality, that accomplishes its results through backroom settlements, and that is dominated by members of the elite professional group that it is designed to control." Again the absence of openness. "In a sense," says Alschuler, "this system resembles the disciplinary committee of a country club."

Pursuing his analogy, Alschuler points out that "some members of the club will inevitably resist" the suggestions of the committee, and "the committee may conclude that a public dispute would tend to bring discredit upon the entire club. Although a 'friendly suggestion' to a fellow club member ordinarily seems harmless enough, an overt attack on one who has been anointed may be viewed as a threat to the anointers and a challenge to the very concept of anointment."

A disciplinary-commission official in another state told me that the commission's work was hobbled by the excessive circumspection of the commissioners—not only the judicial members but also the lawyers and laymen, who are often businessmen. "They look at it defensively," he said. "They make a very conservative interpretation of their responsibility. It's like a club—there's a tremendously high threshold of outrage and a willingness to look at things from the judge's point of view." One judicial member of a discipline commission came under investigation himself because of a physical disability. He was finally persuaded to retire. "They're so conscious of the delicate line," the official continued. "There was one judge who had a terrible temper. We got several complaints about him. He finally offered to resign if the commissioners found him embarrassing, but they didn't pick it up."

The arrival of discipline commissions has clearly been felicitous for the course of justice, but it is not the millennium. There is still a double standard of judgment, one for judges and another for lawyers and the rest of us. Contempt citations are a handy tool to use on irresponsible lawyers and litigants, but no comparable sanction exists for judges. "In practice," says Alschuler, "the trial judge's position, which should carry special responsibilities, carries special immunities. . . . The trial judge's responsibility is usually enforced with moral exhortations while the responsibility of lawyers and litigants is enforced with jail sentences."

The lodge and the lodge mentality reign supreme, and one of the cardinal tenets of the lodge is that you don't criticize your brother. Discipline commissions are useful, and can become even more so—Frankel suggests broadening their membership, adding the power to suspend a judge from office for a kind of probationary period, and incorporating the new code of judicial ethics into their charter, among other changes. But they stop a good distance short of satisfying our restless yen for perfection.

"Justice," said the late Dean Roscoe Pound of Harvard, "is an alloy of men and mechanisms in which men count more than machinery." The most artful attempts to improve the judiciary, the most effective discipline commissions, the most advanced systems of judicial selection are in the end no more than tolerable accommodations with our own helplessness. Our only guarantee of justice is a judge's character, quality, humanity—his spirit. Emile Zola said that art is nature through the medium of a temperament. Justice, most tantalizing of the mystiques we live by, may be law through the medium of a temperament. No "mechanism," no "system" can help us measure or predict the splendidly complex ingredients of that temperament.

Acknowledgments

T H I S list will be shorter than it should be because of the phantom legion who helped me only on condition that I preserve their anonymity. They pop up in these pages constantly, offer an unattributed idea or observation, then trail off into the shadowless mist. I couldn't have done it without them, and I want them all to know that they are anonymous but not forgotten.

It is more satisfying, if less mysterious, to salute the three dozen or so identifiable people who were especially helpful to me in the preparation of this book. They opened doors, made suggestions, set me straight, and provided information and encouragement.

Of those in or about judicial robes, I am particularly indebted to: Judge David Jacobs of the Connecticut Circuit Court; Judge Irving Younger, New York Civil Court; Jack Frankel of the California Judicial Qualifications Commission; Thomas Russell and Laurance Hyde of the National College of the State Judiciary; Judge Franklin Flaschner of Massachusetts District Court; Allan Ashman of the American Judicature Society; Judge Frank Montgomery of North Carolina District Court; Ernest Winsor and Allan Rodgers from the Massachusetts Law Reform Institute, and Virginia Demmler of the Nanette Dembitz campaign staff.

My benefactors in academia include Howard Sacks and Leonard Orland of the University of Connecticut Law School; Sheldon Goldman of the University of Massachusetts; Stuart Nagel, University of Illinois; Beverly Blair Cook, University of Wisconsin-Milwaukee; Harold W. Chase, University of Minnesota; Herman Schwartz, New York State University at Buffalo; Mark Denbeaux of Seton Hall; Allan K. Butcher of the University of Texas-Arlington, and Anthony Amsterdam of Stanford.

397

I am grateful to my journalist friends William Lambert, Steve Gelman of *New Times*, Don Thackrey of United Press International, Philip Hager of the Los Angeles *Times*, Madeleine Nash of *Time*, Wayne Woodlief of the Norfolk *Ledger-Star*, and Ralph Olive of the Milwaukee *Journal*. Thanks also to non-journalist friends Rollie Rogers of Denver, Seth Brody of Newtown, Connecticut, Bayard Hooper of the Louis Harris organization, and James Sheehan of Northwestern University.

My father, Z. B. Jackson, and my brother, Allen Jackson, both attorneys in San Francisco, bravely endured my questions, tolerated my prose, and had grace enough not to offer too many suggestions. I owe an enormous debt to an old and valued friend, Terry Crowley of the Toledo University library school, who guided me through acres of library research.

Herman Gollob of Atheneum Publishers contributed the original idea for the book, consistent encouragement, and wily suggestions. John Hawkins of the Paul Reynolds Agency made it possible for me to do it. Tom Hyman of Atheneum, an old comrade from *Life*, was a thorough and sensitive editor. Darlene Jackson from my house, closest comrade of all, typed the manuscript, participated all along the way, and finally pulled me through.

Source Notes

10 "I define a good judge": Interview with William Kunstler, Jan. 3, 1973

10 "The most important prerequisite": Interview with Judge Irving Younger, Nov. 3, 1972

10 "A good judge": Interview with Herman Schwartz, Jan. 19, 1973

10 Still other judges: Marvin Frankel, "Lawlessness in Sentencing," *University of Cincinnati Law Review*, 1972

10 "The horrible thing": G. K. Chesterton, "The 12 Men," *Tremendous Trifles*, p. 56

13 These courts too bear: *Judicature*, November 1972

13 They are constitutionally empowered: "The United States Courts," U.S. Government Printing Office, 1971

14 "A judge," in Curtis: Quoted by Martin Mayer, *The Lawyers*, p. 466 (Dell ed.)

14 In France and most: Gerhard Mueller and Fré le Poole Griffiths, "Judicial Fitness: a Comparative Study," *Judicature*, December 1968

15 "Historically, we've always": Schwartz interview, Jan. 19, 1973

15 None of the thirteen: Glenn Winters and Robert Allard, "Judicial Selection and Tenure in the United States," *The Courts, the Public and the Law Explosion*, pp. 148–9; Glenn Winters, "Selection of Judges—An Historical Introduction," *Texas Law Review*, June 1966

16 By 1973 the currents: The state-by-state breakdown was compiled with the assistance of the American Judicature Society and its research director, Allan Ashman.

16 It's a changing vista: American Judicature Society, "Election Day 1972: The Judicial Issues," *Judicature*, December 1972

17 "We see the judges move": Quoted by Sybille Bedford in *The Faces of Justice*, p. 11

17 "Judges think the law": Interview with Judge Franklin Flaschner, Aug. 16, 1972

17 "All their lives, forces": Benjamin Cardozo, *The Nature of the Judicial Process*, p. 12

18 A judge's own past: Jerome Frank, *Courts on Trial*, p. 151

CHAPTER 2

19 In 1970 twenty-three judges: Paul E. Wilson, "A Square's Night Behind Bars," *The Nation*, Feb. 15, 1971

19 The following year: *Time*, Sept. 6, 1971

19 But with that: Interview with Laurance M. Hyde, Aug. 15, 1972

23 By 1972 the college: *Ibid.*

29 "We wanted the best": *Ibid.*

29 The Institute for Judicial Administration: Warren E. Burger, "School for Judges," 33 Federal Rules Decisions, 1963

30 "The schools arose": Hyde interview, Aug. 15, 1972

CHAPTER 3

38 Herron is living proof: Quoted by Martin Mayer in *The Lawyers*, p. 460

43 "Men of property and prestige": Goldwin Smith, *History of England*, p. 278

43 "Never in any commonwealth": Quoted in Smith, *History of England*, Ibid.

43 The JP system was transported: Institute for Judicial Administration, *The Justice of the Peace Today*, 1965

43 New York University's: *Ibid.*

44 The opponents began: *Ibid.*

44 Another 10 states: Correspondence with James G. McConnell, American Judicature Society

44 "No one knows how many": Quoted in *The Justice of the Peace Today*, p. 117

44 In Alabama, Arkansas, Kentucky: *Martindale-Hubbell Law Directory*, 1972

45 "The squire has to satisfy": Interview with Ron Wilson, March 22, 1972

45 The President's Crime Commission: The President's Commission on Law Enforcement and Administration of Justice, Task Force Report, *The Courts*, 1967, p. 34

45 "That's okay if you want": Interview with Justice Edward E. Pringle, Aug. 1, 1972

45 "A judge personally": Quoted in *Journal of the American Judicature Society*, February 1965

46 Dean Dorothy Nelson: Declaration filed with petition by California Rural Legal Assistance, Inc., Jan. 5, 1971

46 In San Andreas: San Francisco *Chronicle*, Feb. 2, 3, 1973

46 Justice John Klarich: San Francisco *Examiner*, Nov. 2, 10, 1972

46 In Norristown: Correspondence with Carol Stone, American Civil Liberties Union, Norristown, Pa.

46 "I don't know anything": Riverside (Calif.) *Press-Enterprise*, Dec. 10, 12, 1968

47 Another California justice: Los Angeles *Times*, April 3, 1970

47 "You have a personal": Declaration by Rick Romero filed with petition by California Rural Legal Assistance, Inc., July 28, 1970

47 "I delve into something": *New York Times*, Oct. 27, 1971

48 "If the JPs go": Interview with Martin Bogarad, March 21, 1972

48 Perhaps, as Martin Mayer: Mayer, *The Lawyers*, p. 443

48 When West Virginia Supreme Court: Charleston (W. Va.) *Gazette*, Feb. 17, 1972

48 Professor Willard Lorensen: Interview with Willard Lorensen, March 24, 1972

CHAPTER 4

73 Leonard Downie summed it up: Leonard Downie, *Justice Denied*, p. 23

74 "The system of criminal justice": Richard Pious, "Pretrial and Nontrial in the Lower Criminal Courts," *Current History*, July 1971

74 Chief Justice Warren E. Burger: *Santobello v. New York*, 1971, quoted in *Judges' Journal*, January 1973

74 Hammurabi complained: Maurice Rosenberg, "Court Congestion: Status, Causes, and Proposed Remedies," *The Courts, the Public and the Law Explosion*, p. 30

75 The simple expedient: San Francisco *Chronicle*, Aug. 17, 1972

75 Increasing the daily: Portland *Oregonian*, Nov. 11, 1971

75 The chief judge: *New York Times*, April 30, 1971

75 When the year was up: *Time*, May 8, 1972

75 President Nixon has proposed: *New York Times*, March 12, 1971

75 Senator Henry M. Jackson: *New York Times*, June 5, 1972

75 "I think there is": *New York Times*, Aug. 21, 1971

79 Ribicoff's court-reform bill: Joseph I. Liebman, *The Power Broker*

79 On one occasion: Hartford *Courant*, May 1965

80 When a stripper: Hartford *Courant*, Bridgeport *Post*

80 But his biggest burst: Hartford *Courant*, September 1964

80 Eielson became nationally: Rodney Eielson, "Sins of the Parents," *McCall's*, January 1965

81 The judiciary committee: Interviews with Bernard Avcollie, June 29, 1972, and John Carrozzella, June 21, 1972

82 It was a "public display": Hartford *Courant*, March 28, 1969

82 The floor debate: Transcript of General Assembly debate, March 26, 1969

83 By 1973 most of the forty-four: Connecticut Citizens for Judicial Modernization and Connecticut Bar Association, Report of the Joint Committee on Judicial Modernization, March 1972

84 One result is that: *Ibid.*

85 A Judicial Review Council: Interview with Judge John Daly, June 21, 1972

85 In 1972 an *ad hoc* group: Report of the Joint Committee on Judicial Modernization, March 1972

85 The Connecticut legislature: Interview with James Bingham, Oct. 18, 1973

CHAPTER 5

95 Texas political scientist: Interview with Allan K. Butcher, Nov. 16, 1972

CHAPTER 6

111 When Elreta Alexander: "Black Judges in the South," *Ebony*, March 1971

111 Of 136 federal judges: Beverly Blair Cook, "Black Representation in the Third Branch," *Black Law Journal*, Winter 1971

111 Nationally there are 314: The figure for black judges is from Judge George Crockett. The figure for all full-time judges is an estimate based on data from the American Judicature Society, American Bar Association, *The Book of the States*, and a statement by Chief Justice Warren E. Burger (quoted in *Newsweek*, Dec. 25, 1972)

111 Discrimination by the American: Revius O. Ortique, Jr., "The National Bar Association—Not Just an Option," *Judicature*, April–May 1970

111 So few blacks: *Ebony*, March 1971

111 "The low number": Interview with Judge George Crockett, Dec. 11, 1972

111 The first was: George Crockett, "Black Judges and the Black Judicial Experience," *Wayne State Law Review*, September 1972; Cook, "Black Representation in the Third Branch"

111 It was 1924: Crockett, "Black Judges and the Black Judicial Experience"

112 It was a fraternity: *Time*, Aug. 23, 1971

112 The federal bench: Cook, "Black Representation in the Third Branch"

112 "A Negro involved": William H. Brown III, "Racial Discrimination in the Legal Profession," *Judicature*, April–May 1970

112 The sea of white: Crockett, "Black Judges and the Black Judicial Experience"

112 "A judge is a product": Crockett interview, Dec. 11, 1972

112 "We're experts in human": Interview with Dr. Sedrick Rawlins, March 1970

113 As many as a dozen: Cook, "Black Representation in the Third Branch"

113 The Negro population: U.S. Department of Commerce, 1970 census

113 Political scientist Beverly Blair Cook: Cook, "Black Representation in the Third Branch"

113 "I think that race": Crockett interview, Dec. 12, 1972

114 In the late sixties: *Ebony*, March 1971

114 By 1972, when the city: *New York Times*, Jan. 23, 1972

114 Thirty-six more: Correspondence with George Crockett, *New York Times*, Feb. 4, 1973

115 A temporary commission: Interview with Allan Rodgers, Jan. 26, 1973

115 The council asked: Release from the Judicial Council of the National Bar Association, April 27, 1972

116 "It was given": Crockett interview, *Black Law Journal*, Winter 1971

116 "I have always favored": *Ibid.*

116 "I don't think revolution": *Ibid.*

116 A judge, he believes: Crockett, "Reflections of a Jurist on Civil Disobedience," *The American Scholar*, Autumn 1971

117 "Who are we": Marvin Frankel, "An Opinion by One of Those Softheaded Judges," *The New York Times Magazine*, May 13, 1973

117 "Sometimes the idea": *Ebony*, March 1971

117 Crockett was the duty: Crockett interview, Dec. 12, 1972; Crockett, "A Black Judge Speaks," *Judicature*, April–May 1970

118 "There are only two": *Black Law Journal*, Winter 1971; Washington *Post*, Jan. 17, Feb. 17, 18, 1972

119 Judge Bruce McMarion Wright: *Black Law Journal*, Winter 1971; Bruce Wright, "A Black Brood on Black Judges," *Judicature*, June–July 1973; *Time*, Jan. 15, 1973; *New York Times*, Dec. 28, 1972; *Civil Liberties*, March 1973

119 In one sense these: *New York Times*, March 11, 1973

120 Harry Alexander was: Washington *Post*, Jan. 17, 1972

120 Bruce Wright was: *New York Times*, Nov. 18, 1971

120 He says the attacks: Crockett, *Judicial Council Newsletter*, March 1972

120 There are 22 black: "The Black Judge in America: A Statistical Profile," *Judicature*, June–July 1973

120 President Kennedy: Harold W. Chase, *Federal Judges*, p. 21

121 When Georgia's Republican: *New Republic*, Aug. 15, 1970

122 During his 1960 campaign: Cook, "Black Representation in the Third Branch"

122 To get Eastland's: Victor Navasky, *Kennedy Justice*, p. 245

122 "The brothers had to pay": Interview with Ed Brown, Jan. 3, 1973

122 "If he was Eastland's": Mary Curzan, *A Case Study in the Selection of Federal Judges: The Fifth Circuit, 1953–63;* Navasky, *Kennedy Justice*, p. 265

122 McCree, sponsored by liberal: Crockett, "Black Judges and the Black Judicial Experience"

122 A poll of 362: Chicago Council of Lawyers, "Survey of Lawyers Concerning the Performance of Judicial Officers in the Federal District Court," November 1971

123 Robinson was a professor: *New York Times*, June 20, 1972, Sept. 11, 1973

123 Constance Baker Motley: *Black Law Journal*, Summer 1971. Five of the six women federal judges are named in Chapter 12; the sixth is Charlotte Murphy of the U.S. Court of Claims.

123 Damon Keith of Detroit: *Black Law Journal*, Winter 1971; *New York Times*, June 20, 1972

123 At least one black lawyer: *Congressional Quarterly*, Dec. 16, 1972

124 David Williams of: Alvin Gershenson, *The Bench Is Warped*, pp. 68–74; *New York Times*, Dec. 15, 1972
The first salvos: *New York Times*, Feb. 4, 1973

CHAPTER 7

135 "Judges ought to be": Sir Francis Bacon, "Of Judicature," in *Handbook for Judges*, p. 25
135 The House of Commons: Joseph Borkin, *The Corrupt Judge*, p. 213
136 "I do plainly": *Bartlett's Familiar Quotations*, p. 119
136 Their lordships fined him: *Encyclopaedia Britannica* (1971), Vol. 2, p. 994
136 It "poisons the well": Borkin, *The Corrupt Judge*, p. 17
136 As Bacon's contemporary: William Shakespeare, *Measure for Measure*
136 The Kerner story: *New York Times*, Dec. 16, 19, 1971; Jan. 4, 10, 14, 21, 28, Feb. 11, 20, April 20, 1973; Chicago *Daily News*, Nov. 13, 1972; Feb. 17, 18, 19, 1973; *Time*, Dec. 13, 1971, March 5, 1973; *Newsweek*, March 5, 1973
139 Joseph Borkin: Borkin, *The Corrupt Judge*, pp. 11–15
139 Borkin documented: *Ibid.*, pp. 219–58
139 Three of the 55: *Ibid.*, pp. 95–186
140 Manton was a judicial: *Ibid.*, pp. 23–93
141 In a year of: *New York Times*, July 15, 1969; *New York Times*, July 6, 1973; New York *Daily News*, July 5, 1973; *Wall Street Journal*, Oct. 20, 1970
141 Edward J. DeSaulnier: Boston *Globe;* letter from Judge DeSaulnier to Gov. Francis W. Sargent
142 Mitchell Schweitzer: *Life*, March 12, 1971; *New York Times*, Nov. 19, 1970; July 22, 30, Sept. 24, 25, Oct. 19, Nov. 21, Dec. 11, 23, 1972
143 In 1965 four justices: *New York Times*, May 11, 12, 13, 1965; *Newsweek*, May 24, 1965
143 In 1968 Judge Glenn Sharpe: American Judicature Society, *Judicial Disability and Removal Commissions, Courts and Procedures*, 1972, p. 411
143 Probate Judge Clem McClelland: Murray Teigh Bloom, *The Trouble with Lawyers*, p. 248 (Pocket Books ed.)
144 In Oregon, District Judge: *Ibid.*, p. 260; Jack Frankel, "Judicial Discipline and Removal," *Texas Law Review*, June 1966
144 The ties between organized: *New York Times*, Feb. 19, 1973
144 Ralph DeVita: *New York Times*, Dec. 3, 10, 1969; April 11, 15, May 28, 1970; interview with Hyman Isaac, Oct. 18, 1973
144 Judge Louis W. Kizas: William Braithwaite, *Who Judges the Judges?*, pp. 102–4
145 In 1972 a Los Angeles: Los Angeles *Times*, Nov. 29, 1972; California Commission on Judicial Qualifications releases of Dec. 26,

1972, June 11, 1973, Aug. 2, 1973; correspondence with Jack Frankel

145   Seymour R. Thaler: *New York Times*, Dec. 22, 24, 26, 1971; March 10, 16, 17, 24, 26, Aug. 9, 1972; interview with Ira Postel, Oct. 18, 1973

146   "In the case of judges": *New York Times*, Oct. 6, 1972

146   According to a newspaper: *New York Times*, Dec. 14, 1972
District Judge Clyde R. Ashworth: Fort Worth *Star-Telegram*, Feb. 5, 1970

149   The following week: *New York Times*, July 13, 1972, Dec. 30, 1973

149   The American Bar Association's: American Judicature Society, "Canons of Judicial Ethics," June 1969, p. 1

149   The new canons: American Bar Association, "Code of Judicial Conduct," May 1972

149   The National Conference: San Mateo (Calif.) *Times*, Aug. 12, 1972

150   "The public has": Interview with Roger Traynor, Aug. 31, 1972
Justice Roy J. Solfisburg: *New York Times*, July 15, Aug. 1, 1969; *Time*, Aug. 29, 1969; Braithwaite, *Who Judges the Judges?*, pp. 106–11

151   When Delmar Shelby: Braithwaite, *Ibid.*, pp. 30–3
Judge Ross L. DiLorenzo: Interview with Mark Denbeaux, Oct. 6, 1972; *Village Voice* (N.Y.), Nov. 9, 1972; *New York Times*, April 4, 1972, Aug. 10, 1973

152   The canons flee: American Bar Association, "Code of Judicial Conduct"

152   Justice Traynor's views: Traynor interview, Aug. 31, 1972

152   Judge Leland Geiler: California Commission on Judicial Qualifications release, Aug. 29, 1972, Oct. 25, 1973; San Francisco *Chronicle*, Aug. 30, 1972

153   Judge James H. Edgar: San Francisco *Examiner*, Sept. 6, 1972; Report of Michigan Judicial Tenure Commission, June 29, 1972; statement by Chief Justice Thomas M. Kavanagh, Sept. 6, 1972

153   Edward A. Haggerty, Jr.: American Judicature Society, *Judicial Disability and Removal Commissions, Courts and Procedures*, 1972, p. 388

154   Judge John J. McDonnell: Mike Royko in Chicago *Daily News*, Nov. 30, Dec. 7, 1972; Chicago *Daily News*, Dec. 5, 6, 17, 1972; interview with Ray Breen, Illinois Judicial Inquiry Board, Oct. 18, 1973; report of Illinois Judicial Inquiry Board

155   The idea that the sins: Harry W. Jones, "The Trial Judge—Role Analysis and Profile," *The Courts, the Public and the Law Explosion*, pp. 137–8

155   "Glaring down from": Herman Schwartz, "Judges as Tyrants," *Criminal Law Bulletin*, March 1971

155 If the judge is arrogant: Jones, "The Trial Judge—Role Analysis and Profile"

155 Judge L. Jackson Embrey: Harvey Katz, "Some Call It Justice," *Washingtonian*, September 1970

156 Judge Floyd Sarisohn: Braithwaite, *Who Judges the Judges?*, p. 7

156 When a lone dissenting: *New York Times*, Jan. 14, 1973

156 Judge Edward Beard: Katz, *Washingtonian*, September 1970

156 Allan K. Butcher: Interview with Allan K. Butcher, Nov. 16, 1972

156 "If they want to": Katz, *Washingtonian*, September 1970

156 Superior Court Judge Gerald S. Chargin: California Commission on Judicial Qualifications, release and inquiry concerning a judge, April 3, 1970, June 10, 1970

157 The most encouraging: American Judicature Society, *Judicial Disability and Removal Commissions, Courts and Procedures*, 1972; correspondence with Allan Ashman

157 Jerome P. Troy: "Report on Investigation into Dorchester Municipal Court," Chief Justice Franklin Flaschner, Massachusetts District Court; interview with Judge Franklin Flaschner, Aug. 16, 1972; *Time*, June 5, 1972; *New York Times*, Oct. 9, Nov. 8, 1973; interview with Ernest Winsor, Nov. 9, 1972

CHAPTER 8

160 The Superior Court combines: "The Modernization of Justice in the District of Columbia," *American University Law Review*, December 1970–March 1971

161 Deputy Attorney General Richard Kleindienst: Washington *Post*, Sept. 23, 1970

161 The only grumbles: *Ibid.*

162 The forty-four Superior Court judges: Interview with Judge Harold Greene, Oct. 16, 1972

163 The one significant difference: Mary Lawton, "Juvenile Proceedings—the New Look," *American University Law Review*, December 1970–March 1971

164 In Washington, with its: Interview with Lee Simovitz, Oct. 16, 1972

166 "Most judges," says Stanford: Correspondence with Anthony Amsterdam

170 But as a judge: Harold W. Chase, *Federal Judges*, p. 187

175 The Supreme Court acknowledged: Daniel A. Rezneck, "The Rights of Juveniles," National College of the State Judiciary, 1972

175 Chief Judge David L. Bazelon: David L. Bazelon, "Racism, Classism, and the Juvenile Process," *Judicature*, April 1970

175 *New York Times* reporter: *New York Times*, April 2–5, 1973

175 A West Virginia judge: Interview with Judge Callie Tsapis, March 16, 1972

176 Former Family Court Judge: James Mills, "The War Against Children," *Life*, May 19, 1972

176 Mediocrity on the bench: Maurice Rosenberg, "The Qualities of Justices—Are They Strainable?", *Texas Law Review*, June 1966

CHAPTER 9

177 But in early 1972: *New York Times*, Oct. 16, 1972

178 To her considerable: *New York Times*, June 22, 1972

184 When the electorate spoke: *New York Times*, Nov. 9, 1972

186 "We won because": *New York Times*, Nov. 13, 1972

186 "If there's anything": *New York Times*, Nov. 9, 1972

186 Five months later: *New York Times*, April 15, 1973

186 Between 1968 and 1972: *New York Times*, Oct. 6, 22, 1972

186 The most malodorous: New York *Post*, Oct. 14, 1972; *Village Voice* (N.Y.), Nov. 9, 1972; *New York Times*, July 28, 1971, Oct. 31, 1971, Oct. 6, 1972

187 Criminal Court Judge: *Village Voice*, Nov. 16, 1972

187 In 1960 a scholarly: Wallace S. Sayre and Herbert Kaufman, "Courts and Politics in New York City," *The Life of the Law*, p. 207

187 In 1966 Martin Mayer: Martin Mayer, *The Lawyers*, p. 467

187 "It doesn't happen all": *New York Times*, June 23, 1970

188 "I'm convinced it": *Ibid.*

188 A more predictable: *Ibid.*

188 Thus the New York Democratic: New York *Post*, Oct. 14, 1972

188 The New York Crime Commission: *New York Times*, June 23, 1970

188 An investigation by: *Village Voice*, Nov. 9, 1972

188 "The legislators prefer": Interview with Clinton Dominick, Jan. 4, 1973

189 Political kinfolk: Jack Newfield, "The Ten Worst Judges in New York," *New York*, Oct. 16, 1972

189 The commission surveyed: *Village Voice*, Feb. 8, 1973

189 Another investigative agency: *New York Times*, Sept. 25, 1972 Nicholas Gage of the: *Ibid.*

190 Manhattan Supreme Court Justice: *New York Times*, March 15, 1973

190 New York judges were: Newfield, "The Ten Worst Judges in New York"

190 Fino was rated: *Village Voice*, Nov. 9, 1972

191 Newfield's piece: *New York Times*, Nov. 29, 30, 1972; *New York*, Nov. 13, 1972

191 Legal Aid attorney: *Life*, March 12, 1971, July 28, 1972

191 Another victim: *New York Times*, Oct. 4, 5, 28, 31, Nov. 11, 1972

192 Lindsay's pulpit: *New York Times*, Oct. 5, 1972; Andy Logan, "Around City Hall," *New Yorker*, June 10, 1972; New York *Post*, Jan. 25, 1972

192 His portfolio: Interview with Mark Denbeaux, Oct. 6, 1972

192 Drohan was among: *New York Times*, July 28, Aug. 28, 1973

193 "Landlord-and-tenant": Interview with Judge Irving Younger, Nov. 3, 1972

195 "We can't say that": New York *Post*, Oct. 14, 1972

195 A committee of legal luminaries: *New York Times*, Feb. 4, 1972

195 Former Mayor Lindsay: *New York Times*, Dec. 28, 1972

195 The *New York Times*: *New York Times*, Feb. 15, July 27, 1973

195 The state bar association: *New York Times* (letter), March 23, 1973

195 A month later: *New York Times*, April 23, 1973

195 New York's Court on: William Braithwaite, *Who Judges the Judges?*, pp. 56–80; *New York Times*, Sept. 13, 1973

196 The commission spent: Interview with Clinton Dominick, Jan. 4, 1973

196 Since 1916 the senior: *New York Times*, Feb. 23, 1973

197 Breitel was promptly: *New York Times*, March 7, 1973

197 A deal was made: *New York Times*, March 3, 1973

CHAPTER 10

203 His chance at a judgeship: Interview with Harry Lawson, Aug. 1, 1972

204 The new plan established: *Constitution of the State of Colorado*, pp. 34–5

204 As of 1972: Lawson interview, Aug. 1, 1972

204 "A lot of good lawyers": Interview with Justice Edward E. Pringle, Aug. 1, 1972

204 State legislators: Lawson interview, Aug. 1, 1972

204 Pringle believes: Pringle interview, Aug. 1, 1972

205 "One of the big": Lawson interview, Aug. 1, 1972

205 More than thirty: Duke Dunbar, speech at Colorado Judicial Nominating Commissioners' Institute, 1972

205 "There are some parts": Interview with Robert Yegge, Aug. 2, 1972

205 Through 1972: Lawson interview, Aug. 1, 1972; "Merit Retention Elections in 1972," *Judicature*, January 1973

205 "It's better than": Pringle interview, Aug. 1, 1972

205 The qualifications commission: Lawson interview, Aug. 1, 1972; Saul Pinchick, speech at Colorado Judicial Nominating Commissioners' Institute, 1972

206 "If someone could guarantee": Pringle interview, Aug. 1, 1972

CHAPTER 11

222 Archbishop Joseph McGucken: San Francisco *Examiner*, Aug. 10, 1970

222 Haley had been presiding: *New York Times*, Feb. 18, 1973
223 On the day of: San Francisco *Examiner*, Aug. 10, 1970
223 In the 1920s: H. L. Mencken, "Justice Under Democracy," *Prejudices* (Fourth Series)
224 Political trials: Albert W. Alschuler, "Courtroom Misconduct by Prosecutors and Trial Judges," *Texas Law Review*, April 1972
224 Gary presided: Jason Epstein, *The Great Conspiracy Trial*, p. 5 (Vintage ed.); *Encyclopaedia Britannica* (1971), Vol. 5, p. 482
224 D. C. Westenhaver: Ray Ginger, *Eugene V. Debs*, pp. 378–95; Mencken, "Mr. Justice Holmes," *The Vintage Mencken*, p. 189
225 Earlier that year: Herbert Ehrmann, *The Case That Will Not Die*, pp. 472–4; *Encyclopaedia Britannica*, Vol. 19, p. 858
225 In 1972 the National Park: *Time*, April 16, 1973
226 At the time: Harold Medina, *Anatomy of Freedom*, p. 1
226 ". . . If they succeeded": *Ibid.*, p. 5
226 "That whole courtroom": *Ibid.*, p. 8
226 "The men who thought": *Ibid.*, p. 12
227 "We've learned this": Interview with Tom Hayden, February 1968
227 "A fair trial": *New York Times*, June 5, 1972
227 It was the difference: J. Anthony Lukas, "The Second Confrontation in Chicago," *New York Times Magazine*, March 29, 1970
228 When Dr. Spock: Daniel Lang, "The Trial of Dr. Spock," *New Yorker*, Sept. 7, 1968
228 Writer Jessica Mitford: Quoted by Herman Schwartz in "Judges as Tyrants," *Criminal Law Bulletin*, March 1971
229 The LeRoi Jones trial: Kenneth Dolbeare and Joel Grossman in *Political Trials*, edited by Theodore Becker, p. 227–47
229 New York Judge Arnold Fraiman: *New York Times*, May 10, 1973
230 "We came to Chicago": Lukas, "The Second Confrontation in Chicago"
230 His co-defendant: Tom Hayden, *Rebellion and Repression*, p. 15
230 In Tacoma, Washington: *Time*, Dec. 20, 1970
230 Spectators at a: *New York Times*, Sept. 10, 1968
230 When New York judge: *New York Times*, April 27, 1973
230 A murder defendant: Washington *Post*, Oct. 27, 1972
231 "Some individuals": Judge Luther Glanton, Jr., "Pistol-Packin' Judges," *Judges' Journal*, April 1972
231 "Our strategy": Lukas, "The Second Confrontation in Chicago"
232 "Hoffman was not": Alexander Bickel, "Judging the Chicago Trial," *Commentary*, January 1971
232 Hoffman's manner: Lukas, "The Second Confrontation in Chicago"
232 After the trial: Epstein, *The Great Conspiracy Trial*

232 In a speech: Quoted in *Justice in America*, edited by William Lineberry, p. 177

232 The Seventh Circuit: *New York Times*, May 12, Nov. 22, 1972

232 Earlier Judge Hoffman: *Life*, Jan. 14, 1972

234 Byrne handled: *New York Times*, April 27, May 12, 1973; *Time*, Feb. 12, 1973

235 Questions were raised: *New York Times*, May 1, July 27, 1973

235 Federal-court judges: *Newsweek*, Jan. 15, 1973

235 A conference of: "Special Problems in the Judicial Function," p. 258, National College of State Trial Judges

235 Four sheets: *Newsweek*, Jan. 15, 1973; *New York Times*, Dec. 15, 1972

236 A woman reporter: San Francisco *Chronicle*, Aug. 24, 1972

236 The American Bar Association: *New York Times*, Feb. 13, 1970

236 Attorney Louis Nizer: Louis Nizer, "Order in the Court," *Reader's Digest*, July 1970

236 The administrative justice: *Judicature*, April 1972

236 Patrolling another front: "Chief Justice Warren Burger on Lawyers," *Current History*, August 1971

237 Reviewing the chief justice's: *New York Times*, June 10, 1971

237 A study of courtroom security: *New York Times*, May 9, 1972

237 The ABA issued: American Bar Asociation, *The Function of the Trial Judge*, 1972

237 The New York City: *New York Times*, Aug. 9, 1971

237 Harvard law professor: *Ibid.*

237 Federal Judge A. Leon Higgenbotham: Quoted by Herman Schwartz, "Judges as Tyrants," *Criminal Law Bulletin*, 1971

238 "A few appellate judges": Quoted by Richard Harris, "Reflections," *New Yorker*, March 25, 1972; correspondence with Anthony Amsterdam

239 "All I expect a judge": Interview with William Kunstler, Jan. 3, 1973

240 When Abbie Hoffman: *New York Times*, Sept. 24, 1971; *Time*, Oct. 4, 1971; *Civil Liberties*, November 1971

241 Justin Ravitz is: Interviews with Justin Ravitz, Dec. 13, 1972, March 30, 1973; "A Mini-Manual of Criminal Justice," Ravitz for Judge Committee, 1972; *New York Times*, March 10, 1973; Detroit *Free Press*, March 29, 1973

243 Judge George Sullivan: Interview with George Sullivan, Nov. 9, 1972; Report of Massachusetts Supreme Judicial Court, July 8, 1971

CHAPTER 12

248 "You can tell": Interview with Herman Schwartz, Jan. 19, 1973

248 The membership roster: "The United States Courts," U.S. Government Printing Office, 1971

248 "There is really": Robert Carp and Russell Wheeler, "The Freshman Socialization Process for Federal District Judges," presented
to Midwest Political Science Association, April 1972

248 President Harry Truman: Beverly Blair Cook, "Black Representation in the Third Branch," speech to Judicial Council of National
Bar Association, April 21, 1972

250 A federal judge "may fashion": Quoted by Walter F. Murphy and
C. Herman Pritchett in *Courts, Judges and Politics*, p. 324

251 "The federal judiciary": Interview with George Edwards, March
29, 1973

252 Roughly one out of five: The data on the backgrounds, ages, partisanship, religions, etc., of federal judges was assembled from a
variety of sources including *Who's Who in America*, American
Bar Association records, the U.S. Senate Judiciary Committee,
articles in newspapers, magazines, and law journals, and a questionnaire I sent to a large number of federal judges.

252 Political scientist: Sheldon Goldman, "Johnson and Nixon Appointees to the Lower Federal Courts: Some Socio-Political Perspectives," *The Journal of Politics*, 1972

253 There were only 183: *1971 Lawyer Statistical Report*

253 "It makes a lot": Interview with Alan Dershowitz, Nov. 10, 1972
F. Lee Bailey believes: Interview with F. Lee Bailey, Jan. 26,
1973

254 Professor Goldman found: Goldman, "Johnson and Nixon Appointees to the Lower Federal Courts"

255 Leading law firms: Quoted by Murphy and Pritchett, *Courts,
Judges and Politics*, p. 81

255 After a year: *New York Times*, Jan. 23, 1973

255 "They are the next-best": Correspondence with Anthony Amsterdam

255 "If it were a genuine": Dershowitz interview, Nov. 10, 1972

255 They found that: Carp and Wheeler, "The Freshman Socialization Process for Federal District Judges"

256 "After you become": *Ibid.*

258 Lyndon Johnson: Murphy and Pritchett, *Courts, Judges and Politics*, p. 71

258 John McClellan of Arkansas: Harold W. Chase, *Federal Judges*,
p. 85

258 The late Senator Robert Kerr: Victor Navasky, *Kennedy Justice*,
p. 253

258 Hugh Scott and Richard Schweiker: Interview with Martin Ham-
berger, Oct. 26, 1972

259 "I gambled": Quoted by Murphy and Pritchett, *Courts, Judges
and Politics*, p. 95

259 A negative FBI report: Interview with John Duffner, Oct. 26,
1972

260 The Senate fulfills: Philip Kurland, "Our Troubled Courts," *Nation's Business*, May 1971

260 Thirty-two new judges: U.S. Senate Judiciary Committee records

260 "I can write": Duffner interview, Oct. 26, 1972

260 "I have the impression": Interview with Sheldon Goldman, Oct. 9, 1972

261 Another scholar: Richard Burke, "The Path to the Court: A Study of Federal Judicial Appointments," *Dissertation Abstracts*, 1958

261 Eisenhower's appointments: Chase, *Federal Judges*, p. 179; *Congressional Quarterly*, Dec. 16, 1972

261 Robert Grant: Sheldon Goldman and Thomas P. Jahnige, *The Federal Courts as a Political System*, p. 57

261 Myron Gordon: Milwaukee *Journal*, Jan. 13, 1967
Ex-Senator Jack Miller: Jack Miller, "The Iowa Story: Reform in the Exercise of Senatorial Courtesy," *Judicature*, March 1972

262 "Kennedy ruined": Kunstler interview, Jan. 3, 1973

262 Eisenhower rated: Chase, *Federal Judges*, pp. 89–110

262 The pre-Watergate John Sirica: *New York Times*, Jan. 16, 1973; *Newsweek*, May 7, 1973; Harvey Katz, "Some Call It Justice," *Washingtonian*, September 1970

263 "I want for our": Chase, *Federal Judges*, p. 51

263 Nicholas Katzenbach: Navasky, *Kennedy Justice*, p. 256

263 Victor Navasky, author: *Ibid.*, pp. 244, 269

263 Political scientist Mary Curzan: Mary Curzan, *A Case Study in the Selection of Federal Judges: The Fifth Circuit, 1953–63*, (Summary) pp. 36–42

264 The Kennedy men: Chase, *Federal Judges*, pp. 48–88

264 Francis X. Morrissey was: *Ibid.*, pp. 173–7

265 The committee moves: Interviews with Lawrence Walsh, Nov. 3 and 21, 1972

265 "We try to get": *Ibid.*

266 The ABA's influence: Joel Grossman, *Lawyers and Judges*, p. 80

266 Critics have focused: *Ibid.; New York Times*, Feb. 9, 1972

266 "Their standards are": Dershowitz interview, Nov. 10, 1972

266 "My impression": Correspondence with Anthony Amsterdam

266 Law professor Herman Schwartz: Schwartz interview, Jan. 19, 1973

267 Walsh concedes: Walsh interview, Nov. 21, 1972

267 "If there are marginal": Goldman interview, Oct. 9, 1972

268 "In the summer of 1970": Dominick interview, Jan. 4, 1973

269 If and when he completes: *Congressional Quarterly*, Dec. 16, 1972

269 In 1973 a subcommittee: *The Third Branch*, August 1973

270 As a presidential candidate: Chase, *Federal Judges*, p. 74

270 Judges who dissented: *New York Times*, March 11, 1973

270 "The Nixon administration": Goldman interview, Oct. 9, 1972

271 One was Samuel Conti: San Francisco *Examiner*, April 14, 1971
271 Joe Ingraham compiled: Curzan, *A Case Study in the Selection of Federal Judges*
271 Robert Varner: *New York Times*, Dec. 16, 1970; July 6, 17, 1973
272 Richard McLaren's appointment: U.S. Senate Judiciary Committee records
272 "I've heard other lawyers": Bailey interview, Jan. 26, 1973
272 "He tested us": Interview with Judson Miner, Dec. 7, 1972
273 He spent one four-week: Washington *Post*, Aug. 14, 1972
273 Richey's name: *Newsweek*, June 18, 1973
273 The longest-standing: Correspondence with Beverly Blair Cook
274 "The general level": Dershowitz interview, Nov. 10, 1972
274 The Chicago Council: Chicago Council of Lawyers, "Survey of Lawyers Concerning the Performance of Judicial Officers in the Federal District Court," November 1971
274 Professor Harold Chase: Chase, *Federal Judges*, p. 208
274 Former Senator Joseph Tydings: Interview with Joseph Tydings, Jan. 10, 1973
274 Sheldon Goldman: Goldman interview, Oct. 9, 1972
274 "Asking whether": Tydings interview, Jan. 10, 1973
275 Chase estimates: Chase, *Federal Judges*, p. 189
     Former Justice John Marshall Harlan: Jack Frankel, "Removal of Judges—Federal and State," *Judicature*, September 1965
275 As one federal judge: Chase, *Federal Judges*, p. 30
275 Judges of the Sixth Circuit: Cleveland *Plain Dealer*, June 2, 1965
275 District Judge Stephen Chandler: Chase, *Federal Judges*, p. 192; *Time*, Feb. 4, 1966; *Hearings on the Independence of Federal Judges*, U.S. Senate Judiciary Committee, 1970, p. 952
275 Nixon appointee: New York *Daily News*, July 5, 1973; *New York Times*, July 6, 10, Sept. 18, 1973
275 Senator Hugh Scott: Sheldon Goldman, "Political Selection of Federal Judges and the Proposal for a Judicial Service Commission," *Judicature*, October 1968
276 President Eisenhower suggested: Chase, *Federal Judges*, p. 194
276 Tydings favors: Tydings interview, Jan 10, 1973
276 "Senators are not": Goldman interview, Oct. 9, 1972

CHAPTER 13
283 "Shots rang out sharply": Dean S. Jennings and A. J. Zirpoli, "The G-Men Strike," *Famous Detective Cases*, September 1935
284 Zirpoli became a highly: San Francisco *Chronicle*, 1951–61
284 He was a ubiquitous: San Francisco *Chronicle*
286 "There was a time": Interview with Don Thackrey, Aug. 21, 1972
287 When several hippies: Wall Street *Journal*, Dec. 14, 1970
288 "We were shouting": *Ibid.*

289 "Zirpoli has a sense": Interview with Martin Glick, Aug. 30, 1972
289 Still another: Wall Street *Journal*, Dec. 14, 1970
294 One Zirpoli interpretation: San Francisco *Chronicle*, 1968
296 In 1964: San Francisco *Examiner*, Oct. 30, 1968
298 He described the conditions: San Francisco *Chronicle*, May 18, 1972
298 "If the state cannot": *Ibid.*
300 "The law suffers": quoted by Jerome Frank in *Courts on Trial*, p. 176

CHAPTER 14
303 "A judge's life": Learned Hand, *The Spirit of Liberty*, p. 33 (Vintage ed.)
304 Yet beauty exists: Hand quoted by Philip Hamburger, "The Great Judge," *Life*, Nov. 4, 1946
305 "Appellate judges": Interview with Delmar Karlen, Oct. 5, 1972
305 Decisions of an appellate: Quoted by Sheldon Goldman, "Conflict and Consensus in the United States Courts of Appeals," *Wisconsin Law Review*, 1968
306 "We seek to arrive": Interview with George Edwards, March 29, 1973
306 Political scientist: Goldman, "Voting Behavior on the United States Courts of Appeals, 1961–64," *American Political Science Review*, June 1966
306 "It's difficult to describe": Edwards interview, March 29, 1973
     It is a reclusive: *Bartlett's Familiar Quotations*, p. 708
307 "I would argue against": Edwards interview, March 30, 1973
307 "The payoff is": Interview with Andrew Watson, Dec. 12, 1972
307 The appellate brotherhood: *The Book of the States*, 1972–73; U.S. Department of Justice, *Register of Department of Justice and the U.S. Courts*, 1973
308 Most cases in appellate: Quoted by Martin Mayer in *The Lawyers*, p. 483
308 "It is when the colors": Benjamin Cardozo, *The Nature of the Judicial Process*, p. 21
308 "It takes me longer": Edwards interview, March 29, 1973
308 Attorney John Frank: Quoted by James E. Clayton in *The Making of Justice*, p. 87
309 "A well-written product": Edwards interview, March 29, 1973
309 State appeals judges are chosen: American Judicature Society, "Judicial Selection and Tenure," August 1971 and revisions.
309 Their salaries range: *Judicature*, November 1972
310 In the Tenth Circuit: U.S. Department of Justice, *Register of Department of Justice and the U.S. Courts*, 1973
310 Sheldon Goldman reports: Goldman, "Characteristics of Eisenhower and Kennedy Appointees to the Lower Federal Courts,"

Western Political Quarterly, December 1965; "Johnson and Nixon Appointees to the Lower Federal Courts: Some Socio-Political Perspectives," *Journal of Politics*, 1972

310   A profile of state supreme: Bradley Canon, "Characteristics and Career Patterns of State Supreme Court Justices," *Case & Comment*, July–August 1972

310   In 1960 Stuart Nagel: Stuart Nagel, *The Legal Process from a Behavioral Perspective*, pp. 200–8

312   They are selected with: Data collected from *Who's Who in America*, American Bar Association, and other sources.

312   "Most are men": Goldman interview, Oct. 9, 1972

312   Delmar Karlen: Karlen interview, Oct. 5, 1972

312   Friendly and Kaufman: Interview with Herman Schwartz, Jan. 19, 1973; Goldman, "Judicial Appointments to the United States Courts of Appeals," *Wisconsin Law Review*, Winter 1967

312   Kennedy wanted to appoint: Goldman interview, Oct. 9, 1972

313   Nixon selected: *Who's Who in America;* Goldman, "Johnson and Nixon Appointees to the Lower Federal Courts"

313   George Mackinnon: Washington *Post*, July 31, 1969

314   Senator Hiram Fong: *Congressional Quarterly*, Dec. 16, 1972
       Edwards' confirmation hearing: Harold W. Chase, "The Johnson Administration—Judicial Appointments 1963–66," *Minnesota Law Review*, April 1968

320   Edwards had the backing: *Ibid.*

321   He derives pleasure: George Edwards, "Exorcising the Devil of Appellate Court Delay," *American Bar Association Journal*, February 1972

322   His opinion endeared: Bailey interview, Jan. 26, 1973

CHAPTER 15

327   It is impossible: Ernest Havemann, "Storm Center of Justice," *Life*, May 22, 1964

328   (Former Chief Justice Charles Evans Hughes: Martin Mayer, *The Lawyers*, p. 494

328   They have been: John R. Schmidhauser, "The Background Characteristics of United States Supreme Court Justices," *Judicial Behavior* (Glendon Schubert, editor), p. 206.

329   Justice William Johnson: Walter F. Murphy, "Leadership, Bargaining, and the Judicial Process," *Judicial Behavior*, p. 399

329   Even the court's size: *Encyclopaedia Britannica* (1971), Vol. 21, p. 434

330   Andrew Jackson named John McLean: *Ibid.*, Vol. 14, p. 539; Schmidhauser, *Judicial Behavior*, p. 227

330   He found another place: Arthur Schlesinger, Jr., *The Age of Jackson*, p. 91 (Mentor ed.)

330   To succeed him: *Ibid.*, p. 31

330 Jackson's selection of: Dean Acheson, "Removing the Shadow Cast on the Courts," *American Bar Association Journal*, October 1969

330 The New York *American:* Schlesinger, *The Age of Jackson*, p. 125

331 "Some justices": Alan Dershowitz, "They Will Affect the Nation for Years to Come," *New York Times*, Sept. 26, 1971

331 The judge, Cardozo said: Benjamin Cardozo, *The Nature of the Judicial Process*, p. 141

331 "I hate justice": Quoted by Mayer in *The Lawyers*, p. 490

331 "I remember once": *Ibid.*

332 In fact the turnover: Joel Grossman, *Lawyers and Judges*, p. 167

332 Charles Evans Hughes: James F. Simon, *In His Own Image*, p. 52

333 Justice Catron: Murphy, *Judicial Behavior*, p. 409

333 One of his nominees: Carl Sandburg, *Abraham Lincoln: The War Years*, Vol. II, p. 65

333 Chase's presidential ambition: *Ibid.*

334 A 1905 decision: *Encyclopaedia Britannica* (1971), Vol. 21, p. 437

334 Holmes was: *Abrams v. United States*, 250 U.S. 616, 630 (1919)

335 "His judicial philosophy": Quoted by Walter F. Murphy, *Wiretapping on Trial*, p. 73

335 "Certainty generally is illusion": Oliver Wendell Holmes, *The Path of the Law*, p. 709

335 When Louis Brandeis: Grossman, *Lawyers and Judges*, p. 54

335 Brandeis was the first: Schmidhauser, *Judicial Behavior*, p. 220

335 "I told him long ago": Murphy, *Wiretapping on Trial*, p. 74

335 Holmes and Brandeis rank: *New York Times*, Nov. 19, 1972

335 He sponsored wide-ranging: Murphy, *Wiretapping on Trial*, pp. 62–81

336 On the margin: Murphy, *Judicial Behavior*, p. 404

336 Taft described him: Murphy, *Wiretapping on Trial*, p. 76

336 He carped at Justice: Murphy, *Judicial Behavior*, pp. 407–8

336 "McReynolds was": Harlan Phillips, ed., *Felix Frankfurter Reminisces*, p. 101

337 McReynolds violated: Murphy, *Wiretapping on Trial*, p. 76

337 Similarly, Chief Justice Burger: *Time*, July 10, 1972

337 Holmes reacted: Murphy, *Judicial Behavior*, p. 397

337 Assignments have been withheld: *Ibid.*, p. 409

337 McReynolds' final act: Phillips, *Felix Frankfurter Reminisces*, p. 101

337 Hostility between: Murphy, *Judicial Behavior*, p. 407

337 The philosophical differences: *Newsweek*, May 8, 1961

338 Harvard law professor: Lance Liebman, "Swing Man on the Supreme Court," *New York Times Magazine*, Oct. 8, 1972

338 Stone, a Coolidge appointee: Murphy, *Wiretapping on Trial*, p. 81

339 "American presidents": Simon, *In His Own Image*, p. 17

339 When he headed east: James E. Clayton, *The Making of Justice*, p. 256

339 Douglas was a non-conformist: Barrett Prettyman, Jr., *Death and the Supreme Court*, p. 32

339 Political scientist John Schmidhauser: Schmidhauser, *Judicial Behavior*, p. 225

340 "A legal system": Havemann, "Storm Center of Justice," *Life*, May 22, 1964

340 Three of Truman's: *New York Times*, Nov. 19, 1972

341 "I always knew": Havemann, "Storm Center of Justice," *Life*, May 22, 1964

341 "He told the story": Mayer, *The Lawyers*, p. 512

342 Both were Ivy League educated: Schmidhauser, *Judicial Behavior*, p. 213

342 Kennedy's advisers suggested: Clayton, *The Making of Justice*, pp. 50–1

343 Robert Kennedy later explained: *Ibid.*, p. 52

344 Denunciations of the court: Simon, *In His Own Image*, p. 70

344 Fortas was charged: Robert Shogan, *A Question of Judgment*, p. 3

345 Like Nixon, he grew up: Jules Duscha, "Chief Justice Burger Asks, 'If It Doesn't Make Good Sense, How Can It Make Good Law?' ", *New York Times Magazine*, Oct. 5, 1969

345 In a 1968 talk: *New York Times*, June 20, 1969

346 He displayed the suspicious: *Newsweek*, Oct. 15, 1973

349 Haynsworth's designation: Simon, *In His Own Image*, p. 104

350 As a candidate: Richard Harris, "Decision," *The New Yorker*, Dec. 5, 12, 1970

351 "The question arises": Simon, *In His Own Image*, p. 99

351 President Grover Cleveland: *Encyclopaedia Britannica* (1971), Vol. 17, p. 514

351 He turned instead: Simon, *In His Own Image*, p. 141

352 "Both men reached": Dershowitz, "They Will Affect the Nation for Years to Come," *New York Times*, Sept. 26, 1971

352 Senator Edward Kennedy said: Simon, *In His Own Image*, p. 222

352 Alan Dershowitz wondered: Dershowitz interview, Nov. 10, 1972

353 Lawrence Walsh's ABA committee: Walsh interview, Nov. 21, 1972

353 After the result: American Bar Association, "Report of the Standing Committee on the Federal Judiciary," Oct. 31, 1971

353 He had responded: Simon, *In His Own Image*, p. 237

353 A former president: Lewis Powell, speech to ABA prayer breakfast, Aug. 13, 1972

354 Frankfurter once described: *New York Times* editorial, Oct. 31, 1972

354 The Nixon justices voted: *New York Times*, June 28, 1973

354 Douglas reportedly protested: *Time*, July 10, 1972; *New York Times*, July 5, 1972

355 The most serious incident: *Time*, July 10, 1972

355 Until 1972 each justice: *Time*, Dec. 11, 1972

355 Burger commissioned: *New York Times*, Dec. 20, 1972, May 7, 24, 1973; Detroit *Free Press*, Dec. 6, 1972

356 "Burger seemed prepared": Simon, *In His Own Image*, p. 140

357 "The new conservative majority": *Ibid.*, pp. 288, 281

CHAPTER 16

358 "I had a case": Interview with Judge Richard Greene, July 26, 1972

360 The maximum penalties: Martin Mayer, *The Lawyers*, p. 180; The President's Commission on Law Enforcement and Administration of Justice, Task Force Report, *The Courts*, 1967, p. 25

360 "By any quantitative standard": Harry W. Jones, "The Trial Judge—Role Analysis and Profile," *The Courts, the Public and the Law Explosion*, p. 139

361 "Not only do you not know": *New York Times*, Sept. 26, 1972

361 "It's a puzzle": Interview with Judge David Jacobs, May 24, 1972

361 "But this way of": Jones, *The Courts, the Public and the Law Explosion*, pp. 140–1

361 Municipal Judge Philip Saeta: Philip Saeta, "The Philosophy and Premises of Sentencing," National College of the State Judiciary, 1972

361 "Nothing tells us": Marvin Frankel, "Lawlessness in Sentencing," *University of Cincinnati Law Review*, 1972

362 The American Bar Association: American Bar Association, *Sentencing Alternatives and Procedures*, 1968, p. 61

362 But, as Frankel: Frankel, "Lawlessness in Sentencing"

362 "I'm considered a judge": *New York Times*, Sept. 26, 1972

362 "The purposes of sentencing": *Ibid.*

362 Judge Saeta, who led: Saeta, "The Philosophy and Premises of Sentencing"

363 "We are divided": James Q. Wilson, "If Every Criminal Knew He Would Be Punished If Caught," *New York Times Magazine*, Jan. 28, 1973

365 In Reno, Judge Saeta: Saeta, "College Cases," National College of the State Judiciary, 1972

367 The causes, Judge Frankel: Frankel, "Lawlessness in Sentencing"

367 A survey by Boston: Stephen Bing and S. Stephen Rosenfeld, "The Quality of Justice in the Lower Criminal Courts of Metropolitan Boston," 1970

367   A 1972 federal-court: Whitney North Seymour, Jr., "1972 Sentencing Study: Southern District of New York"

367   The average sentence: Charles Morgan, Jr., "Dual Justice in the South," *Judicature*, April–May 1970

367   Whitney North Seymour, Jr.: Seymour, "1972 Sentencing Study: Southern District of New York"

367   A man found guilty: Howard James, *Crisis in the Courts*, p. 144

367   A *New York Times* survey: *New York Times*, Sept. 27, 1972

367   Another study: *Ibid.*

368   Half the federal judges: The President's Commission on Law Enforcement and Administration of Justice, *The Courts*, p. 23

368   Judges as a group: Frankel, "Lawlessness in Sentencing"

368   On a single day: Pittsburgh *Post-Gazette*, Dec. 13, 1972

368   Opposite urges: *New York Times*, Oct. 21, 1972; Jan. 28, May 16, 1973; *Time*, June 4, 1973

369   "I suppose I shouldn't": Interview with Judge Richard Greene, July 27, 1972

369   U. S. District Judge Jack Weinstein: *New York Times*, Oct. 7, 1972

369   Superior Court Judge Alfred Burka: Washington *Post*, Jan. 17, 1972

369   During the Vietnam War: Willard Geylin, *In the Service of Their Country*, pp. 323–7; *New York Times*, July 3, 1972

369   Fourteen hijackers: *New York Times*, July 12, 1972, Feb. 12, 1973

370   The next spasm: *New York Times*, May 22, 1973

370   "Sentencing churns": Interview with Andrew Watson, Dec. 12, 1972

372   John Hogarth: John Hogarth, *Sentencing as a Human Process*, pp. 319–78

372   "He's in prison now": Lewis Carroll, *Through the Looking Glass*, A. L. Burt Edition, p. 241

373   The three judges took: *New York Times*, Oct. 13, 1972

374   Sentencing panels: *New York Times*, Oct. 3, 1972

374   Circuit Judge Alfonso Sepe: *New York Times*, Sept. 10, Dec. 28, 1972

374   Michigan Judge John Roskopp: *New York Times*, Jan. 7, 1973

374   Federal Judge Philip Neville: *New York Times*, May 5, 1973

374   State judges in Portland: Correspondence with U.S. District Judge James Burns

374   Judge Stanley Fuld: *New York Times*, Sept. 28, 1972

375   Professor Leonard Orland: Interview with Leonard Orland, March 3, 1972

375   Appellate review: American Bar Association, *Appellate Review of Sentences*, 1968

375   But Judge Frankel: Frankel, "Lawlessness in Sentencing"

376 Piero Calamandrei: Piero Calamandrei, *Eulogy for Judges*, pp. 72–3

CHAPTER 17

377 "There are, obviously": Sybille Bedford, *The Faces of Justice*, pp. 70–2

378 "There is no character": Quoted in *Handbook for Judges*, p. 36

378 "The greatest scourge": Quoted by Arthur Vanderbilt in *Judges and Jurors*, p. 24

379 "It isn't fair": Interview with Herman Schwartz, Jan. 19, 1973

379 "If my sampling": Howard James, *Crisis in the Courts*, p. 4

379 (22 states introduced: Interview with Allan Ashman, Dec. 8, 1972

379 "Our judges are as honest": James F. Simon, *In His Own Image*, p. 10

380 Merit selection is: "Election Day 1972: The Judicial Issues," *Judicature*, December 1972

381 What they *have* shown: Stuart Nagel, "Comparing Elected and Appointed Judicial Systems," 1972

381 "The problem is not": Correspondence with Anthony Amsterdam

382 In a 1952 special election: Emmett Bashful, *The Florida Supreme Court*

382 That same year: Alvin Gershenson, *The Bench Is Warped*, p. 264

382 "The popular vote": John Paul Stevens, speech to the Chicago Council of Lawyers, Dec. 6, 1972

382 Just how blunt: *Judicature*, March 1971

383 Politicos and reformers: *New York Times*, May 21, 1973; *Judicature*, July 1973

383 The main ingredients: Glenn Winters and Robert Allard, "Judicial Selection and Tenure in the United States," *The Courts, the Public and the Law Explosion*, p. 150

383 As of 1973: Interview with Allan Ashman, Dec. 8, 1972; correspondence with Allan Ashman

383 "There is probably": Glenn Winters, "Selection and Tenure of Judges," *Michigan Alumnus Quarterly Review*, Spring 1948

384 "So long as we": Warren Burnett, "Observations on the Direct-Election Method of Judicial Selection," *Texas Law Review*, June 1966

384 "The trial judge's job": Martin Mayer, *The Lawyers*, p. 474

384 But in practice: "Merit Retention Elections in 1972," *Judicature*, January 1973; Burnett, "Observations on the Direct-Election Method of Judicial Selection"; interview and correspondence with Allan Ashman

385 Warren Burnett: Burnett, *ibid.*

385 Their most important finding: Richard Watson and Rondal Downing, *The Politics of the Bench and the Bar*, p. 6

385 "The Missouri Plan will not": *Ibid.*, p. 319
385 The one black judge: *Ibid.*, p. 149
386 "Every system so far": Interview with Sheldon Goldman, Oct. 9, 1972
387 Two New York University: Gerhard Mueller and Fré le Poole Griffiths, "Judicial Fitness: A Comparative Study," *Judicature*, December 1968
387 "Picking judges is": Schwartz interview, Jan. 19, 1973
388 In Massachusetts: Interviews with Ernest Winsor, Nov. 9, 1972, and Allan Rodgers, Jan. 26, 1973; John Robertson and John Gordon, "Merit Selection of Judges in Massachusetts: The Experience of the Ad Hoc Advisory Committee," 1973
389 The 1500-member: Interview with Judson Miner, Dec. 7, 1972
389 Their report concluded: Chicago Council of Lawyers, "The 107 Cook County Magistrates Who Are Scheduled to Become Associate Judges of the Circuit Court," 1971
389 Working through a committee: Chicago Council of Lawyers, "Judges Seeking Retention in November 1972," 1972
390 Most merit-selection: Correspondence with Allan Ashman
391 "When the human elements": Jerome Frank, *Courts on Trial*, p. 261
391 "If merit selection": Ashman interview, Dec. 8, 1972
392 Only three impeachments: William Braithwaite, *Who Judges the Judges?*, p. 13; *Newsweek*, May 24, 1965
393 The swing to discipline: Interview with Jack Frankel, Aug. 23, 29, 1972
393 The idea so captivated: Ashman interview, Dec. 8, 1972
393 The principal grounds: *Constitution of the State of California*, Article VI
393 In practice: Interview with Roger Traynor, Aug. 31, 1972
393 The California panel: Frankel interview, Aug. 29, 1972
394 Texas law professor: Albert Alschuler, "Courtroom Misconduct by Prosecutors and Trial Judges," *Texas Law Review*, April 1972
395 Contempt citations: *Ibid.*
395 "Justice," said the late: Quoted by Maurice Rosenberg, "Improving Selection of Judges on Merit," *Judicature*, January 1973

Index

423

Donald Dale Jackson

*Donald Dale Jackson was born in San Francisco in
1935. He received an A.B. degree from Stanford
University in 1957, and a Master's degree from the
Columbia School of Journalism in 1958. After a 21-
month stint in the Counter Intelligence Corps of the
U.S. Army, he worked for two years as a reporter
for United Press International in its San Francisco
bureau, and then, in 1963, became a reporter for*
Life *magazine in New York. During his years at* Life
*he contributed major articles on a vast variety of
people and subjects: from Lee Harvey Oswald to
F. Lee Bailey; from Nelson Rockefeller to Richard
Nixon; from Dr. Spock's conspiracy trial to a Colorado
death-row inmate; from the American wilderness to the
American cowboy; from the Connecticut parole board
to the 1972 Winter Olympics in Sapporo, Japan. In
1965 he received a Nieman Fellowship to Harvard.*

Mr. Jackson is presently a Contributing Editor for
New Times *magazine. He lives in Newtown, Connecticut, with his wife, Darlene, and their two children.*

67765

KF
8775
.J3

Jackson, Donald
Judges.

DATE DUE

Fernald Library
Colby-Sawyer College
New London, New Hampshire

GAYLORD   PRINTED IN U.S.A.

BRODART PRINTED IN U.S.A.   23-520-002